D1103762

Cornell Studies in Civil Liberty

ASPECTS OF LIBERTY

Essays Presented to Robert E. Cushman

ROBERT E. CUSHMAN

ASPECTS OF

LIBERTY

Essays Presented to

ROBERT E. CUSHMAN

Edited by MILTON R. KONVITZ

and CLINTON ROSSITER

CORNELL UNIVERSITY PRESS

Ithaca, New York

Reprinted with the permission of Cornell University Press

JOHNSON REPRINT CORPORATION
111 Fifth Avenue, New York, N.Y. 10003

JOHNSON REPRINT COMPANY LIMITED
Berkeley Square House, London, W. 1

Preface

ROBERT E. CUSHMAN'S retirement after forty years of teaching has moved a group of his friends, students, and colleagues to express their admiration for him in the form of this volume of essays. Our common subject, quite properly, is human liberty—the chief concern of his scholarly labors, the guiding star of his public service, and the delight of his gentle spirit.

Professor Cushman has been a pioneering scholar in the field of civil liberties. As the bibliography in this volume proves at a glance, he started to work many years ago on important but neglected aspects of the Bill of Rights. Through his accomplishments he has helped to make research in civil liberties a highly respected field in political science and constitutional law, and he has opened lines of inquiry that others have found rewarding to follow. In 1943 Professor Cushman launched the Cornell Studies in Civil Liberty with a grant from the Rockefeller Foundation. Since that time more than a dozen books devoted to problems of American liberty have appeared under his supervision. In conceiving, directing, and editing these studies, he has proved beyond a doubt that scholarship can shed decisive light on political developments that trouble our lives and institutions.

This book is both a mark of our respect for Professor Cushman and a small payment of our debt to him—for the example of his inspiring teaching, for his active enlistment of us and others in the exploration of sensitive problems, and for his demonstration that the scholar need not and cannot be a mere "summer soldier and sunshine patriot." His

Preface

career is proof that a scholar's life may show dedication and courage. We dedicate these essays to Robert E. Cushman with abiding respect and affection. He has brought dignity to scholarship, distinction to teaching, and strength to the cause of ordered liberty.

THE EDITORS

Cornell University
March 1958

Acknowledgments

THE editors thank the following publishers and publications for granting permission to quote from the books and articles listed: Commonweal Publishing Co., Inc., and Harcourt, Brace & Co., Inc., *Catholicism in America;* Macmillan & Co., Ltd., *Sadhana* by Rabindranath Tagore; The Times Publishing Co., Ltd., an editorial in *The Times* of April 23, 1954; *New Statesman,* extracts from the issues of June 23, 1956, and October 26, 1957; Brown University Press, *Constitutional Reason of State* by C. J. Friedrich; and Alfred A. Knopf, Inc., *Freedom and Responsibility in the American Way of Life* by Carl Becker.

Contents

Contents

IV. INTERNATIONAL ASPECTS

V. COMPARATIVE ASPECTS

VI. JURISDICTIONAL, INSTITUTIONAL, AND PROCEDURAL ASPECTS

I

THEORETICAL ASPECTS

1

THEORETICAL ASPECTS

[ROBERT M. HUTCHINS]

THE FUND FOR THE REPUBLIC, INC.

Ideas, Institutions,

and American Liberty

SOME forty-five years ago, when Robert Cushman was teaching me ancient history in Oberlin Academy—a dark chapter in his life, but a bright one in mine—we knew what was wrong with the world. It was full of underdogs, easily identifiable as such. They were the poor, the workers, the Negroes, the aged, the immigrants and aliens, the defrauded, the unfortunate—the powerless who were being pushed around by the powerful. The task of right-minded men was to come to their rescue.

The New Freedom for which Woodrow Wilson was campaigning at the time was freedom for the underdog. What made a man an underdog was chiefly low wages, long hours, bad conditions of work, and economic insecurity. The principal test of right-mindedness in that epoch, therefore, was the attitude one took toward organized labor.

The efforts of the liberalism, or "underdoggism," in which I was raised have largely succeeded. The obvious groups of the downtrodden and oppressed have almost vanished. In particular, labor unions have achieved enormous power. Who is an underdog now?

The answer appears to be that everybody is. Consider the remarks of the British Socialist magazine, the *New Statesman*, on June 23, 1956:

For a Socialist the problem of freedom has always been theoretically simple. The bourgeois revolution established certain notions about personal liberty and toleration which are of permanent value for all forms of society. It also

3

established an acquisitive society in which individual liberty was closely linked to the individual ownership of property. In such a society men might be legally free, but powerless to enjoy their freedom. Effective freedom could, therefore, only be secured by extending public welfare. What is simple in theory, however, is far from simple in practice. The denial of human rights in Communist countries is a final warning of the dangers of over-organization and unchecked bureaucracy.

In England we are rightly proud that the welfare state has brought a vast increase in freedom to millions. But where does the danger now lie? While we carry through this vast and beneficial change, we are aware that the individual, while benefiting from greater security, often feels powerless in the face of the huge and complex organizations of modern society. Power is concentrated not merely in the state and in big business which in the individual's point of view are scarcely distinguishable from the state itself, but also in such near monopolies as the press and radio, the trade unions, and even in the democratic political parties. To the ordinary citizen, the bureaucrat and the oligarch are *they* over whom *we* have little control.[1]

The problem now, according to the *New Statesman*, is that the individual is powerless when confronting the concentrations of power— government, business, press, union, political party—that make up the society in which we live. These concentrations deprive us of our autonomy, and if they treat us unjustly, we may be unable to do anything about it. It would seem that Socialism cannot solve this problem; for Socialism in its only precise meaning requires state ownership of the

---

[1] On October 26, 1957, the *New Statesman* published the following: "A lady who is trying to send four shillings to Belgium for a photograph of a Pieter Brueghel picture has just sent me a round-by-round account of the enterprise up to now. . . . Her first inquiry brought an invoice for 27 Belgian francs . . . from the Archives Centrales Iconographiques d'Art Nationale in Brussels. She went with this to her local post office to get an international postal money order, and they said she must go to the one in the nearest big town. Here she was told to write to the Accountant-General's Dept., GPO, Bickley, Kent. The reply she got from there was that she must get an import license from the Board of Trade at 43 Marsham Street, SW1. She wrote for this on 27 September. Three weeks later she received a batch of forms, on which she was to apply for a license to import Goods other than Vehicles, Exposed Cinematograph Films, Machinery, Plant, Scientific Instruments and Parts for which special application forms are used. Among these forms was the blank for the import license that she still hopes to get one day. She has to make it out herself, but it will not become a license until the Board of Trade has nerved itself to the point of 'validating' it. Then she can start again, I suppose, on the post offices. Let us, then (may I suggest to her?) be up and doing, With a heart for any fate; Still achieving, still pursuing, Learn to labour and to wait."

principal means of production. The bureaucratic oligarchy of the state might be able to control other oligarchies, but the individual would be powerless still.

In England and the United States there has clearly been a change over forty-five years. Efforts to maintain that there has not been a change everywhere in the West or to suggest that the welfare state may not be enough to guarantee freedom and justice have a certain air of disingenuousness about them. This is the impression that Jean-Paul Sartre gives in an interview published in the *Listener* of June 6, 1957. He says:

> I take it that one cannot go beyond Marxism today because the really important questions of contemporary philosophy are still within a Marxist framework. As long as scarcity remains a problem for the people's democracies and for us, the exploitation of man by man remains a living problem, and one cannot go beyond the great Marxist problems, and therefore, their solutions.

Sartre says that he regards philosophy as "the way the rising class looks at the world, the way this class sees and depicts itself, its self-awareness, a method to solve the real problems of life *and* a weapon against other opposing classes." The rising class (the underdogs) is still the proletariat; the real problem of life is still scarcity; scarcity results from the exploitation of man by man; the exploiters are the capitalists, and the exploited are the workers; scarcity results from exploitation; therefore the Marxist problems and the Marxist solutions to them must remain the preoccupation of philosophers and, presumably, of all right-minded men.

This analysis seems inapplicable to Britain, if the *New Statesman* is to be believed, and still less to the United States. According to the *New Statesman,* whatever may be said of classes, the main issue is no longer scarcity and the economic exploitation of man by man; it is the control of everybody by uncontrollable oligarchies; it is the sense of powerlessness. In the United States, classes, if they exist, have little self-awareness. The individual struggles; the family may struggle; groups struggle with groups. But the society is fluid and open, taxes are high, and the struggles are not ideological. They are struggles for competitive advantage or security within a system that all "classes" appear to sanction. Here the "great Marxist problems" do not present themselves. Our problem is abundance, rather than scarcity. In this country it is not always easy to tell who is exploiting whom. Some corporations doubtless deal more equitably with those affected by them than certain "working-class" organizations do with their members, their employers, and the public. In this country it is not always possible to tell who are the employers and who the employed. The Teamsters Union, for example, actually runs the industy that the so-called employers "own."

An industrial society in which the economic relation between employer and employee is no longer the paramount problem is one that in Sartre's own terms must "go beyond Marxism." Sartre's terms, however, are not quite the same as those of Marx. In the same interview, Sartre says, "I am a Marxist. That, to be absolutely precise, means that I cannot attempt not to be one without falling back on old notions such as abstract freedom or equality of rights."

Why should surplus value be abolished? Marx replies that it is exploitation. What is the matter with exploitation? Marx replies that it is unjust. The worker is entitled to the total product of his work. Marx rested his case on old notions such as abstract freedom or equality of rights. They are the source of his moral fervor.

II

The *New Statesman* concludes the editorial from which I have quoted by condemning the political party to which it gives its nominal adherence. It says, "To ask the right questions, one must have a theory of society, not a set of *ad hoc* responses to particular abuses. And Labour today seems to have no such theory, but only a rag-bag of philosophical ideas which are wearing very thin."

There is a fairly prevalent notion that everybody in the West is carrying around a rag bag of thin ideas, even though there is an equally popular view that Marxist ideas are thinner still. Thus on April 10, 1956, Dr. A. J. M. van Dal of The Hague, Secretary-General of the International Commission of Jurists, called for "a simple set of fundamental principles expressing in a readily understandable way the common denominator of our legal-political beliefs." He said that leaders of the democracies lacked definite purpose and clear conceptions of what they stood for. Consequently, he said, the masses do not often believe in any deep-rooted ideal. He said this situation frequently resulted in "too much improvising, too much taking a stand on incidental issues, too much changing of ground, too much confusion, disagreement, and disappointment."

With the rest of the world looking to the United States for leadership, we have not been able to make striking contributions on any but the economic and military levels. Ideas and ideals that we suppose were clear to our ancestors have tended to become forms of words that are useful as rhetorical flourishes or political weapons but that do not have much visible effect in our daily lives. When we are asked what we stand for, our reply is likely to sound like a cliché or a slogan. The severity of the shock to American public opinion administered by the announcements that Russian satellites were circumnavigating the globe can be taken to mean that we had had confidence only in our scientific and technological superiority, in our power and wealth, and, when that was shaken, we had nothing to fall back on. In particular, we could not fall back on the superiority of our theory of society, because we could not clearly remember whether we had a theory, or what it was, or why it was superior.

The American theory of society is set forth in the Declaration of Independence and the Constitution. They have been able to appeal to persons of different religious faiths, philosophical positions, traditions, and races. Everybody says he is for these documents. Yet the grave clashes among groups that proclaim their dedication to the same principles suggest that clarity about these principles is missing.

In Carl Becker's last work, *Freedom and Responsibility in the American Way of Life*, he has this to say about the American theory of society as it stands today:

Admirable as the American system of government is, and particularly because it is so admirable, we need to be reminded that a system of government designed to meet the problems of the eighteenth century is not necessarily in all respects suited to meet the problems of the twentieth. We need to be reminded of this more especially because we are rather too apt to regard our constitutions as sacred tablets handed down from Mount Sinai—documents revealing those fundamental principles of government which, being universally applicable, need never be re-examined. It is as if in the eighteenth century we discovered and labeled our liberties, locked them safely away in oak-ribbed and riveted constitutions, placed the key under the mat, and then went cheerfully about our private affairs with a feeling of complete security. . . .

To revere the founding fathers is all very well, but it would be better if we followed their example by re-examining the fundamental human rights and the economic and political institutions best suited to secure them. . . .

If the civil liberties, or some of them, are denied every day to someone, and few people bother about it unless they are directly concerned, and most of us feel that those who do bother about it must for that reason be Jews, Reds, or crackpots—if that is the way we take it (and by and large it is), then less than nothing is gained by reflection that our civil liberties are secure because they are abstractly defined in the same archaic phraseology in forty-nine bills of rights and may be defended in as many courts of law.

According to Becker, America is a society that should be re-examining its theory of itself. The old notions of freedom and justice as they were embodied in our basic documents and applied in the early stages of our history are not to be impugned; but it is not to be supposed that because "freedom of the press," for example, is an effective slogan with which to belabor the Secretary of State or the Secretary of Defense or the Russians or the price of newsprint it supplies an answer to the question of how the people are to obtain vital information and carry on vital discussion today.

The problem with which the founding fathers dealt was how to protect the liberty of the citizen against the government. Becker suggests that the American people are now largely indifferent to the accomplishment of that object. He also suggests that another question may be even more important: whether the institutions through which the rights of the people must be exercised are conducted in such a way as to deprive the people of the effective use of their freedom. This, in effect, is the question raised by the *New Statesman*. Becker says, of the freedom of the press, "In our time the practical problem has to do, not so much with those who may freely assemble and speak their minds, but rather with those who may acquire a virtual monopoly of collecting and disseminating information."

Woodrow Wilson made the same point in his campaign speech, "The Old Order Changeth," in 1912:

The life of the nation has grown infinitely varied. It does not center now upon questions of governmental structure or of the distribution of governmental powers. It centers upon questions of the very structure and operation of society itself, of which government is only the instrument. . . . Today, the everyday relationships of men are largely with great impersonal concerns, with organizations, not with other individual men.

Since Wilson spoke, and even since Becker wrote, the size and scope of government have swollen beyond recognition. The world has become polarized, and we live in a state of continuous international tension. We cannot relegate the problem of coping with government to a secondary position. The ordinary citizen on his lawful occasions finds himself encountering government at every turn. An American who wants to feel powerless should try winning an argument about what he owes the government on his income tax.

It remains to be seen whether the American reaction to the Russian Revolution, which was strikingly similar to the reaction to the French Revolution, will take a similar course and die as the Alien and Sedition Acts did. For the first time in our history we have run in "peacetime" into the problem of "reason of state," which has been translated into "national security." Renewed insistence upon national security will undoubtedly follow the flight of the Russian satellites. But the official representatives of the newspapers have announced that no considerations of national security can be permitted to interfere with the freedom of the press. They have done this although the press as a whole has not been quick to protest against interference with the freedom of the citizen in the name of national security. The Supreme Court now appears of a mind to insist that there are limits to what government can do to individuals and organizations in that name. But what are the limits, and, if the danger grows greater, will the limits grow broader?

But as Wilson and Becker suggest, government today is not the only problem, perhaps not even the main one. The tremendous fanfare about national security, which of necessity keeps the government on the front pages all the time, should not hide from us the fact that in other areas of our lives the state may be withering away. Even a Marxist could not think that this was a good thing at this stage. The cumbersome and ineffective efforts of government to deal from time to time with institutions that it has itself chartered, the failure of government in a field like education, the doubts and hesitations of government that have followed the decision of the Supreme Court on segregation—all may be attributed, in part at least, to an unreasoning notion that the state should wither away as far as possible. In the case of institutions chartered or empowered by government, such as corporations and labor unions, it is sometimes difficult to tell who is doing the controlling. The infiltration of government by the institutions that it should control has become an American commonplace. It may be that an effort to figure out the role of government in this society should begin with the analysis and application of Lincoln's statement that "the legitimate object of government is to do for the people what needs to be done but which they cannot by individual effort do at all, or do so well, for themselves."

We are a nation of employees, and what the corporations don't do to us, the unions will. We live in cities, with nobody to talk to. We have no means of appraising the reliability of the information supplied us by the media of communication. We have the opportunity, of which we all avail ourselves, of sending our children to school, but we can say nothing effective about the education they receive. We are supposed to make ourselves felt through political parties, but they are just as huge and remote and insensitive as the government itself. The atmosphere in which we live is anonymously created, but deeply felt: we don't know how we know what is not to be done or said, but we know all right. The institutions that dominate our society have made underdogs of us all.

The remedies that achieve popularity are likely to be mere slogans. We chant, for example, about the right to work, ignoring the fact that right-to-work laws have had little or no effect, or about democracy as the cure for injustices that union members suffer, ignoring the fact that perhaps the most democratic union, the International Typographical, is one of the most antisocial.

The institutions that should help us to understand and improve our society, such as the university and the press, have been swallowed up by it. In the last generation the universities have become service stations, rather than beacons. Their principal interest appears to be money, and they will engage in any activity that seems likely to provide it. So we are without centers of independent thought and criticism. The highly specialized and diffuse character of the universities prevents them from becoming centers, and their eagerness to sell themselves prevents them from being independent. This process has gone very far and seems irreversible. It is altogether unlikely that the American universities can become centers of independent thought. It would be simpler, and more hopeful, to establish new institutions for the purpose than to try to reform the universities to the extent that would be required.

Rising costs have driven many newspapers from the field, have made standard in the United States the one-publisher town, and have put the publisher in the driver's seat. As the case of Boston shows, there is no necessary connection between competition and equality. Boston has had more newspapers, and more poor ones, than any city of its size. The Commission on the Freedom of the Press, though lamenting the tendency toward fewer newspapers in fewer hands, saw no hope in the antitrust laws or in any other method of arresting or reversing this tendency. The best that the commission could do was to propose a continuing private agency to appraise and report on the performance of the press. One of the aspects of the agency's work would be to appraise the performance of the press as a purveyor of information, and another would be to appraise the performance as a forum of criticism and discussion. These mild suggestions infuriated the publishers, who took the view that nobody outside the newspaper business was entitled to criticize it or was competent to do so and that criticism in any event was unnecessary because the American people criticized the newspaper every day in making up their minds whether or not to buy them. The obvious absurdity of this reply—the part about freedom of choice must have seemed especially laughable to the inhabitants of one-paper towns—did nothing to diminish its popularity in newspaper circles.

The Commission on the Freedom of the Press wrote its report before television had burst upon the eyes and ears of the American public. If the commission had known what television would be like it would have been more melancholy than it was—it would have had more reason to be—but it would not have changed the general tenor of its report. Television is young enough so that the possibility of social invention, which was quickly lost in the case of radio, may not yet have wholly escaped us. The potentialities of the educational stations and of subscription television deserve examination. But the uniformity with which the managers of networks and stations assert that they know what the public wants and that the public is getting what it wants suggests that commercial television will go the way the movies have gone: it will become an insignificant factor in supplying information or providing a forum of criticism and discussion.

The great conflicts about contemporary institutions seem to center around what their purpose is. A generation ago the Michigan Supreme Court condemned the suggestion of Henry Ford that a corporation might have other motives than profit. This year Walter Reuther condemned the automobile manufacturers because, he said, their only motive was profit. Is the purpose of the labor union to fight the employers, to give the worker status, or to provide a relatively amicable and satisfactory method for making rules for industry? Is the purpose of a professional association to restrict competition or to elevate the standards of the profession in the interest of the public? Is the purpose of a university to supply the services that vocal groups appear to want or to illuminate the pathway of mankind? Hard, practical thinking about what institutions are for must precede, or at least accompany, any attempts to help them meet the requirements of a free society.

Social actions affecting freedom and justice have so far outrun social thought about them that those who would do something about freedom and justice are compelled to bring thought about them up to date. Gardner Means has pointed out that contemporary economic theory cannot account for any of the major phenomena of contemporary economic life. If we phrase our question in the broadest possible terms and ask what America is all about, the problem is the same. Consider the brilliant book by C. J. Friedrich, *Constitutional Reason of State*. He says:

On the one hand there are those who would go to any length to defend the United States against her enemies within and without; on the other hand are those who, regardless of the consequences, would maintain the American belief as embodied in the rights guaranteed by the constitution. The believers in *Fiat justitia, pereat mundus* glare at those who coldly observe that *Inter arma leges silent*. The Republic is being rocked to its very foundations by this controversy. Why? Because the United States, like the churches, is an organization which *rests upon a moral belief*.

Mr. Friedrich then goes on to indicate what the moral belief is upon which the United States rests:

The United States is, however, basically committed to a position different from that of the Catholic Church. It is committed to a faith in the common

man, in the capacity of human beings to work together effectively by granting to each member of the community a substantial amount of freedom,
freedom to search out the truth for himself, to argue and to be wrong. The
United States is committed, through its constitution, to the proposition that
we do not know the truth, except in comparative terms. The final truth is
there, but no man or group of men is in possession of it. God is there, but
no man or group of men can speak with greater assurance about Him than
any other. We know that one proposition may contain more truth than another, but we do not know that this proposition is final, and the presumption
is that it is not.

Although the assertion that the United States is committed, *through
its Constitution,* to the proposition that we do not know the truth, except in comparative terms, would seem to deserve somewhat closer
scrutiny than Mr. Friedrich gave it, his statement represents a rather
common Protestant view. But if this is the moral belief upon which
the United States rests and if the Roman Catholic Church is committed to a different belief, how can we escape the conviction that
devout adherents of that church are un-American and un-American
in a most basic kind of way?

John Cogley, writing on "Catholics and American Democracy" in
Catholicism in America, has this to say:

But *can* the American tradition of Church-State separation be reconciled
with Catholic teaching? The answer is yes, provided one does not identify
the American idea with an extreme and doctrinaire liberalism that would
turn "democracy" into a full-blown ideology and root our political liberty
in the proposition that skepticism is the only true religious philosophy for
an American, indifferentism the only true religious attitude, relativism and
subjectivism the only true outlook on morality.

For instance, it seems in some circles to be good "liberal" doctrine that
"man is a law unto himself," or, in other words, that individual judgment
and choice confer upon the one making them a moral "right" to do, or write,
or say what he pleases. This, of course, is based on the notion that there is
no objective wrong or right or, if there is, that the line where the moral law
is drawn is too hazy for modern man. . . .

But is the American concept of civil liberties, or civil rights, rooted in such
a philosophy? I think not.

If men equally devoted to freedom and justice can differ so deeply
about the philosophy in which our rights and liberties are rooted, we

may well fear for the safety of these rights and liberties in our new society and our polarized world. The first step that would seeem to be necessary is an effort to clarify the underlying issues. We do not have to agree, but we must have intelligent debate. The role of government, the limits of pluralism, the requirements of unity, and the nature of the moral belief on which the United States rests—these are issues that must be clarified if intelligent debate is to take place.

[CLINTON ROSSITER]

CORNELL UNIVERSITY

The Pattern of Liberty

THE task I have set myself in this essay is to trace the pattern of liberty in Western civilization. My intention is to discuss liberty as both a personal aspiration and a social situation. I am concerned with the disciplines, ethical and intellectual, to which a man must submit if he seeks personal freedom; with the conditions, practical and spiritual, under which he may seek it most hopefully; and with the relations, moral and legal, between the man who seeks it and the society that promises it.

What makes such a man? What makes such a society? What are the obligations of each to the other? These are the timeless questions to which I address this inquiry.

My answers, it should be noted, will be framed largely in ideal terms. I consider it both the delight and the duty of the political theorist to rise occasionally above the reality of his own society, which from his usual angle of vision is almost always grim, and to put his thoughts in the language of warmhearted hope rather than of tough-minded analysis. Certainly the present state of American liberty is full of soft, indeed corrupt spots, and I would not have it thought that I am blind to even the least painful of these. Yet I do not see how we can deal successfully with the problems of real liberty if we have not imagined the pleasures and challenges of ideal liberty, and that is what I propose to do in this paper.

I know that I am slogging my way back over a road which the best minds of the West have traveled in search of truth and justice. I justify this undertaking by assuming exactly what these men assumed: that

15

every generation must take up the study of liberty as if liberty had never been studied before. Aristotle made it impossible for the wisest man of our age to say anything very original about the distinction between liberty and license; Hobbes described the "escape from freedom" with a savage clarity that makes imitators of us all; the first page of Rousseau's *Social Contract* cast the paradox of liberty and authority in a form that still shapes all our debates. But neither they nor Plato nor Locke nor Mill spared us the exacting task of doing our own creative thinking about liberty—of asking their questions in our words, of applying their insights to our problems, of drawing their distinctions with our materials. They would be the first to say that the conditions of our civilization called for new thinking about old truths; they would be the last to insist that we publish our thoughts in the form of commentaries on the Great Books.

This inquiry is largely a product of my own experience, observation, and reflection. I could not and would not cleanse my memory of the thoughts on liberty we all have read in Plato, Cicero, Augustine, Aquinas, Hobbes, Locke, Jefferson, and Mill, but I did refrain consciously from refreshing my recollection of the lessons of the giants or from acquainting myself with the writings of those who have worried about liberty in our own time. Like the *Leviathan* of Hobbes, this piece is the product of a man's brain rather than of his bookshelves. It may be that a mouse rather than a whale will come forth from these labors; if so, let it be judged the fault of the man and not of the method.

A DEFINITION OF LIBERTY

My first task is to define liberty, a task as difficult as it is necessary. Liberty is like electricity: we all know what it is and how it works and what happens when it is turned off and on, but we find it impossible to construct a short definition that is readily intelligible. My own answer to the question "What is liberty?" is essentially this: Liberty, like truth and justice and all the other great abstractions, cannot be defined but can be understood, and the first step toward understanding is to identify the most important uses of the word. As I hear men talk of liberty, especially as I hear them defend our civil and economic and political liberties against the stresses of the age, they seem to have one or more or all of four things in mind: independence, privacy, power, opportunity.

The Pattern of Liberty

Independence is a situation in which a man feels himself subject to a minimum of external restraints on his freedom to make and pursue decisions in the course of his existence. In this sense, liberty is defined largely in negative terms; it is the freedom *from* a whole array of compulsions—freedom from coercion, freedom from oppression, freedom from fear, freedom from psychic and physical insecurity. The free man is the self-confident, self-controlling man. Few men in modern society can hope to maintain a relationship to the men who surround them on every side that can honestly be described as autonomous; indeed, the fact of growing interdependence is one which we must face honestly and often even gratefully. But the free man still pursues the laudable end of reducing his dependence on other men—whether these be friends or relatives or colleagues or policemen or politicians or suppliers of services—to a level at which he can practice self-reliance to a meaningful degree.

Privacy is a special kind of independence, which can be understood as an attempt to secure autonomy in at least a few personal and spiritual concerns, if necessary in defiance of all the pressures of modern society. It is an attempt, that is to say, to do more than maintain a posture of self-respecting independence toward other men; it seeks to erect an unbreachable wall of dignity and reserve against the entire world. The free man is the private man, the man who still keeps some of his thoughts and judgments entirely to himself, who feels no overriding compulsion to share everything of value with others, not even with those he loves and trusts.

Independence and privacy are only one-half of liberty, and the negative half at that. A man may be independent; he may achieve a real measure of privacy. But if this is all he is and does, he is far from enjoying liberty as we understand it today, a fact to which almost any American Negro can bear eloquent witness. Liberty is also a positive thing. It implies energy, motion, creation; and we must therefore think of it in terms of *power*. The free man is the able man, the man who is not simply exempt from the direction of others but capable of directing himself. He is the man who sets his goals and has the power to reach them; and the more efficiently he reaches them, the freer man he is likely to be.

To close the circle of liberty, we should think of it also in terms of *opportunity*. If self-directed action is the end product of liberty, as surely it is for most men in modern society, then liberty is a condition

17

in which a man is permitted to act, has the capacity to act, and—this is the added dimension—is encouraged to act by the external situation. The most important element in opportunity would seem to be choice. The free man is the man with alternative courses of action; and the more courses he may have to choose among in a particular situation, the more genuine liberty he may be said to enjoy. Opportunity for purposeful activity, opportunity for self-realization, opportunity for work and rest and love and play—this is what men think of as liberty today.

I have been much too taxonomic about this most noble of man's earthly aspirations, and I therefore hasten to fit these four pieces—independence, privacy, power, opportunity—back together into a unity that I have picked apart only in fancy. Liberty is an exciting blend of qualities and situations, and the blend gets its final strength from the provident fact that it is self-nourishing, that each of its elements feeds upon all the others, that its positive and negative elements are held in a state of fruitful tension. The emphasis in classical Liberalism, to be sure, is on the negative aspects of liberty. Liberty is thought of almost exclusively as a state of independence and privacy. But this is precisely one of those points at which classical Liberalism no longer serves, if ever it did serve, as a wholly adequate instrument for describing the place of the free man in the free society. Such a man must be free *from*, but he also must be free *to*—and no explanation of his liberty can fail to give a place of first importance to his power to act and to the situation in which he exerts this power. Indeed, unless we give this place to power and opportunity, we must agree with those men, more sad than wise, who insist that we are not as free as we were in the days of Coolidge or McKinley. We are, it is true, much more dependent on the pleasure of men and on the whim of forces over which we have no effective control; we have been forced to surrender most of the joys of privacy to employers and tax men and draft boards and peer groups. Yet we are freer—much freer, as almost any woman or child or worker can testify—principally because both our powers and opportunities have expanded so fantastically. The total content of liberty, understood in this broad and realistic sense, has never been greater than at the present moment.

If liberty still confuses and defies definition, so be it. All great words confuse and defy definition, which may be one reason why they remain great words. In any case, I shall be speaking about liberty as I have analyzed it here: a blend of elements no one of which can safely be put aside, a blend within which a shift is going on from negative to positive.

THE DISCIPLINES OF LIBERTY

Out of this exercise in definition there now emerges—at least in my field of vision—the substantial figure of the free man, the man of independence, privacy, power, and opportunity. No one man has exactly the same amount of liberty as any other man, nor does his liberty have exactly the same inner proportions. Some men are plainly freer than others—and not simply because some are bachelors and others have five children, some are rich and others poor, some are free to wander and others pledged to stay and serve. They are freer because, morally and practically, they are less dependent on the commands and suggestions of others, more intent upon staking out a preserve of privacy, better equipped to select and pursue their ends, more favorably situated to choose among alternative ends and to reach them successfully. The variations of liberty in a free society are as numerous as the men who inhabit it. The situations of men range from near-perfect freedom to near-absolute subjection, and there are fewer men who achieve the former than endure the latter. Not every man in a free society is free himself.

I do not mean to question the splendid doctrine of inherent, inalienable, even God-given rights. No belief has had more meaning for American democracy and Western civilization than the enlightened assumption that all men are created equal and that what they are equal in is freedom. But it is one thing to have freedom in the abstract, which we all have as children of God, quite another to use it and enjoy it, which we all do not as children of the world. The capacity for liberty dwells in every man, but no one of us cultivates this capacity with exactly the same skill and intensity as does any other, and many of us do not cultivate it at all.

Then we may ask: What are the means of cultivating freedom? How does a man achieve it? How can he achieve even more? What, in short, are the things he must have done and must continue to do in order to be truly free?

Aspects of Liberty

The question is the oldest in the history of liberty, and so, too, is the answer: A man must have practiced and must continue to practice genuine self-discipline. The price of liberty is self-sacrifice, self-reliance, and self-control; nothing has happened in modern society to relieve the free man of responsibility for the state of his own freedom. Rather, the shift toward power and opportunity within the equation of liberty makes the practice of self-discipline even more essential. To say this is not in the least to deny the immense influence of environment on the state of liberty. But we cannot permit ourselves to become so bewitched by the truth that liberty is socially influenced as to forget the companion truth that liberty is also personally cultivated. Different men enjoy different amounts of liberty in the same environment. Men on their own may long to escape from freedom; men in legal bondage may stake out an area of privacy in defiance of all the odds. Liberty is an intensely personal thing. It is conditioned by the society, but it is achieved and practiced by the person. It is most securely achieved and effectively practiced by men who submit to certain forms of self-discipline.

The first and most essential of these is the discipline of *faith:* A man must want to be free. Liberty is at bottom a quality of the spirit, and all else depends upon the mysterious process through which a shaky instinct is raised to a firm belief. The free man believes intensely in freedom—freedom for himself and freedom for others. If he cannot believe in it for himself, if he assigns it only a modest position on the scale of human values, he will be unwilling to submit to the other kinds of self-discipline that give him independence and power. If he cannot believe in it for others, if he aspires to one state for himself and concedes a lesser one to his fellows, his faith is twisted into something ugly and inhuman. It perishes for want of the nourishment it must get from his sense of identity with other men. Nurture has conspired with nature to put steel in the free man's spirit for the exertions that make him free. The essential ingredient in the steel is an unshakable belief —which must often be maintained in the face of depressing evidence to the contrary—that men are born to be free.

The second is the discipline of *knowledge:* A man must learn to be free. First guided by the love and kindness of others, then spurred by his own faith, he must pass and repass through those processes and experiences—reading, writing, listening, thinking, observing, acting, adventuring, suffering—that lead him to measured knowledge about himself and the world. For knowledge is the essence of power, and power is the creator of opportunity. The free man has learned many things, how to work and play, how to love truth and honor it, how to know the good and cherish it, how to live bravely and die content. He has learned about society, about its gifts and temptations. He has learned about liberty, about its challenge and promise. Most important of all, he has learned about himself—about his urges, talents, strengths, and weaknesses, about the distance his spirit can safely bear between reach and grasp.

Let me demonstrate the importance of this discipline with a simple analogy—ten men in the middle of a pool. They are all free and equal in the water, just as they are on land. Those who have learned how to swim can enjoy their freedom; and the more they have learned, the more delightful their freedom is. Those who have not learned how to swim, who have not submitted to the discipline of knowledge and training—well, they, too, can enjoy their freedom, at the bottom of the pool. Otherwise they must suffer the indignity of being rescued and the frustration of being thereafter forbidden a part of their potential freedom. Knowledge is not freedom, but next to faith it is the most essential ingredient, not least because it raises faith to a new level of dignity.

Implicit in the discipline of knowledge is the discipline of *effort:* A man must work to be free. He must toil and spin to achieve independence, never relax in his attempt to maintain privacy, strive ceaselessly to acquire power and then to use it. I have spoken of the "escape from freedom," a phrase that seems to imply that men generally abandon liberty through an act of positive surrender. The fact is, of course, that one can escape from freedom and surrender himself into dependence or even subjection simply by sitting quietly in dull or cheerful sloth. Freedom is a magnet, but so is bondage, and freedom will not draw a man to itself without help from him. It can be argued, of course, and argued persuasively, that many men achieve a large measure of liberty through the efforts of others. There is no doubt that we get off to quite different starts along the road to independence and power, no doubt that some of us are born to opportunity, others must achieve it, still others have it thrust constantly upon them. Yet no amount of effort by family and friends, no measure of inherited status or present fortune, can spare a man the final necessity of sweating for his liberty—if liberty be understood in any positive sense.

The other forms of self-discipline are held together and given direction by the discipline of *purpose:* A man must have a reason to be free; indeed, he must have a variety of reasons. Knowledge for what? Effort for what? The free man has asked and answered these searching questions by constructing a foundation of values and goals that supports his quest for self-realization. The purposes of men are as varied as are their natures and capacities, and certainly some men achieve more freedom than others because their purposes are higher. Yet any man, or so we must believe, can cultivate enough intellectual and moral purpose to move him powerfully in the direction of liberty. The importance of purpose is never so apparent as when we observe men who lack it. We all know men, especially young men, who have a measure of faith in freedom, a respect for knowledge, and a capacity for effort, and yet who are so purposeless as to exist almost like mindless, amoral vegetables. They are unfree as only thoroughly frustrated men can be, and they will be set free only when purpose takes hold of their lives.

Finally, we must pay our respects, as the best minds of the ages have paid theirs, to the discipline of *virtue:* A man must be decent to be free. The importance of morality to liberty is usually demonstrated in terms of its benign influence on the social order, but the case for virtue can also be argued in terms of the individual and his spiritual health. The man who is fair-minded, kind, decorous, and honest, whose whole cast of mind is turned toward the practice of the acknowledged virtues, is visibly freer than the man who lies and cheats and indulges his every whim and lust. The good man's independence is a source of comfort and self-confidence, the wicked man's is a breeder of fear and self-pity. The good man's power begets more power in the using, the wicked man's is wasted in maintaining his defiant position. Most important, the good man's spirit is strengthened by his respect for the liberty of others, the wicked man's is withered by its essential inhumanity. It is impossible for a man whose thoughts are dissolute and actions furtive, whose relations with other men are poisoned by contempt and spite, to have that sense of psychological security which pervades the spirit of genuine liberty. The free man is the good man, and goodness is a state that most of us reach only through persistent self-discipline.

The Pattern of Liberty

Faith, knowledge, effort, purpose, virtue—these are the challenges that every man must meet in order to be free. No one of them can be ignored, no one answered too impetuously. The discipline of liberty, like liberty itself, forms a seamless web, each part of which strengthens and is strengthened by all the others. The man who fails to practice any one of these self-disciplines, the man of no faith or no knowledge or no virtue, weakens his will and ability to practice the others. The man who practices any one of them too zealously, the man of blind faith or undigested knowledge or overbearing virtue, loses sight of the ultimate goal. In the pursuit of the disciplines of liberty, as in the enjoyment of the fruits of civilization, harmony must inspire and prudence govern every man's conduct.

THE CONDITIONS OF LIBERTY

This dissection of the personal aspects of liberty has gone far enough, and I turn now to consider the social context within which men can practice it most successfully. Liberty has neither real existence nor abstract meaning outside society, for it is essentially a posture toward one's fellow men, a relationship with the other members of a community. The very idea of the free man implies the presence all about him of other men.

The importance of society for personal liberty goes much deeper than that. Social environment has a determining effect on the practice of liberty. To carry the thought in the preceding paragraph one step further: The very idea of the free man implies the presence all about him of other free men, and such men can arise and flourish in meaningful numbers only in an environment that encourages them to cultivate the self-disciplines. Liberty is social as well as personal; it needs the protection and respect of society as well as the faith and effort of the person. The potentially free man becomes the actually free man only in a society that respects his independence, honors his privacy, stimulates his power, and, above all, presents him with broad opportunity.

And so the next major question comes: What are the characteristics of this society? In what kind of community can a man hope to be free, and have no one to blame but himself (or gross bad luck) if his hope is frustrated? What is the ideal social context for the pursuit of personal liberty? And the answer, surely, is a community—more precisely, a chain of communities stretching from neighborhood to nation—that can discipline itself even as its citizens discipline themselves, that can resolve to travel the hard road to democracy rather than the easy one to tyranny, that can sacrifice present indulgence to future good. The marks of such a community would appear to be these:

First, a *faith in freedom* governs the climate of opinion. The faith of a free nation is the sum of the faiths of all the people in it; it finds expression in the words and deeds with which they carry on the practical business of living from day to day. But the faith of a free nation is also something larger and more splendid than the practices of the moment; it finds expression in ideas and institutions and folkways over which the people have no immediate influence—in constitutions, customs, laws, traditions, values, myths, and rituals. If these were conceived in liberty and continue to honor it, the men who inherit them, who bask in their benign warmth from their earliest years, are particularly well started on the quest for personal liberty. To be born and raised in freedom is no guarantee of success in this quest. A free man, like a free nation, can sell the birthright of liberty for a mess of tinsel glory or false security, but at least we may say that he was given a special chance to practice freedom and that if he spurned the chance he betrayed his community as well as himself. The gap between practice and faith in a community must not loom too wide or persist too long, but the capacity of faith to close the gap should never be underestimated. Let India stand as an example of the power of faith in liberty to overcome the most adverse environment.

A close corollary of the nation's faith in freedom is a widespread attitude of *good will.* Certainly no condition is more favorable to a man's practice of the self-disciplines of liberty than the secure feeling that his fellows wish him well. Their good wishes may be expressed both negatively and positively—negatively as the spirit of tolerance, which supports his claims to independence and privacy; positively as the spirit of respect, which places power in his hands and opportunity at his feet. The importance of tolerance for the practice of liberty needs no demonstration. The importance of respect, which is felt most sharply in the expectations of one's fellows, needs only this piece of evidence, the condition of woman in modern society. Why is she demonstrably freer than women of even a generation ago? The answer, quite simply, is that we expect her to be freer and that she is proving anew the capacity of the individual to be drawn upward to self-liberation by the expectations of others.

The nation's faith in freedom finds its most exacting test in the willingness of its citizenry to support the means of *education*. If knowledge is the great self-discipline through which men seek the power of freedom, the environment in which they live must encourage them to "gladly learn and gladly teach." The nation must be prepared to assign a healthy portion of its treasure to the use of its schools and colleges— and by treasure I mean not only money but men—or open the door of the future to all the enemies of liberty, to ignorance, sloth, vice, and fanaticism. I know no magic number that expresses the percentage of its income which a society should devote to education, but I do know that no society has yet risen very far above the minimum in the direction of the optimum. Nor has any society given enough hard thought to the purposes for which it should make this sacrifice, especially to the central purpose of raising up young men and women to live as self-respecting citizens who show respect for others. Education in the delights and challenges of liberty is one of the certain conditions of human freedom. And need I add that education begins at home, that much is asked of the family in the training of children for liberty? How fortunate the society in which the common practice is, not to take the easy way out of teaching children to submit or the even easier way of permitting them to run wild, but to train them to make self-reliant choices within the bounds of law and order.

A fourth condition for the flourishing of liberty is the capacity of the society to sponsor candid, rational, informed *discussion* of the issues that face it. This is one of the most important skills in which free men must be educated—to gather information efficiently, to state opinions judiciously, to listen to the opinions of others respectfully, to stay within the limits of fair-minded debate, to leave their minds open to persuasion, to change their minds gracefully when persuaded of error, and to honor the truth for its own sake. The social justification for freedom of expression is a matter of common knowledge: genuine progress in all the areas of human concern is best achieved in a society that ventilates its problems thoroughly. The personal justification is no less certain: the willingness of free men to inform, criticize, and persuade one another in a spirit of mutual respect leads to an ever-growing independence of mind and power of decision in all but the most obstinate or cowardly.

Liberty finds political expression through the institutions of representative democracy, and the great guardian of these institutions is the spirit and forms of *constitutionalism*. Like the other conditions that I have been discussing, constitutionalism is a servant of both social and personal liberty. To the society it guarantees that decisions will be made and pursued through sober, predictable methods. Democracy is grounded on common agreement to proceed slowly through discussion and compromise and to avoid steps that cannot be retraced. In this sense, constitutional prescriptions stiffen the democratic process by forcing men to think, talk, and bargain before they act. To the individual it offers shelter against the whims of the current majority. Bills of rights carve out an area in which men can enjoy independence of thought and decision in defiance of all the dominations and powers the state can bring to bear. The rule of the majority remains the vital principle of republics, but constitutionalism sees to it that the majority is persistent and undoubted on all occasions, extraordinary on extraordinary occasions, and powerless on those occasions when the issue is a man's liberty of conscience.

Still another mark of the free society, and thus a condition for the effective practice of liberty, is widespread *economic security*. By "economic security" I mean a condition of material well-being whose price is something less than subjection to the will of other men, whether they be public or private; and by "widespread" I mean a condition that most men have achieved or at least find within their reach. No man can be expected to give much thought to liberty if liberty gives him nothing but exhausted privation. No man can be expected to give much allegiance to democracy if democracy leaves him in degrading poverty. Rather, he needs opportunity to acquire and hold private property by reasonable effort, insurance against poverty that is caused by events beyond his control, and a sense that equity if not equality marks the distribution of the wealth of the nation. The free society needs a surplus of wealth to provide education, information, leisure, and culture for its citizens. Economic well-being makes neither men nor nations free, but it does provide the stable foundation on which they can wrestle with the other disciplines of liberty and have some hope of victory.

The Pattern of Liberty

Finally, the machinery of the free society, like the mind of the free man, is directed by a sure sense of *morality*. This sense governs all those in power, especially those whose power is political. The men who make the laws are noted for their persistent devotion to the public interest; the men who execute them are fair-minded, skilled, frugal, and upright; the men who interpret and enforce them are no respecters of persons except as persons. The laws themselves, which articulate the ideals and folkways of the people, are sound, just, and workable, and equitable if not always equal in application. I have already noted the central position of the self-discipline of virtue in the mind and heart of the free man, and it seems almost banal to add that such a man, unless he be one of those rare spirits who flourishes on the "outside," can practice private virtue consistently only in a context of public morality. No man will submit to this exacting form of self-discipline unless he is genuinely confident that his efforts are likely to be rewarded, and no society can ask him to display that measure of confidence unless it assures him that its hands are clean, that it deals with him as it deals with all men, that it is prepared to encourage virtue and punish vice— especially in high places. The key to order and stability in a free society is a glad consensus on the fundamentals of the democratic process; and this kind of consensus, which inspires men to go far beyond and above the letter of the law in the conduct of their daily lives, will arise only in an atmosphere in which personal decency and public integrity support one another.

No society has ever existed or ever will exist in which all these conditions are perfectly realized, but I think it has served a useful purpose to describe these seven conditions for a democratic Utopia. If all of them are goals we can never expect our nation to reach, all of them are also standards against which to measure the public efforts of the men around us to preserve and increase our measure of liberty. All men cry "Liberty!" but not all men serve it by working for conditions in which liberty can flourish.

The true friends of liberty, it seems to me, are those who have studied our tradition and made it a force in their own lives, who make an effort to stay within the bounds of tolerance when thrown into contention with men of contrary opinions, and who lend active support to education for right living and high thinking. They defend the freedoms of thought and expression against the relentless assaults of envy;

they cherish due process of law and all other instruments of constitutional government; they protest against chicanery in public office, even or especially when practiced by their friends.

Such men, the true friends of liberty, are in fact the most necessary condition of all to the health of a free society. Such men are few in number but mighty in influence.

THE OBLIGATIONS OF LIBERTY

The essential interdependence of the free man and the free society calls upon each to honor certain obligations to the other. I have already touched upon the obligations of the society, which may be summed up as dedicated cultivation of the conditions of liberty. The free man has a right, inherent in his freedom, to expect the society to encourage and reward his pursuit of freedom, particularly to create ever-widening opportunities for him to exploit his largely self-acquired powers. But what of his obligations to society? What does he owe in return for protection, care, and respect? The answer is that society can ask him to make an honest attempt to practice the self-disciplines of personal liberty. He owes faith, knowledge, effort, purpose, and virtue to himself; he also owes them to his society, to his fellow men—unless, of course, he is a hermit or outlaw who asks nothing of society. And he owes, in addition, three special obligations.

The first is the obligation of *duty:* A man who enjoys the privileges and immunities of a free society should pay for these in the hard cash of service. Duty beckons to different men with different degrees of urgency, and men may answer in different ways. Some men make a career of public service, and for those who pursue it with zest and integrity a free society must ever be grateful. Most men, however, live essentially private lives; of them the obligation of duty asks only these things: that they recognize the ways in which their calling serves the public and cultivate these ways with particular intensity; that they meet the common demands of citizenship, especially the challenge of the suffrage, with intelligence; that they meet the more exacting demands, such as payment of taxes and military service, with understanding if not always zeal; and that they sacrifice a meaningful portion of their energies over a meaningful span of years to the charitable, cultural, or civic activities of their community. There is no doubt that a man can choose to pursue freedom in isolation from his fellows or that a healthy society can tolerate the presence of many such men, men who will not vote, will not serve, will not lift a finger for their fellows. Yet it is as plain as such things can be that these men get something for nothing, which is to say that they are not entirely honest, and that such a society is not as healthy as it could be, which is to say that it is sicker than it should be. For this reason, no development in recent political thought in this country has been so welcome as the revival of interest in the correlation of rights and duties, of the recognition of the kinship of freedom and responsibility. The free society has an insatiable appetite for men who can serve it intelligently in every area and at every level of existence, and no free man can fail consistently to answer the call of duty.

The second is the obligation of *obedience:* A man who is sheltered by the equitable laws of a free society should honor these with unforced compliance. One of the enduring commonplaces of our political tradition is the notion that freedom is intelligent obedience to the laws we make for ourselves. For all purposes, this means the laws for which we could conceivably have voted had we been lawmakers over the years. It is absurd, of course, to ask the free man to approve every detail in the great mass of laws and ordinances to which he is subject in the modern community, yet he is bound by every dictate of democratic logic to observe them as best he can—the good ones with grace, the bad ones with a grimace and a determination to have them altered or abolished. A familiar example will serve to illustrate the measure of increased freedom we gain from obedience to a law we may be said to have made for ourselves, the law that places traffic lights at busy corners. Which man in fact is freer—the driver in a lightless city, whose route to work is a string of gambles with disaster, or the driver in a regulated city, whose route is safe, predictable, and probably twice as quickly traveled? Our freedom to act in this highly social situation arises from the expectation that others will obey the law as willingly as we. The law is the fact and symbol of civilization, and those who obey it rationally demonstrate their readiness to seize the opportunities that civilization offers. Need I add that none but the civilized shall know freedom in civilization?

And the third is the obligation of *loyalty:* A man who enjoys the fruits of liberty in a free society should pledge steady allegiance to its first principles. The squabbles over loyalty that have soiled our post-war politics have discredited the truth that every community needs an extra layer of spiritual cement to hold it together and that no cement is more adhesive and less expensive than the spontaneous loyalty of a grateful citizenry. Loyalty is something more than the mere absence of treason, but just what that something is we find it hard to say. Certainly it is easier, thanks to the inanities of the past decade, to say what it is not. It is not conformity, not orthodoxy, not ritualism, and certainly not chauvinism; it is not an outward display of love of country to hide an inward hatred of many of the people in it. It is, rather, the cutting edge of that strong faith in freedom which guides the thoughts of the free man and the values of the free society. It is persistent devotion to the hard core of these values—to truth and justice, to virtue and charity, to constitutionalism and democracy—even if such devotion means challenging the assembled orthodoxy of the times. If the challenge is issued in behalf of an alien despotism or native obscurantism, the count of disloyalty may perhaps be leveled. But if it comes in behalf of a genuine regard for the acknowledged principles of the nation, the count of disloyalty is untrue, irrelevant, and itself disloyal. Loyalty to a free society, to be specific, loyalty to America, is loyalty to the practices and ideals of rational, ordered, constitutional liberty.

I realize that these words—duty, obedience, loyalty—have been the stock in trade of all the tyrannies that ever arose to rob man of his birthright to liberty. Yet we must not be driven by our contempt for tyranny too far in the other direction, or we may find ourselves standing on the untenable ground of anarchy. I realize, too, that I have produced no useful answer to the hard question of when a free man may or must refuse to do his duty, refuse to obey the law, refuse to engage in the rituals of loyalty. I console myself with the thought that the question is essentially unanswerable, that both the rebel with cause and the rebel without it will get their just deserts from history or heaven. All I have tried to say is that the free man has substantial obligations to the free sociey and that a consistent refusal to pay them out of spite or selfishness or ignorance is a kind of spiritual suicide.

There are a hundred morals I could draw from this inquiry into the disciplines, conditions, and obligations of liberty, but I will limit myself to two—each of them an appeal of sorts to the men who think and write about problems of liberty in modern America. Although neither is really any more original than the entire cast of this paper, each takes on a certain freshness from its special urgency for our times.

The first is the observation that we have all been much too casual about the place of the state, by which I mean society and government, in the total pattern of human liberty. Our zealous attention to the rituals of the cult of American individualism has left us nearly blinded to the immense debt of the free man to the community all about him. We have forgotten the lesson of history: that we see as far as we do only because we stand on the shoulders of generations, that liberty was an abstraction until our ancestors earned it for us, that all the knowledge we apply to the practice of liberty is the gift of others. We have neglected a fundamental of our ethics: that the great law of moral equilibrium commands the reciprocity of rights and duties. We have ignored one of the plainest facts of political and social science: that what keeps us from slipping into tyranny by way of anarchy are the institutions of society—colleges, churches, corporations, unions, associations, schools, libraries, courts, police, even the bodies that make laws and collect taxes. And whatever became of such concepts as friendship and such realities as the family? Have we ever paid them their due as supports of individual liberty?

I do not mean to carry this minor display of indignation too far. I am as aware as the most unreconstructed Spencerian that the state is a massive threat to liberty. But there are states and states, and the one I am talking about is quite remote in fact and faith from the Communist and Fascist Goliaths that have swallowed up government, society, and individuals in the disgusting maw of totalitarianism. The price of liberty is just what it always has been, but it is high time we directed some of that famous "eternal vigilance" to the dangers to liberty that arise in the disorganized and despised community: ignorance, violence, insecurity, and disorder. Our quest must be for a state neither adored nor despised but entrusted prudently with uncommon responsibility for the conditions of liberty, and we would do well to make this quest in theory even as we make it in practice.

My concluding observation is intended to refix attention on the integer of liberty—the free man—and this observation is simply that he cannot hope to gather the fruits of liberty unless he is willing to cultivate it consistently with energy and intelligence. The test of most social action in our time appears to be the liberation of the individual, but the individual must still decide for himself whether he really wants to be liberated, whether he will choose creative liberty or comfortable inertia. If he chooses liberty, he chooses self-discipline, and far too many men are unwilling to make the right choice because it is the hard choice. That is why I would direct a second appeal to our political thinkers—to imagine the ways, moral and intellectual and emotional, in which men can be encouraged to choose liberty over sloth or surrender. We need to do more thinking than we have done in recent years about the moral aspects of individual liberty. And as we do, we should remember the advice of Edmund Burke, who told us that liberty cannot endure "unless a controlling power upon will and appetite be placed somewhere; and the less of it there is within, the more of it there must be without." To this warning I would add: The more of it there is within, the less of it there will need to be without. Idle men may talk of liberty as a handsome gift; the men who know it best have noted and paid the price on the cover: relentless, purposeful, prudent self-discipline.

[JAMES HART]

UNIVERSITY OF VIRGINIA

The State and Human Freedom

IT is proposed to consider what the relation of the state to human freedom ought to be. The inquiry presupposes that man can obtain and
act upon moral or ethical as well as empirical knowledge. He acquires
knowledge of the ought by making explicit the norms, criteria, or
principles of conduct which are logically implicit in his chief end as
determined by his nature.

Man is that animal whose endowment of reason transforms all his
other qualities. His chief end is to glorify God and enjoy Him forever,
to live the good life, to develop his best self by realizing to the fullest
those potentialities which represent his humanity rather than his mere
animality. Since, moreover, man means every man and since the person of every man, because he is made in the image of God or because
he is possessed of reason, is of intrinsic worth, no man can glorify
God or follow reason without trying, so far as in him lies, to ensure
the opportunity of all men to seek their chief end.

Ethics, or systematic study of the ought, makes the assumption,
which man cannot help acting upon, that he has within himself the
capacity, albeit limited, of making choices. That capacity is the internal freedom which the theologians call free will and without which
man's conduct would be wholly the product of determinism.

Since, however, man is an animal as well as a rational being, he is
characterized by an inner tension between reasonableness and intem-
perate desire, between reason as the teacher of humility and charity
and reason as the tool of pride and avarice. In resolving this tension
he may choose the noblest or the most degrading course; but it is only

when he follows the good life that he finds that happiness which his nature makes available to him alone among God's earthly creatures.

The chief end of man can be stated in terms which are demonstrably valid deductions from his nature only if they are highly abstract. From these abstract principles more specific moral precepts may be derived; but they are not unqualifiedly applicable *semper et ubique*. For man's moral understanding is fallible; and there is vast variety in the general circumstances and the particular situations to which it has to address itself. Yet even abstractions take rich meaning from our heritage of philosophical, moral, and spiritual insight; and our past experience with their application furnishes concrete norms which we are under moral obligation to bring to bear, as John Dewey would say, even upon novel situations.

These premises have been stated in part in theological terminology in the belief that Christian theology, all question of its validity at the literal level aside, expresses at the allegorical and moral levels profound truths and in the Passion of Christ gives at the anagogical level an epic view of man's relation to the universe which renders life so meaningful that it deserves to be accepted by men at least on an *als ob* basis.

Nec meus hic sermo est; for it summarizes that part of our Western tradition which is among the noblest achievements of the human spirit.

Though we assume man's free will, or internal capacity of making choices, we must recognize that his practical opportunity of making them is greatly affected by external causes. This opportunity constitutes his external freedom and includes both the possession of the means necessary to the making of a choice and the absence of constraint upon the exercise of that choice.

Necessary means of making choices include an education which supplies the basic skills for living and for seeking the good life, the accessibility of fundamental cultural assets of the world, the purchasing power required for a minimal standard of living, and leisure from the task of earning a living sufficient for varied forms of self-development. Possession of these means may be adversely or favorably affected, and constraint upon the exercise of choice may be produced, by the choices of other men in the exercise of their freedom or by impersonal causes. These impersonal causes embrace the natural environment, including the operation of the laws of nature in man considered as a biological organism; the social environment, particularly the economic order and dominant group opinion; and the state of advancement of the arts and sciences, the technologies and economic techniques, ethics and philosophy, and, indeed, every aspect of civilization. The threat, as a means of compelling certain conduct, of physical coercion or of economic, social, political, or other detriment is the mode by which constraint upon the exercise of choice is exerted by other men. The actual employment of such coercion or the causing of such detriment has the effect of curtailing the means of making choices. The threat or employment of such coercion may exact economic wealth as taxation.

When the management of a corporation fires an employee for joining a union, a means of making choices is taken away by the choice of other men; but when that same management is compelled by a decline in the demand for the product which the corporation manufactures to lay off employees, the same means is taken away by the impact of the economic system. Though the men are laid off by the action of other men, that action is not the result of choice but of a practical necessity which makes it essentially impersonal.

Both constraint upon a man's exercise of choice and action which affects his possession of the means of making choices may be taken by those members of an organized group of which he is a member who are recognized as having authority to act in the name of the group; or they may be taken, without the sanction of such recognized authority, by other men as individuals or on behalf of an organized group of which he is not a member.

Organized groups, or organizations, which are characterized by having organs with recognized authority, are of many sorts, one of which is the modern state. A modern state may be formally defined as the organization of a group of people for the making and enforcement of rules and decisions of supreme authority with respect to all the relations of all the people within its territory and for the conduct of its relations with other like organizations.

The modern state is accordingly a unique organization in that its function is to provide an over-all ordering of the relations which subsist among individuals and groups within a society. It is differentiated from organizations of all other kinds by the comprehensiveness and supremacy of its authority and by its virtual monopoly of the physical coercion of man by man as a recognized means of regulating social relations.

Since the differentia of the state gives its action profound consequences for man's freedom, the first problem is the moral justification of the state as opposed to anarchy, or having no state at all.

Whether the state is morally justified must depend wholly upon whether it is a means to the chief end of man. The idea that the state is an end in itself and hence can be justified apart from the chief end of the individual human beings involved is a denial of the very premises of ethics. Even as a means to the chief end of man, moreover, the state cannot give him the good life, which by nature is attainable only by individual self-development. It can at best be a means to that external freedom which makes individual self-development possible.

For the sake of simplicity this part of the discussion will be confined to freedom as the absence of constraint by other men upon a man's exercise of choice. Social contract writers took the problem to be how to get from an assumed absolute moral right to freedom on the part of every individual to the moral right of the state to limit his freedom. They saw that there was no way to make that jump unless by the consent of every member of every generation or even of every citizen whenever a law is passed. John Locke sought to find the former in tacit consent, Jean-Jacques Rousseau the latter in the *volonté générale*. But tacit consent is consent which is attributed to men rather than consent which they themselves freely give; and the continuing consent of the general will is so paradoxical an expression of the rationale of the democratic process that it frightens us, as W. Y. Elliott does well to imply, by the ease with which it can be manipulated into majoritarian totalitarianism.

If the free and express consent of all were a prerequisite, then no state would have a moral basis. But we cannot admit that it is. For on the premise that the consent of every man is necessary, if any man refuses his consent he may then use his absolute right to constrain the exercise of choice by his fellow men and hence their chance to seek their chief end.

T. H. Green and W. W. Willoughby make it clear that the assumption is untenable that the individual has an absolute moral right to freedom. Willoughby points out that Thomas Hobbes was right in saying there is no morality in a nonsocial state of nature, but that this means that to discuss ethics at all we must begin, not with such a state of nature, but with a society whose members recognize in principle each other's right to that freedom of choice which alone makes the search for the good life possible. Reciprocal recognition of moral rights carries reciprocal recognition of the correlative moral duties or obligations. It is this reciprocity or mutuality of recognition which is the germ of truth in the myth of the social contract; but that myth cannot be taken in any legalistic or literalistic sense.

However, even if reciprocal recognition of rights to freedom is habitually followed by most men most of the time, that is not enough. For it is predictable from the nature of man that all men will fall short of that goal some of the time and some men most of the time. If man is not, as held by John Calvin, totally depraved, neither is he, as held by the Enlightenment, naturally good. He may resolve the tension within himself contrary to as well as in favor of reciprocity.

Men accordingly make conflicting as well as common and mutual claims to freedom and seek to settle these conflicts by efforts to bring constraint to bear upon one another's exercise of choice. It was the genius of Hobbes to see that this fact carries the threat of social disruption. The situation is saved, however, by the fact that every man is born into a family and other organized groups and joins or even helps to form organizations concerned with various social relations. For every organized group has organs with recognized authority to exercise in recognized ways some form of constraint upon the exercise of choice by its members. While, therefore, conflicting claims to freedom may lead to violence between individuals and between groups, the canalizing of freedom by R. M. MacIver's magic of authority avoids the *bellum omnium contra omnes* of Hobbes.

Even before we get to the modern state, moreover, authority is justified as a feature of organized groups from the point of view of freedom itself. For the individual's freedom to seek the good life is doubly protected. In the first place, authority, by furnishing continuity in the dividing line between freedom and constraint, enables men, as Jesse S. Reeves puts it in his *La Communauté Internationale,* to discount the future and thereby offers them a breathing spell in which to give some attention to the quest for their chief end. In the second place, the constraint produced by authority, so far from necessarily resulting in less freedom, may greatly increase it. Constraint upon A may be necessary to prevent his so using his freedom as to constrain B, C, D, and E in the exercise of theirs; and this operates in either of two ways. If the five of them are about equally powerful, then authority may protect the freedom of each against constraint by any. If, however, A is the one who is powerful, constraint upon him may be the only way of securing the freedom of the others, even while it leaves him free in other respects. If the freedoms thus protected are necessary for the development of the best in the several individuals, then support of authority becomes the ethical duty of all concerned.

Over-all regulation of social relations by the state has the advantages, noted by Willoughby, of being paramount, systematic, comprehensive of all social relations within a more or less wide territory, and definable in general principles and rules which are as impartially administrable as human frailty allows.

The comprehensiveness of the state's authority is succinctly expressed in Dante's *De Monarchia: Et ubicunque potest esse litigium, ibi debet esse iudicium.* Since the state's constraint upon the exercise of choice may aid freedom, the comprehensiveness and supremacy of its authority are both quite consistent with a reasonable adjustment between freedom and constraint. Indeed, embodiment of these elements in the legal order of the state is a necessary condition of men's not being diverted from cultivation of their highest talents to mutual aggression because of fear of each other.

Physical coercion, by the threat of which the supremacy of the state's authority is supported, is of course, as Willoughby points out, a crude instrument; but the sole alternatives are public coercion by the state and private coercion presumably by society's most aggressive individuals and groups. The prohibition by the state to all private individuals and groups of the freedom to exert physical coercion over others allows the state itself normally to reserve this sanction for the last resort and thus normally to prevent that general recourse to violence which Hobbes so feared.

It is apparent, then, that to speak of man versus the state is to pose a false issue. For authority, including that of the state, is an indispensable means to the chief end of man precisely because it is the only way of making an adjustment between freedom and constraint which protects men generally in the external freedom to seek their chief end.

The next problem, that of what the state ought to do and how it ought to be organized to do it, thus becomes one of seeking the ideal adjustment between freedom and constraint. Recognizing with Reeves

The State and Human Freedom

that the elements in this ideal adjustment, or *res publica*, are *securitas* and *iustitia* as well as *libertas*, we can relate them rationally by the grand generalization that the state ought to give all men security in that freedom to which they are justly entitled. It is possible, moreover, to go a certain distance in making explicit the implications of this theorem.

Security is the present assurance of future freedom. The common defense builds in the present protection of the whole people's freedom from future external aggression. Law and order, domestic tranquillity, security of person and property—these enable us to make choices in private planning with the reasonable expectation that freedom to enjoy the fruits of our planning will not be jeopardized by failures in enforcement of the rules or by sudden and sweeping changes in the rules themselves. So-called social security guarantees to individuals future purchasing power, as a necessary means to their having choices which befit a human being, against destruction by presently foreseeable catastrophic casualties.

Insofar as this present assurance of future freedom is given men by the state, it enables them so to discount the future as to be able to resolve their inner tension in favor of seeking their chief end rather than trying to shore up their security for themselves by getting through fair means or foul all they can of wealth and power.

The premise that man is duty-bound to conform to the rationality which distinguishes him from the other animals prescribes that the adjustment between freedom and constraint be not merely viable but just. Justice implies equity, equality in the sense of no irrational discrimination, and, in the meaningful phrase of Chief Justice Hughes, fair play. Fair play is both substantive and procedural; or, what amounts to the same thing, there ought to be fairness both in the general principles by which the state makes the adjustment and in their application to particular instances.

Substantive fair play relates to the principles and rules of law which are to be applied as occasion arises. Of course whatever the state enacts is positive law; and it is one's duty in most circumstances to obey even an unjust law rather than defy authority, especially if there is freedom to criticize the inequity and to try to have it changed by orderly processes. Yet we must agree with Cicero in the thought that if the mere fiat of the people or anybody else could make conduct just then it would be just to commit robbery and adultery and the forgery of wills if the fiat said so.

To deny the existence of principles of justice is as false as to affirm that they are infallibly to be given universal application. They share the features that all moral principles have been shown to possess. It may be hard to decide which of two moral rules applies to a novel case. Fallible judgment has to define the limits of a rule such as "Thou shalt not kill" and to distinguish the circumstances in which abstract norms of justice are and are not relevant.

When the worker depended for compensation for injuries sustained in the course of employment upon a common-law damage suit against his employer, the courts followed the principle that no man ought to be held liable without fault. That that principle is binding whenever it is pertinent is a precept of reason. Under the modern statutory arrangement, however, it is recognized that the principle is not applicable; for the insurance method is employed to transfer the expense to the consumer, on the reasonable ground that it is a part of the cost of production and hence ought to go into the price.

That procedure is fair, that process is due, which provides that in every controversy over the application of the law to a given instance an independent third party shall furnish both sides due notice and an opportunity to be heard in an impartial manner and shall on that basis make the decision through an effort to be objective in finding the facts and in interpreting the law as it may apply to the facts so found.

It is only by giving fair play to others that the individual can realize his best self; but it is beyond the strength of character of most men to give fair play unless there is reason to expect fair play in return. For the state, therefore, to exercise its authority justly and to constrain men from gross injustice to one another is for it to enable them to feel that they may themselves be just without self-injury.

Equality is not an end in itself, but is an end only because and insofar as it is an aspect of justice. Equal protection of the laws is basic to justice. So also is equal provision that all shall have, by earning it when possible, the minimal means of self-development, to the extent that this is economically feasible. Sometimes justice calls for proportionate equality: it is not just for everybody to pay the same amount of income tax or even for the rate to be the same for all brackets of income. Ability to pay is a proportionate ability.

The State and Human Freedom

A. N. Whitehead says in his *Dialogues* that, though men are in fact unequal and unalike, the craving for equality is founded on the infinite variety of human abilities. He calls it error to assume that genuine ability consists in the forms of aptitude which lead to economic achievement. This implies that systematic means ought to be taken to discover and encourage everybody's talents of a non-money-making character and to give to those who are endowed with them in high degree the freedom from financial worry which will enable them to develop their gifts and thereby simultaneously realize their potentialities and benefit mankind.

It will clarify the problem of how to give all men security in the freedom to which they are justly entitled, and furnish partial solutions, if note is taken of the distinction, derived from Reeves, between the different ways in which the claims of different men to freedom from constraint by others may be related to each other. Unless they happen to be unrelated, they are common, conflicting, or mutual.

When men share as against others the claim to a freedom, such as national independence or freedom from external aggression, they have a common claim to freedom. If, on the other hand, they have claims to freedom which are both different and incompatible, their respective claims are conflicting. Within a nation partial groups are organized in which the members of one share a common claim to freedom which conflicts with a common claim shared by the members of another. Common claims lead to co-operation, conflicting claims to threats of economic or other forms of detriment or to efforts to have the law threaten physical coercion.

Still again, the freedom which each claims for himself may be precisely analogous to and entirely compatible with the freedom which every other claims for himself. In this event one or more may, indeed, claim both this freedom and the freedom to deny its analogue to others. The conflict of claims which so unreasonable an attitude involves becomes transformed, however, into a mutuality of claims if the attitude changes to one of recognition by all that each is entitled to have his freedom in this regard respected. Their claims are then mutual because they agree to place them on a basis of reciprocity or live-and-let-live. Examples are the First Amendment freedoms: freedom of religion, of speech, of the press, of assembly, and of petition. Besides having a political significance presently to be mentioned, these freedoms broaden out into the wide field of what MacIver would call cultural freedoms.

Cultural claims to freedom are at least potentially mutual, whereas economic ones are often inevitably conflicting. The explanation of this difference lies in the fact that cultural wealth is not scarce, whereas economic wealth is. The ideas and values embodied in art and literature can be appropriated without diminishment, without deprivation of others; indeed, they are multiplied by appropriation:

> *O maraviglia! che qual egli scelse*
> *L'umile pianta, cotal si rinacque*
> *Subitamente là onde la svelse.*

Economic wealth, on the contrary, consists, as John Stuart Mill said, of all those useful and agreeable things which cannot be obtained in the quantity desired without labor or sacrifice. It is characterized by scarcity as well as utility; and so is the economic power which the possession or control of economic goods gives. To be sure, every man may cultivate his own vineyard and refrain, or be constrained by the state, from interfering with the like freedom of his neighbor. This mutuality of claims, however, relates only to men who own vineyards. If a few own the vineyards and employ the rest to tend the vines, conflicting claims to freedom are unavoidable. In short, as between those who have comparable shares of economic wealth or power, mutuality of claims to economic freedom is applicable; but otherwise conflicts of claims arise inevitably out of the factor of scarcity.

With regard to the role of the state in the light of these distinctions, that organization is patently an indispensable means to common claims which are shared by the bulk of the community, as when it provides for the common defense.

In the case of civil and other cultural freedoms, the state is an indispensable means of maximizing and equalizing freedom by keeping it upon a mutual rather than a conflicting basis. Its legal order can stabilize the just principle of mutuality by making it illegal for anybody to interfere with the exercise by another of a cultural freedom he claims for himself and by providing a bill of rights, enforced by judicial review, which puts cultural freedom for all beyond the reach of those who control its political government.

More difficult is the case of conflicting claims. The claim by the managers of a corporation of the freedom to hire and fire at pleasure conflicts with the claim by the employees of the freedom to organize for collective bargaining so as to redress the economic inequality of bargaining power as between the corporation and its individual employees. Present interest lies not so much in the merits of such conflicts as in the fact that the problem is merely evaded by the remark that the state should keep hands off. For the modern state comprehends within its authority employer-employee relations along with all other social relations within its territorial limits. By the very nature of its function, therefore, the state must take a stand as between all conflicting claims to freedom. Thus employer-employee relations were once regulated by the common law, which the courts interpreted as allowing the employer to insist that the employee agree in the contract of hire not to join a union; but in time the common law was modified by statutory provisions forbidding as an unfair labor practice the imposition of such a condition of hire. When the state changed sides, those whose former freedom was restricted complained in the name of "the" freedom of "the" individual; but in this area the question always is, whose freedom to do what shall be protected, and whose restricted, by the state and why?

In sum, whereas the application of the ideal to common and mutual claims to freedom is reasonably clear, what justice demands in the case of conflicting claims depends upon empirical knowledge so difficult to arrive at and upon moral judgment so apt to be beclouded by selfish interest that differences of opinion abound. It is the duty of those trained in political theory to analyze this problem so thoroughly that the issues will be sharpened and such implications as are clearly deducible from the ideal will be brought out to refute irrationalism. Otherwise, the problem of conflicting claims becomes one of so organizing the authority of the state as to maximize the probability that in the long run the ideal will stand the best chance of being approximated.

Insofar as freedom is the possession of means of making choices, what is the role of the state in furnishing those means?

To begin with, justice suggests that the state provide for all men certain essential means of self-development, among which are education and the accessibility, through such means as public libraries, of the cultural assets of mankind.

C. H. McIlwain points out that Aristotle was right in saying that man needs leisure for the higher things of the mind and the real life of the state, while greater economic productivity and broader vision have made it possible for the manual laborer to have the leisure which Aristotle thought he could never have. The modern state recognizes that every man is entitled to earn both leisure and the purchasing power needed for a minimal standard of living when it puts a ceiling over hours and a floor under wages.

The modern state also protects purchasing power as a means of choice by cushioning the blow of those catastrophic casualties which take away the means of earning a living: industrial accidents, serious illness, disability, retirement, old age, and involuntary unemployment. It does so by entering the spheres of workmen's compensation, hospitalization and disability aid or insurance, unemployment and retirement insurance, and assistance to the aged.

How far the state should go in promoting the arts and advancing the sciences may vary with circumstances. Of late it has, for the sake of the common defense, spent large sums upon certain forms of scientific and technological research.

All these ways of furnishing or safeguarding freedom in the form of the possession of necessary means of making choices involve constraint upon the exercise of choice. Education is compulsory. Wage-and-hour legislation narrows the range of choice of employees and of employers. The insurance principle is finding ever wider uses; and people are often required to be beneficiaries of insurance plans. It calls for no elaboration, however, to show that under modern conditions, at least, to participate or not to participate is not a mere self-regarding choice.

Insurance beneficiaries should, where possible, be required to pay part of the cost through premiums, lest the state tempt them to take the distorted view that the world owes them a living. Yet public spending is in one way or another always involved, and the state must therefore exact economic wealth in the form of taxation. Taxation has precisely the same moral justification as other constraints upon freedom exercised by the state—its necessity as a means of giving men a chance to seek the good life. In deciding how far this means ought to be used, it is to be remembered that taxation decreases the freedom of the taxpayer in two ways: it reduces his means of making choices and enforces the exaction by threatening or employing physical coercion.

The fact that taxation and public spending to supply necessary means of making choices impinge differently upon different men puts this whole subject definitely in the area of inescapably conflicting claims to freedom to the extent that the modern sense of justice has not reduced this conflict to disagreement over details.

Society changes and produces new relationships. Not only do economic and other claims often conflict, but new conflicts emerge from time to time. Under changing circumstances, moreover, justice and security may become competing emphases concerning freedom. Altered conditions may give rise to the contention that the security which the law gives, and may long have given, to certain freedoms enables some men unjustly to defeat claims to freedom on the part of others or unjustly withholds from others necessary means of making vital choices. Even when this contention is valid, however, the wont and use which Edmund Burke cherished may not wisely be abandoned in a sudden and wholesale fashion. For it is the very basis upon which continuity and hence rationally guided readjustment of the boundary between freedom and constraint, as distinguished from blind, impulsive action, depends.

Herein lies the paradox of social change which Whitehead in his *Symbolism* stated in these words: "Those societies which cannot combine reverence to their symbols with freedom of revision, must ultimately decay either from anarchy, or from the slow atrophy of a life stifled by useless shadows." In our efforts to resolve this paradox reason and experience join in counseling us to follow the Greek ideal of moderation in all things, to strive for that mean which the *maestro di color che sanno* called the way of virtue. Lest, however, those of us who are satisfied with the status quo distort the doctrine of the mean into an excuse for doing nothing, we ought ever to remind ourselves of the words of Alessandro Manzoni: *Predicano sempre che la perfezione sta nel mezzo; e il mezzo lo fissan giusto in quel punto dov'essi sono arrivati, e ci stanno comodi.*

Although the number whose decisions are final may be one, a few, or many, MacIver points out that in the nature of the case the exercise of the state's authority is always in the hands of a few. Accordingly, the grand difference between governments depends upon whether these few are or are not responsible. This difference is nonetheless fundamental because it is one of degree.

Reflection and history tell us that to have men's freedom to seek the good life at the mercy of an irresponsible few poses a threat to the chief end of man which is intolerable. The responsibility which is called for, however, is of two sorts: constitutional and political.

Constitutional responsibility finds its basis partly in positive law but even more importantly in what Lindsay Rogers is fond of calling constitutional morality. It means the exercise of the authority of the state in accordance with principles of constitutional government which are historically traceable to Locke and philosophically deducible from the premise that the state is a means of making it feasible for every man to seek his chief end. These principles, which have already been indicated, may be restated. The adjustment between freedom and constraint ought to be defined in rules which apply equally to all concerned. In their content, these rules ought to provide for the common defense, guarantee mutuality in men's claims to cultural freedoms, and embody in the compromises of conflicting claims whatever norms of substantive justice reason may impose. The application of the rules to particular controversies ought to be made in conformity with procedural justice; and the rules as thus applied ought in the last resort to be enforceable by physical coercion, which, however, ought to be subject to the sanction of an independent judiciary. Such physical coercion and the threat thereof ought otherwise to be banned as a means of regulating social relations.

In this realm of constitutional responsibility, political responsibility has no place; for to submit the rational requirements of constitutional government to men's desires and opinions would be irrational and immoral. Political responsibility is, therefore, confined to conflicting claims and applies even to them only because and to the extent that liability to partiality and limitation of empirical knowledge leave issues which are unresolvable by an appeal to reason.

That even to this extent officialdom ought to bear political responsibility to the community is a meaningful conclusion only if the community has attained a minimal political maturity. This ought, however, to be the goal for all communities, for the reason that it is more likely in the long run than any alternative to keep alive the aim of giving all men the opportunity to seek their chief end.

Conflicting claims, however, divide the community; and the fact that freedom has a chance to thrive only under domestic tranquillity means that they must somehow be peaceably resolved. Some specific mode of resolution ought, therefore, to be fixed in advance by law. Since the issues involved, moreover, are *ex hypothesi* matters of opinion, the law ought not, except for special reasons, to deny anybody a vote in electing the officials charged with resolving them or to give a vote on one side a different weight from a vote on the other.

At the same time any idea that the majority is entitled to throttle the minority is immoral. There ought to be means of making officialdom responsible to the whole community. Probably the basic means is for a nation's economic policy to aim at promoting or keeping the strength of the middle class. Arthur N. Holcombe has often pointed out that Aristotle's hypothesis that a strong middle class makes for the mean is verified in American experience. We have two parties principally because the bulk of the voters are in the middle, economically and psychologically, and hence electoral majorities are to be won by a brokerage in compromise and an avoidance of extreme positions. Within this framework freedom of speech, freedom of the press, freedom of assembly, and freedom of petition are necessary to broaden political responsibility as well as to ensure individual opportunity of cultural self-development. These freedoms then unite with the freedom of the ballot to produce a fluidity in majorities which inspires the minority of the moment to acquiesce in a mode of resolving conflicts which may soon favor its own members.

To say, however, that in this area officialdom ought to be made responsible to the community is to say no more than that it ought not to be allowed to stand irresponsibly above the rest of the community. It cannot rationally be taken to imply that the governors and the experts who advice them ought to be reduced to the status of mere automatons who adopt as public policy the lowest common denominator of mass opinion or the curbstone reactions of a majority of "sample" citizens. Rather is the responsibility of officialdom to a rough consensus sharpened, and the likelihood that the prevailing opinion will be a reasoned opinion at the same time increased, by general recognition that official-

47

dom has the right and duty to exercise leadership. Without this recognition the influence which belongs to the official governors tends to fall into the hands of unofficial and irresponsible ones. In this connection the doctrine of the mean calls for an interplay of leadership and responsibility which is so nicely harmonized as to join in a creative manner expertness and common sense, tutorship and public response. This is a result which obviously can come only from an attitude to politics which a mature people ought to cultivate.

[GEORGE E. G. CATLIN]

MC GILL UNIVERSITY

On Freedom

THE curse of political language has been the bias toward rhetoric. No word, unless it were love, has been so much abused in this fashion as liberty, which for Rousseau was "the noblest of human faculties" [1] As Lincoln excellently said: "The world has never had a good definition of the word 'liberty.'" In terms of political philosophy we may indeed hold that freedom and liberty have value, imponderable value, even infinite value. But whether this be the case will in large measure depend upon how we choose to define these words. In Biblical language freedom is described as service. The Stoics had the same view. For S. Clemens Alexandrinus, by implication the clever salesman, who stimulates a desire for satiety in material goods, is a slave-master and the greediness he incites is an active cause of human unhappiness.

One of the first duties imposed upon us by the logical analysis of political science is to decide in what sense we are going to use our terms. Even if an element of the arbitrary, and of lexicography rather than of logic, is left in our final choice, nevertheless one elementary requirement for scientific advance is that our usage shall be consistent. When we say A we must go on saying A, and not change the meaning to A'. Another requirement, of a prudent and Ockhamite economy, is that our definition shall not be so "loaded" or sophisticated as to go beyond the element common to all the manifestations which, by com-

---

[1] This essay should be read in connection with the author's article "Critique of Authority," in *Authority*, C. J. Friedrich, ed. (Cambridge, Mass.: Harvard University Press, 1957). The reference to "la plus noble des facultés de l'homme" will be found in the *Discours de l'Inégalité parmi les Hommes*, Garnier, ed., p. 83.

mon usage, we may be expected to study. Perhaps freedom *ought* to mean in practice this or that; but the question will remain whether actions, or lacks of impediment to action, which do not possess this ethical value may not, nevertheless, indubitably be instances, however licentious, of liberty.

The first step in clarification is to make a distinction, which even if arbitrary is useful and not without precedent, between Freedom and Liberty. It will give precision and abbreviate much of the discussion, for example by writers such as D. G. Ritchie, about whether we can have "rights," sometimes called "natural," prior to the establishment, whether by "covenant" or otherwise, of a social order. By liberty we shall mean such freedom as is recognized within the social order. There may, indeed, be legitimate debate about whose recognition is necessary for the establishment of civil liberties and about whether the government may not be usurping powers which infringe upon what are constitutionally recognized as the civil liberties of individuals. Civil liberties yet only obtain within the established civil order or, at least, within what the wider social order, through its constitutional morality, has shaped the civil or state system into being. Natural rights, as has been pointed out against T. H. Green, may be claims, moral or according to positive sociological requirements (usually with a concealed moral postulate,) based upon the fundamental psychology of man and the consequent requirements of his social health. They can be prior, not indeed to *all* social order, but to any *particular* and established social or civil order. We move here into the less committed and less limited field of Freedom—as indeed we do in most of the common affairs of everyday life, where we speak, not of our liberties, but of our freedom to act.

In our definition of freedom I can see no reason to advance beyond the elementary and stripped terms of Hobbes, devoid of emotional overtones: "[Freedom] signifieth the absence of opposition." This usage admittedly is negative, but it is precise. It conforms to the deep distrust of government and "minimalist" theory of legislation, amid which Anglo-Saxon liberalism grew up. Hence it came to be lauded uncritically and is now suspect in a more collectivist and optimistic age. But this fluctuation of sentiment, which explains the valuation placed on this currency, is no argument why the definition should be wrong.

There can indeed be among philosophers a positive usage, which is sometimes an indication to show that "freedom" is rightly used as a "praise-word" and is unqualifiedly "a good thing" like "1066." As Montesquieu writes (and Rousseau agrees), freedom is a faculty "which can consist only in the power of doing what we ought to will"; and, as Milton said, no one can love it "but good men." For Spinoza it means following "the dictates of reason alone"; and for Kant it is "independence of anything other than the moral law." A political theorist may prefer to say that freedom *is* by no means necessarily a good thing (save as a facility for vital energy), but that in those particulars only in which it is a good thing it *ought* to be recognized, tacitly or explicitly, as within the field of civil liberties, which are established and defined by social authority. With de Jouvenel, we may agree that liberty and authority, even as polar, must yet be coupled. The usage, about positive freedom, of the philosophers is not that of common speech. It does, indeed, say something of high importance; but what philosophers call "true freedom" would be better called "the exercise and enjoyment of the virtue of self-discipline" or "voluntary submission to rational authority." Politically it is not entirely helpful, since it is with difficulty adjusted to societies where there is no agreement on the public philosophy of what is rational authority or what are the behavioral consequences of rational authority (self-law).[2]

II

From the point of view of political science these definitions, offered here, of freedom and of liberty have not only the merits of extreme simplicity, without emotional load, and of logical clarity. The definition of freedom also permits a satisfactory connection to be established

[2] Reference may be made here to the excellent little book by Maurice Cranston, *Freedom* (New York, 1953). Mr. Cranston's own conclusion is: "I am tempted to think that freedom from the constraints that emanate from the non-rational parts of our own natures is indeed the most important freedom we can have or strive for." Mr. Cranston's conclusion is that indeed of Christian dogmatic orthodoxy, but it is by no means uncontroversial; it would not appeal to the advertising men of Madison Avenue; and is in apparent flat conflict with President Eisenhower's remark, in his Oklahoma City address (November 13, 1957), which praises "the promise to each man that he will be allowed to be himself, and to enjoy, according to his [actual] own desires, the fruits of his own toil." There is a "permissive" anarchist-individualist element, good or bad, in the typical American philosophy which here is merely not confronted.

with psychological and even physiological empiricism, so that we can understand, not merely that men wish to be free, but why and in what sense they wish to be free. Although there is a plentitude of references in political literature to men's natural rights (or claims) and "instinctive" demands, it is very seldom, indeed, that these so-called "instincts" are to be understood in any precise and scientific sense. But in the present case this is not so. One of the results of the work of Pavlov, in his *Conditioned Reflexes,* is to show that, beneath even psychological drives, there is a biological instinct to struggle when bound, an instinctive reflex action of the muscles to any condition of bondage at a lower level than that of conscious decision. It is no metaphor to say that man struggles against being "in chains." Moreover, complete bondage, so that the limbs become immobile, is so contrary to the vital process that it will result in death. While our attention here may be positivistically concentrated upon observing what happens and we may truly say that, were the bonds a means to preventing (let us say) murder, we could value these bonds as means to a good end, nevertheless we may note as a general hypothesis that the logical extreme of bondage, since it spells death, is "a bad thing" and freedom *pro tanto* good. This hypothesis is made on the assumption, repudiated, indeed, by Buddhists and some very old people, that life is good—an assumption general enough and made, as fundamental, by the medical profession. Insofar as human power protects human freedom, despite Fénelon and Acton, such power to be free also by its nature would seem to be primarily good, although political science, as science, may have no need for such a postulate.

A profitable discussion of human freedom, and of how far it *a priori* deserves recognition in society as liberty, apart from the actual use which Smith or Jones may make of the liberty, would seem to involve an awareness of the psychophysical origins for the demand. Certainly we can reject as not only inadequate, but nonsense, the proposition of some lawyers, with its totalitarian implications, that a liberty is an action which is authorized by the state (and hence has moral validity) *because* the state has not chosen to forbid it. It is permitted and, indeed, recognized as a liberty by the state and like social organizations; but its moral validity springs from its conformity to the behavior in society of a rational human nature. What is that nature and how is it rationally shaped? To use the terminology of Erich Fromm, what is "a sane society"?

Put briefly, we may say that every man tends by his will to implement and realize his wishes, which also take shape in his dreams and imaginations. This is a matter of degree. So many men, and even entire peoples, for better or worse, are content to live much of their lives in a dreamworld of imagination. This is a "free," utopian, and unbounded world, with "no opposition." Sometimes, again, it does make an impact on the objective world, as a messianic scheme of perfection which will force that world to its own shape. Or, at least, we have a dream of the forceful reshaping of that world. This is that "myth of revolution," of which Professor Raymond Aron writes as besetting the French mind, just as the myth of the Roman Reich beset the German mind. It is also the Bolshevik obsession, compensating the perpetual Russian inferiority complex about being remote Muscovites. There is a long history of utopias and of the relation of the perfectionists to revolution. Those who will not descend from the infantile or adolescent imagination (or who are animated quite literally by an antifather fixation, such as seems to explain, for example, the philosophy of H. J. Laski toward authority) refuse to accommodate themselves to the actual material of the home and world and become, as Professor Aron says, historical *a priori* pessimists, however much they may be visionary optimists.

In some measure, however, every child as he grows has to leave behind the Eden of what is called "an oceanic omnipotence," where there is an innocent self-love and where, when asking for the moon, the infant expects to be gratified, and has to meet the objective resistances of that-which-is-not-himself, "the reality principle." It is here that the great decisions of character are taken, whether due to nature or nurture. The fortunate child develops his accommodation to parents, society, God and reality in an atmosphere of trust—or what Dr. Fromm, with reminiscences of Horace, likes to call the exercise of an "art of loving." [3] His distrusts or fears are of a kind that have ob-

---

[3] For the word "trust" which I use here Erich Fromm, in his *Art of Loving* (New York, 1957), uses the more loaded or expensive word "love." We could indeed say that the observed phenomena are of trust and distrust, reciprocated trust producing love as its consequence and this love, in turn, engendering trust. Both Fascist

jective grounds in the reality of evil, and are rational. The unfortunate child grows up in no such balanced relationship, and his habits and choices harden from fear into distrust. Not wrongly was "freedom from fear" reckoned among the four basic freedoms. If he falls into the hands of Marxists, he is provided with an ideology of distrust to give him what sociologists would call a rationalization of his negative or "bloody-minded" conduct. The rebel as such is exalted—first Ishmael, then Cain. Or, as in Baudelaire, there is the attraction of evil precisely as such and the cult of Satanism.

Permeated by fear, as Plato said the soul of a tyrant or tyrant state was permeated, the growing child overcompensates, for lack of confidence, insecurity, and self-hate, by an obsessive desire for dominative and even sadistic power. The obsessive desire for domination in any culture, whether political, economic, or familial, is the end of love and its religion. On the other hand, it is those nurtured in trust, loving themselves with an innocent vitality, who have the outgoing faith or confidence to love others. Love involves a duality, but to love another "as oneself" involves being on terms of love and joy with oneself. The enigma of power here is how one shall resist those who hate, and yet resist only in accordance with the power of a rational justice and without accepting in defensive fear (just as a medical man may be infected by the plague) the enemy's psychosis and social disease.

The first experience, after the infantile glory of a world of wish, in which subject and object are not distinguished, is that of a restriction or obstacle. Then follows the need for *freedom* to consummate the impeded wish—to be without this restraint. We are still moving in the

---

and Marxist philosophies produce an emotional and rationalized condition of distrust or, as Russell says, hate which, in turn, rots their roots. It will be noted, however, (a) that the trust here commended is a rational trust, focused on certain central intuitions or *principles*, confirmed by experience and tradition (what Fromm calls a "discipline"), and not an indiscriminate trust; and (b) that Dr. Fromm's "love" is speedily distinguished by him from what he calls "biological symbiosis" and from the "erotic love"—"the most deceptive form of love there is"—which can be this symbiosis or an "egotism *à deux.*" Indeed it ends as something much closer to the benevolence of a monk than to the sentiment of a family man. The undoubted and theological truth in Dr. Fromm's identification needs in practice careful handling. "Love" has also to include care and the principle of justice as well as that of mercy. Nor must we end, with some early Christian (and pagan) sects, in the general love of erotic orgy. Reference may also be made to R. E. Money-Kyrle's *Psychoanalysis and Politics* (New York, 1951) which, although controversial, is also suggestive.

thought world of wish, although this may be accompanied by general bodily gestures. Then follows a desire for *power*, objectively to overcome the obstacles; a rising to consciousness of a deliberate will to possess this power; and a co-ordination, not only instinctive, but deliberate and conscious. The will for power to assure our freedom to achieve our wish is born—whether parentally and socially aided in trust, or in distrust and even as a neurotic will to dominate. The freedom is neutral and neither good nor bad, save in that general sense already mentioned in which it connects with vitality and growth—the unfolding of a personality, which is not good *eo ipso* but which may be rich or may be cancerous. For the unfolding powers *can* be cancerous—an observation overlooked by some liberal moralists such as Fromm himself. Insofar as the will, sprung from the primitive Eden, is one of distrust and pride, biased toward power over and against others, then that will (as Freud has so well insisted) is biased by the original sin of self-will against rational reality (or civilization) and is bad. The political scientist, however, is only concerned to study its actual operations both in men and in nations—nor let us, with Reinhold Niebuhr, or Luther, wrongfully exaggerate the distinction of the two.

III

The guarantee which power offers for our freedom to enjoy our wishes is *control* and, in the case of social undertakings, the establishment of that enduring and recognized power over others, which is authority.[4] If this linkage between freedom and authority—and again of authority with the freedom recognized by authority as liberty and civil liberties—is dialectically valid, then there is, indeed, a polarization; but the contradiction rhetorically stated between freedom and authority as such is quite false. The whole elaboration of political science stems from a recognition of its falsity. The political market which authorities offer would not be there, were men not thereby guaranteed freedom and did they not reckon up their competitive costs. Nevertheless, that such a contradiction between freedom and authority, on a historically formidable scale, is made in the rhetorical

[4] This entire argument is further developed in the chapter "Freedom and Authority," in my forthcoming *Elementa Politica*.

literature and debate of politics is clearly shown in Professor Aron's *Opium of the Intellectuals*, a book of which it must be said that its very brilliance sometimes obscures the clarity of the detailed arguments. M. Aron writes: "Each [French political type] regards itself as the embodiment of a perennial human type. The one invokes family, authority, religion; the other equality, reason, liberty." The unspoken implication, as M. Aron underlines, is that it would be possible for society to get along *without* the family or authority, or *without* reason and liberty. The comment is that both types, and indeed all Frenchmen, are anxious enough to be free to acquire certain political goods and that both sides would be quick enough, each in its turn, to invoke authority, if this would serve its purposes. Prudence indicates that the tendency toward monopoly of power by all governments and bureaucracies is so great that the actual individual consumer is best protected by "division of powers." But this doctrine, when it issues in the logical extreme of weak government and few goods, seldom appeals to any political groups in a hurry toward their objectives. (Indeed the complete division of power, uncorrected by a locus of authority instead of the unbalance of decision obtaining in the international field, is the recipe for continuing anarchy and recurring war.) The market continues to higgle and oscillate.

In the dreamworld of imagination, of course, in utopias and indeed in some subjective or socially irresponsible forms of religion, since there is no impingement upon social life and its impediments, freedom has no bounds or need of guarantees; and there is no need for authority, since it is without basis or function. Much "otherworldly" or nonsocial religious thought takes place at this level. The same comment holds for the mythical political world of the idealist revolutionary and *avante-garde* rebel. Against this dream utopia, which regards even reason as a tyrant, must be set the dictum of an objective revolutionary such as Lenin: "There is nothing more authoritarian than revolution."

In the popular philosophy of certain extreme schools of existentialism, such as that of Sartre, which are indeed far from being either what we may call "social-existentialist" or "real-essentialist," we find presented what is rather a kind of dream ideal of narcissism, that finds even in the rule of reason a tyranny. Here more stress is placed upon a generalized freedom to do *anything* than upon the actual and objective implementation in society of a *specific* wish (unless it be the exhibitionist wish of a narcissist who looks for some public to act as his mirror). This species, however, of stress on totalist freedom does not correspond to any common human need; and it is more than questionable whether it is urged dialectically *de bonne foi* and not to score a Nietzschean point. It is not irrelevant that much twentieth-century dictatorship traces its philosophy of force, at least in part, from the qualified nihilism of Nietzsche and the unqualified nihilism of Netchaev. No other way out is, therefore, left than the irrational leap into action. We may agree that the ideal authority, civil or religious, is the one which I not only recognize by assent but have myself chosen by deliberate and free (if responsible and educated) judgement and consent. But what matters here is that the social authority which exists shall rationally explain itself. To say that no authority is valid unless the individual "sees the reason why" is to ignore the reality of history as objective to ourselves and the fact that authority has not only a dream function of being our own dream command but a social function, whether we like it or not. Not even a trade union will admit, for its members, this policy of conditional anarchy and free withdrawal of obedience. What we can do, if we dislike a functioning authority, is to withdraw support on the market, short of excessive cost. But costs there will be, unless another alternative authority can perform the function.

The fundamental contention, it would seem, of any systematic political science is that there is a linkage, not accidental but necessary, between authority and freedom. Authority is that species of power and control which guarantees the freedom that an individual's power cannot win for itself, to implement our wishes. As a guarantee or security we desire it. We *wish* for authority. Or, rather, we *will* it. As something that has to be paid for in costs, and that can restrict ourselves by the same law by which it restricts our competitors, we yet detest it. It is ambivalent. And hence our object is to purchase as much of the political goods which we desire, and which it provides, for the minimum cost on the market. Like power itself (save in some specialized sense) it is neither good nor bad, but the neutral provider of commodities. If we like the goods, we approve of the authority. If we need the goods, we pay the charges of supporting the authority. We do this unless these charges are too monopolistic and extortionate and unless some other competitive authority, in fact or at least on paper in some political party's advertising catalogue and price list of goods or program of sales, offers us a better bargain.

It may be well to follow the school of the *politiques* and rather to be cool than excited about the matter. We have here an affair of means. Where we shall require moral inspiration is in that choice of ends— of our "good goods"—which we have to make *ourselves*. We must not blame the shop, whether of this political party or that, if we willfully chose the goods it had to sell, while what we really wanted was some- thing quite different. From a bourgeois democracy one can buy op- portunities for smelling the chance of private success, but scarcely the satisfaction of a disciplined public philosophy. From a dictatorship one can buy partnership in some five-year plan of economic advance- ment, but scarcely, for example, sure freedom from conscription for military ventures. From a balanced democracy one may be able to obtain leadership, but at the cost of responsible performance of many tedious civic duties.

IV

"Man is not born to be free." So, in reply to Rousseau—who had also said, with histrionic pessimism, that "everywhere man is in chains"— Goethe wrote, in his *Tasso*. "All men are created equal and inde- pendent," originally wrote Jefferson, in the draft of the Declaration of Independence, until someone in the Continental Congress pointed out that indeed no mother's son had ever been born "independent." Alex- ander Herzen quotes Goethe's warning phrase—Herzen himself being a champion of freedom to the verge of anarchism, a precursor of the Russian Revolution—and then Herzen goes on to write, of Rousseau's view: "I see in it a violation of history and contempt for facts. I find that intolerable. . . . I do not deem it necessary out of politeness to humanity to attribute to it imaginary virtues and splendours, so I hate phrases. . . . We accept them on trust and march on, leaving these treacherous beacons behind us, and lose our way."

It is the professional business of political scientists not to lose their way, whatever may be the popular route. As Herzen says, the prime obligation here is to truth. And "Are men free?" is a nonsense question, unless we ask or state, "Free for what?" Perhaps Herzen, a Byronic dilettante whom yet Sir Isaiah Berlin acclaims as the first modern man, the protoexistentialist, is not to be taken too seriously. His dialogue, of the revolutionaries of 1848, concludes, as in the logic of the quest for truth contemplated in tranquillity, "I shall go to America." "It is very boring there." "That's true . . ." But this is no reason why *we* should not take the matter seriously, or should fail to recognize the distinctive and challenging role played in this matter of civil liberties by the country of Jefferson and also of Whitman, with their vision of a great experiment, noted by de Tocqueville, and of a pattern of social life increasingly recognized, even in the darkest South. In passing, we may note that it is surely odd that freedom should be found boring. And again we shall reply to ourselves, "Freedom for what?"

Democracy is indeed in danger when it may no longer be criticized, any more than Marx-Leninism by professors in Russia, and when it has become a sacred cow. Or when, perhaps, in capitalist democracy it has become a golden calf. Let us, therefore, in approaching this question of "Freedom for what?" choose some recent instances of decisions reached within the field of civil liberties and see what enlightenment they provide.

Let us begin at the modest level of the folk art of burlesque.[5] The Constitution of the United States guarantees that there shall be no abridgment of freedom of speech or of the press. This guarantee could be held to extend to the theater, films, and television and, by analogy, to other forms of expression and communication besides speech, such as might be used in these media. Certainly it cannot be supposed that the guarantee, given to the press, does not include other means of shaping the public mind, invented since the First Amendment was passed but even more influential in effect. Plato, we may recall, held that nothing was more influential on manners than music; and a study of juvenile habits may show how right he was. In the United Kingdom a censorship of the press would be regarded as most contrary to the spirit of the constitution but (for reasons in part fortuitous) there is a long-standing practice of compulsory censorship of the theater under the Lord Chamberlain's office. There was also a recent practice, so long as the British Broadcasting Company enjoyed a monopoly, of very effective censorship of speech and action on radio and television, in part under an officer magnificently called the Director of the Spoken

[5] Adams Newark Theatre v. Newark, 354 U.S. 931 (1957).

Word. These checks and censorships, as distinct from the right to proceed ex post facto against obscenity and like conduct held to be contrary to "the public welfare" (including atheistic blasphemy), have been no part of American practice. What is *le bien commun* is vague. A voluntary censorship in films is the compromise reached. But have the legislature and the courts the constitutional right to prevent, ahead of performance, theatrical scenes which are (like some in *Titus Andronicus*) morally repulsive or salacious or which verge on the obscene? And who is to define these words? The present answer in America, on appeal, is that the courts will define, in conjunction with the police, and that the Constitution—whatever may have been the practice of that veteran pagan, Mr. Justice Holmes—does not protect the art of burlesque.

This decision is not isolated. In the related field of literature, alleged to be obscene and corrupting, but so difficult to define, the courts have recently held that the Constitution, in guaranteeing freedom of the press, does not guarantee the right of any publisher to make money out of obscenity.[6] The British Parliament has gone further. Methods of voluntary restraint among newspaper proprietors having broken down, the law has stated that divorce cases, to prevent objectionable sensationalism, may not be reported in detail unless the words of the court record are followed—the assumption being that the words of any court record would be too dull to have sales appeal to the Sunday morning bedtime reader in search of lubricity. Certain British newspapers, such as the *News of the World*, which have raised their circulation to eight million by strict attention to the themes of sex and crime, proud of the noble principle of the freedom of the press and devoted to the task of educating the public, adult and otherwise, in the facts of life and adultery, have contrived to conform to the law in a fashion admirable by its almost surgical purity and terseness of style. Other newspapers, such as Lord Beaverbrook's, praise themselves for avoiding all dirt and corruption. They merely feature articles indicating that the divorce barrier to political advancement has now been broken and that the practice of successive polygamy is indeed fashionable in the highest society. Any divorcee, leaving the court wreathed in smiles like a bride, is assured of the publicity of a photograph. It is reserved for *Pravda* and *Izvestia*, and also for the *Osservatore Romano*, to be con-

[6] Roth v. U.S., Alberts v. Calif., 354 U.S. 476.

spicuous by maintaining a more severe puritanism of outlook in rejection of bourgeois decay. Whom, then, do we support? *Pravda* and the *Osservatore Romano,* or the *News of the World?* The American courts, as cited, incline to support *Pravda*—although in the case of *Confidential* the jury's indecision perhaps indicated the current mental muddle. Are the American courts right? At least it may be submitted that the contrary views of Professor Walter Gellhorn, in the *Columbia University Forum,* are wrong—not because pornography, promoted by all the resources of commercial greed, is not appropriate and stimulating reading matter, but because, far from enlivening the public mind to deeper insights in the great debate of politics and morals (which is the ethical justification), it drugs it. It has, therefore, *no inherent justification* as a special ethical right. To maintain the contrary, with or without benefit of the First Amendment, is the emptiest form of liberal doctrinairism and lack of sense for the public realities.

Despite certain frivolous aspects of the matter, the answer can penetrate deep to the heart of liberal philosophy. Before, however, endeavoring to see what the answer may be, we may take another recent issue of civil liberties. Although the category is dissimilar, the problem is not dissimilar and may serve to indicate the dimensions of the questions involved. Let us take the case of the civil liberties of Army Specialist Third-Class William Girard, of Ottawa, Illinois, and the issue whether these rights of his, as an American citizen, precluded his being surrendered to the jurisdiction of an alien (in the particular instance, Japanese; in a comparable case, Chinese) court of criminal justice. The point was made by the defense that Girard committed his alleged offense "in the cause of duty" and that, therefore, he was subject to trial by American court-martial.[7] But it seems to be questionable whether, if his constitutional civil liberties as an American protected him from cession to an alien court for alleged offenses affecting the citizens of that alien power, they might not protect him whether his actions were "in the course of duty" (no "offense" by definition being the consequence of official duties) or not, provided that he was in the country, not of his own free choice, but under the orders of the United States Government.

In the course of the *Girard* case it became clear that it would not only be highly embarrassing to the American Administration if an

[7] Wilson v. Girard, 354 U.S. 524 (1957).

agreement made under international treaty, affecting American troops present in friendly countries, could not be implemented owing to the municipal constitutional rights of individuals. Not for the first time the American Constitution has been found to be a millstone around the neck of the American Government, since the Constitution is primarily concerned with individual citizen rights in abstraction from a competitive international situation. It can be argued that it is as archaic as eighteenth-century machinery, shaped in a horse-and-buggy age. Indeed, a situation could arise, due to this insistence on the civil liberties of individual citizens, endangering the strategic security of the United States, where the removal of all such troops from their territories might be demanded by the friendly sovereign Powers. A problem arises of alleged constitutional rights versus *raison d'état,* here involving national power and security. It arises, not as in the instances of the "copperhead" cases during the Civil War, as a matter of domestic balance between the rights of the individual and the chances of victory for a government at war; but the balance involved is between individual rights and an international situation involving sovereign countries which had no interest whatsoever in these constitutional legal rights of American specialists (third class). The question is one of the adaptation of the Constitution of the United States (according to what has been alleged to be the correct interpretation) and the overriding realities of international power. The courts, indeed, held, on appeal, that Girard's constitutional rights had not been infringed; but several legislators remained of the view that the law should be so amended as to extend protective rights to him and to all armed forces in like position. The question, then, becomes one of whether Girard does not enjoy an absolute constitutional right, or has not an absolute moral right which should be legally implemented, whatever its repercussion upon the strength of his country.

I have chosen this case of the civil liberties of the person to certain forms of trial (the alternative to which could be regarded an arbitrary detention) because it raises the question, in a fairly emphatic fashion, how far civil liberties are absolute individual rights (approximating to "natural rights," based on Natural Law) for the protection of the actual freedom of the human unit or how far they are always to be construed in the context of the welfare of the whole, itself to be determined not by the actual wishes or the actual wills of so-called sovereign electors—in the words of David Lawrence, "it is the people who ultimately decide what is the Constitution"—but by the natural or social realities of the total situation.

It is, of course, doubtless true that there are many countries in which justice, as understood in common law, cannot be relied upon in the domestic courts and in which the inhabitants would not recognize a "human right" even if it leaped up and bit them. We are, however, here concerned with cases where the United States Government and Senate have chosen to negotiate treaties and to form the judgement that the rights of its nationals, whatever these nationals may individually feel, can properly be risked. The issue raised earlier was the different but allied one, whether the courts themselves are entitled, in the interest of what they conceive under law to be "the public welfare," to curtail personal freedom of expression, verbally, artistically, or in the press and like media of opinion, exercised according to the actual wishes and private good judgement or obstinacy of individual free citizens. Whatever the competent authority, in all these cases the competence is at stake of that authority to override the actual freedom of individuals, in what at least can be pretended to be rights so fundamental as to be constitutional, in the interest of what that authority may decide to be the real welfare of the whole. In passing, it will be noted that it can be objected that this "whole" can be that of the entire human community, and not solely the *raison d'état* of a local or national part, be it Little Rock, Oklahoma, the South, or the United States, all of them being "communities."

V

When, then, we use the words "freedom" or "liberty," not in the precise sense of political science, but in a rhetorical or indeed a valuational sense, what is it that we assume or imply? Often, indeed, what is meant is national freedom or independence from any other sovereign power. This usage, with its implications in international law and relations, and the degrees of its relativity or absoluteness, I do not propose to discuss here. How far is Mississippi sovereign? However, when Patrick Henry or the apostles of the French Revolution used the words, although they may have referred to this national meaning also, they primarily had in mind personal rights. The dual usage, indeed, of the words breeds much confusion—although it can, of course, be well argued that the philosophy of the moral rights to independence of the group flows from the philosophy of the natural, inalienable, and indefeasible rights of the individual.

Nor is the school of neo-Hegelians, from T. H. Green on, who have pointed out that these rights are social rights, not valid against community welfare—and it may be added (although this they did *not* point out) that national rights are social rights not to be held valid against humanity's welfare—a school that is to be adjudged by now, for all reasonable men, to have won the day. For are there not rights, rational and rooted in human nature itself and its empiric health—conditions, as Fromm and Money-Kyrle have insisted, for any "sane society"—which take logical precedence of all temporary claims, forcible exactions, and cultural *mores* of the ruling classes in any given particular and transient organization of human society? Must we not recognize the claims of empiric and rational Natural Law? No one who has given attention to the pluralist criticism of claims made for the state community alone to define rights can evade these issues. We may say that all civil liberties are merely those liberties which the state or its courts, or its electorate acting in the framing of its constitution, chose to recognize to be rights and which the courts *and* police will enforce. But this only passes us on to the question: What freedom, objectively and naturally, *must* a human being enjoy in order to be a healthy member of a healthy society (which is an issue for nature and science, and not for any sovereign despot or people to decide); and what freedom, therefore, *ought* a sane and rational constitutional morality to recognize, in good and just laws?

The claim for natural freedoms, as providing the flesh and stuff for recognized civil liberties, often goes beyond these rational or empiric demands, biological and psychological and formulated as Natural Law, which have already been discussed. Fromm and Riesman alike, following a liberal tradition that traces from Locke, Milton, and the Puritans, but also a humanist tradition that, through John Stuart Mill and von Humboldt, traces back to Goethe, speak of the need for the kind of laws, customs, and liberties that lead to the development of the independent, responsible, autonomous, rounded personality, fully developing all its powers "into a harmonious whole." Archibald MacLeish, in his *Freedom Is the Right to Choose*, while stopping short of the excess of a Nietzsche or a Netchaev, and indeed elsewhere speaking of joint collaboration in building the work of civilization, has yet spared nothing in emphasizing a man's absolute right to shape his action and his belief upon the conclusions that he happens to think out on his own. Indeed, he calls this rugged individualism in ideas "the American Proposition." I submit that this "progressive" nineteenth-century view is facile, misleading, and false. Such an eminent American as Lewis Mumford, in his *Condition of Man,* rightly criticizes this species of left-wing Protestantism, verging on moral nihilism. Shall we, then, move to the "more progressive," nonbourgeois, twentieth-century, revolutionary, and left-wing view of the Bolshevik Revolution and hold that what is the welfare of the community, "the common good," will be decided by "the politically conscious, revolutionary vanguard," as assembled in the conclaves of the Soviet Presidium and in the more secret places of the Kremlin and as voiced from day to day by *Pravda* and *Izvestia?* My answer will again be, "no."

As one reads the writings of contemporary, self-styled neohumanists, with their praise of self-development and autonomy, one is impressed by a major contrast between them and the great humanists of the past. The great humanists, of whom we can take Pico, Erasmus, and Goethe as outstanding examples, had a sense for tradition, cultural form, history. Goethe had immensely such a feeling for history, which he connected with his sense for art. Tradition yielded patterns and shapes, and it was the business of modern man to soak and discipline himself with the tradition of accumulated wisdom, the drama of culture. The petty temporary tyrannies and superstitions must be subject to, and critically exposed by, this mighty measure in their cheapness, vulgarity, provinciality. There is nothing here, in Goethe, of the hysterical desire for the self-development of the individual self-will, which is a species of lust for power, whether in untutored isolation or in no less unfitting exhibitionism. "Auto-nomy" means a law, if it is a law or *nomos* which the educated self, educated out of philistinism, becomes mature enough to choose. The development of the powers is a disciplined development, *not* into fulfillment of the actual, un-educated, willful self in accordance with its actual animal wishes, but into harmony, the harmony of the personal whole *secundum naturam et rationem* in accordance (as Goethe would surely have insisted) with the cosmic whole, which only genius can intuit in the vision of poet and rare sage.

Frankly, Goethe's humanism is highly aristocratic, with the aristocracy, not of status, but of education in "shape"—a matter on which L. L. Whyte lays right emphasis. It is not at all Mr. MacLeish's "American Proposition," and maybe not that of David Riesman either. Professor Riesman is so rightly critical of direction by the Joneses; but maybe he only substitutes, for heteronomy by the Joneses, the more frightful autonomy of the natural Jones, unredeemed by grace. According, indeed, to Professor Julian Huxley, what we require is not grace, but natural science and study of biological evolution from the amoeba to the Huxleys, so much that in the end the whole human race will conform, in spiritual monolith-wise, to one set of views which could be called "scientific humanism" or religion without tears. This is not my judgement. Nor do I believe that this elimination of the tragic sense of life could have been Goethe's view or that of the great earlier humanists.

Much of the philosophical discussion of the values of freedom turns on this inherent moral right to self-expression, as part of the dignity of man. (There is much philosophical talk about "the dignity of man," although it is noteworthy that the cartoonists, as interpreters of the bourgeois-democratic mind, usually depict for us the "ordinary man" as humorous but, with straggly moustache and battered hat, almost the precise antitype to "the dignified.") But contemporary moral and political philosophers have given quite inadequate attention to what may be the rational rights to self-expression of those who have nothing, or nothing desirable, to express and whose dignity is conspicuous by its absence. Dignity is not automatic for every biped, nor are all what the Confucians called "superior persons," with an aspiration to discipline and excellence. That anything inarticulate in human nature must be good if it is made articulate is a thesis that belongs to a pre-Freudian age. We here verge upon the issues, and these we cannot now discuss, of the principle of tolerance, which may spell patience "until the harvest" or may mean a cautious agnosticism or may mean indifference. We do well to digest the comment of an eminent historian, A. J. P. Taylor: "The truth is that toleration springs only from indifferentism." [8] A distinction must be drawn between the three fields of private moral taste, of civil peace in which the coercive law has place, and the intermediate field, to which political philosophers have attended too little,

[8] Quoted from a review in the *Observer*, London (September 1, 1957), by A. J. P. Taylor, of M. Ashley's *The Greatness of Oliver Cromwell*.

where the public pattern of life is affected and where organized social approval or disapproval is relevant, using perhaps techniques, comparable to the medical, of social hygiene.

In the great hall at Delhi the inscription runs: "Liberty is a blessing that must be earned before it can be enjoyed." Is this the case? Or is the rational claim to it, for example in the context of politics, religion, and social behavior, automatic and resting on men's actual and casual wishes? It may, indeed, be argued that, whatever men *ought* to seek to express in public life (provided that we could even get agreement about this "ought"), in fact they have *actual* wishes and opinions which, in a democratic society, they should be free to express, unless others thereby are directly harmed. This "wonderfully free" society, it will be remembered, is precisely what Plato, in certain famous pages of satire, and Aristotle parenthetically, attacked as the weakness of an unprincipled democracy. On the historical record, democracy is one of the more unstable forms of government, when as in Athens and Florence —but not only in Athens and Florence, and sometimes today in Europe —it is combined with imperialism; and we get here a peculiarly unstable version of it. Indeed, with its own Peloponnesian War—with two civil wars to its credit in a generation—a pessimist might say that twentieth-century Europe (unless it can learn the discipline of unity) bids fair to extinguish itself.

The theme of John Stuart Mill, in his essay *On Liberty*, despite the quite Victorian pruderies and reservations which he inserts when it comes to morals, has often been criticized on the ground that he assumes all men to be Mills. Insofar as liberalism adopted this theme, is not its sociology wildly unrealistic? We find that, so anxious are people to "express themselves," they will commit murder—whether like Loeb and Leopold for the direct pleasure or in order to find their names headlines in the papers. This is admittedly no modern depravity. One recalls the Renaissance tyrant of a small Italian town who, on his deathbed, repented that, having the Pope and Emperor once with him on the top of a tower, he had not thrown them over, "so that his name would have lived forever." The human desire for publicity is of incredible intensity among the neurotic; and few men are not neurotic in some measure. The contemporary hero of the ill-bred press is the criminal who, having news to sell unlike honest fellows—vice being news for the public, and virtue not being news—can always command big money from that press. A sensational divorce is a less costly method of achieving the same publicity and makes the world of Hollywood, the great fashioner of our modern public ethics, philosophy, and taste, go round and round. A formidable case can be made that Western bourgeois-democratic society is decadent when a serious writer must, like a mountebank or like Bernard Shaw, turn somersaults in the street, so as to attract attention, acquire a "name," and therefore have the least weight attached to his views by the media of mass information. As touching mass publicity the reader is referred to Vance Packard's *The Hidden Persuaders*. The Soviet system, being a blunt class oligarchy, as Trotsky and Djilas have well shown, is subject to no like temptation of playing to the democratic gallery. Press proprietors who prate about the sacredness of freedom of the press—freedom, for example, to embarrass the American Government and to publish Kremlin propaganda at a time opportune for the Kremlin, because this represents a great "scoop" for circulation—such newspaper proprietors observe, with entire frankness and as wisdom, that the task of a newspaperman is "to give the public what it wants," and to be quicker than competitors in supplying this. A like comment can be made on television commentators who create international embarrassment by impertinently quizzing Foreign Ministers of great Powers for fun [9]—or to attract advertising. Is it a "free press," claiming absolute and sacred rights as a Fourth Estate, or "a responsible and free press," *insofar* as this contributes to the quest for truth, that is justified?

It may quite gravely be asked whether, however detestable a Soviet moral despotism with its contempt for all freedom of the press, responsible or irresponsible, this Communist puritanism is not cleaner than the lust for the sweet smell of success? Indirectly, this question is raised by Professor C. Wright Mills, in his *Power Elite*, with his denunciation of "the higher immorality" and of "organized irresponsibility." Is Soviet puritanism, with is doctrinal "vanguard" of excellence, not more moral than the undignified cultivation of the opinion of the Joneses insofar as it may contribute to this private success, assessed by irresponsible private judgements—what MacLeish calls "the truth as it appears to each of them"? It can be argued that the weakness of

[9] The reference is to the embarrassment arising from London ITN's Mr. Robin Day, in his "tough" cross-examination of Mr. A. Fujiyama, the Japanese Foreign Minister, as reported in the London *Daily Mail* of September 28, 1957.

Britain at the present time is a national laxity which construes freedom as "doing what one damn-well likes" and taking one's leisure. Also it can be argued that the present weakness of the United States is the flattery to the vanity of untrained men which leads them to think that their "opinion" on any issue is as good and weighty as that of those trained and skilled.

There must be limits, not least limits in principle, to the anarchy of moral relativism. The true existentialism sets out to solve actual problems, instead of the abstract logical conundrums of the schools. The false existentialism denies that there are any human principles in accordance with which problems should be solved. Marxism (as I said in *What Does the West Want?*) may be "the opiate of the proletariat." But at least, even if intolerably narrow and with hate-laden and force-laden values, with its test of "What does a man contribute to the community?" it is arguable that it is better than this degeneration of freedom. The basic argument is as old as Plato.

VI

Mr. Walter Lippmann, commenting on the discussions of a decade ago between General Eisenhower, as he then was, and Marshal Zhukov, remarks that it is untrue that the liberal democratic order permits everyone to "do anything." *Laissez faire*, he says, even in its wider sense as more than freedom of production, it should have been pointed out to Marshal Zhukov, operates "within an environment of laws and customs." There is, in short, says Lippmann, a public philosophy, if a philosophy of liberalism itself, with appeal to debate and reason. "A hundred flowers may bloom," but (as General Mao adds) when a flower is not a flower, but a poisonous weed, its blooming is not tolerated. Zhukov and Eisenhower, Lippmann suggests, might agree upon a soldierly altruism which puts duty to the community first; but yet our good society would—as against Zhukov—be one reasonable, shaped by free (*if responsible*) debate, not a totalitarian state. We are not free to "do anything" or to express ourselves in any way, because this would be neither customary nor reasonable; and it is the personality of the cultivated and reasonable man, and certain extraordinary standards of human *excellence*, which we respect. The conclusion is neither anarchist nor Sartrean. It is not a MacLeishian "American Proposition," which is a false proposition. There is an objective something which is the judgement of the reasonable man. And, since this judgement is not solely an affair of logic or, again, of instinct, it is also shaped by regard for the accumulated and cultivated experience in the major or grand tradition of values to be found in history. This indicates and delimits the more fundamental civil liberties, which are those of a reasonable and morally responsible man (*not*, be it added, those of every news-paper proprietor or hot-dollar merchant). Increasing psychological knowledge indicates with increasing clarity how these civil liberties rest upon demand for freedoms springing from the objective nature and real character of man in a condition of health and from the de-mands of a corresponding sane society.

If a group of men seeks to change this system, not by rational de-bate, but by appeal to force, then a reasonable freedom can and should (as Locke said) defend itself. In wartime in Britain, following great tolerance in discussion, Communist and Fascist, some people found, not witch-smelling debated, but their persons apprehended so speedily that they scarcely knew where they were. They found themselves de-tained without trial and without compensation (but also without re-peal of habeas corpus) for several years. In peacetime, in Britain, there is neither First nor Fifth Amendment to be debated, and Royal Com-missions (as the American Bar Commission has pointed out) have powers of arrest that congressional committees on un-American activi-ties never had. Senator Joseph McCarthy emerged as a bungler, when it came to the real job. Wire-tapping, according to the latest Privy Councilors' Report (with the Opposition in agreement) will be con-tinued. So presumably (subject of course to "the proper safeguards") will be the opening of letters. There is a felicitous combination of ex-treme freedom up to a rational limit, with extreme speed and toughness beyond it. The civil liberties of the individual are what the law says they will be. If Parliament says the individual will be, not of course a prisoner, but "detained" without trial, he will be so detained. The law being clear, appeal would be pointless. One may not arrest on general warrant. But one can rearrest on a specific warrant.

Is this conclusion satisfactory? It has a great historical exemplar, and the system has run not badly but, if anything, with too much tolerance for the seditious. And in the British system delation and witch-hunting have existed (more in the First World War than the Second), but they

70

have been held within close bounds. Its strength has lain not so much in its formulas as in the tradition of practical administration, which can override technicalities but yet can be liberal in the face of unpopularity. On the one hand, Joyce was hanged although he was probably not technically a British subject and, therefore, not guilty of treason. On the other hand, Oswald Mosley was released while the war was still on because, the crisis having abated, there was no proper ground for detaining him, unless the charges against him could be sustained in a court of law. It is a legal system that is not hypnotized, like much of the American, by legalism. Nevertheless, it can be argued that the powers of Parliament are dangerously great and that civil liberties should not only be enunciated and constituted by law and within law. Not only—as we see from the contrary case of "Nazi" South Africa— should a great and important fight be waged for the supremacy of the judiciary. Civil liberties must also be related to, and will ever spring as political demands from, the more fundamental Natural Law and the actual and rational nature of man. What, however, it may be said, is intolerable is the claim to the right to be irrational, in the name of individualism and of the caprice of private opinion.

Liberties may properly be limited by the needs of the security of the nation and the Constitution. This limitation, however, springs from the assumption that the Constitution is freely chosen and, as touching possible amendment, the right to vote freely exercised. Otherwise we have an oligarchy which provides no constitutional means for its own replacement. Action against such an oligarchy may well produce the kind of breaches of law which should be a matter for trial by jury. But the jury must be of one's peers. In a society of first- and second-class citizens, for example, a trial of second-class citizens as defendants, under the Magna Carta principle of trial by "peers" or *pares,* would require second-class citizens only as jurors, for example all-Negro juries in the Deep South. Within these requirements of freedom, however, there is no ground in liberal principle why an authentically liberal system should permit itself to be attacked without using equally potent powers of defense. Mr. de Valera has put members of the I.R.A. behind barbed wire in Ireland in order to educate them in the way he was educated himself. Contributions to the Fascist Party or movement were outlawed in Britain.

There is, then, no ground on principle, but only in expediency, against suppressing by law the Communist Party (or the Ku Klux Klan) insofar as it takes any active steps to overthrow the Republic or to intimidate its agencies of justice. It cannot be said that, by this argument, Lord North was equally justified in taking steps to suppress George Washington, since George III was not elected nor were his Ministers constitutionally voted in by the colonists, who (like most Englishmen at the same time) were left without remedy save in revolution. Under such circumstances even St. Thomas said that revolution by force might be moral—if it were also successful.

VII

What position, then, have we reached? The moral basis (and limitation) for the claims of civil liberties lies in their being not only stated, as "civil," by positive law, but also in their being reasonable in Natural Law. Who, then, decides what is reasonable? The Communists have a persuasive case in saying that the excesses, exhibitionism, and avarice of bourgeois decadence are unreasonable and morally an affront. By "bourgeois decadence," for instance, the Communists can mean a desire, not only for money, but for notoriety so avid that men will commit murder to reach the headlines. The photographs, here, in the free press, go to other quarters than to the best factory worker, "according to his benefit to the community." If murder is too costly, publicity of a desirable character can always be achieved—although in smaller measure, since the supply is so vast—by those who can emerge with a smile from those divorce courts by which some states fiscally sustain themselves. The Communists will, however, not mention the proletarian decadence of those afraid to deny power to *gopak*-dancing vulgarians, or to triumvirs of tyrants for whom the rulers of the equalitarian and proletarian Roman Empire offered appalling and no less bloody prototypes. The Communist puritans and "vanguard" would jail, for example, newspaper proprietors, advertisers, Madison Avenue men, and all who might encourage this deplorable way of life, dominated by the desire for individual success, judged by cheap standards. They have a case. I would always hesitate to say that the Communist approach was too right-wing. The Catholic Church has usually held a like view, except that it has preferred on principle to hand over miscreant and blasphemous men to the secular arm for liquidation.

I can but say that, in my view, "reasonable" is that which an aristocracy, not a status or oligarchic power but of reasonable, disinterested, and cultivated men, a community of highly reasonable and cultivated beings, consulting the human record of history, is prepared to call reasonable. I would hold that many journalists are unreasonable and would probably be best jailed, as corrupters of good manners and invaders of the sacred right of privacy, hired footmen of the vulgar and anonymous tyranny of public prurience. But others, who hold that all men are naturally good and of equal intelligence and judgement, will hold that a Gallup poll, taken from the Eskimo to the Hottentot, will suffice.

Further, a rational freedom may, and perhaps should, be defended by such resolution, courage, authority, and physical force as the situation requires. (The defense, of course, under the name of "freedom," of some absolute and unqualified national sovereignty is a defense of freedom divorced from the context of international law and authority, that is, a defense of anarchy.) The notion that the maintenance of civil liberties, defined and authorized by law, involves any laxity or hesitation in maintaining the authority of law itself seems to involve some kind of confused thinking. It was an error of the old Polish constitution to assimilate liberties with anarchy; and to fail to recognize that authority itself springs from the very demand to assure some of our freedoms by power. Every guaranteed liberty rests upon the strength of authority.

VIII

Finally, we may turn from the speculations of philosophy about what kind of liberties we ought to desire in the good society and ask whether the political scientist should not see all liberties, constitutional rights and the like, as merely manifestations, fluctuating and temporary, of the *power* which particular bargaining groups have at a given time. The political philosopher may have brought our notion of freedom, if not to the verge of the Hegelian and Marxist view that it is the recognition of necessity, at least into accord with the older notion that it achieves substance and particular development in society, as a rational form of self-chosen service. But then, as we have said, what is rational? The political scientist may inquire whether, if we accept in public life a Marxist or an anti-Marxist view of liberty, this is not actually a function of who is in power. When it comes to the use of words, as Humpty Dumpty said, the question is, "Who is the master?"

If the Kremlin re-establishes its power in Hungary, then "the freedom fighters of the revolution" become "the counterrevolutionaries fighting against the defenders of freedom." To object to Malenkov in 1955 is to be a conservative, if not fascist, reactionary. To side with Malenkov today is to be a conservative, if not fascist, reactionary. What will be meant by a purge of society in the interest of moral reform will depend upon whether the Communists, the Catholics, or those well-known champions of purer morals, Mr. Dave Beck and Mr. Harrison of *Confidential*, are in charge or decisively influential. Who is in control of power will decide what is done; and the right names and Paretoan rationalizations will be supplied afterwards. The strong government which we dislike is called tyranny; and the freedoms which those in power like are called sacred liberty—and the rest is called license.

Even those with no desire to indulge in an empty cynicism can accept much of this statement as descriptive of actualities. If, however, it is to be understood as a statement about purposes in society, then it is false. No aristocracy or "vanguard," Marxist or the reverse, can accept an analysis of purpose solely into pursuit of power beyond power, without cutting the ground from beneath its own feet. It must maintain the validity of its own picture of what is rational—for example the connection of the civil liberties it recognizes with Natural Law, the empirically discoverable nature of man, and the conditions of his health. It must seek to persuade others of its views. Ideas must have their role, and it can be decisive in a political world which is always a world of human choice. It will not admit utter moral relativism, of which the issue is always the appeal to force and the Aristotelian transition from an unprincipled democracy to an unscrupulous dictatorship.

What, however, shall we say of the statement as adequate scientific description of actuality? Shall we here agree with the determinism of Bentley or of Marx? Clearly not. Where we have a society strongly permeated by a sense of purpose, its authority will arrange the assemblage of interests in the political market and actually override the conflict of classes or groups. In the last resort Bentley's analysis into "apathy"—"the spreading atrophy"—and "individual self-interest" is an eighteenth-century analysis. The directive purpose will shape the notions of desired freedoms in that market and will decide the ensuing liberties that are recognized. Only when this common purpose is absent, or too balanced, will other interests (even Bentley's "apathy" and "selfish interest of the individuals") take over.

This purpose yet requires power; and it is circumscribed by the immemorial techniques of power. The rules of the political market are not abrogated. It must offer men such freedom to pursue to fruition the wishes which they actually have, according to the actual distribution of these men's power and needed support—support in quantity, although even more support in organized and persistent quantity. This is true, even if the propaganda of public philosophies may convert men to having the wishes which it indicates and preaches. Education may change men's actual wishes but, until changed, their actual wills, according to degrees of determination, still provide limits.

The issue, then, is not one *merely* of power, but *as well* a vision (a position which the Marxist dogmatically denies, but practically accepts); but it is yet *also* one of power. Our recognized freedoms will be just those which we have the power to get our social authorities to approve; and what authority here provides is not static but will go on changing with the market. The detached philosophy of Montaigne and the *politiques* holds true. There are no sacred and immutable civil liberties any more than, in the changing contexts of civilization and as the groups shift of which the support has to be catered for, political demand remains unaltered. We must not say, with Shaw's Broadbent, "I see no evils in the world—except, of course, natural evils—that cannot be remedied by freedom, self-government and English institutions." Freedom can mean, precisely, the way to achievement of anything one wishes. It is the demand of a Gandhi and of a Stalin, of yogi and commissar. Self-government can spell the remedy of objective evils according to the realistic wisdom of those who govern themselves and according to what species of self they develop and what kind of powers. With all homage to Magna Carta, English institutions will or will not at any time provide remedies, whether to barons, merchants, or Irish peasants, according to what kind of remedies the market at any given time requires. All that can be said is that, by their constitutional morality and habits, the institutions provide a less monopolistic market than some—than, for example, what the American South, despite inherited English institutions, sometimes provides to the Negro political consumer, who also happens to be a human being. The "sovereignty of Parliament," in the United Kingdom a possible blessing for a wide electorate, is, in South Africa, a sorry curse. Of old, "English institutions" regarded only the baron as *liber homo* and ignored "those with no stake in the country."

What we can yet add is that, whatever the temporary play of the market and whatever his civil liberties of the moment, the citizen as a man will always be pressing for freedom, which urge springs direct from his self-will. And he will always be concerned, less or more, with the objective techniques of power to implement this will. It is for his educators, the responsible leaders or aristocrats of this society, not to fail in the responsible task of so shaping his imagination that what he freely wills is compatible with social health and equilibrium, as distinct from addiction to sniffing the licentious, sweet smell of personal success, understood as notoriety. This last undertaking of leadership may yet involve a complete reconstruction of our present system of economic rewards and a reconsideration of the relations of democracy, which trusts the judgement of the ordinary man as the best protection against the ravages of power, with the discipline of education which, as Shaw said, is always by its nature aristocratic.

*

II

METHODOLOGICAL ASPECTS

[MILTON R. KONVITZ]

CORNELL UNIVERSITY

The Use of the Intelligence
in Advancement of Civil Rights

THE despair of truth, wrote Nietzsche in his "meditation" on Schopen-hauer, confronts every thinker who begins from Kant's philosophy. A "gnawing and crumbling skepticism and relativism" will attack the mind; and to an active and noble spirit, Kantianism will bring the ex-perience of a spiritual upheaval and the intellectual "despair of all truth." As an example of the latter, Nietzsche cited the effect of Kant on Heinrich von Kleist. Wrote Von Kleist:

Not long ago I became acquainted with Kant's philosophy; and now I must tell you of a thought in it, inasmuch as I cannot fear that it will upset you as profoundly and painfully as me. We cannot decide whether that which we call truth is really truth or whether it merely appears that way to us. If the latter is right, then the truth we gather here comes to nothing after our death; and every aspiration to acquire a possession which will follow us even into the grave is futile. If the point of this idea does not penetrate your heart, do not smile at another human being who feels wounded by it in his holiest depths. My only, my highest aim has sunk, and I have none left.

In the political thinking of Americans, the Constitution has been a set of fixed, immovable dogmas, far beyond the reach of intellectual skepticism or moral relativism. Everything about us might change, yet the Constitution remained undisturbed. The Constitution was the unmoved mover in the political metaphysics of the American mind.

79

"We may be tossed upon an ocean where we can see no land—nor, perhaps, the sun or stars," Daniel Webster said in a speech in 1847. "But," he continued, "there is a chart and a compass for us to study, to consult, and to obey. That chart is the Constitution." Three years later Henry Clay told the Senate that the Constitution was made not merely for the generation that existed in 1789, "but for posterity—unlimited, undefined, endless, perpetual posterity."

In 1954, however, when the Supreme Court announced its unanimous decision in the school desegregation case,[1] many Americans felt themselves shaken out of their dogmatic slumbers. The effect of the decision on their minds was like that of Kant's philosophy on Heinrich von Kleist.

First of all, they were called upon to face a world in which white and Negro children, boys and girls, would be going in the morning, with their books tucked under their arms, to the same school; and these boys and girls, white and Negro, would meet and play together in the school gymnasium and on the school playground. To this threat to their racial pattern of life their reaction could, perhaps, best be described in the words of a Governor of South Carolina some fifty years ago: "Whenever the Constitution comes between men and the virtue of the white women of South Carolina, I say," said the Governor, "—to hell with the Constitution!" The choice was not a difficult one, as any sensible person can see. When the issue is put in such terms, who can but be on the side of the virtue of the white women of South Carolina?

But there was more than this to the Supreme Court's decision. The virtue of the white women can yet be protected and preserved—a difficult but not an impossible task, especially if a simple device such as racial segregation is taken by worrying fathers, brothers, and husbands as the guarantee of virtue. It will take more than solemn words to shatter racial segregation. But what has happened to the Constitution? Suddenly, what Gladstone spoke of as "the most wonderful work ever struck off at a given time by the brain and purpose of man" became to many Americans, as the Kantian philosophy became to Von Kleist, the source of a gnawing and crumbling skepticism and relativism and of intellectual despair. From *Plessy v. Ferguson*,[2] for two generations, racial segregation in the schools had been constitutional, and now, by

[1] Brown v. Board of Education of Topeka, 347 U.S. 483 (1954).
[2] Plessy v. Ferguson, 163 U.S. 537 (1896).

the decision in 1954, it was unconstitutional. They could not—and cannot—decide whether that which they had called constitutional was really constitutional or whether it merely had appeared that way to them. If the Constitution was appearance and not reality, a mere phenomenon and not a thing-in-itself—not pre-eminently *das Ding an Sich* —then all values are in flux, and there is no chart or compass, there is nothing that is "endless" or "perpetual." The Constitution becomes like the river to Heraclitus—something without sameness, something that is a mere becoming—there is no Constitution, only change; there is no *ens realissimum*, there is no truth, there is not even simple, yeomanry honesty of statement, but only hypocrisy parading as sincerity and brutality parading as justice and law. As a consequence, the world projected by the Constitution

> Hath really neither joy, nor love, nor light,
> Nor certitude, nor peace, nor help for pain;
> And we are here as on a darkling plain
> Swept with confused alarms of struggle and flight,
> Where ignorant armies clash by night.
> —MATTHEW ARNOLD

Sophisticated citizens were not so startled by the decision in *Brown v. Topeka*. They knew with Justice Hughes that although we are under a Constitution, "the Constitution is what the judges say it is," and they were aware of the fact that in its long history the Supreme Court had often overruled its own prior decisions. In order to make room for the New Deal, the Court had to follow the advice that Franklin D. Roosevelt gave to a committee of the House of Representatives in 1935: "I hope your committee," wrote the President, "will not permit doubts as to constitutionality, however reasonable, to block the suggested legislation." Both Congress and Court followed the President in disregarding constitutional precedents standing in the way of social legislation. But on the whole, the American people, I would say, have refused to draw broad or radical conclusions from these events. They insist on living, constitutionally, in a pre-Kantian era, in which a happy people have a sense of certainty, feeling that their feet are on solid ground and that they are not exposed to the nonsense of metaphysicians with their finespun theories of now-you-see-it and now-you-don't. As Dr. Johnson refuted Bishop Berkeley's "ingenious sophistry" of the nonexistence of matter by "striking his foot with mighty force against a large stone" and saying, "I refute it *thus*," even so Americans persist in refuting what to their minds is the Court's sophistry by pointing to the document known as the Constitution and saying, "We refute it *thus*."

Thus the Court's decision and the Court itself are attacked from two different standpoints. They are attacked by those who are for racial segregation or white domination—no matter what. These persons are not concerned with the Constitution but only to maintain existing racial patterns. The decision and the Court are also attacked by persons whose conception of the Constitution allows no room for dramatic or sharp reversals of judicial precedents. They would amend Roscoe Pound's famous saying, so that it would read: "The law must be stable and must stand still." The latter group is made up of defenders of white supremacy, like the 19 Senators and 81 members of the House of Representatives who issued the "Southern Manifesto" on March 11, 1956, who cloaked their argument in words about the Constitution, and of others who, though they have deep convictions for racial equality, are bewildered by recent constitutional developments.

This bewilderment has led, among some persons, to a cynicism respecting law and justice. Like Thrasymachus in Plato's *Republic*, they see justice as the interest of the stronger; or, with Hume, they see reason as only the slave of the passions. Not out of conviction but out of a deep cynicism, they would adapt Luther's famous dictum and say: "Whoever wants to be a judge should tear out the eyes of his reason." With Luther they would say that reason is a whore—it has a price, and it can be bought to do the bidding of passion. Thus, it is contended, the Supreme Court Justices had made up their minds to outlaw racial segregation. They reached this decision without regard to the intent of the framers of the Fourteenth Amendment, without regard to precedents, constitutional norms, or history. After reaching their decision, they looked for support and found it in the works of Gunnar Myrdal and other sociologists and psychologists which showed that racial segregation in the schools has detrimental effects on Negro children by affecting their motivations to learn, by retarding their educational and mental development, and by depriving them of the tangible and intangible benefits they would receive in a nonsegregated school system. From this body of sociological and psychological facts the Court concluded that separate educational facilities for Negro pupils are "inherently unequal"; therefore, there could not be "separate but equal" facilities; therefore, separate facilities, made compulsory by state law, are a denial of the equal protection of the laws guaranteed by the Fourteenth Amendment. These conclusions, say the critics, are not based on legal reasoning. They start from a passion for racial equality, and they end in a constitutional conclusion of racial equality, and the union between passion and law was effected or consummated by social science or nonlegal factors.

This argument assumes that the law moves about in a special realm of pure legal reasoning. In this realm all the values or ends are fixed for all time by the Constitution and the constitutional tradition that has been built up by the great body of decisions and opinions of the Court. It is a self-enclosed and all-sufficient body of knowledge, and the Justices have no business going outside their windowless monad to look for facts, insights, values, norms, or principles. They are to live and think in a world from which human passion or feeling is absent; a world in which experience counts for nothing unless, in earlier cases, it had been reduced to a rule of law; a world in which there is no hunger or desire, no outbursts of emotion or nature, no ecstasy or dejection, but only a judge's tidy mind, laid out with eternal principles, doctrines, and decisions, all making up a beautiful pre-established harmony in which dissents are a concession to an unfortunate pride of intellect.

From this point of view, the Court has no right to look to experience for guidance, once it has been settled by decision that the Constitution requires "separate but equal" facilities. The constitutional rule is a value, and experience is not a source of values; only the Constitution is the source of constitutional values. As Bertrand Russell has said: "Science [read here "sociology and psychology"] has nothing to say about 'values' [read here "constitutional doctrines"]. . . . Questions as to 'values' lie wholly outside the domain of knowledge."

This criticism of the Court is without substance, as I shall now attempt to show:

The Fourteenth Amendment says nothing about "separate but equal facilities." It provides that a state may not deny to any person within its jurisdiction "the equal protection of the laws." Whether or not an action of a state is a denial of equal protection may be a complicated question of fact, the answer to which may involve many questions of judgment. *But what the Constitution guarantees is, not separate but equal facilities, but equal protection of the laws.* The difference is consequential. The meaning and import of the difference can best be brought out by considering Justice Brandeis' dissenting opinion in *Burnet v. Coronado Oil and Gas Co.*[3]

In 1914 the State of Oklahoma leased to Coronado Oil and Gas Company certain gas and oil lands. First the State received 50 per cent, and then 12.5 per cent, of the gross production. This income was used for the establishment of the public school system. The Commissioner of Internal Revenue assessed income and excess profits taxes upon the net income of the company from these leased gas and oil resources. The company contested the assessment. The Supreme Court, in a 5-4 decision, upheld the claim of the company. The decision was based on the principle of the Court's decision in *Gillespie v. Oklahoma.*[4] In the *Gillespie* case Justices Brandeis and Clarke dissented; in the *Coronado* case Justices Stone, Brandeis, Roberts, and Cardozo dissented. Our interest here is in the Brandeis dissent in *Coronado.* Justice Brandeis' reasoning was as follows:

(1) Under the *Gillespie* decision of 1922, he said, vast private incomes were given immunity from federal and state taxation. That case, he said, was wrongly decided and should be frankly overruled.

(2) The rule of *stare decisis* should not stand in the way. The rule is not an inflexible one. It is always in the discretion of the Court to decide to follow a precedent or to overrule it. *Stare decisis,* he said,

is usually the wise policy, because in most matters it is more important that the applicable rule of law be settled than that it be settled right. . . . This is commonly true even where the error is a matter of serious concern, provided correction can be had by legislation.

(3) In the *Gillespie* case the decision to exempt from taxation the state's lessee of gas and oil lands was not based on any statute, but on the Constitution. (It was held in that case that a state may not tax the net income derived by a lessee of Indian lands, since the lessee was an instrumentality used by the United States in carrying out duties to the

---

[3] Burnet v. Coronado Oil and Gas Co., 285 U.S. 393 (1932).
[4] Gillespie v. Oklahoma, 257 U.S. 501 (1922).

Indians.) In cases involving the Constitution, correction through legislation is impossible. For this reason, the Supreme Court has frequently overruled its earlier decisions. (Justice Brandeis cited fifteen cases that overruled prior decisions on constitutional grounds. One of these cases had been law for twenty-seven years and had been cited with approval fifteen times by the Supreme Court. In addition, he cited thirteen cases in which decisions based on the Constitution had been qualified in subsequent cases, and three cases in which there were striking departures from constitutional doctrines previously established, without specifically overruling or qualifying earlier decisions. These cases, it should be noted, were cited by Brandeis in 1932; today many more cases could be added to his list.) In overruling its earlier decisions that involved constitutional provisions, said Justice Brandeis, the Court bowed to the lessons of experience and to the force of better reasoning and recognized that the process of trial and error, fruitful in the physical sciences, is also appropriate in the judicial process.

Justice Brandeis quoted with approval the following passage from an opinion by Chief Justice Taney:

After such opinions, judicially delivered, I had supposed that question to be settled, so far as any construction of the Constitution ought to be regarded as closed by the decision of this Court. I do not, however, object to the revision of it, and am quite willing that it be regarded hereafter as the law of this court, that its opinion upon the construction of the Constitution is always open to discussion when it is supposed to be founded in error, and that its judicial authority should hereafter depend altogether on the force of the reasoning by which it is supported.[5]

(4) Justice Brandeis distinguished cases that involve applying the Constitution from cases that involve interpreting the Constitution. There are strong reasons for not relying on *stare decisis* in cases that involve applying the Constitution to some set of facts. This, he said,

is strikingly true of cases under the due process clause when the question is whether a statute is unreasonable, arbitrary or capricious; of cases under the equal protection clause when the question is whether there is any reasonable basis for the classification made by a statute; and of cases under the commerce clause when the question is whether an admitted burden laid by a state upon interstate commerce is so substantial as to be deemed direct.

[5] Passenger Cases, 7 How. 283 (1849).

These issues resemble, fundamentally, that of reasonable care in negligence cases, the determination of which is ordinarily left to the verdict of the jury. In every such case the decision, in the first instance, is dependent upon the determination of what in legal parlance is called a fact, as distinguished from the declaration of a rule of law. When the underlying fact has been found, the legal result follows inevitably. The circumstance that the decision of that fact is made by a court, instead of by a jury, should not be allowed to obscure its real character.

Applying this reasoning to the question before the Court in the *Coronado* case, Brandeis said that

the question whether it would interfere substantially with the functions of the state government to permit the general income tax of the United States to include profits derived from the lease involves primarily the determination of a fact, not the decision of a proposition of law. . . . the decision of the Court, if, in essence, merely the determination of a fact, is not entitled, in later controversies between other parties, to that sanction which, under the policy of stare decisis, is accorded to the decision of a proposition purely of law. For not only may the decision of the fact have been rendered upon an inadequate presentation of then existing conditions, but the conditions may have changed meanwhile. . . . Moreover, the judgment of the Court in the earlier decision may have been influenced by prevailing views as to economic or social policy which have since been abandoned. In cases involving constitutional issues of the character discussed, this Court must, in order to reach sound conclusions, feel free to bring its opinions into agreement with experience and with facts newly ascertained, so that its judicial authority may, as Mr. Chief Justice Taney said, "depend altogether on the force of the reasoning by which it is supported."

This language and reasoning of Justice Brandeis apply forcefully to the school segregation issue that the Court faced in *Brown v. Topeka.* The case involved the application of the Equal Protection Clause to a set of facts, namely, the social, economic, and psychological effects of separate schools on Negro pupils. This was a question of fact. In 1896 the Court resolved the question of fact to support segregated schools, concluding that "separate but equal" schools answered the constitutional command of equal protection. The question of fact may then have been answered "upon an inadequate presentation of then existing conditions," or it may have been answered upon the extent of the knowledge then obtainable. In any case, fifty-eight years later the facts were different. During these intervening years segregated schools had been tried, and they have been found wanting. The trial and error method was used, with the result that segregated schools were exposed as a failure in constitutional equality: they did not fulfill the constitutional command of equal protection of the laws.

This reasoning is implied in Chief Justice Warren's opinion in *Brown v. Topeka*. It is regrettable that he did not put more flesh on the dry bones. The pattern for the Court's decision and opinion in 1954 had been set with masterly skill by Justice Brandeis in 1932. In the school segregation case the American people should have been taken more intimately into the confidence of the Court, so that they might have a better, more satisfactory understanding of the judicial methods and thinking involved in the decision-making process.

We have said that the criticism of the Court is without substance. We have considered one reason for this judgment, namely, a radical misunderstanding of the nature of the judicial method in cases involving application of the Equal Protection Clause. I would like now to state another reason for my judgment.

Justice Brandeis was, I submit, right in placing a strong emphasis on the factual nature of the questions that come up under the broad clauses of the Constitution, such as Due Process or Equal Protection. But there is more to the factual issues involved under these clauses than was spelled out by Justice Brandeis. A conclusion on the facts as to racial equality, for example, may be influenced, to use the language of Brandeis, by "prevailing views as to economic or social policy." What facts are to be selected as relevant, what weight is to be given to some facts, where reliable facts are to be found, how facts are to be interpreted, what causal connections exist between sets of facts—these and other problems point up the truth that facts and values are often inextricably mixed. One may conjecture that the facts that seemed convincing to the Court in 1896 were seen through a social policy that did not place much value on the ideal of racial equality. It is doubtful if any member of the Court at that time, except Justice Harlan, saw an inexorable command of racial equality in the Equal Protection Clause. Today the opposite is the case. Today's experience with racial questions arises out of a different set of values than that which obtained two generations ago.

This argument does not weaken, but rather strengthens, the conclusion of Justice Brandeis. The Justices of the Supreme Court today must see a charge of denial of equal protection to persons because of their color or race quite differently from the way of their predecessors of two generations ago. Our sensitivity to such charges is much greater; our reading of the constitutional guarantee is directed by values that were considerably weaker until events of recent years both at home and in other parts of the world. In other words, not only are the facts different, but different also are the values through which the facts are seen. The only thing that has not changed is the language of the Fourteenth Amendment.

In considering an issue such as that before the Court in *Brown v. Topeka*, facts and values are not found in separate worlds. The values that are summarized by the phrase "racial equality" have come to be recognized because of the happening of many events, including the consequences of racial segregation in the schools. The ideal of equal protection of the laws, guaranteed by the Fourteenth Amendment, has received clarification through the struggle of the Negro in the United States for racial equality and through the struggle of subject peoples throughout the world for recognition as equal partners with the white race and the powerful nations in the enjoyment of life, liberty, and the pursuit of happiness. Our constitutional ideal of equal protection, in other words, received meaning as a goal as men made the effort to achieve the goal. The full meaning of equal protection was not known in 1868 when the Fourteenth Amendment was ratified; nor is its full meaning known today. Meanings are forced out of it by events, by facts—even as events or facts are forced out of values. There is an inextricable interplay between facts and values, between events and ideals, between means and goals. Our ideals are never wholly set; our goals are never wholly fixed—they undergo changes as people seek to attain or to defeat them. And facts are never altogether cold, neutral, or profane, as if they had never been touched by values. Facts make policy even as policy makes facts.

This being the case, the Supreme Court cannot, in a case like *Brown v. Topeka*, see only and be bound only by its own precedents. It would be a fearful thing for a judge to make a decision on a constitutional issue if he thought that he was deciding not only the case before him, but all similar cases that might come before his successors for countless years ahead. Precedents are, of course, to be reckoned with; so is history; so is tradition. But there is no escape from the need to use the intelligence creatively. This, essentially, is what Justice Brandeis said in his opinion in *Coronado,* and this is, too, what Chief Justice Warren meant to say in his opinion in *Brown v. Topeka* when he cited psychological and sociological studies of the effects of racial segregation in the schools.

It is the use of the intelligence creatively that gives dignity to the judicial function and that makes it one of the supreme examples of human responsibility. This creative intelligence is not that of a disembodied soul; it is not abstract reason. It is informed by passion even as it is informed by logic; it is moved by goals even as it searches for and creates or changes goals; and it is moved by facts even as it seeks to direct the creation of conditions from which will emerge new facts —new facts, new goals, new values, and even new passions, new conflicts, and new loves.

Now that the "separate but equal" rule has been discarded, it is important to recall that this rule was not an absolute evil; it was only an imperfect good, for it gave recognition to the ideal of equality. The emphasis, constitutionally, was not on separation but on equality. For this reason, we should bear in mind what Tagore has said:

An imperfection which is not all imperfection, but which has perfection for its ideal, must go through a perpetual realisation. Thus, it is the function of our intellect to realise the truth through untruths, and knowledge is nothing but the continually burning up of error to set free the light of truth. Our will, our character, has to attain perfection by continually overcoming evils, either inside or outside us, or both; our physical life is consuming bodily materials every moment to maintain the life fire; and our moral life too has its fuel to burn. This life process is going on—we know it, we have felt it; and we have a faith which no individual instances to the contrary can shake, that the direction of humanity is from evil to good. For we feel that good is the positive element in man's nature, and in every age and every clime what man values most is his ideal of goodness.[6]

[6] Rabindranath Tagore, *Sadhana: The Realisation of Life* (London, 1921), p. 53.

[JOSEPH TANENHAUS]

NEW YORK UNIVERSITY

Social Science in

Civil Rights Litigation

ONE of the lesser controversies stirred up by the Supreme Court's epochal holding in the school segregation cases concerns the part played by social science in the decision. A backward glance puts the problem in perspective. In 1896 the Court, in *Plessy v. Ferguson,* held that segregating Negroes from whites on railroad coaches did not violate the Equal Protection Clause of the Fourteenth Amendment, as long as the facilities provided to the races were substantially equal.[1] The *Plessy* doctrine, although never squarely judged applicable to state-supported schools, seemed to have received implicit Court endorsement where they were concerned.[2] In 1950, in *Sweatt v. Painter,* the Supreme Court began to tack.[3] The Court in the *Sweatt* case ordered admission of a Negro to the University of Texas Law School even though a separate law school for Negroes had been established within the State. In explaining its decision the Court was not content merely to point to the larger faculty, the more adequate library facilities, and the richer curriculum in the white school. The highly regarded white school also possessed advantages "incapable of objective measurement," such as "reputation of the faculty, experience of the

[1] 163 U.S. 537 (1896).

[2] Cumming v. County Board of Education, 175 U.S. 528 (1899); Gong Lum v. Rice, 275 U.S. 78 (1927); Missouri ex rel. Gaines v. Canada, 305 U.S. 337 (1938).

[3] Sweatt v. Painter, 339 U.S. 629 (1950).

administration, position and influence of the alumni, standing in the community, traditions and prestige." [4] Since differences of this nature were manifestly impossible to overcome, the Court had in effect ruled that segregation in law schools was inherently a denial of equal protection of the laws.

This reliance on intangibles pointed the way to a frontal assault on segregation in the entire public school system. If the Court could be persuaded to rule that segregated schooling at any level, no matter how equal the physical facilities, faculty, and curricula, deprived Negro children of an education fully comparable with that received by white children, then the legal underpinnings of the whole system of segregated schooling would be swept away. In the series of cases immediately set in motion as a result of *Sweatt v. Painter,* lawyers for the Negro children presented as expert witnesses a number of psychologists and other social scientists, who testified that legally enforced segregation harmed the Negro child and impeded his educational progress. [5]

When these cases were appealed to the Supreme Court, appellants, in their briefs and in oral argument, stressed the testimony of the social scientists. A group of social scientists, including some who had testified in the trial courts, also prepared a statement of their own which was appended to appellants' briefs. [6] The Court, in declaring segregated schooling "inherently unequal," endorsed a finding by one of the trial courts that legally sanctioned segregation in the public schools tends to retard "the educational and mental development of Negro children and to deprive them of some of the benefits they would receive in a racial[ly] integrated school system." [7] The trial court's finding, observed the Supreme Court, "is amply supported by modern [psychological] authority," and to this observation was appended the now-famous footnote 11 citing several publications by social scientists, but none of their testimony or their formal statement. [8]

[4] 339 U.S. at 634.

[5] See in particular the Record in Briggs v. Elliott, No. 2, and Davis v. County School Board, No. 4, United States Supreme Court, 1953 Term.

[6] This statement, entitled "The Effects of Segregation and the Consequences of Desegregation: A Social Science Statement," is reprinted in 14 *Minnesota Law Review* 427 (1953).

[7] Brown v. Board of Education of Topeka, 347 U.S. 483, 494 (1954).

[8] *Loc. cit.*

Just what the sentence and the footnote reveal about the value, if any, that the Justices attached to the testimony and writings of the social scientists has been the subject of rather extreme claims and charges and, more recently, of some highly thoughtful commentary.[9] No attempt to add to the speculation on this intriguing subject is made in this essay. Our purpose rather is to examine some problems in admitting and weighing social science data which have arisen in the segregation cases and other civil rights litigation.

ADMISSIBILITY OF SOCIAL SCIENCE DATA

Just half a century ago the State of Oregon invited Louis D. Brandeis to defend its statute establishing maximum hours of work for women before the United State Supreme Court. Brandeis was convinced that law had "not kept pace with the rapid development of our political, economic, and social ideals" [10] and that the reason for this was clear. "The judge came to the bench unequipped with the necessary knowledge of economic and social science, and his judgment," Brandeis said, "suffered likewise through lack of equipment in the lawyers who presented the cases to him." [11] Accordingly, the brief that Brandeis submitted to the Court in *Muller v. Oregon* [12] contained but two pages of legal argument, whereas more than 100 pages were devoted to recounting legislative experience here and abroad and to detailing economic, social, and medical data designed to illustrate the harmful effects of long working hours on women. His oral argument was in similar vein.

The Court, through Justice Brewer, in sustaining Oregon's law, commented favorably upon Brandeis' brief with its elaborate reliance

[9] The more worth-while analyses include Arnold M. Rose, "The Social Scientist as an Expert Witness," 40 *Minnesota Law Review* 205 (1956); Jack Greenberg, "Social Scientists Take the Stand: A Review and Appraisal of Their Testimony in Litigation," 54 *Michigan Law Review* 953 (1956); Jerome Frank in "The Lawyer's Role in Modern Society: A Round Table," 4 *Journal of Public Law* 1 (1955); and two remarkable essays by Edmond Cahn, "A Dangerous Myth in the School Segregation Cases," 30 *New York University Law Review* 150 (1955), and "The Lawyer, the Social Psychologist, and the Truth," 31 *New York University Law Review* 182 (1956).

[10] In an address before the Chicago Bar Association, January 3, 1916, quoted by Alpheus T. Mason in *Brandeis: A Free Man's Life* (New York, 1946), p. 246.

[11] *Ibid.*, p. 247.   [12] 208 U.S. 412 (1908).

on "other than judicial sources." [13] Brewer's remarks prompted Professor Felix Frankfurter to observe, a few years later:

The *Muller* case is "epoch-making" not because of its decision, but because of the authoritative recognition by the Supreme Court that the way in which Mr. Brandeis presented the case . . . laid down a new technique for counsel charged with the responsibility of arguing such constitutional questions, and an obligation upon courts to insist upon such method of argument before deciding the issue.[14]

Actually Frankfurter's comment subsequently proved to be something of an overstatement. The "Brandeis brief" did become a fairly widely used technique, but the bar did not utilize it as fully as it might have. "If anything appears in the opinion," complained Justice Stone during his first years on the Court, "it is because some member of the Court takes the time and energy to go on an exploring expedition of his own. . . . [If we should catch up with our docket] some of us could become real students of the social and economic development of the United States, whether counsel are interested or not." [15] One reason for the failure of the bar properly to exploit social science was a lack of competence in working with its materials. Probably more important, however, was a change in the Court's personnel that resulted in a majority that characterized such data as "interesting, but only mildly persuasive." [16] In any event, even where courts were little impressed by social science findings, they did not seek to block their submission in appellate litigation.

Introducing social science testimony in trial courts, on the other hand, has proved more obstacle-laden because of evidentiary practices concerning hearsay and relevancy. Each of these difficulties merits rather extended consideration.

The hearsay obstacle is well illustrated by *State v. Irvin.*[17] In Lake County, Florida, in the fall of 1949, three Negroes were convicted of raping a white girl. The trial took place in an atmosphere of such prej-

[13] 208 U.S. at 419.

[14] "Hours of Labor and Realism in Constitutional Law," 29 *Harvard Law Review* 353, 365 (1916).

[15] Quoted by Alpheus T. Mason in *Harlan Fiske Stone: Pillar of the Law* (New York, 1956), p. 241.

[16] Adkins v. Children's Hospital, 261 U.S. 525, 560 (1923).

[17] 66 Fla. 288, 66 So 2d 288 (1953).

udice and violence that Justice Jackson, with Justice Frankfurter concurring, referred to the case as "one of the best examples of one of the worst menaces to American justice." [18] Three of the defendants were convicted, and two were sentenced to die. These latter, Samuel Shepherd and Walter Irvin, appealed ultimately to the United States Supreme Court, which reversed, apparently on the technicality that Negroes had been discriminated against when the jury was selected. A retrial was ordered by the State, and a change of venue to neighboring Marion County was granted.

Irvin's lawyers (at this juncture Shepherd was shot to death while "attempting to escape") sought still another change of venue, this time to a more remote part of Florida. They did not think that Irvin stood much more chance of winning acquittal in Marion County than he had had in nearby Lake County. The counties were not only contiguous, but in the same judicial district, and this meant that the prosecuting attorney who handled the first case would again represent the State. At the suggestion of one of Irvin's attorneys, Jack Greenberg of the NAACP Legal Defense and Educational Fund, the Elmo Roper Research and Public Opinion Organization was engaged, at at cost of more than $7,000, "to find out whether any large majority of the population of the State or of Marion County was prejudging the guilt or innocence of this defendant." [19]

With a leading professional pollster, the late Dr. Julian Woodward, as survey director, the Roper organization undertook to provide the desired data by "absolutely the same standard research technique" that it had used on behalf of many scores of clients, among them some of the country's leading business firms.[20] The interview schedule included a number of questions of general interest unrelated to the *Irvin* case and was pretested in Jacksonville, Florida, before the final forms were printed. Trained interviewers, who had no knowledge of either the client's identity or the purpose of the survey, administered the questionnaire to more than 1,500 adults in Lake and Marion counties and in two other counties, Jackson and Gadsden, in distant

[18] Shepherd v. Florida, 341 U.S. 50, 55 (1951), concurring in *per curiam* order.
[19] The facts are taken primarily from the case records made available to the writer by the NAACP Legal Defense and Educational Fund. The quotation appears in Transcript of Record, Florida v. Walter Lee Irvin, vol. 1, p. 25. See also Julian L. Woodward, "A Scientific Attempt to Provide Evidence for a Decision on Change of Venue," 17 *American Sociological Review* 447 (1952).
[20] Transcript of Record, Florida v. Walter Lee Irvin, vol. 1, p. 15.

parts of the State. Persons interviewed in each county (all white with the exception of a special sample of Negroes in Marion) were selected by quota sampling, with sex, age, occupation, and area as controls. In accordance with normal practice, the names of the interviewees were not recorded.

The results of the sample survey convinced Irvin's lawyers that they had been correct in thinking that his chances for acquittal would improve if the trial were moved far from the Lake-Marion region, and they sought to have the survey considered by the trial judge in deciding whether to grant a change in venue. Woodward was sworn as an expert witness and permitted to explain at length the way in which the survey had been designed, administered, and processed. His field supervisor, Dale Anderson, was also permitted to testify that the survey was carried out in the field under his personal supervision and that he had witnessed from a distance some of the interviews taking place. The results of the poll itself, however, were then excluded as hearsay because Woodward and Anderson did not know of their own personal knowledge what had transpired between interviewers and respondents. The Supreme Court of Florida, in sustaining the refusal to admit the sample survey, said it amounted to "hearsay based upon hearsay." [21]

The law is generally reluctant to consider a statement without an opportunity, as it were, to take the measure of its author. His appearance on the witness stand gives judge (and jury) an opportunity to observe his demeanor and permits cross-examination to test his acuteness of perception and memory, his narrative ability, his sincerity, and his veracity. In *State v. Irvin,* Woodward and Anderson could testify of their own knowledge only as to how the survey had been planned and carried out. For the attitudes of the persons polled they had to rely on the forms filled in by the interviewers.

A few courts have recently held that surveys are admissible if some of the interviewers take the stand. [22] What a survey does, according

[21] State v. Irvin, 66 So 2d 288, 291.

[22] For example United States v. 88 Cases More or Less Containing Bireley's Orange Beverage, 187 F. 2d 967 (1951); People v. Franklin National Bank of Franklin Square , 200 Misc. 557, 105 N.Y.S. 2d 81 (1951). The cases are discussed in Frank R. Kennedy, "Law and the Courts," in Meier and Saunders, *The Polls and Public Opinion* (New York, 1949), pp. 92 ff.; Robert C. Sorensen and Theodore C. Sorensen, "The Admissibility and Use of Opinion Research Evidence," 28 *New*

to these courts, is merely to record the attitudes of the persons interviewed. Whether these attitudes are well founded or factually justifiable is quite beside the point, and the credibility of the respondents, therefore, is not at issue. Only the credibility of those who did the interviewing needs to be assessed. If these latter submit themselves to cross-examination on the faithfulness and accuracy with which they reported what the interviewees said, then a survey is not hearsay at all.

This argument is based on two assumptions (both of which, as research has amply demonstrated, are open to challenge).[23] One assumption is that some persons may misunderstand the questions posed or be too misinformed about them to give useful answers. It is quite possible, for example, since no filter questions were used to protect against this, that some of those polled may have confused the *Irvin* case with another which had recently required a change of venue from Gadsden County or that others who knew nothing at all about the case answered the questions anyway instead of refusing an opinion simply because they did not wish to appear ill-informed. The second assumption is that respondents necessarily offer honest replies to the queries made. A person who knew in his heart that he would never vote to acquit a Negro of a charge of rape might feel that the interviewer would not respect him unless he paid lip service to the myth that a man under indictment is presumed innocent[24] and so might give a false answer.

Despite the fact that sample surveys may be hearsay, however, there is good reason for admitting them as one of the numerous exceptions to the hearsay rule. After all, the exclusion of hearsay can be justified only on the ground that cases ought to be decided on the best possible kind of evidence. When a court is faced with assessing

York University Law Review 1213 (1953); Lester E. Waterbury, "Opinion Surveys in Civil Litigation," 17 *Public Opinion Quarterly* 71 (1953); Note, "Public Opinion Surveys as Evidence: The Pollsters Go to Court," 66 *Harvard Law Review* 498 (1953).

[23] See, for example, Herbert H. Hyman, *Interviewing in Social Research* (Chicago, 1954); Stanley L. Payne, *The Art of Asking Questions* (Princeton, 1951); Hugh J. Parry and Helen M. Crossley, "Validity of Responses to Survey Questions," 14 *Public Opinion Quarterly* 61 (1950); Herbert Hyman, "Do They Tell the Truth?" 8 *Public Opinion Quarterly* 557 (1944).

[24] See the discussion of this popular myth by Charles T. McCormick in *Handbook of the Law of Evidence* (St. Paul, 1954), pp. 647–649.

the state of the public mind, the traditional approach has been to hear a parade of "public witnesses" usually carefully selected by lawyers to suit their purposes.[25] Such witnesses, no matter how brilliant the cross-examination, can hardly be considered to provide a better kind of evidence about the state of the public mind than a sample survey designed and directed by highly qualified personnel and administered through trained interviewers, with no knowledge of the client's identity or the purpose of the survey, to persons whose anonymity is guaranteed.

The second obstacle to admitting social science evidence at the trial stage is "legal relevancy." To be legally relevant, evidence not only must be logically pertinent to the problem under consideration, but also must possess at least enough probative worth to outweigh the mischief that may attend its admission. Testimony may be denied admission if it is unrelated to the facts at issue, or so likely to mislead or confuse the jury, or so time-consuming to hear, or of such dubious scientific standing, that its probative damage would probably outweigh its probative worth. The question where relevancy is concerned is not how much value should be attached to the evidence, but only whether, when all counterweights are balanced against it, the evidence is worth considering at all. *In re News Syndicate Company,* a case handled by the Federal Communications Commission, points up significant facets of this important cluster of evidentiary rules.[26]

The News Syndicate Company, publisher of the New York *Daily News,* was one of nearly a score of applicants for five available FM channels in the New York metropolitan area. The American Jewish Congress (AJC) filed a petition to intervene in opposition to the granting of a license to the *Daily News* because its "past activity in the newspaper publication field tends to prove that applicant would use the requested facilities as a means of furthering its hostility to those of the Jewish faith and to other minority groups."[27] Its petition denied, the AJC appeared as a public witness at hearings held in the summer and fall of 1946. Over vigorous protest by the *Daily News* that its

[25] Waterbury, *op. cit.,* p. 74.

[26] Docket No. 6175, Final Decision, 12 F.C.C. 805 (1948).

[27] The facts are taken primarily from the case records made available to the writer by the American Jewish Congress. The quotation appears in the AJC's Petition to Intervene, March 15, 1946, p. 2. The case is discussed in Note, "Content Analysis—A New Evidentiary Technique," 15 *University of Chicago Law Review* 910 (1948).

freedom of press was thereby violated, the trial examiner permitted the AJC to submit evidence that the *Daily News* had displayed consistent bias and hostility against Jews and Negroes.

The evidence presented by the AJC consisted in major part of a comparative content analysis covering a period of six months selected at random. The content analysis purported to be a systematic classification of all items dealing with Negroes and Jews appearing in the editorial and general news columns of the five New York City morning papers of general circulation—the *New York Times,* the *Herald-Tribune,* the *Mirror, PM,* and the *Daily News.* Eight categories were established. Five were favorable news: (1) achievements of individuals; (2) political or community activities; (3) persecution and discrimination; (4) intergroup good-will activities; (5) miscellaneous favorable. Three were unfavorable news: (6) crimes; (7) intergroup antagonism and clashes; (8) miscellaneous unfavorable. An experienced content analyst placed each item in one of these categories unless it semed to be neutral or balanced. (But in violation of the best-established procedures, no independent classifications of the newspapers by additional trained analysts were made.[28]) The results were tabulated and tables constructed comparing the material appearing in the five papers by the total number of stories, the total number of column inches, the ratios between favorable and unfavorable stories in each of the papers, and in several other ways.

The results of the content analysis, the AJC maintained, proved that the *Daily News* as compared with the other papers displayed consistent bias against minority groups and gave a distorted image of them. Counsel for the *Daily News* so completely discredited the AJC analysis on cross-examination that a new one was prepared. The second analysis, although somewhat less vulnerable than the first, was also subjected to devastating cross-examination.

Upon motion of the *Daily News,* the Federal Communications Commission, one member dissenting, ordered the content analysis stricken from the record, but one year later reversed itself. The Commission's reasoning is instructive. Its first order excluding the evidence as devoid of probative value, and therefore irrelevant, was made so that the "record may be clear that it has not entered into our decision upon

---

[28] On content analysis and its procedures see Bernard Berelson, *Content Analysis in Communications Research* (Glencoe, Ill., 1952); Harold D. Lasswell, Nathan Leites, and Associates, *Language of Politics* (New York, 1949).

the merits" of the *Daily News* application for an FM license.[29] Two justifications for exclusion were offered. For one thing, no satisfactory criteria had been presented for determining the significance of the study results. The Commissioners simply were not persuaded that an average based upon the *New York Times*, the *Herald-Tribune, PM,* and the *Mirror* provided any usable standard for what an unbiased newspaper should do. Their other justification for refusing to admit the data was that the categories "rest only on personal and inexpert opinion, the reliability of which has not been demonstrated" and that "subjective" standards were used in assigning news items to one or another of the several categories. "Under these circumstances it is essential to have judgments of the type involved checked by such additional procedures as a second independent analysis of the same material by another analyst." Without such an "experimental demonstration of reliability," the content analysis was incompetent and legally irrelevant.[30] The dissenting Commissioner, Clifford Durr, although agreeing that no satisfactory standard for the unbiased paper had been established and that an independent check by a second analyst should have been made, believed that the evidence carried some weight and should be admitted.[31]

In its final decision of April 7, 1948, the Commission reversed itself and agreed to admit the evidence.[32] It was no less persuaded than before that the technical deficiencies of the AJC study "fully explored in cross examination" left it without probative value. But, the Commission explained, a proceeding before an administrative body is like a trial before a judge sitting without a jury in that findings of fact are made on the basis of "reliable, probative, and substantial evidence" appearing in the record. As a result, any reliance on legally insufficient evidence can be reversed on appeal. In the language of the Commission:

Findings and conclusions of an expert body thus leave no room for the surmise and speculation about the possibilities of prejudice which a general verdict may engender and cannot dispell. Under such circumstances there

---

[29] In re News Syndicate Company, Docket No. 6175, Memorandum Opinion, April 9, 1947, p. 4.

[30] *Ibid.,* p. 3.   [31] *Ibid.,* p. 10.

[32] In re News Syndicate Company, Docket No. 6175, Final Decision, 12 F.C.C. 805, 828 (1948).

exists no necessity for insulating the special fact finding body from relevant evidence which may turn out to be insubstantial.[33]

The absence of any generally accepted systematic theory for the admissibility of social science evidence has left judges with considerable expanse in excluding as irrelevant evidence which they do not consider worth the candle. The FCC's thoughtful reasoning suggests a possible approach not only to legal relevancy, but to admissibility where hearsay is concerned as well. When an administrative expert or a judge sitting alone tries a case, there can be little danger in admitting any sort of sample survey or content analysis, projective tests like the one with black and white dolls employed by Professor Kenneth B. Clark in the South Carolina school segregation case, and such other social science data as a lawyer might deem useful in presenting his case. There would be little likelihood that testimony of dubious scientific standing would be overvalued by these specialists, and the possibility of misleading or confusing a jury would of course be absent. In any event there is the added protection, as the FCC pointed out, of judicial review of findings that must be based on sufficient probative evidence in the record.

Not only can there be little harm in a liberal policy of admitting evidence when no jury is involved, but also it has very definite advantages. If the evidence is admitted, then the judge or administrator can reflect upon it at his leisure, check authoritative works, consult with specialists if there is need; and perhaps, in the case of an administrative body with an adequate staff, as Commissioner Durr has suggested, an impartial corroborating investigation of its own might even be undertaken. Opposing counsel, moreover, if admission could be anticipated, would be on notice to prepare for a searching cross-examination on the merits of the testimony—the substance of which could be made available to him in advance together with all working papers, data sheets, and whatever else may be involved. If such advance warning for any reason could not be given, then an adjournment would always be in order until the necessary preparation could be made.

Where juries sit, there is need for more caution. Motions to admit or exclude social science evidence should be handled at a pretrial conference. Not only would the necessity for snap rulings during the

[33] In re News Syndicate Company, Docket No. 6175, Memorandum Opinion, April 7, 1948, 12 F.C.C. 837, 844.

course of a trial be obviated, but also, if the testimony is to be admitted, this procedure would give opposing counsel adequate time to prepare his case. A higher standard for admitting evidence in a jury trial is also essential because balancing the limitations against the worth of some social science data requires more sophistication than the ordinary juror might be expected to have attained.

Wide judicial discretion in deciding whether to submit social science evidence to a jury is probably unavoidable, but a useful rule of thumb might be as follows: When there is need to determine such intangibles as the state of the public mind or the moral standards or feeling of the community, sample surveys, planned and executed by qualified personnel, may be admitted—even if they did not make use of the most powerful tools available. Where alternative kinds of evidence would be of considerable probative value, as they generally are in jury cases, the courts would do well to insist upon standards for social science evidence stringent enough to satisfy most or even virtually all experts in the field.

If the suggested rule of thumb were followed, a content analysis like that prepared by the AJC would not be submitted to a jury, but more sophisticated ones, such as those prepared under the direction of Professor Harold Lasswell and used in several criminal prosecutions during the Second World War,[34] probably would not be barred.

WEIGHT OF SOCIAL SCIENCE DATA AS EVIDENCE

Once social science evidence has been admitted, the question arises as to how much weight it should carry. The answer must depend on two variables—the character of the evidence and the purpose for which it is used. If the constitutionality of a statute is at stake, courts are generally ready to agree with the doctrine set forth by Mr. Justice Washington in 1827. "It is but a decent respect to the wisdom, integrity, and the patriotism of the legislative body, by which any law is passed, to presume in favor of its validity, until its violation of the Constitution is proved beyond all reasonable doubt." [35] It was just this

---

[34] United States v. Pelley, 132 F. 2d 170 (1942); United States v. Auhagen, 39 F. Supp. 590 (1941); Harold D. Lasswell, "Propaganda Detection and the Courts," in *Language of Politics,* pp. 173 ff.

[35] Ogden v. Saunders, 12 Wheaton 213, 270 (1827).

presumption (which Holmes fought so hard to get the Court to honor) that gave thrust to the Brandeis brief. As Brandeis himself put it during oral argument in *Stettler v. O'Hara:*

In answer to the question, whether this brief contains also all the data opposed to minimum wage laws, I want to say this: I conceive it to be absolutely immaterial what may be said against such laws. Each one of these statements contained in the brief in support of the contention that this is wise legislation, might upon further investigation be found to be erroneous, each conclusion of fact may be found afterwards to be unsound—and yet the constitutionality of the act would not be affected thereby. This court is not burdened with the duty of passing upon the disputed question whether the legislature of Oregon was wise or unwise, or probably wise or unwise, in enacting this law. The question is merely whether . . . you can see that the legislators had no ground on which they could, as reasonable men, deem this legislation appropriate to abolish or mitigate the evils believed to exist or apprehended. If you cannot find that, the law must stand.[36]

Where a presumption of constitutionality is granted, social science data need only be persuasive enough to warrant reasonable men in acting as they did. Under these circumstances social science can be an impediment to civil rights as readily as a bulwark, for statutes can circumscribe freedom as readily as they can enhance it. To justify a "liberal" Court in exercising judicial self-restraint when economic regulation was challenged, while at the same time abandoning restraint when statutes infringed upon basic freedoms, a sizable number of Justices for a time endorsed an ingenious new formulation by Justice Stone.[37] According to this doctrine the presumption of constitutionality extends to all legislative acts except those touching upon the First Amendment. For legislation affecting these "preferred" rights, the presumption was reversed and clear necessity had to be demonstrated before the enactment would be permitted to stand.

During those years when both presumption doctrines seemed to have the support of a Court majority, the odd possibility arose that social science evidence weighty enough perhaps to sustain a statute if challenged as contravening one section of the Constitution would not be adequate to protect this same statute against an alleged violation

[36] 243 U.S. 629 (1917). Quoted by Samuel J. Konefsky in *The Legacy of Holmes and Brandeis: A Study in the Influence of Ideas* (New York, 1956), p. 61.

[37] United States v. Caroline Products Co., 304 U.S. 144, 152, n. 4 (1938).

of the First Amendment.[38] In 1943 the Hawaiian territorial legislature passed a law prohibiting, in effect, the teaching of any language other than English to children under ten years of age. The statute contained a legislative finding that the study of foreign languages by young persons of average mentality impaired their ability to learn English and created emotional disturbances as well. Chinese language schools attacked the law as an arbitrary interference with the right of parents to have their children taught foreign languages, in conflict with the Due Process Clause of the Fifth Amendment. The Territory produced a psychiatrist, a psychologist, and educators as expert witnesses to support its argument that the legislature had acted in a reasonable and appropriate manner. A. L. Wirin, counsel for the foreign language schools, with the apparent purpose of showing that the expert witnesses had yielded to ugly racist pressures, sought to impeach their credibility in trenchant cross-examination.

A three-judge district court found for the language schools, and the Territory appealed—alleging that since the First Amendment was not involved the constitutionality of the statute should be presumed. In its Supreme Court brief the Territory argued:

As part and parcel of the presumption of constitutionality, where there is a conflict of opinion as to the facts upon which the statute is based the legislature alone has the prerogative of deciding which body of expert opinion it will follow. In the present case the legislature adopted that body of expert opinion which holds that bilingual instruction is harmful to a young child. Such opinion accordingly cannot be rejected by the Court even though the members of the Court, were they sitting in the legislature, might be disposed to reject it.[39]

Entering the case as an *amicus curiae,* the American Jewish Congress filed an admirable brief based on a thorough canvass of relevant psychological studies.[40] The AJC agreed with the Territory that there was some authority on its side. Nevertheless, the AJC maintained, religious schools were not exempt by the statute, and a First Amendment freedom had thereby been impaired. The evidence, consequently, was not weighty enough to save the law. Said the AJC:

[38] Po v. Stainback, 74 F. Supp. 852 (1947); rev'd 336 U.S. 368 (1949).

[39] Appellants' Brief, Stainback v. Po, No. 52, United States Supreme Court, 1948 Term, p. 79.

[40] The preparation of this brief is discussed in Tracy S. Kendler, "Contributions of the Psychologist to Constitutional Law," 5 *American Psychologist* 505 (1950).

Evidence to support a finding that bilingualism causes retardation or maladjustment lacks by far the clarity and cogency required to justify legislative restriction on the free exercise of religion. . . . The restriction on religious liberty imposed by the Hawaiian legislature has not been shown to be clearly necessary or appropriate to meet the evil.[41]

In disposing of the case on other grounds the Supreme Court found no need to discuss the weight of the evidence or the question of presumptions.

Even in areas where the applicability of the traditional presumption doctrine has never been challenged, the Court may refuse to pay it homage—sometimes to the distinct profit of civil rights. In *Sweatt v. Painter*, the Texas law school case, the State argued in its Supreme Court brief that segregation by race was a reasonable classification and, therefore, not violative of the Fourteenth Amendment. Among the materials relied upon to support its position that there "are at least sufficient [grounds] to show substantive evidence of the reasonableness of the classification" was a sample survey by the Texas Poll, a professional opinion research organization.[42] The survey reported that four-fifths of the white persons and nearly three-fifths of the Negroes in Texas favored segregated universities. One of the main reasons whites offered for continuing with segregated universities was a "fear of racial trouble." And in *Davis v. County School Board*, the Virginia school segregation case, counsel for the State produced a clinical psychologist, a child psychiatrist, and the Chairman of Columbia University's Department of Psychology, for a similar purpose. The witnesses did not deny that segregation did or could hurt the Negro child. They maintained, nonetheless, that, given the state of mind in Virginia at the time, Negro high school students would suffer less psychological distress and get a better education in physically equal schools of their own.[43]

In neither the law school nor the public school segregation case did

[41] Brief of the American Jewish Congress, Amicus Curiae, Stainback v. Po, No. 52, United States Supreme Court, 1948 Term, p. 22.

[42] Respondent's Brief in Opposition to Petition for Writ of Certiorari, Sweatt v. Painter, No. 44, United States Supreme Court, 1949 Term, p. 59. The poll appears at pp. 62–63, 86–87.

[43] Transcript of Record, Davis v. County School Board, No. 4, United States Supreme Court, 1953 Term, pp. 529, 538, 555, 569.

the United States Supreme Court make even the vaguest reference to a presumption of constitutionality in favor of the statutes requiring segregation—although Justice Reed disclosed considerable interest during oral argument in the motives which the state legislatures had in enacting them.[44] But certainly if the Court had decided against invalidating segregated schooling, it could have invoked the presumption of constitutionality doctrine and pointed to the social science evidence presented by Texas and Virginia as showing that, however wrongheaded their policy, the state legislatures in requiring separate schooling had not acted in a totally capricious manner.

Data that can justify rational men in marking out a course for legislative policy do not need to be highly authoritative or refined. However, when judges set about determining the wisdom of establishing one judge-made rule in preference to others (and frequently this is just what they do when they decide whether or not to yield to a presumption of statutory validity) or when questions of fact are at issue—for example whether bilingualism or school segregation retards the learning process—the elegance of the evidence is of cardinal concern.

Much of the evidence offered by social scientists in civil rights cases has been difficult to assay with any precision because, though the opinion of experts, it is without mensurable base. As Mr. Justice Frankfurter observed during oral argument in *Gelbart v. Belton,* the Delaware school segregation case:

If a man says three yards, and I have measured it, and it is three yards, there it is. But if a man tells you the inside of your brain and mine, and how we function, that is not a measurement, and there you are. . . . We are here in a domain which I do not yet regard as science in the sense of mathematical certainty. I do not mean that I disrespect it. I simply know its character. It can be a very different thing from, as I say, things that are weighed and measured and are fungible. We are dealing here with very subtle things, very subtle testimony.[45]

And again in reply to NAACP counsel Jack Greenberg's statement that the testimony of the expert witnesses in the Delaware case had not been contradicted, Frankfurter observed:

[44] For example, Transcript of Oral Argument, Briggs v. Elliott, No. 2, United States Supreme Court, 1953 Term, pp. 65–66.

[45] Transcript of Oral Argument, Gelbart v. Belton, No. 10, United States Supreme Court, 1953 Term, pp. 68–69.

But the testimony of a witness is subject to intrinsic limitations and qualifications and illuminations. The mere fact that a man is not contradicted does not mean that what he says is so.[46]

Not all social science data are by any means so imprecise. They may not carry the conclusive weight that blood tests for nonpaternity do some 50-odd per cent of the time, but their reliability—the extent to which repeated measurement of the same phenomenon turns up highly similar or identical results—can often be determined. Take, for instance, the Roper opinion survey in *State v. Irvin*. One key question (8 a) read:

You've probably heard about the case of the white girl, Norma Padgett, who has accused four colored men of attacking her down in Groveland. Which of these statements comes closest to describing how you feel about the case? [interviewee handed card]

a) I feel sure the men are guilty
b) I think they're guilty, but I'm not completely sure
c) I really don't know if they're guilty or not guilty
d) I think they're not guilty, but I'm not completely sure
e) I feel sure they're not guilty [47]

Table 1. Prejudgment by white adults of Irvin's guilt in selected Florida counties

	Marion	Lake	Jackson	Gadsden
a)	43%	63%	17%	25%
b)	20	14	13	15
c)	25	16	26	29
d)	1	2	1	2
e)	—	*	1	—
Never heard of case or refused to answer	11	5	42	29
	(N = 518)	(N = 424)	(N = 258)	(N = 254)

* Less than .5%.

The response to this question is reproduced in Table 1. If true random sampling had been used and all other factors had remained constant,

[46] *Ibid.*, p. 68.
[47] Elmo Roper Research and Public Opinion Organization, "A Study of the Attitudes of Florida Citizens on Some Current Issues," February 1952 (mimeo.), p. 22.

the probabilities are that in 95 polls of every 100 the percentage who expressed certainty that the men were guilty would have ranged as follows: Marion County, 39–47 per cent; Lake, 59–67 per cent; Jackson, 13–21 per cent; and Gadsden, 20–30 per cent.[48] Although the Roper organization did not use true random sampling, the area controls it did employ were refined enough to make it unlikely that the sampling error was much larger than has been indicated. The reliability of the content analysis submitted by the American Jewish Congress in the *Daily News* case could also have been computed if a number of trained analysts had independently coded the same newspapers.

In fact one of the serious shortcomings of social science testimony tendered in civil rights litigation has been the failure to base it on reliable studies even when these could have been readily undertaken. *Tudor v. Board of Education* is a good example of this deficiency.[49] Gideon's International desired to distribute copies of the King James version of the Bible to those public school children in Rutherford, New Jersey, whose parents would permit acceptance of them. In an effort to circumvent the constitutional restrictions governing state aid to religion,[50] slips were distributed to each pupil which, if returned with the signature of a parent, would entitle the child to receive a Bible. The volumes were to be distributed after school hours. In all, 615 of the approximately 2,200 who received the slips returned them properly signed.

Counsel for Tudor, who was seeking to enjoin the distribution as unconstitutional, claimed that Protestant Bibles so distributed would "inevitably" end up in the hands of Jewish and Catholic children and injure them psychologically. To support his contention he presented as an expert witness psychologist Isidore Chein. Excerpts from the testimony follow:

Q: I ask you as a psychologist what effect the receipt of such a slip would have on the average public school child in respect to the distribution of

[48] The standard error is given approximately by $\sqrt{\dfrac{PQ}{N}}$, in which P equals the sample percentage, Q equals $100 - P$, and N equals the number of cases. When the standard error is multiplied by ± 1.96, the products give the probable range of all samples at the 5 per cent level of confidence.

[49] 14 N.J. 31 (1953), cert. den. 348 U.S. 816 (1954).

[50] Robert F. Cushman, "The Holy Bible and the Public Schools," 40 *Cornell Law Quarterly* 475 (1955).

the New Testament and its sanction and authenticity as far as the public school is concerned?

A: Well, I would expect that a slip of this kind, distributed under the authority of the school, would create a subtle pressure on the child which would leave him with a sense that he is not quite as free as the statement in that slip says, in other words, that he will be something of an outcast and a pariah if he does not go along with this procedure.

Q: Would you say that there would be a number, not necessarily how many, but a number of Jewish and Catholic children who would, on the basis of your testimony, either themselves seek to obtain the New Testament or urge their parents to sign the request slip in order for them to obtain the New Testament?

A: I most certainly would. I think that they would be in a situation where they would have to play along with this or else feel themselves to be putting themselves in a public position where they are different, where they are not the same as other people, and the whole pressure would exist on them to conform.[51]

Now Dr. Chein may well have been right, but after all it would not have been such an arduous task to check every third or fourth slip in an effort to find out just how many had been returned by Jewish and Catholic children and to analyze those children in an effort to determine whether psychological pressures, or perhaps the desire to own a literary masterpiece, or some other reason had been responsible for their requesting King James Bibles.

Nor, one may add, is it to the credit of adversary counsel that such matters as these, or even of Dr. Chein's knowledge of the system for distributing the Bibles, were never probed. In the *Tudor* case, as in a number of other civil rights cases involving social science testimony, cross-examination has left something to be desired.

Highly reliable data are certainly desiderata. Yet reliability, however impressive, cannot be of great moment unless the data are also valid, unless they go some way toward solving the problem set for them. Take the Roper survey in *State v. Irvin*. The survey was designed to measure the degree of prejudgment of the defendant in Marion as compared with several other counties. On the not unreasonable assumption that

---

[51] Transcript of Record, Gideon's International v. Tudor, No. 745, United States Supreme Court, 1953 Term, p. 43 a. Cf. Professor Cahn's discussion of Dr. Chein's testimony in the Girard College Case, "The Lawyer, the Social Psychologist, and the Truth," *op. cit.*, pp. 186 ff.

errors caused by respondents' dishonesty and interviewers' recording of the responses rendered would be constant for the several counties and with allowance for a rather generous sampling error of 4 per cent for each county, the differences between those convinced of Irvin's guilt in Marion as compared with Jackson and Gadsden are still highly significant statistically. They could be expected to occur by chance less than one time in one hundred.[52] Insofar as the state of prejudgment is concerned, then, the survey is quite valid.

Still the state of prejudgment in itself is not really the underlying question. Rather more basic is whether Irvin stood a better chance of acquittal if venue were changed to Jackson or Gadsden than if the trial took place in Marion. Would, in other words, a jury drawn at random from Marion, after hearing all the evidence, be more likely to reach a verdict of guilty than a jury similarly selected in Jackson or Gadsden? Any meaningful answer requires some knowledge of at least two factors in addition to the degree of existing prejudgment. First, just how much did the persons polled know about the earlier history of the case? There is reason to suspect that Irvin's prior conviction and its reversal on a technicality were much more widely known in Marion and Lake than in the two far-removed counties. This differential in knowledge, which would have been quickly eliminated if the case were moved into Jackson or Gadsden, may have been largely responsible for the differences in the survey results. Unfortunately, because the survey did not use a filter question to separate out those who knew about the prior conviction from those who did not, this factor must remain a matter for speculation.

The survey did, however, anticipate the second factor, the freedom of a juror once convinced of the defendant's innocence to vote for his

---

[52] Statistical significance for the data was determined by use of the Chi Square test for 2×2 tables. The allowances for sampling error reduced the percentage of those certain of guilt in Marion County to 39 per cent and increased the percentages in Jackson and Gadsden Counties to 21 and 25 per cent respectively. Since in all cases the smaller of the expected frequencies was greater than five, the following formula was used:

$$x^2 = \frac{N(AD - BC)^2}{(A + B)\ (C + D)\ (A + C)\ (B + D)}$$

The data for Marion and Jackson yield a Chi Square of 19.49, and for Marion and Gadsden of 7.21. A Chi Square larger than 6.64 indicates the probability that the difference would have occurred by chance less than one time in one hundred. See Quinn McNemar, *Psychological Statistics* (New York, 1949), pp. 200 ff.

acquittal, and the results are worth attention. The question (8 b) read: "Do you think anybody on the jury in the [Irvin] case would get away with it if they voted 'not guilty' or do you think something might happen to them if they did?" [53] The response appears in Table 2. The striking thing about the figures in this table is that in those counties where

Table 2. Consequence of a juror's voting to acquit Irvin anticipated by white adults in selected Florida counties

	Marion	Lake	Jackson	Gadsden
Would get away with	60%	65%	31%	42%
Something might happen	16	16	23	20
Didn't know or refused to answer	24	19	46	38
	(N = 518)	(N = 424)	(N = 258)	(N = 254)

there was the most prejudgment, Marion and Lake, there was the greatest belief that a juror could "get away with" a vote to acquit. These figures, which are just as significant statistically as those on prejudgment,[54] may not seem so bizarre if one is aware that contempt and hostility toward the Negro are much more pronounced in Jackson and Gadsden than in either Marion or Lake.[55] Irvin's prospects for acquittal may not have been very good in Marion County, but they may have been even worse in Jackson or Gadsden. The survey, in short, offered no valid basis for changing venue to one of these two counties, though if more progressive counties had been polled, stronger grounds for a change might well have been turned up.

The content analysis submitted by the American Jewish Congress in the *Daily News* case, if one were to assume its reliability, raises similar problems of validity. The purpose of the content analysis was to determine whether the *News* displayed a consistent bias against Jews and Negroes as compared with four other New York papers. Holding that it had made its case, the AJC in its *Memorandum in the Nature*

[53] Elmo Roper Research and Public Opinion Organization, *op. cit.*, p. 35.

[54] The data for Marion and Jackson yield a Chi Square of 30.69, and those for Marion and Gadsden of 6.73.

[55] Professor Manning J. Dauer several years ago, for the use of the State's Attorney General, grouped Florida counties in accordance with their readiness for desegregation. Marion and Lake fell at about the middle of a seven-point scale, and Jackson and Gadsden were in the bottom group.

of Proposed Findings [56] presented several tables comparing the *Daily News* and an average of the *Times, Herald-Tribune, Mirror,* and *PM*. The first AJC table [57] dealt with the ratio of favorable to unfavorable stories about Jews and Negroes and is reproduced here as Table 3.

Table 3. Ratio of favorable to unfavorable stories about Jews and Negroes appearing in the *Daily News* and an average of four other New York newspapers

	Favorable	Unfavorable
Daily News	65	35
Average of other papers	89	11

The differences between the *Daily News* and the average of the other four papers would have occurred by chance less than one time in one hundred. But is it legitimate to compare the *News* with an average of the *Times, Herald-Tribune, Mirror,* and *PM?* The raw figures from which the AJC table was computed suggests that it is not. These figures are shown in Table 4.

Table 4. Classification of stories about Jews and Negroes appearing in the news and editorial columns of five New York newspapers °

	Favorable categories						Unfavorable categories			
	1	2	3	4	5	Total	6	7	8	Total
Daily News	31	32	9	22	1	95	45	6	0	51
Mirror	22	32	18	18	0	90	38	3	0	41
New York Times	62	228	44	108	5	447	26	3	0	29
Herald-Tribune	58	103	40	88	1	290	36	4	3	43
PM	13	35	62	98	2	210	10	2	1	13
Total	155	398	164	312	8	1132	110	12	4	177

° Adapted from Table 3 of the second AJC content analysis, dated September 24, 1946 (mimeo.). The categories to which the numbers refer are listed above, p. 99.

Close examination of Table 4 reveals that only one unfavorable category (6) is large enough to have any meaning, and this deals with

[56] Filed on November 12, 1946, at the direction of the Federal Communications Commission.

[57] *Ibid.*, p. 58.

crime. Assuming that a crime story involving a Negro or a Jew ought to be considered unfavorable to the minority group to which he belongs—and the assumption is not unassailable—the differences between the *Daily News, Herald-Tribune, Mirror,* and *Times* are not impressive, especially when one has in mind that sensationalism is a main dish of the tabloids. Of the favorable categories, four are large enough to warrant consideration: (1) achievements of individuals; (2) political or community activities; (3) persecution and discrimination; and (4) intergroup good-will activities. In none of these does the *Daily News* differ dramatically from its sister tabloid, the *Mirror,* nor does either deviate much from *PM* in the first two categories. What really weights the average against the *News* is, first, the extended treatment which the *Times* and *Herald-Tribune* give to political and community affairs and to intergroup good-will activities and, second, the repeated campaigns against bigotry and intolerance by *PM,* more a journal of opinion than a newspaper. The data show, if they show anything at all, that the *Daily News* and the *Mirror* are very similar. The *Daily News* may very well have displayed a consistent bias against Jews and Negroes in 1945–1946, but the AJC content analysis does not prove it.

Nor did Professor Clark's research with his doll test demonstrate that school segregation per se harmed the Negro child. Clark presented pictures of Negro and white dolls to sixteen Negro children in South Carolina and asked them to select the doll that "you like best or that you'd like to play with," the "nice" doll, the "bad" doll, the doll that "looks like a white child," the doll that "looks like a colored child," the doll that "looks like a Negro child," and the doll that "looks like you," in that order. The choices of these sixteen children, he testified, were similar to those of several hundred Negro children in the North. He had never performed the test with white children.[58] But unless the answers given by white children and by Negro children who attend nonsegregated schools differ significantly from the answers given by the South Carolina children, the doll test, however reliable, cannot possibly be of any value in showing the effects on Negroes of school segregation.

[58] Discussion of the doll test appears in Transcript of Record, Briggs v. Elliott, *op. cit.,* pp. 84 ff.; Transcript of Record, Davis v. County School Board, *op. cit.,* pp. 245 ff., 520 ff.; Transcript of Oral Argument, Briggs v. Elliott, *op. cit.,* pp. 48–49; Cahn, "A Dangerous Myth in the School Segregation Cases," *op. cit.,* pp. 161 ff.

CONCLUSION

Several concluding observations may perhaps be in order. Social science has made its most important contributions in civil rights litigation by helping appellate judges to justify one policy over another. In the trial court, where fact finding is most important, social science has thus far carried relatively little weight. This is due, in part at least, to inordinately strict practices in the admissibility of evidence and to the failure of lawyers to recognize when social science can help them.

Yet much of the fault lies with the social scientist. The relative imprecision of many social science techniques is, of course, a major limiting factor; but even more important has been the failure of the social scientist to use the more adequate tools already in hand in a thoroughly satisfactory way. All too often he has proved willing to draw unwarranted conclusions from his data and has opened the profession wide to sarcastic jibes like that of John W. Davis during oral argument in the South Carolina school segregation case: "Social science [is] 'fragmentary expertise based on an examined presupposition.'" [59]

Social science can make a significant contribution in trial court litigation. If it is to do so, however, the social scientist must adhere to just as rigorous standards in giving evidence as he does in presenting research for professional publication. Advocacy should be left to the lawyers. Insofar as civil rights are concerned, social science is neutral. The social scientist who persists in playing the role of advocate rather than expert will in the long run carry no weight with the courts. Nor will he be of service to civil rights.

[59] Transcript of Oral Argument, Davis v. County School Board, *op. cit.*, p. 51.

[JOHN F. CUSHMAN]

DEPARTMENT OF JUSTICE

Mediation and Education

for Equal Economic Opportunity

AT first view, it might seem that as uninspiring a document as a government contract would have little, if any, relationship to civil rights, particularly those aspects which are concerned with the vital problem of eliminating distinctions based on race or color. But firmly embedded amid the multitude of "whereas" and "wherefore" clauses appears the following provision in substantially all contracts to which the Government is a party today:

In connection with the performance of work under this contract, the contractor agrees not to discriminate against any employee or applicant for employment because of race, religion, color or national origin.[1]

The contracting agencies of the Government enter into approximately six million contracts annually, and it is a rare business of any size which does not have occasion to supply either products or services to the Government at one time or another. It has been estimated that perhaps as many as fifty million Americans work for firms which have signed contracts containing this obligation. Since equal economic opportunity is essential if noneconomic discriminations based on race or color are to be eliminated, it is plain that the government contract must be included in any present-day discussion of civil rights in the United States.

[1] Executive Order 10557, 3 C.F.R. (1954 Supp.) 69.

Aspects of Liberty

With respect to the above contract provision, commonly called the "nondiscrimination clause," three questions are commonly asked:

What legal authority, if any, authorizes inclusion of such a provision?

What steps, if any, does the Government take to secure compliance with it?

What impact, if any, has it had on employment opportunities for members of minority groups?

It is the purpose of this paper to attempt a partial answer to these questions.[2]

The present nondiscrimination clause, like those which have preceded it, is required in government contracts solely by virtue of a Presidential Executive Order.[3] Primarily because of this fact, it is sometimes asserted that there is no legal authority for including such a clause, that Presidents Roosevelt, Truman, and Eisenhower all exceeded their constitutional powers in this regard. But as it has recently been observed, "rarely does the contention rise to the level of a carefully formulated legal argument."[4] Rather, it is asserted that because Congress has considered specific FEPC legislation, and has not acted, it is a usurpation of legislative power for Presidents to do by Executive prerogative what Congress has not expressly said shall be done. The recent *Steel Seizure* case has been pointed to in support of this conclusion.[5]

On the other side of the ledger, however, a number of well-established legal principles would seem to compel the conclusion that this is a proper exercise of Executive power. Congress has vested broad discretion in the President and the Executive agencies with respect to the terms and conditions of contracts. The First War Powers Act, for example, empowers the President to authorize any department or

[2] From 1954 to 1957, the author, as a member of the Department of Justice, was privileged to work with the President's Committee on Government Contracts in an official capacity. However, the views and opinions expressed herein are the author's exclusively.

[3] See, e.g., Executive Orders No. 8802 of June 25, 1941, 6 F.R. 3109; No. 9346 of May 27, 1943, 8 F.R. 7183; No. 10308 of December 5, 1951, 16 F.R. 12303; and No. 10479 of August 13, 1953, 18 F.R. 4899, as amended by No. 10482 of August 15, 1953, 18 F.R. 4944.

[4] Robert Pasley, "The Nondiscrimination Clause in Government Contracts," 43 *Virginia Law Rev.* 837, 857 (1957).

[5] Youngstown Sheet & Tube Co. v. Sawyer, 343 U.S. 579.

agency exercising defense functions to enter into contracts without regard to usual restrictions "when he deems such action will facilitate the national defense." [6] Under the Federal Property and Administrative Services Act, negotiated contracts for supplies and services "may be of any type which in the opinion of the agency head will promote the best interests of the government." [7] Both national defense and the public interest have consistently been asserted as among the reasons for promulgating the Orders. Moreover, in the field of contracts it has been recognized that the Government enjoys substantially the same rights and privileges as a private person. Thus the Supreme Court has said:

Like private individuals and businesses, the Government enjoys the unrestricted power to produce its own supplies, to determine those with whom it will deal, and to fix the terms and conditions upon which it will make needed purchases. Acting through its agents as it must of necessity, the Government may for the purpose of keeping its own house in order lay down guide posts by which its agents are to proceed in the procurement of supplies, and which create duties to the Government alone.[8]

Nondiscrimination in employment under government contracts has been required by Executive Order since 1941, notwithstanding the fact that Congress, in the so-called Russell Amendment of 1946,[9] cut off the source of funds used to finance the wartime FEPC. It has been held that Executive construction of its statutory powers is entitled to great weight [10] and that congressional acquiescence in that construction may be inferred from congressional silence.[11]

Beyond any question the nondiscrimination clause is a manifestation of the public policy of the United States. Chief Justice Stone, writing for the Supreme Court, said:

Distinctions between citizens solely because of their ancestry are by their very nature odious to a free people whose institutions are founded upon the doctrine of equality.[12]

[6] 50 U.S.C. App. 611.   [7] 41 U.S.C. 254(a).
[8] Perkins v. Lukens Steel Co., 310 U.S. 113.   [9] 31 U.S.C. 696.
[10] Fleming v. Mohawk Co., 331 U.S. 111.
[11] Norwegian Nitrogen Co. v. United States, 288 U.S. 294; United States v. Jackson, 280 U.S. 183.
[12] Hirabayashi v. United States, 320 U.S. 81.

It would seem extremely doubtful that courts which will not lend their aid to the enforcement of private racial covenants,[13] which have required desegregation of our public school systems,[14] and which have held that Negroes may not be barred from federal housing projects erected by the Government with public nonsegregated tax receipts [15] would hold void a voluntarily assumed contractual obligation and thus sanction racial or religious discrimination in work under government contracts financed by public funds. And this would be true even assuming that a contractor has about the same option in this matter as a state may have in deciding whether to accept a grant-in-aid containing contract conditions it does not like.[16]

The fact that such a provision may validly be imposed as a condition for doing business with the Government would be of little moment, of course, if by custom or otherwise the requirements were relegated to that category of small print which may be ignored or overlooked. Although there is reason to believe that such may have been the case at one time, it is emphatically not true today.

Executive Order 10479 makes the "head of each contracting agency" primarily responsible for obtaining compliance with the nondiscrimination clause. Basically, it is the job of each procurement agency to advise their contractors, and through them any subcontractors, that ability alone must be the criterion to govern their employment practices. Since 1954, all the major contracting agencies have developed specific procedures and instructions to implement this national policy, and the contracting officers have been provided with a detailed manual for their guidance. It has been fully recognized that in the final analysis the success or failure of this program will depend in large part on what transpires when a contracting officer sits down to talk contract terms with a prospective contractor. Every effort has been made to ensure that specific attention is drawn to this obligation and that the Government expects compliance with it just as it expects compliance with all the other terms and conditions.

[13] Shelley v. Kraemer, 334 U.S. 1; Hurd v. Hodges, 334 U.S. 24.

[14] Brown v. Board of Education of Topeka, 347 U.S. 483; Bolling v. Sharpe, 347 U.S. 497.

[15] Vann v. Toledo Metropolitan Housing Authority, 113 F. Supp. 210 (D.C.N.D. Ohio).

[16] McGee v. Mathis, 4 Wall. 143, 155; Stewart Machine Co. v. Davis, 301 U.S. 548, 598.

The Executive Order, however, contemplates that leadership and co-ordinated direction for this program shall come from the President's Committee on Government Contracts. This Committee, which meets officially at least once a month, is composed of fifteen members, nine appointed by the President and one government representative from the Departments of Defense, Justice, Commerce, and Labor, from the Atomic Energy Commission, and from the General Services Administration. That the President is vitally concerned with the success of this program is evidenced by the fact that he named Vice President Nixon to serve as Chairman.[17] That the public members recognize the importance of the Committee work is in part evidenced by the fact that in over four years the only member to resign did so most reluctantly and as a result of his appointment to the federal bench. That affirmative steps are being taken to secure compliance with the nondiscrimination clause can best be demonstrated by considering some of the major activities and accomplishments of the Committee.

One of the first steps taken by the Committee was to recommend to the President the adoption of a revised clause making it plain that the contractor's obligation was not limited solely to hiring practices. The revised clause in Executive Order 10557 now provides that discrimination includes actions with respect to promotion, demotion, transfer, recruitment, recruitment advertising, and other aspects of employment.[18] Thus it is not enough that minority groups may be represented in the work force; if they are denied equal opportunity for advancement into skilled trades, are barred from white-collar jobs, or are not admitted to in-job training courses which are made a prerequisite to such advancement, the contractor is not in compliance.

Under the revised clause, contractors and subcontractors also must agree to post, "in conspicuous places, available for employees and applicants for employment," notices setting forth the terms of the non-

[17] Other present members are Honorable James P. Mitchell, Daniel C. Gainey, Fred Lazarus, Jr., Honorable Perkins McGuire, George B. McKibbin, George Meany, Honorable George T. Moore, James M. Nabrit, Mrs. Helen Rogers Reid, Walter P. Reuther, Honorable William P. Rogers, John A. Roosevelt, Harry S. Traynor, Ivan L. Willis, and White House Liaison Officer Maxwell M. Rabb.

[18] Executive Order 10557 provides that the nondiscrimination clause "shall include, but not be limited to, the following: employment, upgrading, demotion, or transfer; recruitment or recruitment advertising; layoff or termination; rates of pay or other forms of compensation; and selection for training, including apprenticeship."

discrimination clause and the fact that the contractor has agreed to them. This requirement has been implemented by providing all contractors and subcontractors with copies of a poster entitled "Equal Economic Opportunity."

Although it is not possible to isolate the effectiveness of the poster requirement in bringing about compliance with the clause, some indication of its impact may be inferred from the fact that a substantial number of contractors have sought for one reason or another to be excused from this obligation and others have displayed the poster only when specifically requested to do so by compliance officers. It has been contended that to post such a notice would be tantamount to admitting that at one time the company practiced discrimination, an interpretation not shared by the Committee. Others have quite frankly stated that they cannot afford to take a public position on such a controversial matter, even though privately they would be quite willing to agree to the conditions imposed and would work gradually for their implementation. Almost without exception, the Committee has denied requests of this nature.[19] Obviously an obligation of this sort can bear fruit only as those affected by it may be aware of its existence. Moreover, failure to have the poster conspicuously displayed can be readily determined and suggests the existence of noncompliance with the substantive provisions of the clause.

The Committee has given wide publicity to the existence of the nondiscrimination clause. Extensive use has been made of car cards in the busses and streetcars of over 150 major cities publicizing the national equal job opportunity policy. During the 1956 Christmas season, United States mail trucks carried such a placard. Thousands of copies of leaflets explaining the purposes of the provision have been distributed to contractors, social agencies, and state and local employment offices. A "Newsletter" is published each month setting forth current activities and accomplishments. A movie entitled "Commencement" has been distributed and televised. In 1955, the presidents or board chairmen of 55 companies which employ approximately 2,500,-000 people attended an Equal Job Opportunity Conference in Wash-

[19] Section 2 of Executive Order 10557 provides that the clause shall be included in all contracts except "contracts and subcontracts to meet other special requirements or emergencies, if recommended by the Committee on Government Contracts." Under this provision the Committee has granted a very limited number of exemptions to meet special requirements.

ington at the invitation of the President. Members of the Committee and its professional staff are in almost constant attendance at state and local conferences. A branch office has been opened in Chicago.

An essential part of the work of the Committee centers around the elaborate procedures by which any complaint alleging noncompliance with the clause is handled. Such complaints may be filed either directly with the Committee or with the contracting agency. But whichever procedure is followed, once it is determined that the Government has a contract with the alleged violator and the matter has been thoroughly investigated by the contracting agency involved, the complaint, the agency's investigative report, and its recommendations are transmitted to the President's Committee, which makes the final determination as to the action required. Probably in no other government program does a complaint by an individual or association receive such careful attention at such a high level of government.

In the four years from August 1953, 293 complaints have been received.[20] Approximately 200 have been closed, some because the Committee found it was without jurisdiction, some because the actual facts failed to support the allegations, and others because corrective action was taken. Most of the "closed cases" falling in the last category are still open in the sense that compliance reviews are subsequently made to determine whether the policies of the clause are being carried out.

There has been some misunderstanding of the complaint process on the part of complainants and contractors. This has been due to a misconception of its purposes and perhaps to a failure to appreciate the remedy available to the Government where it finds noncompliance.

The Committee is naturally concerned with individual instances of injustice caused by discrimination. If the facts warrant the conclusion that discrimination has been practiced, every effort will be made to persuade management to offer to the individuals involved employment, reinstatement, or advancement, as the case may be. Corrective action in this respect is taken into account in determining whether there is good faith compliance.

But there is no legal power to compel any contractor to hire or promote any particular individual. Even in a case of flagrant violation, the nondiscrimination clause creates no third-party beneficiary rights.

[20] Fourth Annual Report, President's Committee on Government Contracts, November 1957.

The contractor's obligation is to the Government. Stated otherwise, a contractor is free to practice discrimination provided he is willing to forego the privilege of doing business with the Government. In this sense, a complaint, or a particular set of facts, merely serves as a means of alerting the contracting agency to the fact that a company may not be living up to its contractual obligation.

In addition, whether or not a company is in compliance can seldom be determined solely from the facts of an individual complaint. Personnel action with respect to a particular individual can often be justified on some ostensibly valid ground, such as lack of ability, lack of co-operation, or, in the case of denying employment, a union requirement to rehire from a seniority roster employees who have been laid off. Because of the inherent difficulty in determining whether discrimination is practiced in a given situation, the contracting agencies have been instructed to investigate the company's over-all employment practices. A typical case will demonstrate the soundness of this approach.

In an early complaint, an employee alleged that he had been denied employment solely because he was colored. The investigation made was limited solely to the facts of the particular complaint, and the investigator recommended that the case be closed because the individual involved was a chronic troublemaker and had been discharged from numerous jobs. The report was wholly silent on the general employment practices of the company. Upon reinvestigation, made at the request of the Special Subcommittee on Review,[21] it was found that during a period of over twenty-five years no Negroes had ever been employed by the company. This was evidence against the employer. Total absence of any particular minority group may not conclusively establish discrimination, but on the other hand, as the Supreme Court has said in the jury exclusion cases:

That showing as to the long-continued exclusion of Negroes from jury service, and as to the many Negroes qualified for that service, could not be met by mere generalities. If . . . the mere general assertions by officials of their performance of duty were to be accepted as adequate justification for the complete exclusion of Negroes from jury service, the constitutional provision . . . would be but a vain and illusory requirement.[22]

[21] The Committee has created a number of special Standing Subcommittees. See Appendix I to the Second Annual Report.
[22] Norris v. Alabama, 294 U.S. 587.

Equal Economic Opportunity

More serious problems are encountered in the far more common situation where members of minority groups are actually employed. Some contractors believe, contrary to the text of the clause, that as long as there is not a total debarment because of race or color their obligation has been met. This may be illustrated by one contractor who is reported to have told an investigator somewhat heatedly that his company did not discriminate and never had; it just so happened that on the day the complainant applied for work "we had no openings for colored." Here again, the total absence of minority groups from the skilled or better-paying jobs is treated as a prima-facie case of discrimination with the burden on the contractor to demonstrate that his employment policy conforms to the national policy.

The complaint process is only one means by which the Committee obtains information on employment practices. It is well aware of the reluctance of employees to bring what amounts to charges against their employers. During 1957 the contracting agencies conducted compliance reviews of substantially all the Government's principal contractors located in the larger metropolitan areas. The policy was to evaluate employment practices, regardless of whether or not there was reason to believe that discrimination in some form existed. Although these reviews have not been fully analyzed, the Fourth Annual Report of the President's Committee states:

The information compiled . . . gives the Federal Government, for the first time, detailed knowledge of the employment policies and practices of many of its principal contractors. The report reveals the areas of employment being opened to members of minority groups, and directs attention to those situations which will require further effort.

Quite clearly the "areas" requiring further effort are in the skilled trade and white-collar jobs where the percentage of Negroes is described as "strikingly low."

The major criticism leveled against the President's Committee is that despite the filing of some 300 complaints and despite its review of over 500 plants, no contract has been terminated for noncompliance and no contractor has been placed on the list of contractors ineligible to receive further awards. Since, presumably, cases of noncompliance have been found, it is concluded that the program has no teeth and that those who refuse to comply run no risk of loss of contracts. It is also asserted that in any event the Government has no alternative but to do business with the major defense, utility, and transportation companies, so that as a practical matter the Government could not terminate a major contract even if it found deliberate and willful violation.

Although there is a substantial element of truth in these assertions, such a far-reaching condemnation of the Committee and its work would seem to be wholly unjustified. It is true that the Committee has largely followed a policy of education, mediation, conciliation, and persuasion to accomplish its objectives. It has done so deliberately. This is a common-sense approach, particularly when it is recalled that contractors have been under Executive directions since 1941 not to discriminate and that the obligation has been largely ignored, until recently, even by the Government itself. When the contract clause was revised and strengthened and the poster requirement was inserted, a reasonable period of time was necessary to familiarize management with its responsibility and the Government's determination to seek compliance. Thus, where evidence of noncompliance comes to the attention of the Committee, a presumption obtains that the violation is unintentional, the result of an oversight, and since the contractor has agreed to eliminate discriminatory practices, it is assumed that corrective action will follow once the matter is called to the employer's attention. Moreover, where a contractor is attempting in good faith to comply, none of the objectives of the program are served by contract termination or by debarring the contractor from future awards. Continuing jurisdiction depends on continuing contracts.

This period of acclimation appears, however, to be drawing to a close. In the spring of 1957, the Committee announced a firmer policy for the future by requesting the contracting agencies to reject a prospective contractor's bid if the preaward survey (customarily made in all cases to determine over-all responsibility) found that the contractor's employment record disclosed practices inconsistent with the nondiscrimination clause. It further requested the agencies to deny additional awards to existing contractors where clear and convincing evidence of noncompliance was found and to resume contracting only upon receipt of satisfactory evidence that corrective action had been taken. Even prior to the announcement of this policy, the Committee had recommended, and several contractors had been put on notice, that no new awards would be made to them unless they abandoned their discriminatory policies. The companies involved had substantial contracts with the Department of Defense and immediately took affirmative steps to bring themselves into compliance within the time prescribed. Numerous factors suggest that no company is anxious to test the ultimate power of the Government.

A contractor may not of course be held responsible for discrimination over which he has no control. This does not mean that he may put the matter of employing members of a minority group to a vote of his employees, as occurred in one instance. But where a contractor must look to organized labor for his employees and where the unions maintain segregated locals, clearly an employer should not be charged with responsibility for the resulting discrimination unless he actively supports and encourages union practices of this nature.

Both George Meany and Walter P. Reuther are members and strong supporters of the President's Committee. The constitution of the AFL-CIO contains a nondiscrimination provision. Despite this fact and despite efforts made at a national level, a substantial number of locals still practice discrimination. The primary responsibility here lies with labor, and though the Committee has sought and obtained the active co-operation of many responsible union leaders, there is no ready solution to this problem over which contractors can exercise little, and the Committee almost no, disciplinary authority.

Finally, in answer to those who would critize the Committee for not having taken a firmer stand, the record will show that substantial progress has been made under the policy of education and persuasion. Examples follow.

(1) In October 1953, the Board of Commissioners of the District of Columbia agreed to include the standard nondiscrimination clause in all its contracts.

(2) As a result of negotiations conducted by a Special Subcommittee, the Capital Transit Company and the Chesapeake and Potomac Telephone Company have abandoned discrimination practices in employment. Because discrimination tends to follow industry-wide patterns, it is of interest to note that fifteen of the nation's twenty major telephone companies now employ Negro operators.

(3) The oil-refining industry, which has had separate labor departments, one Negro and one white, for a long time, is abandoning this practice as a result of changed practices in one company against which a complaint was filed.

(4) The meat-packing industry now offers white-collar as well as production employment to all minority groups.

(5) Discriminatory job application forms have almost ceased to exist. The Committee has closed 22 of 28 cases filed by the Bureau on Jewish Employment Problems in Chicago, where the complaint was made that contractors discriminated by placing employment-agency job orders which excluded specific racial and religious groups.

(6) The Douglas Aircraft Company at Tulsa, the McDonnell Aircraft Company at St. Louis, and the Western Electric plant at Winston-Salem have all made encouraging progress in advancing Negro employees into skilled and semiskilled production positions, technical posts, and clerical and secretarial work.

(7) Ten major airlines are co-operating with the Committee, and positions have recently been opened to Negroes for the first time as mechanics, as reservation agents, in ticket-sale offices, and in clerical work.

Rich as this nation may be in essential raw materials and productive capacity, we have no manpower surplus. We can ill-afford to sacrifice our skills and talents on the altar of racial prejudice. Far more than the nation's conscience is at stake. Putting into effect a nondiscrimination policy is more than the right thing to do: it is essential to a strong and healthy economy that we promote the fullest potential of all our people. At a time when the eyes of the free world look to America for leadership, it is imperative, as President Eisenhower has recognized, that we "have continued social progress, calmly but persistently made, so that we may prove without doubt to all the world that our nation and our people are truly dedicated to liberty and justice for all." These are the objectives of the nation's policy toward affording equal economic opportunity.

III

HISTORICAL ASPECTS

III

HISTORICAL ASPECTS

[JOHN P. ROCHE]

BRANDEIS UNIVERSITY

American Liberty: An Examination

of the "Tradition" of Freedom

THERE has been no shortage of analyses, to say nothing of tracts, dealing with the general question of American liberty, but viewed *sub specie aeternitatis* they all seem to suffer from a congenital weakness: whether hortatory, monitory, or deprecatory, they deal with abstract Americans acting in accordance with deductively formulated principles. From the professional patriots at one end of the spectrum we hear that American civilization is and always has been the natural habitat of freedom. From the Marxists at the other we learn that American freedom is a fake, a deceptive myth perpetuated by the cunning bourgeoisie for its class ends. One school waves Old Glory, while the other mobilizes data to prove that American dedication to liberty is rank hypocrisy. Useful catalogues of rhetoric—for Independence Day or May Day, depending on one's viewpoint—have thus been compiled, but all hands have engaged in a conspiracy against defining the crucial term "liberty."

Thus, when all is said and done, we have discovered little of what liberty has meant in precise institutional terms to individual Americans or groups of Americans. Instead we have been supplied with primer syllogisms which might be set forth as follows:

The flag shakers
Radical denounces capitalism = subversion of American liberty.

129

Aspects of Liberty

Patriots lynch radical = righteous vengeance of a free people.

The denigrators

Mineowner murders Wobbly = act of capitalist oppression.

Wobblies dynamite mine and owner = working-class blow for liberty.

Although I would never assert that any student could approach his subject matter in a spirit of complete objectivity, I have attempted in the pages that follow to appraise the nature of American liberty without *ideological* bias. In other words, though my angle of vision may have its defects, I have not gone tramping through American history to document a sermon. It is my fundamental contention that only by discovering precisely how liberty was defined by discrete American groups or subcultures can we evaluate the actual meaning of the concept at any given point in our history. Indeed, only in this fashion can we ascertain whether there has in fact been an American "tradition" of liberty.

This matter of traditions deserves some discussion. Frederic W. Maitland was fond of observing that it was Sir Henry Spelman—the great seventeenth-century historian of British institutions—and not William the Conqueror who introduced feudalism into England. In a similar sense, one may suspect that many traditions which we encounter from time to time are in essence the creations of scholars with talent for retrospective symmetry. Clinton Rossiter's *Conservatism in America* comes to mind here, as, for that matter, does Louis Hartz's *Liberal Tradition in America*. To those who feel that the phrase "retrospective symmetry" is too severe, I submit in evidence a statement from the latter work. "When asked concerning his social philosophy," Mr. Hartz asserts, "[President Franklin D.] Roosevelt once said that he was a Democrat and a Christian, which meant, needless to say, that he was as good an irrational Lockian as Grover Cleveland." [1] Though, needless to say, this is a private fight among irrational Lockians, I suggest that a tradition cannot be built on such Delphic pronouncements.

Indeed, it is my contention that, if we are to understand the meaning of such conceptions as liberty, responsibility, equality, and due process, we must look to institutional forms for the ultimate, or at least penultimate, answers. We must investigate actions as well as rhetoric and

[1] Louis Hartz, *The Liberal Tradition in America* (New York, 1955), p. 263.

base our judgments on the degree to which the former match the latter, the degree to which practice conforms to precept. Moreover, if we are to talk meaningfully of a "tradition," we must demonstrate that there is some *institutional* connection between the discrete historical episodes adduced in evidence—not merely rhetorical plagiarism.

To avoid misunderstanding, let me take a historical instance of spurious tradition making. The French Huguenots of the sixteenth and seventeenth centuries, one may learn, belonged to the "constitutional tradition." At this point there appears a footnote citing the *Vindiciae contra Tyrannos*. Now the *Vindiciae* was an assertion of constitutionalism and was in the view of experts the outstanding political essay produced by the Huguenots in their polemical exchange with the Jesuits. But before we tuck the Huguenots in the drawer marked "Constitutionalism" and take passage to England to the next stage of the Tradition—the Common Lawyers or perhaps the Independents—it would be in order to take a closer look at the other tracts produced by the French Protestants, those tracts which have neither the force nor the timelessness of the *Vindiciae*. And these reveal a peculiar twist indeed, for the Jesuits, who at the time of the *Vindiciae* (1577) were chanting *Quod principi placuit legis vigorem habet* from the housetops, subsequently developed a real affection for popular sovereignty, whereas the Huguenots later became strong supporters of the royal prerogative. As Gooch put it, in mid-battle the antagonists "exchanged rapiers," [2] and the rationale was not hard to discover. On to the stage strode Henry IV, a Catholic from real estate rather than real spiritual convictions, from whom the Huguenots expected great things and against whom the Jesuits were prepared to appeal to the overwhelmingly Catholic populace. [3]

This emphasis is perhaps unnecessary, but the uncomplaining past has traditionally been the victim of scholars who trespass *vi et armis* upon the affairs of their ancestors and have a congenital weakness for System which leads them to manufacture traditions and discover "deep

[2] George P. Gooch and Harold J. Laski, *English Democratic Ideas in the Seventeenth Century* (London, 1927), p. 19.

[3] See, for example, the *De Rege* of Juan de Mariana, precisely analyzed in J. W. Allen, *A History of Political Thought in the Sixteenth Century* (London, 1928), pp. 360–366. A seminal discussion of this problem which, despite certain revisions occasioned by subsequent research, still holds up well is John Neville Figgis, *The Divine Right of Kings* (2d ed.; Cambridge, Eng., 1914).

policy in some clerk's flourish." [4] This trespass is essential unless we are willing to learn mathematics and become "behavioral scientists," but it must be undertaken with great caution and with vigorous reliance on Occam's Razor to prevent us from assigning superfluous *teles* to the mute deceased. This suggests a somewhat more haphazard view of life than is common among political theorists (who have, after all, a vested interest in systems and traditions) and may seem like an undue depreciation of the role of ideas in history. Yet it is my contention that ideas are no stronger than the institutions which gave them meaning and that they are frequently subservient to powerful institutional patterns. It was Maitland who pointed out in a luminous essay that the victory of English common law over the Roman law invasion of the fifteenth and sixteenth centuries was due more to the system of legal education in the Inns of Court than to the merits of the common law itself.[5] This may be a depressing conclusion for the man of ideas to accept, but it is nonetheless vitally significant for the history of ideas.

So much for the analysis of traditions. Now we must turn to the question of individual placement. It is my view that in examining the attitudes of an individual it is essential to penetrate the rhetorical surface to the subterranean level of definitions. To take another example from the past, John Milton is often considered, on the basis of his *Areopagitica,* a firm believer in freedom of opinion. But to understand the precise meaning of freedom of opinion in Milton's framework, one must carefully size up his exceptions, the opinions which do not merit freedom or do not qualify as "opinion" in the first place. And his list of exceptions, though short, is qualitatively formidable: Catholics, believers in "open superstition," and any who express views that are "impious or evil absolutely, either against faith or manners." [6] By my reckoning this would include at the very least Catholics, atheists, Unitarians, and Antinomians. Once by definition the field is thus

---

[4] Frederic W. Maitland, *Collected Papers* (Cambridge, Eng., 1911), III, 164.

[5] Frederic W. Maitland, *English Law and the Renaissance* (Cambridge, Eng., 1901). For an analysis of Church-state problems in sixteenth-century England which likewise suggests the subordination of theory to political imperatives, see F. M. Powicke, *The Reformation in England* (London, 1941).

[6] John Milton, *Areopagitica,* in *The Works of John Milton* (New York, 1931), IV, 349–350. I disagree completely with David Spitz's view that Milton was a principled defender of freedom of opinion, a position which can be defended only by burking Milton's exceptions. See David Spitz, "Milton's Testament," *Antioch Review,* Fall issue, 1953, pp. 290–302.

narrowed, it becomes apparent that Milton believed in freedom of opinion for basically right-thinking people. As he put it quite clearly, it was *"neighboring* differences, or rather indifferences" [7] which deserved toleration.

To say this is not to accuse Milton of dishonesty or intellectual chicanery; it is merely to assert that by my standards Milton did not believe in freedom of opinion. Had one confronted him with this statement, I suspect he would have replied, in anticipation of the Smith Act, that to be a papist, atheist, or blasphemer was not to hold an opinion, but to engage in subversive activity. This definitional gambit is at the center of all controversies over the extent of liberty and makes it quite possible for freedom and oppression to walk arm in arm by simply defining detested opinions as subversive actions, *ipso facto* beyond the protection of libertarian principles. There is no necessary insincerity involved in this definitional maneuver; Milton believed firmly in liberty as he defined it. Yet on a wholly impersonal basis I insist that freedom of opinion, to have any analytical significance, must involve freedom for those opinions held to be basically wrong or, in the language of Milton's day, heretical and impious. The reader may disagree with this definition if he so chooses, but he must keep it in mind if he is to understand the framework of the analysis to follow.

With these procedural considerations in mind, let us turn to American political thought and specifically to the nature of American liberty. The remarks that follow must be considered tentative and preliminary, but on the basis of the present data certain general considerations seem to hold up under close scrutiny.

In the first place, it appears that freedom today rests on a radically different institutional base from freedom in preindustrial America. This I have formulated in two hypotheses:

First, the individual liberty which was characteristic of early American society was a function of the openness and pluralism of that society rather than of any libertarian ideology.

Second, the individual freedom of contemporary American society is largely a function of the impersonalization and bureaucratization of social relationships and of the formalization of these interactions in a meaningful, national legal conception—due process of law.

[7] Milton, *op. cit.* (Italics added.)

The remainder of this essay will be devoted to an examination of these two hypotheses. Since the major line of division between the two epochs described is that which separates a predominantly rural society from one essentially urban, the discussion will be broken up into two sections, one dealing with "Freedom in Rural America" and the other with "Freedom in Urban America."

FREEDOM IN RURAL AMERICA

When the historian looks back at the intellectual and social history of the early United States, he notes an enormous diversity of opinion. From this it is an easy step to conclude that there was toleration of divergent views among the population at large. From a different vantage point, however, tolerance as the precondition for diversity seems to be a *non sequitur:* what has been overlooked is the fact that until at least the beginning of the twentieth century, and in extensive areas of the nation later, the United States was an extremely heterogeneous country, dotted with subcultures. It is my contention that the diversity of opinion was a consequence not of tolerance and mutual respect—an over-all ideology of freedom—but of the existence of many communities within the society each with its own canons of orthodoxy. In other words, if one looked hard enough, it was probable that he could find somewhere in the United States a community that shared his own peculiar views—whether religious, vegetarian, polygamous, socialist, or whatever—and, joining it, he could help impose group beliefs on all within reach.

In short, one could find a microcosm to be intolerant *with,* and the United States was notoriously the happy hunting ground of what David Riesman has acutely termed "vested heresies." True, there was no centralized authoritarian state on the European model; for obvious geographical and social reasons, Tudor principles of centralization, like the feudalism they were designed to destroy, did not survive the sea passage.[8] But, as liberal commentators sometimes forget, the centralized state is not the only institution capable of oppression; the parish can be as coercive as the state, and decentralized authoritarian-

[8] See Richard B. Morris, *Studies in the History of American Law* (New York, 1930), pp. 9–68; Clinton Rossiter, *Seedtime of the Republic* (New York, 1953), pp. 3–147; Louis Hartz, *op. cit.*, pp. 3–86.

134

ism can be as severe in its impact on the individual as the centralized variety. One finds few earmarks of libertarianism—of respect for views considered fundamentally wrong—in early American society.

The archetype for many diverse communities later established on the twin principles of freedom for Truth and suppression for Error was "Zion in the Wilderness," the Massachusetts Bay Colony. Unlike the Brownist settlers of Plymouth, who were separatists and refugees from the wrath of the Establishment, the men who built the Bay Colony came to this country to establish the theocracy that the laws of England would not permit, the religious absolutism that was denied them by a latitudinarian spirit in Church and Crown.[9] Indeed, properly speaking, they were not separatists at all; even such a conspicuous theological eccentric as Roger Williams was on his arrival in 1631 technically a priest of the Church of England.[10] The Puritan approach to toleration was summarized with vigor and clarity by Nathaniel Ward, in *The Simple Cobler of Aggawam*, when he stated: "He that is willing to tolerate any unsound opinion that his own may also be tolerated hangs God's Bible at the Devil's Girdle."

Although there was little toleration in the colonies, no one could assert that the countryside seethed with oppression. There was little need for it. Wise Unitarians avoided the Anglican or Puritan establishments; Puritans, unless they were seeking expulsion, steered clear of the Anglican colonies, and devout Anglicans reciprocated; Anabaptists, Quakers, and other sectarians were well advised to confine their proselytizing to Pennsylvania and Rhode Island. Catholics, who were associated in the public mind with the international French conspiracy, had the most difficult time of all. Only in Pennsylvania, where William Penn had established such minimal religious standards as belief in one God and Jesus Christ, was the door consistently open,

[9] Thomas J. Wertenbaker, *The Puritan Oligarchy* (New York, 1947), p. 32.

[10] Williams was a clerk in orders, though of pronounced nonconformist tendencies, in England. He avoided trouble by serving as chaplain to Sir Edward Masham, a Puritan gentleman of Essex. In practical terms, this put him virtually beyond the reach of High Commission, which largely confined its visitations and inquisitions to members of the formal religious hierarchy and tended to ignore holders of endowed chapelries or other private benefices. Williams' separatist tendencies emerged full-blown on his arrival in Boston in 1631, when he immediately became a controversial figure by refusing a pulpit on the ground that the congregation had not separated from the Establishment. See Rossiter, *op. cit.*, pp. 180–183; Perry Miller, *Roger Williams* (New York and Indianapolis, 1953), pp. 19–20.

or perhaps ajar, to those of the Roman faith. Indeed, at the close of the colonial period, the only place where the public exercise of Catholic rites was permitted was Pennsylvania, and this was over the protest of the last governor.[11]

⟶These religious restrictions were not considered, I suspect, as limitations on opinion at all. Theology and politics were woven together in the minds of men like Milton, Winthrop, and Ward so that heretical views were by definition acts of treason. With Catholics the foundation for this charge was obvious and not merely theological: the French, the enemy to the north, were often supporters of the cause of British Catholicism and subventors of several rebellions in Scotland and Ireland in behalf of the Stuart pretenders. The atheist was not considered merely an eccentric with a grudge against God; he was an agent of Lucifer, determined to destroy religion, the basic pillar of legitimacy and stability. The Quaker and the Anabaptist, with their disruptive religious subjectivism which had led in England to James Naylor and on the Continent to the chiliastic nightmare at Münster, were viewed as threats to public order. Even the long-suffering Roger Williams finally slapped a treason indictment against one such "for his open defiance against our charter . . . and for saying that it was against his conscience to yield obedience to any human order amongst men." [12] Religious conviction and political action converge in a sentiment like this, and it is not surprising that a definition of opinion was so drawn as to exclude these, and other, nonconformists from any dispensations to freedom of religion. A later secular age would scoff at the draftsmen for their bigotry and be prepared to tolerate any nonsense from a pulpit, neglecting to note that it applied the same technique of definitional exclusion in areas believed important—only religion was not within the significant ambit.

In the interest of fairness, this point requires further emphasis and exemplification. Thomas Jefferson observed in his *Notes on Virginia:* "It does me no injury for my neighbor to say there are twenty gods, or no God. It neither picks my pocket nor breaks my leg." [13] But with his indifferentism in this area we should compare his agitated insistence

---

[11] Leo Pfeffer, *Church, State, and Freedom* (Boston, 1953), p. 81.

[12] Cited in Charles M. Andrews, *The Colonial Period of American History* (New Haven, 1936), II, 55.

[13] Thomas Jefferson, *Notes on Virginia* (Peden ed.; Chapel Hill, 1955), p. 159.

that the Board of Visitors of the University of Virginia should have the
power to select the textbooks in government used at that institution.
In this connection, he wrote Joseph Cabell:

> There is one branch [of learning] in which we are the best judges, in which
> heresies may be taught of so interesting a character to our own State, and to
> the United States, as to make it a duty to lay down the principles which
> shall be taught. It is that of government. . . . It is our duty to guard against
> the dissemination of [Federalist-Nationalist] principles among our youth,
> and the diffusion of that poison, by a previous prescription of the texts to be
> followed in their discourses.[14]

In other words, while matters of religion seemed to Jefferson to be
wholly without the area of important social functions, political opinions
did pick his pocket and break his leg, and the state could legitimately
act to prevent ideological poison from spreading through the body
politic. Jefferson used the same loaded dice as the Puritans, logically
speaking, but he threw them from a different cup.

Though few people, and fewer public institutions, in the colonial
period were dedicated to religious toleration, the important fact was
that no one corpus of religious belief attained monopoly status. Colonial
America was an open society dotted with closed enclaves, and one
could generally settle in with his cobelievers in safety and comfort
and exercise the right of oppression. Generally speaking there was
open season on Catholics and atheists; where they had the power, the
Puritans harassed the Anglicans, and the favor was returned in those
colonies with an Anglican establishment; and probably a record of
some sort was established in South Carolina where the English Protestants at one time combined against the French Huguenots.[15] But
no one establishment achieved hegemony, and there was a perpetual
clamor for toleration from the various persecuted minorities, a clamor
which had vast political implications, since freedom of speech was

[14] Letter of February 3, 1825, in *The Early History of the University of Virginia
as Contained in the Letters of Thomas Jefferson and Joseph C. Cabell* (Richmond,
1856), p. 339. See also Gordon E. Baker, "Thomas Jefferson on Academic Freedom," *Bulletin, AAUP*, 39 (1953), 377–387. In the shrewd observation of Howard
K. Beale, "Men usually 'tolerate' opposing views on subjects they do not regard
as important, and then rationalize 'intolerance' into necessity when disagreement
involves a matter vital to them" (Beale, *A History of Freedom of Teaching in
American Schools* [New York, 1941], p. xii).

[15] Andrews, *op. cit.*, III, 242.

originally thought of as part of freedom of religion. As Figgis observed, "Political liberty is the residuary legatee of ecclesiastical animosities." [16] The demands for freedom were usually demands for the right to establish true doctrine, but they were demands for freedom nonetheless and contributed to an atmosphere of liberty and toleration.

The striking outcome was that there developed in the United States a political elite prepared to institutionalize this short-run interest in freedom in a Constitution which would make centralized tyranny impossible. In fact it is my contention that Figgis' quasi-mechanical theory of the origin of political liberty was consciously held by those key figures Thomas Jefferson, James Madison, and John Adams and implicitly held by the bulk of the political leaders of the time, including many of the anticonstitutional group. Alexander Hamilton, that lonely prophet of centralization, was the outstanding exception.

The road to freedom in this view lay through diffusion of power. Recognizing that the spirit of liberty may be willing, but that the flesh may and probably will be weak, the key formulators of American constitutionalism did not expect that freedom could be guaranteed by rhetorical exhortations or bills of rights inscribed on parchment. They were too intimately acquainted with the political life of their time to trust abstract guarantees; the Liberty Boys had, after all, dealt extensively and sometimes condignly with un-American activities, broadly defined, as a reading of the statutes passed by the states during the American Revolution will readily demonstrate. This was the heyday of direct democracy, and those who extoll the grass-roots freedom of the town meeting and the frontier and bewail the fact that the growth of the industrial state has created an impersonal civilization too often forget that the other side of the direct democracy of the town meeting was the spontaneous democracy of lynching, that ultimate symbol of the sovereignty of numbers.

Clearly, all loyal Americans believed in freedom; was this not the very point at issue with the British? Yet freedom did not involve the right to be pro-British, and one of the classic definitions of freedom of the press can be found in the demand of the Newport, Rhode Island, Committee of Inspection in March 1775—a year before Independence —that James Rivington's *New York Gazetteer* be boycotted. This Com-

[16] John Neville Figgis, *Gerson to Grotius* (2d ed.; Cambridge, Eng., 1916), p. 118.

mittee, urging that the paper be shunned, justified its stand in terms of freedom of the press, which it defined as "the diffusion of liberal sentiments on the administration of Government." [17] Even more in point were the activities of the Sons of Liberty in dealing with "disloyal," that is, loyal, merchants who refused to co-operate in the nonimportation movement of the early 1770's.[18]

The wartime sedition acts passed by the states were very severe and in no sense limited in scope to overt acts against the American cause. Opinions were treated as overt acts and punished as such. To take but two examples, the Virginia treason statute of October 1776 provided that any resident of the state who "by any word, open deed, or act [defended] the authority, jurisdiction, or power, of the king or parliament [or attributed] any such authority, jurisdiction, or power, to the king or parliament of Great Britain [could be fined not more than £2,000 and imprisoned for not more than five years]." [19] A New York statute of 1781 contained similar provisions, holding it to be a felony knowingly to preach, teach, write, print, declare, or maintain "that the King of Great Britain hath, or of Right ought to have, any Authority, or Dominion, in or over this State, or the Inhabitants thereof." [20]

These statutes were the work of a militant majority determined to stamp out Toryism root and branch, and a further study of the punitive legislation of this period suggests that many of the detailed harassments devised were not generally operative, but were held in reserve

[17] Cited by Sidney I. Pomerantz, "The Patriot Newspapers and the American Revolution," in Richard B. Morris, ed., *The Era of the American Revolution* (New York, 1939), p. 316. Pomerantz does not point out that this phrase was drawn from a 1774 Proclamation of the First Continental Congress or that the Committee excluded diffusion of "wrong sentiments respecting the measures . . . for the recovery and establishment of our rights" from the protection of press freedom (*American Archives*, 4th ser., II, 12–13).

[18] See Herbert M. Morais, "The Sons of Liberty in New York," *ibid.*, pp. 269–289, for a vivid description of the kinds of pressure exerted upon reluctant rebels.

[19] Cited by Willard Hurst, "Treason in the United States," *Harvard Law Review*, 58 (1944), 267. This sort of statute was apparently an old Virginia custom: In 1649 the General Assembly provided that anyone who defended the execution of the late Charles I "by reasoning, discourse or argument" was to be deemed a constructive regicide subject to punishment therefor! Moreover, anyone who defamed the memory of the royal martyr could also be suitably punished by the Governor and Council (*ibid.*, pp. 228–229, n. 6).

[20] *Ibid.*, p. 266.

for use should an opportunity present itself. Thus, if the loyal citizens of Kingston, New York, encountered a particularly sullen Tory who did nothing overtly disloyal, there was a web of repressive measures that could be dropped over his head by the local citizenry. Tories presumably knew the facts of life and either got out or simulated patriotism. Indeed, Walter Millis has suggested that the real function of the militia in the American Revolution was not so much military as paramilitary: it kept anti-British opinion dominant in the countryside by quasi-vigilante activities.[21]

This direct democracy clearly made its impact on the founders of the republic. Hamilton, as one would expect in view of his aristocratic bias, took a very dim view of *vox populi;* Jefferson, who was always far more antimajoritarian in his actions and speculative writings than in his speeches, inveighed against legislative supremacy and by implication against direct democracy in his *Notes on Virginia;* James Wilson was devoting his time and superb organizational talent to revising the radical Pennsylvania Constitution of 1776; John Adams was drafting for Massachusetts a Constitution which was a paradigm of the principle of equilibrium; and James Madison was meditating long and hard on the social and political virtues of conflict, of what might almost be termed institutionalized anomie.

The key question confronting these men and their peers at the close of the war and during the years when the Articles of Confederation were in force was, How could liberty be preserved from the twin disasters of tyranny and anarchy? In their efforts to find the answer, they ransacked the history of the past and collated it with their own experience in a fashion most remarkable. One minute John Adams would be taking note of the activities of fourteenth-century Florentines and the next remarking that this reminded him of the situation in Congress in 1776. There is, indeed, a peculiarly disembodied quality about their thinking on government; it is almost as though they were prepared to admit that they, too, would become tyrants if an opportunity presented itself, but that a government should be devised which would make this impossible. In the Constitution this theorizing came to grips with reality, and the solution evolved for avoiding both the peril of anarchy and that of tyranny was the creation of a mechanical wonder—a dynamic equilibrium. Liberty was to be a by-product of conflict and balance, not a positive creation of public policy.

[21] Walter Millis, *Arms and Men* (New York, 1956), p. 34.

The "Tradition" of Freedom

This view—and the air of disembodiment I mentioned above—appears most clearly in a remarkable issue of *The Federalist*. In Number 51, dealing with the fragmentation of power (which should, incidently, be read in conjunction with Number 10 to get the full impact of Madison's social theory), Madison employs the mechanical analogue with brilliance and precision. After examining the principle of checks and balances within the proposed government (a section recommended to those who talk glibly about the "separation of powers"), the author moves on to the problem of group relations in a republic. "It is of great importance in a republic," he begins, "not only to guard the society against the oppression of its rulers, but to guard one part of the society against the injustice of the other part." [22] The section that follows must be quoted at some length for it is crucial to my argument:

> If a majority be united by a common interest, the rights of the minority will be insecure. There are but two methods of providing against this evil: the one by creating a will in the community independent of the majority—that is, of the society itself; the other, by comprehending in the society so many separate descriptions of citizens as will render an unjust combination of a majority of the whole very improbable, if not impracticable. . . .
>
> The second method will be exemplified in the federal republic of the United States. Whilst all authority in it will be derived from and dependent on the society, the society itself will be broken into so many parts, interests, and classes of citizens, that the rights of individuals, or of the minority, will be in little danger from interested combinations of the majority. *In a free government the security for civil rights must be the same as that for religious rights.* It consists in the one case in the multiplicity of interests, and in the other in the multiplicity of sects. *The degree of security in both cases will depend on the number of interests and sects.*[23]

Now this is singularly cold-blooded political theory, worthy of the great political geometer Hobbes himself, for it assumes rapaciousness in all hands and predicates the survival of liberty on the successful operation of a mechanical principle of conflict and diffusion. Nowhere does Madison say that power in the hands of an enlightened majority

[22] *The Federalist* (Modern Library ed.; New York, 1937), p. 339. This edition still lists Hamilton as a possible author of Number 51, but it was prepared before the definitive analysis of Douglas Adair had appeared. Retrospective omniscience is a cheap commodity, but it still seems difficult to believe that anyone could ever attribute these particular sentiments to Alexander Hamilton.

[23] *Ibid.*, pp. 339–340. (Italics added.)

needs no checkrein; indeed, he explicitly denies the conception of the enlightened majority or, in a different formulation, of a virtuous general will. The survival of freedom thus depends on institutions which guarantee conflict—he conceived of the republic as armed pluralism.

Viewed from another angle, Madison is defining freedom as the absence of *centralized* oppressive power, not as a positive condition of enlightenment. In the same way that religious sects fought each other for the right to coerce, so the many political interests in the republic will pursue their selfish ends and come in conflict with the ambition of their neighbors. Freedom occurs when no individual interest can institutionalize its truth as *the* public interest. In short, we have a political formulation of Adam Smith's economic proposition that the pursuit of individual self-interest results in a public good. To quote Madison again: "In the extended republic of the United States, and among the great variety of interests, parties, and sects which it embraces, a coalition of a majority of the whole society could seldom take place on any other principles than those of justice and the general good." [24] The protection of liberty thus rests on diffusion of the power to oppress rather than on exorcism, or pretended exorcism, of oppression by libertarian formulas. As Madison told the Virginia Convention in reference to freedom of religion, "If there were a majority of one sect, a bill of rights would be a poor protection for liberty." [25]

Although he emphasized governmental more than social structure, John Adams shared fully Madison's conviction that a good mechanism could do far more to preserve liberty than would pious rhetoric. "None but an idiot or a madman ever built a government upon a disinterested principle," [26] observed the dour sage of Braintree, and he set forth his own credo: "Men must search their own hearts and confess the emulation [ambition] that is there: and provide checks to it." [27] His views on the need for equilibrium were set forth endlessly in his various works, notably in the three volumes of *A Defence of the Con-*

[24] *Ibid.,* p. 341.
[25] Jonathan Elliot, *The Debates in the State Conventions on the Adoption of the Federal Constitution* (Washington, 1836), III, 313. Edmund Randolph made this point also at the Virginia Convention (*ibid.,* p. 208).
[26] Cited in Zoltan Haraszti, *John Adams and the Prophets of Progress* (Cambridge, Mass., 1952), p. 220. This is a marvelous book which has not received the attention it merits. Haraszti has culled out the best of Adams's marginalia and presented them in the form of dialogues between author and critic.
[27] *Ibid.,* p. 219.

stitutions of Government of the United States of America (1787–1788), but were neatly summarized in the margin of his copy of Mary Wollstonecraft's *Historical and Moral View of the Origin and Progress of the French Revolution:*

Nothing short of an independent power above the [factious people] able to check their majorities ever can keep them within bounds. It is the interest and the policy of the people for their own safety *always to erect and maintain such a power.* . . . . Power must be opposed to power, force to force, strength to strength, interest to interest, as well as reason to reason, eloquence to eloquence, and passion to passion.[28]

Or, as he summarized the function of government in an incisive phrase: "When cunning and force united are balanced against cunning and force united, reason must be armed to mediate between them. There must be an armed neutrality." [29]

The views of Madison and Adams are complementary: by combining them we get, I believe, a clear insight into the nature of the republic, the republic which had as its *telos* the establishment and maintenance of ordered liberty. An armed pluralism, society, confronted an armed neutrality, government; and the Constitution supplied the ground rules for the conflict that ensued. Out of this conflict, in which the participants had both an antagonistic and a symbiotic function, there would emerge a public policy free from passion, a commonwealth in which it would be impossible for any part to establish dominion over the whole. The great enemy of good government and liberty was "enthusiasm," which these deists rejected in both its religious and political manifestations, and under this heading they included the passions of both the just and the unjust.

As political theory this is both sophisticated and naïve. It is sophisticated in that it essays to put the operation of government and the protection of liberty beyond the reach of even the most dedicated enthusiast, and this is done not by establishing a Platonic republic in which harmony will be imposed by the wise, but by fragmenting sovereignty and setting the wolves to guard each other. Some have seen in this approach an underpinning of Calvinism, of the conviction that man is a wicked and perverse creature, but this seems to me an error. In my view, they viewed man as a mixture of good and evil and were certain that, given the proper institutions, those which would

[28] *Ibid.*   [29] *Ibid.*, p. 203.

143

inhibit his evil tendencies and force reason to the fore, the good in men would triumph. In a sense, they stood Hobbes on his head by insisting that only a government founded on freedom and equilibrium could establish real security and that this involved not suppression but socialization of the *bellum omnium in omnes.*

Yet, as events were to demonstrate, Madison's conception was also profoundly naïve, for it rested on two fundamental but unrecognized principles about the nature of society. First, like Smith's economic theory, there is the assumption of natural harmony, the proposition that when all the fighting is over and all the pluralities have had their licks, a public policy which incorporates "justice and the general good" will emerge. Taken for granted here is a willingness on the part of all participants to play by the rules. A faction may disagree about substantive matters—about the content of particular items of policy— but it will not overturn the card table and shoot the other players. In short, there will be *procedural consensus.* The deists, like their Stoic ancestors, assumed the ultimate sovereignty of *recta ratio,* with the consequence that they found it difficult, if not impossible, to conceive of differences which could not be reconciled if reason were given adequate play.

Second, the Madisonian view assumes multipolarism, the continuing existence of many power centers competing with each other, forming temporary coalitions, then wandering off to join other allies in eternally new configurations. This social fluidity was the clandestine premise of American constitutionalism; monolithic majorities, social stasis, were simply defined out of the American future as a medieval priest would exorcise devils from a newly built castle. But what if a national faction arises capable of capturing a majority of the state legislatures, the presidency, and the House of Representatives? Are not all the delicate balances and ingenious counterweights of the Constitution rendered impotent to protect the minority? This was no academic question, for within a decade the Antifederalists were looking down the barrels of a triple-barreled shotgun in the hands of the Federalists—the combination of presidency, Congress, and courts that passed and enforced the Alien and Sedition Acts [30]—and Madison and Jefferson were desper-

---

[30] For an able and comprehensive examination of this period, see James M. Smith, *Freedom's Fetters* (Ithaca, N.Y., 1956). For a discussion of the Alien and Sedition Acts in the framework of this paper, see my review of Smith, *Harvard Law Review,* 70 (1957), 946–950.

ately engaged in devising a new set of rules to protect a minority when the Constitution went off its tracks. John C. Calhoun's *Disquisition on Government* is a tedious and convoluted effort to achieve the same goal in a later bipolar situation.

I have gone into this in some detail because it seems to me important to realize that the generally accepted view at the time the nation was founded was that individual freedom, far from being protected by transcendent legal principles, depended on two essentially mechanical propositions: first, the strength of one's group, its ability to fight off attempts at domination, and, second, the fragmentation of power among many groups, the absence of monolithic configurations. The freedom which the Constitution was intended to guarantee was corporate rather than individual; constitutional government in the United States was to be incapable of destroying the liberty of its constituent bodies and establishing *centralized* authoritarianism. What went on within the constituent bodies was none of the general government's business, with only limited and ambiguous exceptions, that is, limitations on *ex post facto* laws, bills of attainder, laws violating the obligation of contract, state intrusions into foreign relations, or the establishment of monarchial state governments. The inner life of the states, or of private organizations within the states, was thus beyond constitutional jurisdiction, and a Bill of Rights was added to buttress this exclusion.

It is hard for us today to realize the scope of state power at that time, for we live in the shadow of the Fourteenth Amendment and the nationalizing of freedom that has taken place under its auspices. Recall, however, that except as limitations were provided by state constitutions or state laws, state governments had enormous powers over their inhabitants. Two states, Masachusetts and Connecticut, continued their establishments of religion into the nineteenth century, and had any state, say, chosen to make Catholicism the state religion and execute heretics, or to establish Presbyterianism and hang Catholics, there was no external check that could be constitutionally invoked. The minority could get out or engage in what amounted to civil war in defense of its customs and beliefs.

Formal religious establishments were going out of fashion in the early nineteenth century, but this did not mean that there was full religious toleration in the states. The somber saga of Mormonism, to say nothing of the desperate street fighting between Know-Nothing gangs and Irish Catholic home guards that occurred in most of the large cities of the Northeast as the "True Americans" went forth to burn down Catholic churches, is adequate evidence to the contrary.[31] Even the Masons found themselves momentarily featured as sinister, un-American conspirators and were subjected to various official and unofficial harassments.[32] Without attempting a retread of Gustavus Myers' *History of Bigotry in the United States*,[33] suffice it here to say that the extent to which one enjoyed freedom of religion depended on the degree to which his religious sentiments did not offend his neighbors.

Again it must be emphasized that to say this is not to claim that persecution was rife: the average white Protestant American went through life with complete freedom and reciprocated by bestowing on other white Protestant Americans the blessings of liberty. Moreover, if things got too rough for a minority, it could probably emulate the Latter-Day Saints by finding an isolated spot beyond the long arm of the vicinage and the direct democracy of irate neighbors. And before one weeps too vigorously for the poor, persecuted victims, it should also be recalled that persecution was a two-way proposition: the Presbyterian who attempted to explain the evils of Romish domination to an Irish Catholic community, or the Baptist who tried to explain to the Mormons of Nauvoo or Salt Lake City that Joseph Smith was a blasphemer and forger, was seldom greeted in the spirit of Christian love.

The same principle applied in political matters. If a state, or a section of a state for that matter, chose to persecute political nonconformists, there was seldom any legal or constitutional remedy and then only those supplied by state law. The classic instance of moral *laissez faire* was, of course, the constitutional arrangement which permitted the

[31] The American Party still awaits its historian, but the full flavor of its anti-Catholicism can be found in Ray A. Billington, *The Protestant Crusade, 1800–1860* (New York, 1938). A fine piece of nonscholarly analysis which sensitively recalls the ghetto days of the Irish is John Lardner's "The Martyrdom of Bill the Butcher," *New Yorker*, vol. 30, March 20, 1954, pp. 41–53, and March 27, 1954, pp. 38–59.

[32] See Gustavus Myers, *History of Bigotry in the United States* (New York, 1943), ch. xii, pp. 129–139, for a concise discussion of the anti-Masonic upheaval.

[33] An extremely useful work with the significant drawback that Myers' approach to bigotry was so evangelical that few fine distinctions emerge from his analysis. He appears to have believed that nobody of intelligence or integrity could possibly be bigoted; thus the problem of dealing with intolerance was a simple one of disposing of "bad men" and "bad ideas."

existence of human slavery in any state which chose to permit the practice. In defense of the slave system, Southerners created a body of extreme legislation on the principle that an abolitionist was an agent of a foreign power, and this was reinforced by both "due process of law" and vigorous vigilantism.[34] From *Fettered Freedom*,[35] Russel Nye's fine study of the impact of the slavery controversy on civil liberties, one learns in graphic fashion the meaning of direct democracy, the total absence of protection for the liberty of the nonconformist from the hostility of an aroused countryside. The American legal system has always been vulnerable to community collectivism,[36] and the abolitionists learned the hard way the nature of a law and order founded on the actions of a locally elected sheriff, a locally elected judge, and locally chosen jurors.

Many more examples could be adduced in evidence, but I think these establish the point that individual freedom in early, rural America depended not on a national principle of fair play, but rather on the ability of an individual to find a community where his views would not engender wrath and its inevitable fellows, the tarpot, lash, and noose. Maitland observed that British liberty was founded on "writs, not rights," and the important thing we must remember is that the centralized, national government of our day is a post-Civil War phenomenon. To the extent that the writ of the national government runs to protect individual freedom, it does so on the basis of the Fourteenth Amendment. Before the Civil War the general government was virtually excluded from questions of interpersonal relationships, the federal judiciary—after the collapse of the abortive Federalist effort to establish a common criminal law—rarely became involved in civil rights matters,[37] and local authorities knew who had elected them and for

[34] See Kenneth Stampp, *The Peculiar Institution* (New York, 1956); Clement Eaton, *Freedom of Thought in the Old South* (Durham, N.C., 1940); Howard K. Beale, *A History of Freedom of Teaching in American Schools* (New York, 1941), pp. 111–167.

[35] Michigan State College Press, 1949. For another facet of this situation see the study of the "garrison state" aspects of Southern culture by John Hope Franklin, *The Militant South* (Cambridge, Mass., 1956).

[36] For a discussion of this point, which has been a major influence on my viewpoint, see Alexander H. Pekelis, *Law and Social Action* (Ithaca and New York, 1950), pp. 42–90.

[37] Exceptions were litigation arising under the Fugitive Slave Laws, particularly cases arising out of conflicts between the national law and state "personal liberty laws." See, generally, Charles Warren, *The Supreme Court in United States His-*

what ends. For a brilliant portrayal of the result one need only turn to that section of Alexis de Tocqueville's *Democracy in America* entitled "The Unlimited Power of the Majority and Its Consequences." [38]

This is not to say that there were not efforts made to nationalize individual liberty, usually by asserting that the Constitution was *really* meant to achieve this purpose. The clarion call "It's unconstitutional!" was perpetually emerging from one constituency or another, but the problem was to find a section of the Constitution which could justify such an interpretation. The section most relied upon was that portion of the Fifth Amendment which states flatly that "no person shall be deprived of life, liberty, or property without due process of law." A close student of the Due Process Clause will object immediately that there are two barriers to using the Fifth Amendment in this fashion. First, although the wording was ambiguous, it was clearly intended to limit only the Federal Government and was eventually so explicated by Chief Justice Marshall in *Barron v. Baltimore.*[39] Second, the current meaning of due process of law was procedural rather than substantive, that is, to oversimplify, the limitation was not directed toward legislation duly passed, irrespective of its content, but toward arbitrary, capricious official action. Thus, the Due Process Clause, properly interpreted, could only limit the capricious, arbitrary actions of a judge or an executive officer, and a federal judge or officer at that.

On the first point, I am in full agreement, but with respect to the second, I have my doubts. The distinction between procedural and substantive due process is essentially a law professor's "conceit," [40] invented somewhere in the latter part of the nineteenth century. To

---

tory (rev. ed.; Boston, 1947), II, 206–357. Some specific episodes are vividly discussed by Leonard W. Levy in "The 'Abolition Riot': Boston's First Slave Rescue," *New England Quarterly,* 25 (1952), 85–92; and "Sims' Case: The Fugitive Slave Law in Boston in 1851," *Journal of Negro History,* 25 (1950), 39–74. Occasionally a case would appear before the High Court under some other rubric of the Constitution which might be construed to protect individual political liberty, for example the *ex post facto* clause, but these were rare. Such laws as those passed by the Southern states banishing a manumitted slave from the state and prohibiting the immigration of free Negroes were never brought under constitutional scrutiny by the Supreme Court.

[38] Alexis de Tocqueville, *Democracy in America* (Bradley ed.; New York, 1945), I, 264–280.

[39] 7 Pet. 243 (1833).

[40] In the Elizabethan sense of the word; this phrase has been borrowed from a private communication from Howard Jay Graham.

148

our ancestors, due process of law was undifferentiated, and I suspect that there were more substantive, higher-law overtones than have ever been appreciated. For example, we can find Albert Gallatin rising in the House of Representatives on May 22, 1798, to denounce the proposed alien enemies act as a violation of the Fifth Amendment.[41] Had one queried him on his startling employment of a substantive concept of due process of law, he would probably have been taken aback and replied to the effect that, with all due respect to professors of constitutional law, he just wanted to make it clear that the law was unconstitutional. The superb research of Howard Jay Graham has shown how both the abolitionists and their opponents similarly employed a substantive concept of the Due Process Clause.[42] But the important thing is that, with the exception of a few state decisions[43] and Chief Justice Taney's holding in the *Dred Scott* case[44] that the Missouri Compromise had been unconstitutional as a violation of the Fifth Amendment, the substantive interpretation of due process of law was not incorporated in American public law prior to the Civil War. In precise terms, this meant that there was no higher law of personal freedom which a persecuted nonconformist could invoke in defense of his liberty. Legally he was on his own unless he could persuade a state court to implement a state bill of rights on his behalf.

Although I have referred to the Civil War as though it were the turning point in the nationalization of liberty, this was true only on the symbolic level. The great war amendments to the Constitution were designed to nationalize liberty—and not just for the Negroes; the abolitionists had suffered under the lash of parochial justice too often not to intend protection for whites as well.[45] Acting under the

---

[41] *Annals of Congress,* 5th Congress, 2d Session, col. 1789 (1798).

[42] See his "Early Anti-Slavery Backgrounds of the Fourteenth Amendment," *Wisconsin Law Review,* 1950, pp. 479–507, 610–661; "Procedure to Substance—Extrajudicial Rise of Due Process, 1830–1860," *California Law Review,* 40 (1952–1953), 483–500; "Our 'Declaratory' Fourteenth Amendment," *Stanford Law Review,* 7 (1954), 3–39. See also Jacobus tenBroek, *The Antislavery Origins of the Fourteenth Amendment* (Berkeley, Calif., 1951). The classic statement of the old view —which it should be emphasized has been amended, not repudiated—is Edward S. Corwin, "The Doctrine of Due Process of Law before the Civil War," reprinted in *Selected Essays in Constitutional Law* (Chicago, 1938), I, 203–235.

[43] Cited by Graham, "Procedure to Substance," p. 484.

[44] Scott v. Sandford, 19 Howard 393 (1857).

[45] Graham, "Early Anti-Slavery Backgrounds" *passim.*

seemingly clear authority of Section 5 of the Fourteenth Amendment, Congress passed a series of civil rights bills [46] to put teeth in the principle of national protection. The Supreme Court, however, proceeded to draw the fangs from both the Fourteenth Amendment and the civil rights measures,[47] leaving the great abolitionist dream of nationally guaranteed individual freedom a wreck on the reef of legal sophistry. The development of the Due Process Clause of the Fourteenth Amendment as an instrument for the protection of individual civil liberty had to await its appearance as a shield for individual economic freedom. In a way curiously reminiscent of the growth of British liberty, rights of property, once established, were expanded to protect civil and political freedom.[48] This, however, is to get ahead of the story.

The Civil War, then, was not decisive in the immediate sense, but in long-range terms the Union triumph was vitally important. Not only did Northern victory destroy once and for all the effective power of sectionalism and put the Federal Government firmly in the sovereign's saddle, but it led indirectly to an enormous growth of industrialism in the North and eliminated the halter to industrial expansion which Southern, agrarian political power had previously supplied—the check which had, for example, prevented the passage of a high protective tariff and national subsidization of railroads.[49] The bells which tolled victory for Lincoln's armies simultaneously sounded a requiem for rural, decentralized America. The transformation of the United States into an urban, industrial nation, which had of course begun earlier, proceeded at a tremendous and constantly accelerating rate in the post-Civil War era. The war was, as Charles A. Beard said, "the Second American Revolution."

[46] The history of this civil rights legislation is set forth in brief compass in Maslow and Robison, "Civil Rights Legislation and the Fight for Equality, 1862–1952," *University of Chicago Law Review*, 20 (1953), 363. Technically the first Civil Rights Act was passed before the Fourteenth Amendment was ratified.

[47] Notably in the Slaughterhouse Cases, 16 Wall. 36 (1873), and the Civil Rights Cases, 109 U.S. 3 (1883).

[48] In Britain, royal justice was initially a property of the Crown which was dispensed to subjects for appropriate remuneration. Subsequently the remuneration became ritualized with respect to certain actions; upon payment of standard fees, writs *de cursu* could be obtained. Similarly, an individual's "liberties" were his property rights in himself. See Frederic Maitland, *The Forms of Action at Common Law* (Cambridge, Eng., 1948).

[49] See C. Vann Woodward, *Reunion and Reaction* (Boston, 1951).

The "Tradition" of Freedom

FREEDOM IN URBAN AMERICA

Space will not permit either a detailed examination of the history of due process of law since the passage of the Fourteenth Amendment or an elaborate discussion of the development of an urban, industrial society in the United States. It is my contention that these two parallel institutional patterns have resulted in a kind of freedom for the nonconforming individual that was unknown in rural America. To put it a little too neatly, in rural America, freedom was a function of openness, of the individual's ability to get out of an oppressive environment; in urban America, freedom is a function of impersonalization, of the growth of legal and political institutions which muffle interpersonal and intergroup conflicts. Paradoxically, the collapse of that sense of community so esteemed by sociological commentators seems to have created a new atmosphere of liberty for the nonconformist, who no longer finds himself in face to face relationships with his neighbors or subjected to the coercive power of that rural police agency, the parish church.

The proposition which underlies this section is that, for better or for worse, the anomie of our urban civilization has vitiated, except in the rural areas of the nation and notably the South, the force of direct democracy, of that tyranny of the majority which De Tocqueville limned so brilliantly. I am not denouncing the bucolic virtues of our ancestors or denigrating the Jeffersonian dream of the agrarian commonwealth; I am simply suggesting that, from the viewpoint of the dissenter, individual freedom is today a far more meaningful concept than it was a century or even a half-century ago. A nonconformist in our day is not merely protected when he is in his own ideological hive; he is guaranteed—*de jure* if not always *de facto*—certain minimum protection at the contact points, that is, at the points where he actually carries his gospel into enemy territory. The Jehovah's Witnesses are a walking (and litigating) testimony to the validity of this assertion, and even the Communists today exercise rights that led the old Wobbly, Socialist, or trade union organizer to smile condescendingly when the *Daily Worker* proclaimed the existence of a "reign of terror" in the United States.

To say this is not, however, to engage in jejune optimism about the future of American liberty. Ironically, the very factors which have brought about this new freedom for the dissenter have also made possible for the first time in American history the creation of centralized oppression. The locally entrenched nuclei of power, the "armed pluralism" which was the foundation of the Madisonian construct of liberty, could and did oppress the nonconformist, but they also served as a potential counterforce against centralized authoritarianism. The "security risk" in the North during the time of troubles could always go to the South and to a warm and hospitable welcome; the Eastern economics professor fired for citicizing the gold standard could replace an economics professor at a Western state university fired for advocating monometallism. Given the fragmentation of power and opinion which existed, there was no real possibility of a centralized reign of terror.[50] Conversely, the contemporary breakdown of these bastions of parochialism has eliminated from our political mechanism a veto on the activities of the center which could be exercised for good as well as evil ends. The current struggle over desegregation in the South represents an outcropping of Madisonian theory on a Hamiltonian plain, and Southern spokesmen are not wholly without theoretical justification in pointing out that troops employed to desegregate schools could also be employed to destroy unions.

If I had to summarize my contention in a sentence, I would say that American society today is characterized by what the great Italian political sociologist Gaetano Mosca called a "high level of juridical defense." [51] Although in specific terms this is a legal phenomenon—individuals can go to court, even in the deep South, and get judges to affirm their constitutional rights—in the broad sense the legal manifestations rest upon basic political, economic, and social foundations. The most significant factor seems to me to be the increasing power and jurisdiction of the national government which took place as a concomitant, if not as a consequence, of the increasing urbanization and industrialization of the nation. With the bankruptcy of federalism as an operational concept, decision making on significant matters of

---

[50] I would contend that even the repression that accompanied American participation in World War I was thoroughly decentralized. The Wilson Administration encouraged it in part and discouraged it in part, but the national government and its instruments played a minor role in the actual festivities when compared with state and local governments and private vigilante movements such as the American Protective Association.

[51] Gaetano Mosca, *The Ruling Class* (New York, 1939), pp. 120–152.

American policy became increasingly the monopoly of the national government, and the national government, unlike state governments, was thoroughly insulated against direct democracy.

The framers of the Constitution have often been accused of profoundly conservative leanings, and the charge is not without substance. But their conservatism lay not in their fear of change—they were, after all, superb "social engineers"—but in their dread of sudden, passionate alterations in the political structure. As was suggested earlier, the frame of government they created was contrived above all else to frustrate the sudden seizure of power by any faction, however well motivated. True, this does amount to buttressing the *status quo*, but there is no prescription of the substance of the *status quo*: the system will protect a liberal, internationalist public policy from frenzied assaults as effectively as it will sustain a conservative, isolationist one. State governments, even Congress on occasion, have fallen before sudden political tempests, but the winds have generally died before they could overwash the sea wall of strategic delay built into the Constitution. To change the metaphor, reformers, both sound and unsound from the democratic viewpoint, have had to bide their time at the gates of the constitutional fortress.

The Federal Government is insulated against political passion in a way that is not characteristic of state and local governments, and this insulation has contributed to a difference in attitude and action toward nonconformists. To take a concrete instance, the states and their subdivisions have long been engaged in pursuing those members of the populace designated subversive and un-American. This they do under statutes which would probably horrify by their ambiguity and severity even that stern hunter of seditions, Justice Samuel Chase. A few of the resulting convictions have been invalidated by the Supreme Court over the years,[52] but in general the states have exercised plenary jurisdiction over their subversives, even when the substantive case was as flimsy as it was in *Gilbert v. Minnesota*,[53] *Gitlow v. New York*,[54] or *Whitney v. California*.[55] On the other hand, the antisubversive activities of the national government, whatever one may think of their

---

[52] See, for example, Herndon v. Lowry, 301 U.S. 242 (1937); DeJonge v. Oregon, 299 U.S. 353 (1937).
[53] 254 U.S. 325 (1920). [54] 268 U.S. 652 (1925).
[55] 274 U.S. 357 (1927). For details on these cases, see Zechariah Chaffee, Jr., *Free Speech in the United States* (Cambridge, Mass., 1946).

constitutionality or expediency, have been conducted with an increasing respect for due process of law. Compare the "Red Raids" of Attorney General Palmer with the actions of Biddle, Clark, and Brownell in the same area, and the development becomes strikingly apparent.

This respect for due process has certainly been less true of the administrative "security programs" than of the judicial indictments and trials, but even on this level the national government's activities have been suffused with a minimal respect for the principles of natural justice,[56] and state programs have generally been little more than quasi-judicial lynchings.[57] Indeed, we have recently seen the Supreme Court intervene in the internal affairs of the New Mexico and California state bars to impose certain standards of fairness on the legal profession,[58] a profession one might expect to find in the vanguard of the struggle for liberty. In another case, the Court frustrated the efforts of the State of New Hampshire to impose its high standards of patriotism and internal security on an occasional lecturer at the state university.[59] This sort of intervention is seldom undertaken by state judges and was not until recent years undertaken except on rare occasions by the federal courts.

The growth of the Due Process Clause of the Fourteenth Amendment to the point where it provided legal, if not always practical, protection for the rights of nonconformists should be briefly recapitulated. After initially holding that this clause was purely procedural in content,[60] the Supreme Court, under the vigorous prodding of Justice Stephen J. Field,[61] moved to a view that due process protected

[56] See Eleanor Bontecou, *The Federal Loyalty-Security Program* (Ithaca, N.Y., 1953), pp. 239–240.

[57] See, generally, Walter Gellhorn, ed., *The States and Subversion* (Ithaca, N.Y., 1952). For specific studies, see Lawrence H. Chamberlain, *Loyalty and Legislative Action* (Ithaca, N.Y., 1951); Edward L. Barrett, Jr., *The Tenney Committee* (Ithaca, N.Y., 1951); Vern Countryman, *Un-American Activities in the State of Washington* (Ithaca, N.Y., 1951).

[58] See Konigsberg v. State Bar of California, 77 S. Ct. 722 (1957); Schware v. Board of Bar Examiners of the State of New Mexico, 77 S. Ct. 752 (1957).

[59] Sweezy v. State of New Hampshire by Wyman, 77 S. Ct. 1203 (1957).

[60] Slaughterhouse Cases, 16 Wall. 36 (1873); Munn v. Illinois, 94 U.S. 113 (1877); Hurtado v. California, 110 U.S. 516 (1884). In the Hurtado Opinion the shift toward substantive due process is already noticeable.

[61] See the fine analysis of Field's influence in Howard Jay Graham, "Justice Field and the Fourteenth Amendment," *Yale Law Journal,* 52 (1943), 851.

certain economic rights even against legislation.[62] This was the basis for Justice Holmes's famous wisecrack, in a dissent otherwise barren of constructive content,[63] that the Fourteenth Amendment was not intended to enact Mr. Herbert Spencer's *Social Statics*. In short, certain natural rights of an economic character were put beyond the profane reach of government; but with respect to civil or political rights, the Court retained its procedural approach until 1923, or 1925, depending on how one interprets Justice McReynolds' holding in *Meyer v. Nebraska*.[64] In any event, in 1925 in *Gitlow v. New York*,[65] the Court (while affirming Gitlow's conviction for threatening the foundations of the state with his ferocious tracts) ruled that the freedoms protected from national infringement by the First Amendment were also protected from state invasion by the Fourteenth.

To make a long story short,[66] this was later expanded by Justice Cardozo in *Palko v. Connecticut* [67] to include within the protection of the Due Process Clause of the Fourteenth Amendment not only First Amendment freedoms, but also those other features of the Bill of Rights which are "of the very essence of a scheme of ordered liberty." Although this may strike the reader as a masterpiece of studied ambiguity, it has supplied the Supreme Court with a rationale for overruling outrageous state decisions and has served as a gun behind the door which may have cooled the passions of state judiciaries from time to time. The great gap in protection of individual liberty occurs

[62] See Chicago, M. & St. P. Ry. v. Minnesota, 134 U.S. 418 (1890); Smyth v. Ames, 169 U.S. 466 (1898); Lochner v. New York, 198 U.S. 45 (1905); Benjamin Twiss, *Lawyers and the Constitution* (Princeton, 1942).

[63] Holmes clearly did not reject substantive due process as a limitation on the police power of the states, but refused to join the elaborate, thoroughly documented dissent of Justice Harlan in *Lochner v. New York* to the point that *this* restriction on liberty of contract was justified. Instead, he went off on an intellectual buccaneering expedition which was as epigrammatic as it was irrelevant.

[64] I find McReynolds' Opinion suffused with substantive due process; it is not merely that the state law deprived teachers of their jobs, thus infringing their economic rights, but also that the law was an unconstitutional attempt to invade the educational freedom of the people of the state. Meyer v. Nebraska, 262 U.S. 390 (1923).

[65] 268 U.S. 652 (1925).

[66] Succintly told by Edward S. Corwin, *Liberty against Government* (Baton Rouge, La., 1948), pp. 116–168.

[67] 302 U.S. 319 (1937).

in those cases where the state does nothing to prevent coercion; in American municipal law, unlike international law, a state is not actionable for negligence, but current developments in national equity jurisdiction—notably the desegregation process—suggests that perhaps judicial ingenuity may eventually fill this gap.

The enlargement of the federal jurisdiction by virtue of the Due Process Clause is one of the two prongs of the contemporary attack on the legal powers of the states and their subdivisions. The other is the doctrine of pre-emption, which holds that the exercise of federal authority over certain areas automatically excludes and terminates state jurisdiction. Originating as an interpretation of the commerce power,[68] this rule was applied to the regulation of aliens in 1941 [69] and in 1956, in a very important act of judicial legislation, to laws governing sedition.[70] At one stroke, the Court vitiated the sedition laws of forty-eight states and terminated most prosecutions currently proceeding under their authority. Congress could, if it chose, restore this authority, as it did earlier when the Court similarly undermined state regulation of the insurance business,[71] but to date all proposals to this end have failed of enactment.

To sum up the argument thus far, it is submitted that a major factor in the development of freedom in the United States beyond the "armed pluralism" concept of Madison has been the growth in power of the national government which has accompanied our emergence as an urban industrial commonwealth. Specifically, the growth of federal power has led to the implementation of a principle of national protection of individual liberty against the actions of states or municipalities by the judiciary and to judicial decisions excluding the states from areas of jurisdiction of vital significance in civil liberty. Moreover, with a full recognition of the dangerous potentialities of unchecked national power, it is contended that the national institutions have provided a far higher level of juridical defense and have shown a far greater sensitivity to the rights of the individual than have the states.

[68] Cooley v. Board of Wardens of Port of Philadelphia, 12 How. 299 (1851). See F. D. G. Ribble, *State and National Power over Commerce* (New York, 1937), for an elaborate discussion of this doctrine.

[69] Hines v. Davidowitz, 312 U.S. 52 (1941).

[70] Commonwealth of Pennsylvania v. Nelson, 350 U.S. 497 (1956).

[71] United States v. South-Eastern Underwriters Association, 322 U.S. 533 (1944); immediately modified by Congress in the McCarran Act, 15 U.S.C. 1011–1015.

The "Tradition" of Freedom

Urbanization and industrialization are quasi-automatic processes of a quite unteleological character. Although the growth of industry and of cities has taken place in roughly parallel fashion in various nations, the political institutions which have emerged have differed radically in character from country to country.[72] One need only compare the modern histories of Britain, Germany, Japan, and the U.S.S.R. to see that industrialization can exist under and contribute to a variety of political forms—that is, unless one engages in the Marxist auto-hypnosis of asserting that Imperial Japan, Nazi Germany, Fascist Italy, Britain, and the United States were all basically similar state forms, resting allegedly on an undifferentiated concept of "capitalism." One can, therefore, suggest that, although industrialization and urbanization were necessary preconditions for the development of the type of liberty we enjoy, they are not sufficient explanations of cause. We must look for other, more subjective factors which have also been important and which indeed may supply us with more insight into proximate cause than do these other long-range, impersonal conditions.

On this level of analysis, the level of human action and volition, the most important development of the past half-century seems to me to be the growth of civil liberty elites, that is, leadership groups in the population who are committed to civil rights and who publicly endorse libertarian principles. Outstanding in this category have been lawyers, closely followed by ministers, teachers, and newspaper editors. Perhaps most important of all have been the professors of law, for as the law has become more and more an educated profession (as distinct from the old system of informal "reading" in a lawyer's office), that rigorous emphasis on procedural regularity and due process which is the mark of the great teacher has permeated the consciousness of generations of students. Moreover, law today is the access way to careers in business, labor, and politics even more than was the case fifty years ago, so business, labor, and political strata have been influenced by this climate of opinion.

More important in specific institutional terms has been the infiltration of national government decision-making groups by the legal

---

[72] See the thoughtful and penetrating essay by Clark Kerr, "Industrial Relations and the Liberal Pluralist," *Proceedings of the Seventh Annual Meeting, I.R.R.A.* (reprinted, I.I.R., Berkeley, Calif., 1955).

elite. The great legal migration that took place in the 1930's as a consequence of the mushroomlike growth of the national administration, particularly the rise of regulatory agencies, resulted in thousands of key jobs being held by strong advocates of due process of law and civil rights. There was some truth in the reactionary gibe that the way to power in Washington was to go to Harvard Law School and then "turn left." There was a new atmosphere abroad in the government, a rejection of the *laissez faire* tradition of the Republicans, and able young enthusiasts, who a generation previous would probably have gone unthinkingly into private practice or business, flocked to Washington to build the New Jerusalem.

The full impact of this legal colonization on the civil rights climate of the national government can be only intuitively appraised, for we are here in an area which defies empirical analysis. In practice it meant that the thousands of mundane decisions involving human rights—immigration, naturalization, National Labor Relations Board, Farm Security Administration, Department of Justice are jurisdictions that come to mind—were suffused with a new direction. Felix Frankfurter, Robert H. Jackson, Wiley Rutledge, William O. Douglas, Hugo Black, and that paragon of vigilant libertarianism Frank Murphy [73] took their places on the Supreme Court, and shortly a new note began to echo through the musty pages of the *Reports*. In addition, to throw in a really intangible consideration, the ablest graduates of the best law schools became clerks to members of the judiciary, with all the potential influence that this anonymous function can imply.[74] As De Tocqueville saw the lawyers of his day as a real check on the excesses of local democracy,[75] so we can see the Washington lawyer of the New Deal period as a force for regularized, impartial procedures which incorporated a new attitude toward civil liberty.

In a phrase, the United States for the first time in its history became civil liberty conscious. This is not to say that no lawyers formerly believed in civil rights or held government jobs or to assert that all

---

[73] For a discussion of the varying patterns of judicial liberalism that the Roosevelt Court incorporated, see my "The Utopian Pilgrimage of Mr. Justice Murphy," *Vanderbilt Law Review,* 10 (1957), 369.

[74] One gets some insight into the influence of an able clerk on a Justice in Alpheus T. Mason's monumental biography of Chief Justice Stone, *Harlan Fiske Stone: Pillar of the Law* (New York, 1956), especially at pp. 505, 513, 528.

[75] Alexis de Tocqueville, *op. cit.,* I, 282 ff.

lawyers today are enthusiastic about civil liberties—see *Schware v. Board of Bar Examiners of the State of New Mexico*.[76] It is rather to suggest that more lawyers today accept the basic principles of civil liberties and that more of these lawyers, partially as an outcome of conscious recruitment by agency heads, occupy decision-making positions in government. To take one key agency, the Department of Justice, as an example may be to indulge in biased selectivity, but it does seem immensely significant that this powerful institution was over such an important span of years directed by such civil liberties oriented Attorneys General as Cummings, Jackson, Murphy, and Biddle. The role of Biddle as a defender of civil rights deserves particular mention; as Attorney General throughout World War II, he consistently threw the influence of his office against chauvinistic pseudopatriotism and even refused to conduct the President's program for the exclusion and incarceration of the West Coast Japanese and Japanese-Americans.[77] From the viewpoint of civil liberties, World War II was a "good war," and to Biddle—and, of course, to the President who appointed and retained him—should go much of the credit.

The improvement of the civil liberties climate has also been due to the dedicated efforts of crusading individuals and groups outside of government. It is almost true to say that the American Civil Liberties Union invented civil liberties, for before this organization appeared on the scene shortly after World War I there was little articulated interest in or concern for liberty except among the various congeries of oppressed minorities. Much the ACLU did directly with its lawyers, but above all it supplied a formula, a body of civil rights doctrine around which could be mobilized the teachers, trade unionists, min-

[76] 77 S. Ct. 752 (1957).

[77] There was some ambiguity about Biddle's position. When the representatives of the War and Justice Departments met on February 17, 1942, and the Army spokesman sprang the evacuation plan, Biddle, over the objections of his colleagues present, Edward Ennis and James H. Rowe, Jr., apparently agreed in principle to the proposal (see Jacobus tenBroek *et al.*, *Prejudice, War, and the Constitution* [Berkeley, Calif., 1954], pp. 111–112). But despite this concession, Biddle made it clear that he "thought the Justice Department simply should not be a party to a program in which citizens were to be deprived of their liberties" (*ibid.*, p. 358, n. 65). The Army subsequently complained that the Department of Justice sabotaged their activities and gave them no legal aid in prosecuting violations of the curfew and evacuation orders. Both the Hirabayashi and Korematsu litigations were handled exclusively by Army counsel, even at the Supreme Court level.

isters, editors, and others who had previously lived in atomized impotence. For every dues-paying member, there were possibly a hundred nonmembers of the Union who looked to it for leadership and for the appropriate formulation and who passed this view on to their communities. Roger Baldwin has commented on the fact that, in his visits around the country, ministers in small communities frequently told him how valuable the ACLU's work had been to them and how they tried to pass the civil liberties message on to their constituents.[78]

There are other considerations that a longer analysis would have to take under examination, for example the growth of "liberal" political organizations in the big cities and the big-city states and the impact of World War II and the Cold War on the American self-image, but the evidence adduced above seems to support the contention that civil liberty, individual political freedom, has achieved significant institutionalization in contemporary American society. The conditions of life for the majority of our population are impersonal, that is, the growth of the city saw the disintegration of the rural system of social control based on direct democracy, and slowly a new system of sanctions has emerged, a system which is founded on the bureaucratization of interpersonal and intergroup conflict. The security dismissal has replaced tar and feathers; the Smith Act has replaced the lynching posse. In a real sense, the very impersonalization of urban life is a condition of freedom: it is possible to live differently and believe differently from one's neighbors without their knowing, much less caring, about the deviation. Particularly with the virtual disappearance of the first-generation immigrant, who tended to stick to his ethnic ghetto, there has occurred a breakdown of integrated subcommunities in which direct coercion could be applied, say, to the Jew who sponsored a Yom Kippur ball or the Irishman who denounced the Church. The second- and third- generation Americans have typically broken their ties to old sections and scattered out through the city and increasingly the suburbs.

In short, there are in the city no ready-made instruments of social control, of direct democracy. An aggrieved citizen does not organize a lynching bee, he calls the cops or the health department: he is government-minded and is inclined to leave the protection of his lares and penates as well as his personalty to organs of the state. Typically, he

[78] Private conversation.

will have no arms in his home and no inclination toward bellicosity; even such organizations as the American Legion, which attempt to impose sanctions on various forms of unorthodox behavior, seldom make a significant dent in the great wall of indifference. Nonconformity, a psychological manifestation of strong individualism, is paradoxically sheltered by a blanket of urban, perhaps even urbane, anonymity and indifference. The New York policemen who used to stand around Joe McWilliams, the pro-Nazi agitator, before World War II, as he poured out his venom against "the Eskimos," were symbolic of this new development. A century ago they would have been either leading the mob in lynching McWilliams or beating up his hecklers, but in the New York of 1940 they simply stood like statues, and a police stenographer took down McWilliams' every word in the event that a legal action might ensue. The words of one of these policemen might serve as the epitaph of direct democracy. Pushing off an angry young Jew who rushed at McWilliams with blood in his eye, the statue observed, "If you want a fight, son, join the Marines." [79] Even antisocial behavior has been institutionalized! [80]

CONCLUSION

Although this essay may have wandered through some seemingly unrelated fields, there is a thread that provides consistency and relevance. It is my contention that there is no "tradition of liberty" in the United States, but two traditions. Each of these traditions is founded on its own set of premises and rooted in is own historic and social context. A homogeneous rural society visualized liberty as a by-product of social conflict and defined it as the absence of centralized oppressive power. An increasingly homogeneous urban society defines liberty very differently—as a function of social cohesion institutionalized as due process of law. The Madisonian theory of liberty was not at root concerned with interpersonal relationships; it was aimed at achieving group equilibriums. The modern theory of liberty, in contrast, is vitally concerned with the status of the individual, the indi-

[79] This is based on personal experience as an observer and heckler of Mr. McWilliams; the bellicose young man who received the admonition from the policeman was a personal friend.

[80] See my brief discussion of this interesting phenomenon in "Sgt. McKeon and the Cult of Violence," *New Republic,* August 27, 1956, pp. 16–17.

vidual who is permanently part of a great society and cannot take refuge from his enemies in a safe microcosm. As the symbolic institution of Madison's theory was Deseret, the armed, Mormon enclave, so the symbolic institution of the modern theory is the federal district judge informing the State of South Carolina that it cannot assert the sovereignty of numbers to deprive individual Negro citizens of their fundamental rights and liberties. American liberty, in short, has become a positive goal of national public policy, rather than a fortuitous consequence of fragmentation, pluralism, and social conflict.

[DONALD G. MORGAN]

MOUNT HOLYOKE COLLEGE

The Marshall Court and Civil Liberties

TO suggest that John Marshall and the Supreme Court, over which he presided from 1801 to 1835, had anything very important to say about civil liberties is, of course, unorthodox. That Court is famed for its elaboration of the federal system and the powers of the three branches of the Federal Government. It is credited with but one decision affecting civil liberties directly; and that decision, *Barron v. Baltimore*,[1] in denying that the Bill of Rights applied to the member states of the Union, had a negative effect only.

Was the impact of the Marshall Court on civil liberties, then, negative only? Was the creative role played by the great Chief Justice and the fifteen Associate Justices who came and went during his long tenure confined to the federal structure and the operations of the new national government?

Our answer will depend on how we define the problem of civil liberties. If we mean by it the definition of rights themselves, then that Court played only a limited role. If we extend it to include the social and psychological conditions essential for the realization of rights and the governmental means for securing their protection, then the work of the Marshall Court is substantial and suggestive for our own time. Should the movement of McCarthyism have been met by the assertion of the rights of the individuals selected for attack or by restoring public

[1] 7 Pet. 243 (1833).

163

confidence in government personnel and providing the victims more effective channels of redress? Should racial segregation be combated primarily by a judicial determination of rights or by a steady cultivation of a favorable public consensus in the affected areas and the devising of efficient procedures for enforcement? It is a premise of this paper that implementation should receive the same attention as definition.

Such being the case, my purpose is to explore the concepts concerning civil liberties that dominated the Marshall Court and to evaluate the contributions which that body has made to civil liberties today.

I

Problems of civil liberties occupied a place in the Court of Marshall markedly different from that which they occupy in today's Supreme Court. The subjects that arose for decision and the attitudes of the Justices toward them were alike sharply conditioned. Several of these conditioning factors are noteworthy.

For one thing, by that day in 1801 when John Marshall ascended the bench, the meaning and status of civil liberties had become a battleground of party warfare. Even before the emergence of the parties, while the newly framed Constitution was awaiting ratification, Hamilton and Jefferson had reacted in contrasting ways to the absence from it of a bill of rights. Hamilton preferred to rely on public opinion for the maintenance of civil liberties; he scorned bills of rights, "volumes of those aphorisms which . . . would sound much better in a treatise of ethics than in a constitution of government." [2] In Paris, Jefferson studied the new Constitution and sent Madison his criticisms; first among his objections was the omission of a bill of rights, "which is what the people are entitled to against every government on earth, general or particular, and what no just government should refuse, or rest on inference." [3] In the end, of course, Jefferson had his way.

By 1798 one of the provisions of the Bill of Rights, freedom of the press, had become a key issue between the Federalists and the Re-

[2] *The Federalist,* No. 84 (Modern Library ed.; New York: Random House, 1937), pp. 558–559.

[3] Letter dated December 20, 1787, Jefferson, *Papers,* J. P. Boyd, ed. (Princeton, N.J.: Princeton University Press, 1955), XII, 440.

publicans. Federalists in Congress had passed the Alien and Sedition Acts, and Federalists on the bench were applying them with a partisan vindictiveness. The election of Jefferson in 1800, after a bitter campaign, was taken as a tacit repudiation of those controversial acts. For a generation the Alien and Sedition Acts remained an epithet of politics.[4]

In 1801, at Marshall's advent, the federal courts had acquired a reputation for ignoring individual rights and conducting arbitrary trials. Much that Marshall and his fellow judges did in succeeding years must have been calculated to counteract this unfavorable public attitude.

In the second place, the Justices who dominated that Court had a philosophy of civil liberties more akin to that of the Federalists than to that of their opponents. The views of Marshall—unchallenged leader of the Court—had, of course, the utmost importance. He had evidently been among those who supported the adoption of a bill of rights only because such action would allay public doubts and secure ratification. He disliked the legislation of 1798 because he thought it inexpedient, and not presumably because of any constitutional scruples. In the Virginia convention which ratified the Constitution, Marshall had revealed his own objective. There he had defended the proposed new judiciary: "To what quarter," he asked, "will you look for protection from an infringement on the Constitution, if you will not give the power to the judiciary? There is no other body that can afford such a protection." [5] Marshall then applied the principle to the hypothetical case of a federal law officer who violated the privacy of an individual; he went on to assert not only that a law authorizing such official conduct would be void, but also that the federal courts would offer a haven to the aggrieved individual. Later in the same speech Marshall pointed to the basis of his trust in judicial protection. Said he:

If we can expect a fair decision any where may we not expect justice to be done by the judges of both the federal and state governments? But, says the honorable member, laws may be executed tyrannically. Where is the independency of your judges? If a law be exercised tyrannically in Virginia,

[4] Joseph Story wrote in 1833 that the Sedition Act was still a "theme of reproach." See his *Commentaries on the Constitution* (5th ed., M. M. Bigelow, ed.; Boston: Little, Brown, 1891), sec. 1892.

[5] Elliot's *Debates* (2d ed.; Philadelphia: J. B. Lippincott, 1876), III, 554.

to what can you trust? To your judiciary. What security have you for justice? Their independence. Will it not be so in the federal court? [6]

This preoccupation with the judiciary as the means of maintaining constitutional provisions remained a passion with the Chief Justice. His concern with the sanctity of constitutional forms and processes appears in several recently published letters which Marshall wrote from Europe in 1797. There, as an official emissary, he reported to Secretary of State Pickering on the French *coup d'état* of the 18 Fructidor.[7] He was horrified by that resort to force and the "wanton contempt of rules so essential to the very being of a republic." [8]

It is safe to say that Bushrod Washington, Marshall's fellow Virginian and fellow Federalist, who remained on the Court for twenty-eight of Marshall's thirty-four years, must have shared Marshall's sentiments. Washington had presided at trials under the 1798 legislation and unquestionably deemed it valid.[9] Marshall's conception of the judicial function must have suited the conservative Washington.

From 1812 on, Joseph Story served as one of Marshall's most influential and trusted colleagues. His *Commentaries on the Constitution,* published in 1833, express his considered views on civil liberties. On one hand, he defends the addition of the Bill of Rights to the Constitution against the arguments advanced by Hamilton in *The Federalist,* Number 84, and outlines the values served by a properly framed bill of rights.[10] On the other, his discussion of rights, particularly of

[6] *Ibid.,* p. 559.

[7] Marshall wrote: "In opposition to its [the Constitution's] mandates the members of the legislature have been seiz'd by an order of the directory, without observing any of the forms wisely prescribed; & Without being brought before that court which alone can try them they have been banishd, unheard, by the remnant of a terrified legislature forbidden in express terms to pronounce such a judgment by the very charter which created it. The same violence in equal opposition to the constitution is practic'd on a minority of the executive & on several citizens whose only offence was that they had printed free comments on the conduct of the directory & of the armies. These excesses cannot have been necessary" (Jack L. Cross, "John Marshall on the French Revolution and on American Politics," *William and Mary Quarterly,* 3d ser., 12 [1955], 631–649, at p. 637).

[8] *Ibid.,* p. 638.

[9] See James Morton Smith, *Freedom's Fetters: The Alien and Sedition Laws and American Civil Liberties* (Ithaca, N.Y.: Cornell University Press, 1956), pp. 271, 285, 379, 381, 388.

[10] *Commentaries,* secs. 1858–1862.

freedom of the press, tends to support the validity of the Sedition Act in particular and the need of significant limitations on the scope of rights in general. He deplores the "rage of theorists" to load constitutions with their own "crude and visionary aphorisms of government." [11] And, like Marshall, he lays heavy stress on the independent judiciary as guardian of constitutional rights.[12] Hence Story characteristically believed that the judiciary was bound to incur the attacks of demagogues.

The attitudes prevailing on the Court affected even William Johnson, the most outspokenly Jeffersonian of all the Justices. That Johnson held the basic civil liberties in high esteem appears throughout his career. In his separate opinion in the *Steamboat* case in 1824, he epitomized this conviction. The Constitution, he said, should be construed in the light of its purpose, and: "The great and paramount purpose was to unite this mass of wealth and power, for the protection of the humblest individual; his rights, civil and political, his interests and prosperity are the sole end; the rest are nothing but the means." [13] At the same time, Johnson, like his associates, reiterated the importance of the independent judiciary as the protector of individual rights. During the Nullification struggle in South Carolina, a friend wrote Johnson indirectly accusing the Court of bias in its decisions on state and federal powers. Johnson replied: "Although we are emphatically *the men of the people,* being charged exclusively with the protection of individual rights against unconstitutional laws, yet indirectly we are compelled to pass upon the delicate question of sovereign right, from which may heaven deliver us." [14] The Republican Johnson shared the conviction of his associates concerning the Court's role.

These four Justices—Marshall, Washington, Story, and Johnson—dominated the Court throughout most of the period. Their views, especially in those many areas of law where they stood in agreement, were essentially those of the Court.

[11] *Ibid.,* sec. 1863.
[12] *Ibid.,* sec. 1865. See also sec. 1294, note 2.
[13] Gibbons v. Ogdon, 9 Wheat. 1, 223.
[14] Letter to John Taylor of South Carolina, September 22, 1830, *Niles Register,* 39 (October 9, 1830), 119; treated in the present author's *Justice William Johnson: The First Dissenter* (Columbia, S.C.: University of South Carolina Press, 1954), pp. 264–267. The italics are Johnson's.

Finally, the cases which at that period came before the Court offered all too little opportunity for interpretation of civil liberties. The election of 1800 doubtless alerted politicians to the popular distaste for laws encroaching on civil liberties. Again, it was widely felt that laws touching freedom of expression were for the states alone to enact. Concerned primarily with foreign affairs and foreign intercourse, the Federal Government came into contact with the citizen only spasmodically. Accordingly, it was with matters other than civil liberties that the Court usually had to deal.

The way in which the Justices settled those other issues had immense, albeit indirect, significance for the liberties of later generations. That they interpreted broadly the substantive powers of the national government, that they thus enabled it to meet future crises at home and abroad, that they endowed it within its sphere with supremacy over all local governments—all this in the long run made for stability and for responsiveness to popular needs and, accordingly, for a climate of opinion in which individual freedoms could flourish.

It is with the more direct contributions, however, that this paper is concerned. The low esteem in which the Court was held in 1801, the strong Federalist flavor of several of its key members, and the dearth of genuine civil liberties issues shaped its impact on the problem of maintaining individual freedoms.

II

It is not surprising, therefore, that with few lapses the Marshall Justices worked hard at the task of building a powerful and solidly supported judiciary. Their success in this venture has constituted easily their greatest immediate contribution to the stability of civil liberties. The story is a familiar one. I shall mention only two of the means which the Court chose in pursuing its great end and relate the results more directly to our problem.

From the very beginning, when he persuaded the other Justices to abandon individual opinions in favor of a unanimous opinion for the Court, Marshall strove to impart to the tribunal a reputation for solid unity, harmony, and impartiality. As an old man he told the Virginia constitutional convention in 1829 that the greatest misfortune that could befall a people was "an ignorant, a corrupt, or a dependent Judiciary." [15] Clearly he did his best to make the federal judiciary the exact opposite of such an institution. Accordingly he worked for a Court that would appear to be united. In spite of Johnson's achievement in wresting from the majority a tolerance for dissent, dissent remained the exception rather than the rule. Midway in his career, Marshall wrote Story that he hoped "that the harmony of the bench" would never be upset. "We have external and political enemies enough to preserve internal peace." [16]

The standing of the Court would also be served by judicial aloofness from political controversy. Except for his partisan *Life of Washington* and one venture into self-vindication in the press through the medium of a thinly veiled pseudonym, Marshall himself kept apart from public controversy. The example caught hold, for with occasional departures, especially on the part of the restless Johnson, the other Justices, too, avoided involvement in political affairs generally. Unlike the earlier Justices, they by and large confined their activities off the bench to the "non-controversial." As a result, the Court enjoyed a steadily mounting prestige.

While recouping the reputation of the Court, the Justices simultaneously strove to enhance their power. In the face of protests, occasionally from within, frequently from without, they sought through interpretation to amplify their own jurisdiction. With this they coupled the assertion of judicial review. The effect was to afford to individuals a defense against illegal action originating in three principal quarters: the executive, the states, and, to a degree, Congress itself.

When the owner of a vessel went to court to recover damages from a naval officer who had seized it without legal authority, the Court granted him relief; the Justices rejected the officer's plea that he was acting under orders of the President.[17] In the Burr trial Marshall was soon demonstrating that the Court stood to protect individuals, however unpopular, from arbitrary action by the executive, and in the *Embargo Mandamus* case Johnson was freeing a shipowner from the

---

[15] Albert J. Beveridge, *The Life of John Marshall* (Boston and New York: Houghton Mifflin, 1916), IV, 495.

[16] Letter dated July 13, 1821, Massachusetts Historical Society, *Proceedings*, 2d ser., 14 (1900–1901), 328.

[17] Little v. Barreme, 2 Cranch 170 (1804).

duty to obey illegal detention orders of the Secretary of the Treasury.[18] More sustained and bitter was the Court's struggle to assert the power to review state laws and decisions. The *Martin* and *Cohens* cases stand as monuments to its victory.[19] The mounting outcry from advocates of states' rights and the appearance on the Court of Justices sympathetic with that concept caused the Court in Marshall's last decade to moderate its determined stand against state measures. Yet the precedents had been so firmly established that individuals had come habitually to turn to federal courts for protection from certain forms of state legislation. The Court's authority was now beyond repeal.

Congress was another matter, and here the Court proceeded cautiously. William Marbury, be it noted, failed in his well-known effort to wrest his commission as justice of the peace from the Jefferson Administration; yet in the process of denying him relief, and thus avoiding collision with the President, Marshall boldly asserted the power of the Court to delineate at least some of the powers of Congress itself.[20] Seldom after that did the Marshall Court seriously challenge the authority of Congress, and the precedent was indeed a time bomb destined to explode only after the lapse of a half century and more. Nevertheless, that decision completed, in law at least, the circle of Court power.

Authority went hand in hand with authoritativeness as the Court made the most of its role. Marshall's strategy and timing in all this were acute. He dexterously asserted powers and established principles that were widely denounced at the time, yet were sound and acceptable in the long run, and accomplished this without incurring the rebuffs and frustrations which could easily have destroyed the Court's prestige. To establish the Court's capacity to protect individuals in future cases, he might need to disappoint the individuals in present ones. The *Marbury,* the *Martin,* the *McCulloch,* and the *Cohens* decisions all met with public criticism while simultaneously settling enduring principles. In half these cases the individuals seeking redress met defeat; their loss was the Court's gain.

An incident of 1823 and Marshall's reaction to it illustrate his policy.

---

[18] United States v. Burr, 4 Cranch 470 (1807); Gilchrist v. Collector, 10 Fed. Cas. 355, No. 5420 (1808).

[19] Martin v. Hunter, 1 Wheat. 304 (1816); Cohens v. Virginia, 6 Wheat. 264 (1821).

[20] Marbury v. Madison, 1 Cranch 137 (1803).

Justice Johnson in the lower court sought without success to protect a colored seaman from the harsh provisions of a South Carolina law. While seeking to assert sound constitutional principles in the teeth of a defiant opposition, Johnson met with defeat.[21] On hearing of Johnson's plight, Marshall wrote Story that a similar law existed in Virginia and went on to comment wryly: "A case has been brought before me in which I might have considered its constitutionality, had I chosen to do so; but it was not absolutely necessary, and as I am not fond of butting against a wall in sport, I escaped on the construction of the act."[22] Shrewdly and determinedly, the Court of Marshall established a total pattern for conduct and operation that helped make of the judiciary the principal bulwark, both in the official and the popular minds, for individual rights.

III

At first glance it would seem that the rights which benefited from all this judicial activity were those of property. Most of the time Marshall and his associates seemed bent on construing the fundamental law in such a way as to shield landowners, creditors, and merchants from regulations, particularly as they issued from state legislatures. At times the constitutional grounds for this effort were shadowy, but increasingly the majority came to rely on that constitutional clause that prohibited states from "impairing the Obligation of Contracts."[23] Pursuing a literal reading of the clause, the Court, in such cases as *Fletcher v. Peck, New Jersey v. Wilson, Dartmouth College v. Wodward,* and *Sturges v. Crowninshield,*[24] built a protective wall around property and won for itself the title "defender of vested rights." The process continued until a new majority in 1827 reasserted legislative power.[25]

What has this to do with our problem? It seems probable that this trend of Court decisions lent strength to later efforts to protect rights

[21] Elkison v. Deliesseline, 8 Fed. Cas. 493, No. 4366.

[22] Letter dated September 26, 1823, Story Papers (MSS), quoted in Charles Warren, *Supreme Court in United States History* (rev. ed.; Boston: Little, Brown, 1926), I, 626.

[23] Art. I, sec. 10.

[24] 6 Cranch 87 (1810); 7 Cranch 164 (1812); 4 Wheat. 518 (1819); and 4 Wheat. 122 (1819).

[25] Ogden v. Saunders, 12 Wheat. 213; Marshall with two others dissented.

of a different sort. At least two points of relationship suggest them-selves.

In the first place, the Justices not only saw property rights and personal rights as related each to the other, but also advanced social justifications for the former which were closely analogous to those for the latter. The economic chaos that followed the Revolution and the ill-conceived measures that the states adopted for dealing with it had by 1787 created a sense of uncertainty, insecurity, and mutual distrust which had furnished a prime motive for the framing of the Constitution. The constitutional prohibitions on state laws of that kind appeared to the framers to guarantee peace, order, stability, and economic progress —conditions, in short, for individual development and social health. When Marshall in 1810 came to protect the rights of an innocent purchaser of Yazoo lands from the operation of Georgia's revocation of its own original grant, he said that Georgia would be restrained even if that State were beyond the control of those courts "established for the security of property, and to decide on human rights." [26] Farther on, Marshall explained the purpose behind the restrictions on state power:

Whatever respect might have been felt for the state sovereignties, it is not to be disguised that the framers of the Constitution viewed, with some apprehension, the violent acts which might grow out of the feelings of the moment; and that the people of the United States, in adopting that instrument, have manifested a determination to shield themselves and their property from the effects of those sudden and strong passions to which men are exposed. The restrictions on the legislative power of the States are obviously founded in this sentiment; and the Constitution of the United States contains what may be deemed a bill of rights for the people of each State.[27]

Moreover, there was general agreement at the time that the right of property was to some extent a natural right, hence free from certain forms of governmental regulation.[28] If the security of property affected

[26] Fletcher v. Peck, 6 Cranch 87, 133.

[27] *Ibid.*, 138; Marshall was here referring, of course, to portions of Art. I, sec. 10, of the Constitution. Note his further comments: "Titles, which, according to every legal test, are perfect, are acquired with that confidence which is inspired by the opinion that the purchaser is safe." A contrary holding, he said, would mean that "all titles would be insecure, and the intercourse between man and man would be very seriously obstructed." 6 Cranch, 134.

[28] Compare the several treatments of this subject in Ogden v. Saunders, 12 Wheat. 213.

social health and existed as a natural right, those same justifications could be advanced for personal rights. Rights to free expression and to fair judicial procedure can thrive only in communities where the prevailing spirit is one of confidence, not one of fear.

In the second place, the Court, by making itself a sanctuary for individuals who asserted property rights, established a pattern holding promise for those who might assert other rights. The practice begun by Marshall was continued by Chief Justice Taney. In the end, men were bound to insist, as Lincoln did in 1859, that in a free society personal rights took precedence over property rights.[29] Perhaps it was inevitable, in a democratic society, that the preoccupation of the judiciary with the protection of property rights could lead only to assertions of personal rights.

The relationship is subtle, and yet this very same logic was unfolded later in the decisions under the Fourteenth Amendment. The Court of one generation read the Due Process Clause as prohibiting state laws encroaching on rights of business; the Court of the next extended the clause to protect freedom of expression and rights to fair procedure. That process continues.

Had the early Court not used its new-found power and influence to safeguard the merchant, the banker, and the landowner, it would have been far more difficult for later courts to give aid to the pamphleteer, the victim of the third degree, and the member of a segregated minority.

IV

The case of *Barron v. Baltimore* was, of course, the one decision of the Marshall Court that directly and significantly affected personal rights. Decided in 1833, it rejected the suit of a Baltimore wharf owner whose property had lost its value as a result of public works carried on by the city, by holding that the Fifth Amendment guarantee of just compensation applied to the Federal Government alone.[30] Under the terms of the Fourteenth Amendment, the Court in our own century has decided that some at least of the provisions of the Bill of Rights

---

[29] Letter to Henry L. Pierce & Others, April 6, 1859, *Works*, Roy P. Basler, ed. (New Brunswick, N.J.: Rutgers University Press, 1953), III, 375.

[30] Barron v. Baltimore, 7 Pet. 243.

do apply to the states. Accordingly, the *Barron* case recently has come up for re-examination.[31] In the light of the history of the adoption of the Bill of Rights, was the *Barron* case correctly decided?

In lieu of an answer to this question, a matter beyond the space limitations of this paper, two things can, I think, be said about that decision. First, in spite of state precedents to the contrary, the question at issue was still open in 1833. Justice Johnson had dropped hints earlier that pointed toward a ruling counter to that finally reached. Had the literal kind of interpretation that Marshall and Story had earlier applied to the Contract Clause been similarly applied to the Bill of Rights, the result might have been different from what it was. Members of the bar must have entertained hope of such an outcome, for at this session not one, but two, cases presented the main issue.[32]

Second, the final decision accorded both with the predispositions of the majority of the Justices and with the exigencies of the time. Marshall and Story by that date were having difficulty enough in defending property against state encroachments without multiplying the grounds for review of state laws, and the younger Justices had carried to the Court much of the fervor for states' rights and state autonomy that increasingly characterized public life from the 1820's on. One might be tempted to explain the decision as a concession by the older Justices, and yet the forthright character of Marshall's opinion suggests that it may indeed have been a corporate ruling. Whatever the explanation of the *Barron* decision, the result was clear: it was to exclude from Court surveillance numerous questions which were to return only in our own time.

[31] For example, see William W. Crosskey, *Politics and the Constitution in the History of the United States* (Chicago: University of Chicago Press, 1954), II, ch. xxx; Charles Fairman, "The Supreme Court and the Constitutional Limitations on State Governmental Authority," *University of Chicago Law Review*, 21 (1953–1954), 40–78.

[32] The Barron case, as Professor Fairman has shown, was held over from the previous term (Fairman, *op. cit.*, p. 45). Conceivably this was because, with two members absent, the Court was, on this issue as on others, stalemated, or perhaps it was to allow Johnson, one of the absentees, to participate in a decision of special interest to him. In Lessee of Livingston v. Moore, 7 Pet. 469 (1833), counsel had urged that the Due Process Clause of the Fifth Amendment applied to the states. Johnson gave the Court's opinion soon after the Barron decision and announced that the applicability of the Bill of Rights was "now settled" (*ibid.*, p. 551). Clearly it had not been settled prior to the Barron decision.

The gains made by the Marshall Court in connection with personal rights were thus made in relation to the Federal Government alone. Since there was little opportunity to rule on free expression, the emphasis was on the rights to fair procedure. At numerous minor points the Justices settled issues concerning the procedure of the federal courts. They fixed, for example, some of the outlines and limits for jury trial, habeas corpus, and the ban on ex post facto laws. Most of this work, it seems, was done in the lower federal courts. Throughout the period the Supreme Court Justices rode circuits embracing several states. It was there that trials were held and procedures elaborated. The principles which the Justices discussed and the standards which they worked out at the annual sitting in Washington they carried in person to lower tribunals scattered through the country. The trial which Marshall conducted for Aaron Burr, besides being the most famous of all such federal prosecutions of the period, illustrates this point.[33] In the course of it, Marshall issued rulings touching such varied matters as the meaning of treason, the evidence necessary to establish treason, and the issuance of subpoenas to the President.

If the Court added materially to the vitality of procedural safeguards, some of the Jeffersonians among its members would in all likelihood have gone even further. The case of *Hudson and Goodwin* presented the question whether the federal courts, in the absence of clear authority direct from Congress, could try offences made criminal at the common law, in this instance, criminal libel.[34] The majority held that they could not. The decision had the effect of curbing judicial discretion to define crimes and to this extent redounded to the benefit of individuals; Congress, Johnson declared, "must first make an act a crime, affix a punishment to it, and declare the court that shall have jurisdiction of the offense."[35] Significantly, the Court stood divided, with Story and two others, probably including Marshall, in the minority. Elsewhere Johnson insisted repeatedly on preserving intact trial by jury, for to him this was "one of the most inestimable privileges of a freeman."[36] Furthermore, Johnson's collaboration with the major-

[33] United States v. Burr, 4 Cranch 470 (1807).
[34] United States v. Hudson and Goodwin, 7 Cranch 32 (1812).
[35] *Ibid.,* 34.
[36] Lessee of Livingston v. Moore, 7 Pet. 469, 552 (1833); see Morgan, *Johnson,* pp. 134–135.

ity in overruling state laws affecting property resulted in part, at least, from his detestation of retrospective laws. To him such laws, whether civil or criminal in nature, violated individual rights.

Nevertheless, all the Justices, Federalist and Republican alike, held procedures in high respect. In 1821, when for the first time the Court came to decide whether Congress possessed a power to punish for contempts, it was argued that Congress might misuse such a power and treat individuals with undue severity. Justice Johnson spoke for the Court in upholding the power and had this to say of the contention:

If it be inquired what security is there, that with an officer avowing himself devoted to their will, the House of Representatives will confine its punishing power to the limits of imprisonment, and not push it to the infliction of corporal punishment, or even death, and exercise it in cases affecting the liberty of speech, and of the press? the reply is to be found in the consideration that the Constitution was formed in and for an advanced state of society, and rests at every point on received opinions and fixed ideas. It is not a new creation, but a combination of existing materials, whose properties and attributes were familiarly understood, and had been determined by reiterated experiments. It is not, therefore, reasoning upon things as they are, to suppose that any deliberative assembly, constituted under it, would ever assert any other rights and powers than those which had been established by long practice, and conceded by public opinion.[37]

Apart from the deference to Congress which it reflects, the statement has a special pertinence for procedure. It suggests that the Constitution imposes restrictions on government so ancient and so firmly established in custom that violation would be unthinkable. The safeguards Johnson had in mind must have been in the main procedural safeguards. The procedural rights, one may conclude, thus limited Congress as well as other branches of the government.

By insisting particularly on court processes fair to the accused, the Marshall Justices were spelling out numerous personal rights and at the same time promoting their other objective, the establishment of a Court capable of inspiring confidence in the public.

[37] Anderson v. Dunn, 6 Wheat. 204, 232 (1821).

V

The principal lasting achievement of the Marshall Court in relation to civil liberties had to do more with the conditions for realizing rights than with the rights themselves. Those Justices sought, in a variety of ways, to promote a state of interpersonal confidence and to foster respect for the Constitution and the laws of the land. Their more immediate aim—and their major achievement—was the creation of a sure protector for rights: the judiciary was to be an impartial, efficient, and venerated guardian of the rights of all individuals.

If the Court's elaboration of judicial protection was its most im portant contribution, it was not its only one. It also devoted its energies to safeguarding property rights and to strengthening the fairness of the procedures of the courts themselves. For these, and especially the latter, its influence has been substantial. That it had little to say of the rights of expression, and nothing to say of equality of rights in the modern sense, resulted largely from the absence of such issues from the docket. As already shown, the path which the man of property beat to the Court and the reception he got on arriving there were ready and available to others when times changed.

That the Court succeeded, against heavy opposition, in asserting individual rights for a generation gave a firm grounding to rights. Such guarantees came to form in the popular mind an aspect of the Rule of Law. The concept of a government of laws was seen as a kind of antiseptic spread over officialdom to check those arbitrary impulses which forever thrive where power is held. The Court found the executive the easiest to hold to the test of rights. Localism and the nature of the federal system made the states harder to keep in line, and yet the Court's repeated successes here helped set the practice. The Rule of Law might extend even to Congress, although here the Court proceeded with caution.

Some months after Justice Johnson had ruled illegal certain embargo orders of the Jefferson Administration and had granted clearance papers to a Charleston shipowner, he met with criticism of a somewhat novel sort. The grand jury of the Circuit Court in Savannah, Johnson presiding, formally presented as a grievance his headstrong and ill-founded interference with the execution of the laws. In reply Johnson told the jury:

If you are prepared, gentlemen, to waive the government of the laws and submit without repining to every errour or encroachment of the several Departments of government, avow it to your fellow citizens, and prevail on them to abolish the Constitution, or get into office a feeble and submissive Judiciary. For what cause are we now reproached? For interposing the authority of the laws in the protection of individual rights, of your rights and the rights of succeeding generations.[38]

The passage expresses concisely the aim, the mission, and the achievement of the Marshall Justices. Subsequent history has only accentuated the key role which those Justices imparted to the judiciary in the protection of civil liberties.

[38] Quoted in Warren, *op. cit.*, I, 337.

IV

INTERNATIONAL ASPECTS

[QUINCY WRIGHT]

UNIVERSITY OF CHICAGO

Freedom and Human Rights under International Law

THE difficulties faced by the Federal Government of the United States in efforts to enforce the Fourteenth Amendment are small compared to the difficulties faced by the United Nations in efforts to enforce the human rights provisions of the Charter. The basic problem is the same in both cases, that of the legal competence and social desirability of superauthority intervening in the struggle of man versus the state.

LEGAL AND POLITICAL POINTS OF VIEW

From the point of view of international law, the issue concerns the definition of the terms "intervention" and "domestic jurisdiction." That law permits other governments or international organizations to make representations to a state on any matter which affects their interests, provided that the action taken does not amount to "intervention," and it permits certain forms of intervention on matters which are not within the "domestic jurisdiction" of the state addressed. Thus, an organ of the United Nations is competent to pass resolutions concerning "human rights" unless the resolution is both an "intervention" and an encroachment on the "domestic jurisdiction" of a state.

This principle seems to be accepted, but there has been endless debate on the meaning of these two terms.[1]

From the political point of view, psychological problems are involved which are extremely difficult to appraise. From this point of view a Commission set up by the United Nations General Assembly to consider the racial situation in the Union of South Africa reported in 1954:

Even in quarters basically hostile to any racial segregation and wholeheartedly devoted to international cooperation, the opinion has been expressed that advice from outside could do more harm than good and that it was liable to offend national susceptibilities and to contribute to a stiffening of the positions taken up by the opposing parties. The Commission naturally realizes . . . that any measures to reduce racial conflicts must be the result of efforts initiated within the Union itself; it was in order to meet these views that the Commission, as a preliminary step, collected and analyzed the various solutions suggested by different individuals and groups in the Union of South Africa itself. It cannot believe, however, that such a danger really exists. The work of international bodies on a problem such as the racial situation in South Africa must be regarded as a brotherly endeavor on the part of the human community to help one of its members in difficulties. It is to be hoped that international offers of good offices for the settlement of dangerous racial conflicts or deteriorating colonial disputes will be increasingly understood and appreciated in this light.[2]

The United Nations has recognized the different conclusions which may result from a legal and political point of view on the issue of protecting human rights, but there has been a great difference of opinion as to which point of view should take priority. This difference is reflected, particularly, in the debates on whether claims of "domestic jurisdiction" should be submitted for advisory opinion to the International Court of Justice. In general, United Nations organs have not made such requests, often by very closely divided votes, thus in-

[1] I have summarized this in an article entitled "Domestic Jurisdiction and the Competence of United Nations Organs" in Commission to Study the Organization of Peace, *Charter Review Conference,* Ninth Report (New York, 1955), pp. 42 ff., reprinted in Academia Interamericana de Derecho Comparado e Internacional, *Cursos Monográficos* (Havana, Cuba, 1956), V, 362 ff. An extensive documentation is printed by Louis B. Sohn, *Cases on United Nations Law* (Brooklyn: Foundation Press, 1956), pp. 575 ff.

[2] Second Report of the UN Commission on the Racial Situation in the Union of South Africa, August 26, 1955, *General Assembly Official Reports,* IX, Supp. 16 (A/2719), p. 88; Sohn, *United Nations Law,* pp. 575 ff.

dicating a prevailing opinion that the course to be followed should be controlled by political opinion in the United Nations organ, rather than by legal definition. The result of this attitude has been that, while the General Assembly has frequently passed resolutions calling for a better observance of human rights by member states, the member addressed has often taken the view that in doing so the General Assembly has exceeded its competence by intervening in the domestic jurisdiction of that state and that, consequently, the state is free to ignore the resolution. The problem has been faced particularly in connection with the laws of South Africa discriminating against Indians and natives, and on this problem the impasse, just referred to, has arisen. It is possible that a clearer legal definition by the International Court defining both the competence of the United Nations organs and the obligations of members under the Charter would assist in solution.[3] However, to decide whether it would, more fundamental aspects of the problem must be considered. It must be recalled that in the United States, judicial decisions of the Supreme Court have not solved the problem of racial discrimination in the Southern states.

NATIONAL OR INTERNATIONAL RESPONSIBILITY

It is said on the one hand that each state is sovereign, in the sense that it makes law for those within its territory and that the individuals subject to its sovereignty have no rights except those accorded them by that law. Consequently, the intervention of a superauthority to maintain human rights denies the sovereignty of the state and the authority of its law and misconstrues the nature of legal rights by using the term "human rights."

This argument is sometimes justified by introducing sociological conceptions of the relation of the individual to the society and culture within which he lives. The state is an aspect of that society and its ethical, religious, and legal system is an aspect of that culture. The latter, in accord with the extreme relativism of many anthropologists, provides the ultimate standards of behavior for the members of a society.[4] Attempts to enforce the standards of a different state, society,

[3] See below, notes 49, 50.
[4] E. A. Westermarck, *Ethical Relativity* (London: Kegan Paul, 1932); Q. Wright, *The Study of International Relations* (New York: Appleton, Century, Crofts, 1955), p. 442.

or culture are branded as a form of imperialism, ethically unjustified, because a satisfactory adjustment of the desires of conflicting individuals and the values of conflicting normative systems within the society and the adjustment of the requirements of the society as a whole to these internal conflicts and to the external demands which it faces can only, it is said, be achieved by internal processes of accommodation, whether cultural, social, or legal. Externally imposed standards can never be enduring and will only stimulate frustration or violence. Cultures, societies, and states, it is said, must develop from internal sources. Their very existence is a product of their "self-determination."

To this argument it is answered that no state is completely sovereign. States within a confederation are to some extent bound by federal law, and sovereign nations are bound by international law. Law is a hierarchy of competences, pyramiding up to international authorities administering the basic norms of international law. Furthermore, no state or other human institution exists for itself: it exists for the individuals which it serves. The state is for man, not man for the state; ultimately the rights of the individual flow not from the state, but from the nature of man as a social and rational animal. Consequently, superauthorities can properly intervene to enforce the law of the larger community and to protect the natural rights of individuals when the state ignores them.[5]

Ethical arguments can also be adduced to support this theory. While it may be true, say the philosophers in reply to the anthropologists, that primitive peoples regard the local culture as an absolute standard of values, with the rise of civilization, with the differentiation of religious, ethical, legal, and other value systems, with the increase of communications beyond the group creating an awareness of other cultures and of their different standards, a process of comparison becomes inevitable for rational man, and a criticism of local norms by higher norms emerges from this process. Furthermore, religious and ethical geniuses through introspection and insight into the nature of man proclaim value standards said to be universal and attributed to

---

[5] Hersh Lauterpacht, *International Law and Human Rights* (London: Stevens, 1950); Wright, *International Relations*, pp. 186, 441; R. Elburton Smith, "Value Judgment and the Social Sciences," *Bull. Am. Assoc. University Professors*, 35 (1949), 628.

God, or nature, or history. These also serve as standards for criticizing local or specialized value systems.[6]

This process is said to have been exhibited in the legal history of ancient Rome as that city became a world empire bringing numerous local legal systems into contact. The praetors and jurisconsults criticized the civil law of the twelve tables by reference to the *jus gentium*, discovered by comparing local legal systems, and to the *jus naturale*, discovered in the speculative writings of philosophers and poets, and from this criticism they built the more universal system of law codified by Justinian and inherited in large measure by the principal legal systems of continental Europe.[7]

A similar progressive influence in developing local value systems into higher systems of law and morality, better serving the individual, is said to have marked the course of modern empire, though in this case colonies, insisting upon the right of self-determination, have frequently expressed a different opinion, perceiving in the activities of imperialism and colonialism only a suppression of the genius of national cultures as alleged by advocates of the first theory.[8]

The confusion of these two lines of argument has been manifested in the debate over the question of including the right of "self-determination" in the "human rights covenants." The opponents of this program say that self-determination is not an individual but a collective right, if indeed it is a right at all, and so has no place in the covenants.[9] If, however, this position is accepted, then the question arises, What is the collectivity that has the right? Is it the imperial state recognized as a person in international law? Or is it the colony, minority, or people demanding self-determination and aspiring to such recognition? Clearly, simultaneous "self-determination" by these different collec-

[6] Julian Huxley, *Knowledge, Morality, and Destiny* (Washington, D.C.: William Alanson White Psychiatric Foundation, 1951); Wright, *International Relations*, pp. 444 ff., 451 ff., 485 ff., 510 ff.

[7] James Bryce, "The Law of Nature," in *Studies in History and Jurisprudence* (London: Oxford University Press, 1901), II, 586 ff.; Wright, *International Relations*, p. 450; "Equality in International Law and International Relations," in *Aspects of Human Equality*, Fifteenth Symposium of the Conference on Science, Philosophy, and Religion, Lyman Bryson *et al.*, eds. (New York: Harper, 1957), p. 343.

[8] Wright, *International Relations*, pp. 186 ff.; *Mandates under the League of Nations* (Chicago, 1930), pp. 8 ff., 549 ff.

[9] *Issues before the Eleventh General Assembly*, Anne Winslow, ed., *International Conciliation*, November 1956, pp. 206 ff.; Sohn, *United Nations Law*, pp. 806 ff.

tivities would be likely to precipitate conflict. If, on the other hand, self-determination is an individual right, then all political authority would cease. Every individual could himself determine to change allegiance and to assert his own sovereignty and capacity to make his own law. In any case such individual self-determination would conflict with self-determination by either the nationality group or the imperial state which claims his allegiance. If law is to exist at all, it seems clear that self-determination as an individual right can only mean self-determination, or liberty, under law. This implies that some society—the nationality, the state, the United Nations, or the community of nations—is competent to make, or at least interpret, the law. International protection of the right of self-determination, and indeed of all rights, whether human or group, implies, therefore, superiority of the law of the United Nations or of the community of nations over the law of any particular state, nationality, or lesser group. It is difficult to speak of either law or rights until one has first identified the legal community or legal order and the persons or subjects who have rights under it. It is difficult to do this because, in fact, individuals are related to many societies which interpenetrate in complex patterns. Particular legal orders and their subjects can be isolated from this complex only by somewhat arbitrary decisions maintained by custom, authority, agreement, and a measure of rational analysis.

Consideration of the opposing views concerning the roles of the nation and the society of nations in relation to human rights is likely to induce hesitancy to accept either, without qualification, as a reasonable solution of the problem of human rights. There is virtue in local self-government and local lawmaking, but there is also virtue in the broader understanding of man provided by the experience of larger societies with the opportunity to view man under diversified conditions. A balance between law resting on local experience and law resting on universal experience, therefore, seems desirable. Federalism has sought to achieve this balance in emerging national societies, and the United Nations Charter seeks to achieve it in the modern society of nations.

The history of modern civilization, as of past civilizations according to Toynbee, has oscillated between periods of imperial or humanistic cosmopolitanism when the universal idea dominated and periods of feudal or nationalistic isolationism when the local idea predominated.[10] Between have been periods when international law and international organization have sought to balance the two.

EXPERIENCES OF THE UNITED STATES
AND THE UNITED NATIONS

The parallelism, referred to in the first paragraph of this essay, may be traced in the history of the United States and the United Nations. The concern for human rights by the central organs of the United States and of the United Nations arose from similar circumstances. In the United States the tradition that man is prior to the state, that individual rights derive from nature, and that the Federal Government is concerned with their protection arose from experiences, interpreted as violations of such rights by imperial Britain and denounced in the Declaration of Independence. The Constitution and the Bill of Rights, however, because oppression during the colonial period had been attributed to superauthority, were mainly concerned with protecting individuals against the Federal Government, not against the state governments. It was not until the inconsistency of slavery with the human right of equality, affirmed in the Declaration of Independence, had been vigorously propagandized in the first half of the nineteenth century that the danger of violation of human rights by state laws caused much concern. The issue had, it is true, been raised in connection with the Contract Clause of the Constitution, sometimes with considerable emotional fervor, as in the *Dartmouth College* case. The activities of the abolitionists and the exigencies of foreign policy converted the Civil War, begun as a war to save the Union, into a war for human rights violated by the slave states. It was natural that the victory of the Union should have been followed by amendments to the Constitution providing for the enforcement upon the states of the basic human rights for which the Union had fought.

The modern family of nations originated at the time of the discoveries, the Renaissance, and the Reformation which had shattered the hierarchical feudal system of the Middle Ages and had facilitated the self-determination of national territorial states utilizing the recent

[10] Q. Wright, "Recognition and Self-Determination," *Proceedings,* Am. Soc. Int. Law, 1954, pp. 23 ff., and *A Study of War* (Chicago, 1942), pp. 90 ff., 911.

inventions of gunpowder and the printing press to destroy feudal fortresses and to create a consciousness of national vernaculars. These states, however, accepted the ethical theories of classical Christian civilization and especially the idea of human rights flowing from "natural law." The international jurists of the sixteenth century had no hesitancy in asserting that territorial states, though sovereign, were bound by the principles of that law to respect the natural rights of their citizens. This was, indeed, set forth by Francis of Victoria and other jurists as a justification for the Spanish conquest of Mexico. The empire of Montezuma had, they said, denied the natural right of the Spaniards to engage in trade and missionary activity. To protect this natural right of their subjects, the Spanish monarch was justified in conquest. Bartolomé de Las Casas and others argued, less successfully, that Spain was obliged to respect the natural right of the Indians to freedom from slavery and massacre.

Natural law as a foundation for rights, both of the individual and the state, was the foundation stone of international law, but in the seventeenth, eighteenth, and nineteenth centuries the conception of militant state sovereignty developed through the necessities of power politics in a world only slightly controlled by law and through the propaganda of nationalism in a world in which, after the French Revolution, popular democracy was superseding dynastic government. With this conception of sovereignty the idea that international law protected the rights of man diminished, though it was still to be found in the treatises of Pufendorf, Vattel, and other "Naturalists" and more recently in the school of international lawyers [11] who asserted that individuals are subjects of international law. These writers, however, were a minority. The prevailing doctrine of the nineteenth century was a positivism which conceived international law as flowing from the sovereignty of states and ascribed jural personality only to sovereign states, leaving individuals to the discretionary protection of the state of which they were nationals.[12]

The idea of human rights was, however, kept alive by the incorporation of bills of rights in national constitutions based upon the British

[11] For example, John Westlake, Wilhelm Kaufman, and Nicolas Politis. See Q. Wright, *Research in International Law since the War* (Washington, D.C.: Carnegie Endowment, 1930), p. 32, and *A Study of War*, p. 909.

[12] Q. Wright, "Legal Positivism and the Nuremberg Judgment," *Am. Jour. Int. Law*, 42 (1948), 405 ff.

Magna Carta and the seventeenth-century Bill of Rights and the philosophical speculations of Locke, Montesquieu, and Rousseau, who had turned the classical and medieval conceptions of natural law to more revolutionary purposes. The interpretation and enforcement of such constitutional bills of rights were, however, left to the authorities of the nation. The French Declaration of the Rights of Man and Citizen followed Rousseau in solving the conflict between national sovereignty and human rights by the assumption that in a democracy the "general will" of the nation necessarily conformed to the will of the citizens exercising their natural freedom in voting.[13]

The nineteenth century saw some international protection of human rights by general conventions intended to prevent abuses of minorities and aborigines and to extend some protection to soldiers and workers. It also witnessed the development of diplomatic protection by states of their nationals abroad, on the ground that the national was an interest of the state which could protest if he was denied justice or suffered from a "want of due diligence" in being afforded protection by the authorities of the state of residence. There were also some cases of humanitarian intervention to protect individuals against barbarities which "shocked the conscience of mankind," even when committed by their own government. These recognitions of human rights did not, however, shake the general recognition, accorded by international law, of the sovereignty of states and the subjection of individuals to the jurisdiction and the law of the state of residence.

World War I, though waged mainly to protect the rights of small nations, Belgium in particular, gave a greater recognition to the theory that the international order should concern itself with human rights. The League of Nations provided procedures for protecting minorities and the inhabitants of mandated territories, and the International Labor Organization was established for protection of workers. The latter organization has gradually developed an extensive code of labor rights stemming from the brief declaration on the subject in its constitution.

It was not until World War II, however, that the international protection of human rights became a major issue. This war, it is true, began as a war to preserve the balance of power or the "European

[13] Q. Wright, *Problems of Stability and Progress in International Relations* (Berkeley: University of California Press, 1954), p. 295.

system" against the aggressions of Hitler and his Axis Allies. Thus it had a certain analogy to the initial objectives of the American Civil War. But with the development of public awareness of Hitler's barbarities to the Jews and the announcement of the Four Freedoms by President Franklin D. Roosevelt in January 1941, the war became a war for human rights as had the American Civil War. In his historic message nearly a year before American entry into the war, President Roosevelt said:

In the future days which we seek to make secure, we look forward to a world founded upon four essential human freedoms. The first is the freedom of speech and expression—everywhere in the world. The second is freedom of every person to worship God in his own way—everywhere in the world. The third is freedom from want, which translated into world terms, means economic understanding which will secure to every nation a healthy peace-time life for its inhabitants—everywhere in the world. The fourth is freedom from fear, which translated into world terms, means a world-wide reduction of armaments to such a point and in such a thorough fashion, that no nation will be in a position to commit an act of physical aggression against any neighbor—anywhere in the world. That is no vision of a distant millennium. It is a definite basis for a kind of world attainable in our own time and generation.

The Atlantic Charter was signed by President Roosevelt and Prime Minister Churchill on August 14, 1941, and was later incorporated by reference into the Declaration of the United Nations of January 1, 1942, after American entry into the war. The last two freedoms were explicitly referred to in this document which called for a peace "which will afford assurance that all the men in all the lands may live out their lives in freedom from fear and want." President Roosevelt, in his message to Congress on August 21, 1941, said:

It is also unnecessary for me to point out that the declaration of principles includes of necessity the world need for freedom of religion and freedom of information. No society of the world organized under the announced principles could survive without these freedoms which are a part of the whole freedom for which we strive.

The Four Freedoms were repeatedly referred to during the war by President Roosevelt and other statesmen of the United Nations. Thus, on May 29, 1941, British Foreign Minister Anthony Eden said, "We have found in President Roosevelt's message to Congress in January

1941, the keynote of our own purpose." And Viscount Halifax, British Ambassador at Washington, on March 25, 1941, referring to the American Declaration of Independence and the President's speech, said:

I would assert for all men today: the right to think, speak and act freely within the law, and to have free access to the thoughts of others; the right of free association, both national and international, with their fellowmen; the right to believe and worship as conscience may dictate. It is the vindication of these rights that men passionately desire. . . . And so the principal war aim of my people and of those who are fighting with us is to win this life-and-death struggle for the cause of human freedom.

A statement issued by the Office of War Information of the United States in August 1942 elaborated the meaning and the means of implementation of the Four Freedoms in greater detail, emphasizing that "freedom of whatever sort is relative. Nations united by a common effort to create a better world are obviously not projecting a Utopia in which nobody will want for anything." It said:

The first two freedoms—freedom of speech and freedom of religion—are cultural. They are prerogatives of the thinking man, of the creative civilized human being. Sometime, as in the United States, they are guaranteed by organized law. They are rather clearly understood, and the laws protecting them are continually being revised and adjusted to preserve their basic meaning. Freedom from fear and from want, on the other hand, are not part of our culture, but part of our environment—they concern the facts of our lives rather than the thoughts of our minds. Men are unafraid or well-fed or both, according to the conditions under which they live. This, then, is a credo to which the representatives of twenty-nine nations have subscribed—not a promise made by any group of men to any other group. It is only the people themselves who can create the conditions favoring these essential freedoms which they are now repurchasing in the bazaar of war and paying for with their lives.

It is clear that the difficulties of realization were being envisaged even before the war was over, but it is also clear that the United Nations had committed themselves to the cause of human rights with determination and enthusiasm.[14]

It is, therefore, not surprising that the United Nations Charter, signed before the war was over, should have included the protection

[14] Q. Wright, "Human Rights and the World Order," in Commission to Study the Organization of Peace, *International Conciliation* (1943), pp. 238 ff.

of human rights as a major objective. The Preamble declares that "we the people of the United Nations" are "determined" not only to prevent war but "to reaffirm faith in fundamental human rights, in the dignity and worth of the human person, in the equal rights of men and women and of nations large and small." This close relationship of the rights of individuals and of nations was maintained in subsequent articles which repeat, in no less than six contexts,[15] the objective of "promoting and encouraging respect for human rights and for fundamental freedoms for all without distinctions as to race, sex, language or religion," and a human rights commission is authorized (Art. 68). At the same time the Charter affirms the principle of the "sovereign equality of all its members" (Art. 2, par. 1) and asserts that "nothing contained in the present Charter shall authorize the United Nations to intervene in matters which are essentially within the domestic jurisdiction of any state" (Art. 2, par. 7).

The problem of effectively protecting human rights, while at the same time respecting the sovereignty of its members, has faced the United Nations with a problem that remains unsolved after a dozen years of discussion by jurists and by governments in the General Assembly, the Economic and Social Council, and the Human Rights Commission. Statesmen on both sides of the Iron Curtain profess allegiance to the idea, though with differences of interpretation. The Asian-African group, conveniently referred to as the "Bandung" group, differ from both. The major human right for which they have contended is the right of "self-determination," vigorously opposed by the colonial powers of Western Europe and, when used in a context applicable to its satellites, by the Soviet Union. The Soviet Union and other Communist states have sought to concentrate attention upon economic and social rights, such as the right to work, to eat, to housing, and to social security, and have insisted that civil liberties and judicial protection shall be so qualified as not to interfere with the effective authority of government—a position often echoed by the Bandung group. The United States and the Western powers, on the other hand, emphasize civil liberties, such as freedom of religion, speech, and opinion, with a minimum of exceptions, and rights to protection from unfair judicial or administrative procedures. They have tended to regard economic and social rights and the right of self-

[15] UN Charter, Arts. 1 (3), 13, 55 (6), 56, 62 (2), 76 (c).

determination in a category distinct from the traditional human rights, to be dealt with by wholly different methods.

THE POSITION OF INTERNATIONAL LAW

Apart from the United Nations Charter and other treaties, modern international law seems to deny the individual a status as subject of that law.[16] It recognizes, however, the capacity of states to give him such a status by treaty. It also recognizes the right of states to insist on fair treatment of their nationals by other states. Furthermore, it recognizes a right of states to intervene to protect individuals, whether they are nationals or not, who are enduring brutalities that "shock the conscience of mankind." Finally, it recognizes that individuals who commit offenses against the law of nations, such as piracy, crimes against humanity, and war crimes, are subject to punishment by any state that obtains physical control of them, irrespective of the attitude of the state of which they are nationals. These principles seem to imply that the United Nations or other international organizations may properly facilitate the conclusion of general treaties for the protection of human rights and may take appropriate measures even amounting to intervention in a state's territory in order to protect persons in their official service, to protect individuals against extreme brutality, and to punish offenses against the law of nations. International organizations, especially the United Nations, have assumed authority to take such measures.

There has been a considerable body of international law on the last three of these problems. States whose nationals have migrated, established enterprises, or invested abroad have gained general acceptance of the proposition that the standard of protection due their nationals in foreign territory is determined by international law as it has developed in diplomatic practice and arbitral tribunals and as it is established by the principles of law of civilized nations in their domestic administration. This position has been contested by some states, particularly those of Latin America and Asia, that have re-

[16] Wesley L. Gould, *An Introduction to International Law* (New York: Harper, 1957), pp. 205 ff.; Wright, *Problems of Stability and Progress*, pp. 237 ff.; *Contemporary International Law: A Balance Sheet* (New York: Doubleday, 1955), pp. 19 ff.; Charles De Visscher, *Theory and Reality in Public International Law* (Princeton, N.J.: Princeton University Press, 1957), p. 125.

ceived rather than sent foreign capital and economic enterprise. Such states have tended to insist that the standard to be accorded to aliens is that accorded their own citizens. This position has, however, been accepted in international law as only the minimum. If a state accords treatment to its own nationals below the international standard, it must do better by aliens. Procedures of diplomatic and arbitral practice have developed the terms "denial of justice" and "due diligence" in protection, with a meaning in international law closely resembling the terms "due process of law" and "equal protection of the laws" in American constitutional jurisprudence.[17] The World Court has recognized this standard and its applicability to the protection by the United Nations of its agencies in the performance of official functions in the territory of a state even though a nonmember.[18]

Humanitarian intervention is a less strongly established procedure. It occurred in the nineteenth century and the early part of the twentieth century in cases of extreme barbarities against minorities, such as Armenians in Turkey and Jews in Russia, and to protect natives in colonies against extreme inhumanity, such as the Putamaya Indians in Peru and the Negroes in the Congo. The concept, however, was not so defined as to be free from abuses. The vagueness of the conception of "acts which shock the conscience of mankind" made it possible to utilize such intervention as a justification for policies of imperialist expansion or the discrediting of a rival state. [19]

The concept of offenses against the law of nations appears in the Constitution of the United States [20] and was well recognized in the eighteenth century to apply to piracy and offenses against diplomatic

[17] E. M. Borchard, *Diplomatic Protection of Citizens Abroad* (New York, 1916), secs. 13–15, 133, 138–40; "The 'Minimum Standard' of the Treatment of Aliens," *Proceedings,* Am. Soc. Int. Law, 1939, pp. 51 ff.; Clyde Eagleton, *The Responsibility of States in International Law* (New York, 1931), pp. 176 ff.; Q. Wright, "Due Process and International Law," *Am. Journ. Int. Law,* 40 (1946), 398; E. C. Stowell, *International Law* (New York, 1931), pp. 176 ff.

[18] Reparation for Injuries Suffered in the Service of the UN, Int. Court of Justice, *Reports,* 1949, p. 174; Sohn, *United Nations Law,* p. 249.

[19] Stowell, *op. cit.,* pp. 349 ff.; *Intervention in International Law* (Washington, D.C., 1921), pp. 51 ff.

[20] Art. 1, sec. 8, par. 10. The present writer has defined such an offense as an "act committed with intent to violate a fundamental interest protected by international law or with knowledge that the act will probably violate such an interest, and which may not be adequately furnished by the exercise of the normal criminal jurisdiction of any State" (*Am. Jour. Int. Law,* 41 [1947], 56).

agents. The list of such offenses has been expanded by treaty and was given more general recognition by the Nuremberg War Crimes trials and the Genocide Convention. Such offenses include the counterfeiting of foreign currency, offenses against the law of war, offenses against humanity, and political offenses such as crimes of terrorism and offenses against the peace. The last-named include the initiation of aggressive war and "warmongering" by propaganda and other activities detrimental to peace or international security. Of these offenses, those most closely related to human rights are the offenses against humanity, including the offense of genocide, and similar offenses which so "shock the conscience of mankind" as to justify "humanitarian intervention." [21]

While customary international law gives some protection to human rights through the procedures of diplomatic protection, humanitarian intervention, and universal jurisdiction over offenses against humanity, the principal development of such protection has been through treaties and especially the United Nations Charter and conventions made under its auspices and in pursuance of its purposes.

THE UNITED NATIONS PROGRAM

The United Nations is committed to the promotion of respect for human rights as a purpose second only to that of maintaining peace. These two purposes are in fact closely related. Barbarities that shock the conscience of mankind and persecutions of minorities, especially if they have the nationality of the population in another state, have been an important cause of war. Suppression of freedom of speech and press and terrorization by secret police, characteristic of totalitarian states, tend to prevent contacts of the population so oppressed with other peoples and to create a fanatical and uninformed national opinion, unaware of the attitudes of other nations or of the conditions of world opinion and, therefore, dangerous to the peace.

On the other hand, war is inimical to human rights. All govern-

---

[21] Q. Wright, "War Criminals," *Am. Jour. Int. Law*, 39 (1945), 257, 282; "The Law of the Nuremberg Trial," *ibid.*, 41 (1947), 38, 60; "The Crime of 'War-Mongering,'" *ibid.*, 42 (1948), 128; "International Law and Guilt by Association," *ibid.*, 43 (1949), 746; "Proposal for an International Criminal Court," *ibid.*, 46 (1952), 60 ff.; and Raphael Lemkin, "Genocide as a Crime under International Law," *ibid.*, 41 (1947), 145 ff.

Aspects of Liberty

ments in times of war or high international tension impose some restrictions on civil liberties, and states with aggressive policies continually maintain such restrictions. Respect for human rights has, in fact, developed historically only in periods of law and peace and especially among nations such as Great Britain, the United States, and Switzerland somewhat sheltered from warfare by natural barriers of sea or mountain.

These relationships of human rights and war assume that the major human rights are those usually called civil liberties, implying restraints upon governmental interference with individual freedom. Certain so-called economic and social rights, such as the opportunity to work, to obtain an education, to have sufficient food and housing, to enjoy social security, and to have equality of status, may, under some circumstances, be advanced by socialistic activity of governments, and such activity may sometimes be facilitated by restraints upon individual liberty of speech, economic enterprise, and other civil liberties. Governmental activity of this kind may be less resisted in times of war or high tension, and, reciprocally, the advance of socialistic activity inducing totalitarian government may be productive of aggression and war. Thus, the relationship to war of advances in economic and social rights may be the opposite of advance in civil liberties.[22] General discussions of human rights have, however, interpreted the term to apply primarily to civil liberties. This is clearly indicated by the Preamble to the Universal Declaration of Human Rights, which also indicates the relationship between disrespect for human rights and war.

Whereas recognition of the inherent dignity and of the equal and inalienable rights of all members of the human family is the foundation of freedom, justice and peace in the world,

Whereas disregard and contempt for human rights have resulted in barbarous acts which have outraged the conscience of mankind, and the advent of a world in which human beings shall enjoy freedom of speech and belief and freedom from fear and want has been proclaimed as the highest aspiration of the common people,

Whereas it is essential, if man is not to be compelled to have recourse, as a last resort, to rebellion against tyranny and oppression, that human rights should be protected by the rule of law,

[22] Wright, A Study of War, pp. 1162, 1168 ff.

Whereas, it is essential to promote the development of friendly relations between nations . . .[23]

The first article of the Declaration asserts that "all human beings are born free and equal in dignity and rights. They are endowed with reason and conscience and should act towards one another in a spirit of brotherhood." Civil liberties are then stated first in the Declaration, and the economic and social rights are stated at the end.

This statement, as well as the Preamble to the Charter itself, indicates that the interest of the United Nations in human rights arises not only from the relation of violation of those rights to war, but also as a goal in itself supported by the liberal political philosophy which had developed in modern history and dominated the thinking of the majority of the states that framed the Charter. Respect for human rights is considered essential to the development of individual personality which is considered a prime value of that philosophy. While this philosophy originated in Western Europe, inspired by classical and Christian thought, it is also supported by most of the other great religions and has been recognized in the national constitutions of most states, including even the totalitarian states.[24] This philosophy has also been given recognition in international documents of the nineteenth century inspired by both humanitarianism and liberalism. The Institute of International Law resolved in 1929:

That the juridical conscience of the civilized world demands the recognition for the individual of rights preserved from all infringement on the part of the state; . . . that it is important to extend to the entire world international recognition of the rights of man.[25]

These rights were declared to include equal protection of civil rights; educational and economic opportunity without distinction of sex, race, language, or religion; the free practice of religion; and the free use and teaching of language.

The activity of the United Nations in the field has been a responsi-

[23] The Universal Declaration and other UN documents are conveniently collected in Louis B. Sohn, *Basic Documents of the United Nations* (Brooklyn: Foundation Press, 1956).

[24] Wright, *A Study of War*, pp. 169 ff., and "Human Rights and the World Order."

[25] *Am. Jour. Int. Law*, 35 (1941), 63. A number of international jurists such as Fiore, Martens, Snow, and Benthom have attempted to formulate human rights. See Borchard, *Diplomatic Protection of Citizens Abroad*, p. 15.

bility of the General Assembly, acting on the advice of the Economic and Social Council, in turn advised by the Human Rights Commission and by special subcommittees which have been set up on the status of women, on minorities, and on other subjects. The International Law Commission established by the General Assembly has given some attention to the subject, especially in connection with crimes against the peace and security of mankind and genocide.

The work of the United Nations in this field has been concerned with (1) the definition of human rights, (2) the establishment of legal obligations to respect them, (3) the provision of international procedures to ensure observance of these obligations, (4) education on the subject and, for that purpose, acquisition and distribution of information, and (5) political action to stop notorious violations of human rights.

DEFINITION OF HUMAN RIGHTS

The Charter does not define human rights but identifies them with "fundamental freedoms" and asserts that they belong to "all without distinction as to race, sex, language or religion." The conception of human rights supported by many national bills of rights identifies them with civil liberties or rights of the individual against abuses by the state, whether these abuses involve arbitrary *physical* restraints such as unjustifiable arrest, unfair trial, excessive punishment, unreasonable searches, and seizures or other deprivations of life, liberty, or property without due process of law or arbitrary *moral* restraints such as unreasonable restrictions or discriminations on speech, press, opinion, religion, or association.

This conception, however, has often been broadened to include not merely protection of the individual from the government, but also his protection from abuses by other individuals, such as are involved in crime, social disorder, and inhumane institutions like slavery, peonage, forced labor, and the subjection of women. To meet this responsibility, governments must legislate to eliminate abusive institutions, must maintain police and criminal administration to protect individuals from violence and fraud, and must administer civil law to afford remedies for civil injuries. A want of "due diligence" to meet these responsibilities has long been considered a ground for complaint under international law if, as a result, nationals of the complaining state have been injured. Assumption of a specific obligation of states to punish genocide and other crimes against humanity has been urged by the United Nations, and a convention for this purpose has been widely ratified.[26] The United Nations has also produced a draft code of offenses against the peace and security of mankind and a draft statement for an international criminal court.[27]

But even beyond this, respect for human rights has been said to require a political system which will give the citizen some control over, or at least opportunity to escape from, his government. Political rights such as participation in elections, the possession of a nationality, the right of national self-determination, freedom to emigrate, and the right of asylum have been considered human rights, and most of them have been included in the Universal Declaration. Such positive proscriptions affecting the basic form and policy of government raise more controversial issues and have aroused opposition from some states.[28]

Even more controversial has been the demand for government action to assure *freedom* of economic activity, such as the right to acquire property and to engage freely in economic enterprise, and also *equality* of economic and social opportunity, assured by the right to work, to receive fair compensation, to enjoy social security and leisure, and to be provided education, a minimum standard of living, and cultural opportunities. Most Western countries assure freedom of economic opportunity by protecting the acquisition and use of property, but the constitutions of some states in the late nineteenth and the twentieth centuries under socialistic influence have tended to modify property rights by various guarantees of equality of opportunity. The International Labor Organization has developed an extensive code of labor rights with this objective. In the United States, the "New Deal" initiated an emphasis upon such "social and

[26] In 1957 the genocide convention had been ratified by 55 states including the Soviet Union but not the United States. This offense was included among the "offenses against humanity of the Nuremberg trial" and among the "offenses against the peace and security of mankind" adopted by the International Law Commission in 1954. See Louis B. Sohn, *Cases and Other Materials in World Law* (Brooklyn: Foundation Press, 1950), pp. 1019 ff.

[27] Sohn, *Basic Documents,* pp. 99 ff.; see also above note 21.

[28] See above note 9.

economic rights." The National Resources Planning Board in 1941 proposed a bill of rights with this emphasis,[29] and President Franklin D. Roosevelt demanded freedom from fear and want along with freedom of speech and religion. A number of unofficial organizations proposed bills of human rights during and after the war which generally included provisions of this as well as of the three preceding types.[30]

With this material before it, the General Assembly included all these types of human rights in its Universal Declaration, proclaimed on December 10, 1948, and unanimously adopted by the Assembly, with the Soviet group of countries abstaining.[31] Of the 30 Articles in this document, 15 provide civil liberties, 4 protections against crime or abusive institutions, 4 political rights, and 7 economic and social rights. The Declaration is not presented as law, or even as a draft to become law by the process of treaty ratification, but "as a common standard of achievement for all peoples and all nations." It calls for teaching and education to promote respect for these rights and freedoms and for appropriate national and international measures to secure their "recognition and observance," not only in the home territories, but in the colonies of the member states. Though lacking legal validity, this document has been utilized in a number of national constitutions and in treaties and has been generally thought to define the concept of human rights. It does not include specifically the "right of self-determination," which has subsequently become highly controversial, unless the "right to a nationality" and the "right to change" nationality (Art. 15) and the "right to freedom of peaceful assembly and association" (Art. 20), all applicable in colonies as well

[29] National Defense Planning Board, *After Defense—What?* (Washington, D.C., August 1941). This document was laid before Congress by President Roosevelt on January 14, 1942. See also "Declaration of the Rights of Man" by H. G. Wells, 1940, and "Platform of World Citizenship," in World Citizens Association, *The World's Destiny and the United States,* Henri Bonnet, ed. (Chicago, 1941), pp. 101 ff., 296 ff.

[30] American Law Institute, "Statement of Essential Human Rights," *Annals,* Am. Acad. of Pol. and Soc. Science, 243 (1946), 18 ff.; Commission to Study the Organization of Peace, "Bill of Human Rights," *International Conciliation,* 1946, pp. 558 ff.; H. Lauterpacht, *An International Bill of the Rights of Man* (New York, 1945), p. 230; Sohn, *World Law,* pp. 536 ff.

[31] Sohn, *World Law,* pp. 541 ff., and *Basic Documents,* pp. 132 ff.

as in homelands (Art. 2), can be said to add up to a right of national self-determination.

The Universal Declaration was undoubtedly an important achievement. It has provided the basis for subsequent action, legal, administrative, political, and educational, and presents in tangible form the conception of human rights in the contemporary world.[32]

LEGAL SANCTIONS

The second step in the United Nations program was to give more precise definition and legal sanction to the rights set forth in the Declaration. The extent to which a legal obligation to respect human rights is established by the Charter itself is controversial. Article 56 provides that:

All members pledge themselves to take joint and separate action in cooperation with the organization for the achievement of the purposes set forth in Article 55.

Among these purposes are the "promotion" of universal respect for, and observance of, human rights and fundamental freedoms for all, without distinction as to race, sex, language, or religion. At first the Economic and Social Council authorized the Human Rights Commission to receive complaints of discrimination, apparently contrary to the pledge of Article 56, but this authority was presently withdrawn. A Canadian court held that restrictive land covenants, discriminating for reasons of race, were unenforceable because contrary to the public policy of Canada declared in the Charter,[33] and the Supreme Court of the United States, in holding such restrictive covenants void as contrary to the Fourteenth Amendment, referred to the argument that they were also forbidden by the Charter.[34] The issue also arose in the *Fujii* case in California. A lower court held that the California Alien Land Law, which discriminated against Japanese, was void because of the Charter obligation. The Supreme Court

[32] United Nations, *The Impact of the Universal Declaration of Human Rights,* UN Pub. 1953, XIV, 1.

[33] In re Drummond Wren, Supreme Court of Ontario.

[34] Hurd N. Hodge, 1948, 63 Sup. Ct., 847, 853, *Am. Jour. Int. Law,* 42 (1948), 710; Manley O. Hudson, "Integrity of International Instruments," *ibid.*

of California held, however, that the obligation of Article 56 was not sufficiently precise to be self-executing. Nevertheless it held the land law void because contrary to the Fourteenth Amendment.[35]

There can be little doubt that Article 56 imposes some obligations. Whether the obligation is to respect human rights or to promote respect for them through the United Nations is uncertain.[36] The Supreme Court of the United States has not dealt with the issue, but in dicta it has referred to the Charter provision as strengthening the protections of the Fourteenth Amendment.[37]

In any case, it is clear that the Charter provision requires strengthening if it is to assure legal protection of human rights in either international or national tribunals. The need of supplementary conventions to this end has from the first been recognized by United Nations organs. The first efforts of the United Nations were to conclude a single covenant of human rights which incorporated most of the provisions of the Declaration and was open to ratification as a treaty by the member states. The differences, however, between the Western states, wanting to emphasize civil liberties and property rights, and the Communist states, wanting to emphasize economic and social rights, and the realization that procedures for enforcement of these two types of rights would necessarily be very different resulted in the drafting of two covenants, one dealing with civil and political rights and the other with economic, social, and cultural rights.

Difficulties also arose in the covenant dealing with civil and political rights because of the insistence by some states, not only Communist but also Asiatic, African, and even some Western, on including many qualifications in the interest of government action to assure security and to meet emergencies. Some of these freedoms in the draft Covenant, especially those concerned with forced labor (Art. 8), migration (Art. 12), religion (Art. 18), opinion and expression (Art. 19), assembly (Art. 20), and association (Art. 21), included so many qualifications that they appeared to authorize government intervention rather

[35] Fujii v. Cal. (1950) 217 Pac. 2d 481; 218 Pac. 2d 595; (1952) 242 Pac. 2d 617, 38 Cal. 2d 718.

[36] Manley O. Hudson, "Charter Provisions on Human Rights" *Am. Jour. Int. Law,* 44 (1950), 545 ff.; Q. Wright, "National Courts and Human Rights—the Fujii Case," *ibid.,* 45 (1951), 62 ff.

[37] Oyam v. California, 1948, 332 U.S. 633, Concurring Opinions by Justices Black, Douglas, Murphy, and Ruthledge; *Am. Jour. Int. Law,* 48 (1948), 475.

than to guarantee individual freedom.[38] In spite of the fact that the Covenant specified that it merely established a minimum and would not interfere with prior standards required by national constitutions or laws of a party (Art. 5, par. 2), some states with high local standards felt that these might be jeopardized by the stated exceptions. There was also extensive debate on the applicability of the Covenant's provisions to the states of federations and the dependencies of empires. Eventually the claims of both federal and imperial states were rejected, and the Covenant was made applicable to all the territories of the parties without limitation or exception (Arts. 2, 52, 53).

This situation apparently contributed to the Bricker Amendment movement in the United States, the object of which was to prevent ratification by the United States of human rights covenants for fear that they might encroach upon "states' rights" or impair constitutional guarantees. There was also a fear that such covenants might increase the authority of the Federal Government to protect human rights in the South. While the Bricker movement has failed to amend the Constitution, its supporters influenced the Secretary of State to announce in 1953 that the United States Government had "reached the conclusion that we should not at this time become a party to any multilateral treaty such as those contemplated in the draft covenants on human rights, and that we should now work toward the objectives of the Declaration by other means." [39] This statement had special reference to the Covenant on Civil and Political Rights. It had long been understood that the United States would not approve the Covenant on Economic, Social, and Cultural Rights because of its socialistic implications.

In spite of this discouragement, the Commission continued its efforts, and the two draft Covenants were presented to the General Assembly in 1954, but progress has been halted because of the insistence by the African-Asian bloc on including in each draft Covenant the right of self-determination. This proposal provided not only for the right of colonial emancipation, but also for the sovereignty of nations over their national wealth and resources, a provision which it was feared might justify the nationalization of the property or concessions of

[38] Sohn, *Basic Documents*, pp. 136 ff. The qualifications suggested during the course of drafting are indicated in Sohn, *World Law*, pp. 547 ff.

[39] U.S. Dept. of State, *Bulletin*, 28:579 ff.

foreign corporations. This provision was vigorously opposed by the imperial powers on the ground that self-determination was a principle, not a right, and, in any case, was a collective, not an individual, right. Its inclusion resulted in the practical withdrawal of these states from support of the Covenants. Although it continued discussion of the draft Covenants, the General Assembly in 1957 approved a resolution providing for study of interim measures for preventing violations of human rights.[40]

It is likely that further progress in the legal definition of human rights would be promoted by pursuing a less ambitious method.[41] Regional covenants, like those approved by the Organization of American States and the Council of Europe, are easier to achieve because there is usually less cultural disparity among states in a region. Covenants might be drafted on particular human rights, one after the other, following the method of the International Labor Organization. To this end special studies have been made on forced labor, slavery, women's rights, trade union rights, and minority rights. On the last subject the United Nations has not accepted the position of the League of Nations that social, religious, and national minorities should be entitled to educational and other facilities designed to preserve their distinctive cultures. This claim is to be distinguished from the claim of racial minorities in the United States to the same educational facilities as those enjoyed by the majority. The United Nations has not given support to the principle of special minority privileges, but has insisted on their equality of treatment in the enjoyment of human rights, thus looking toward their assimilation in the national culture rather than toward maintenance of their distinctiveness.

Revision of the slavery convention of 1926 has been considered by the Economic and Social Council and of the forced labor convention of 1930 by the International Labor Organization. Conferences have been proposed to conclude conventions on these subjects.[42] The General Assembly has opened for signature a convention on the nationality of married women and has considered three conventions on freedom of information. The first of these, on the international right of

[40] See above note 9 and *International Organization,* 11 (1957), 333.
[41] Commission to Study the Organization of Peace, Tenth Report, *Strengthening the United Nations,* Arthur N. Holcombe, ed. (New York: Harper, 1957), especially the chapter "Human Rights and Minorities" by Louis Sohn and Inis Claude.
[42] *International Organization,* 10 (1956), 201, 622, 634.

correction, was approved by the Assembly in 1949 and opened for signature in 1953. The second, on international transmission of news, was approved by the Assembly but has not been opened for signature, pending approval of the third convention on freedom of information. This draft has suffered, as have a number of articles in the General Covenant on Civil and Political Rights, from the insistence by many states that the right of the government to restrict freedom of the press in the interests of security and morals be spelled out in detail. On all these conventions the United States, in pursuance of its declaration of 1953, has assumed a nonco-operative attitude.[43]

The achievement of legally binding conventions in the field of human rights has been meager. More has been accomplished in particular regions such as Western Europe and the Americas. Doubtless the drafting and obtaining extensive ratifications of general conventions, even if each deals with only a single human right, will be a long and difficult process.

ENFORCEMENT PROCEDURES

The two draft conventions on human rights include enforcement provisions of different character. That on civil and political rights requires the parties to adopt legislation and all measures necessary to give effect to the rights recognized in the Covenant, including effective judicial and other remedies, and to submit reports to the United Nations on the action taken. An International Human Rights Commission is empowered to deal with complaints of member states, to find facts, seek amicable solution, and, if necessary, report its opinion on the justifiability of the complaint. There may then be an appeal to the International Court of Justice by any state concerned.

This does not go so far as the European Human Rights Covenant, which is actually in force. An optional clause, accepted by seven states, established a Commission before which individual petitioners may bring complaints. There is also a provision for a European Court of Human Rights to hear appeals from this Commission. While ratified by several states, this is not yet in force.

The draft Covenant on economic, social, and cultural rights provides a more gradual approach to realization by national legislative

[43] *Ibid.*, 10 (1956), 318; 11 (1957), 372; above notes 9, 39.

action as resources become available. Periodic reporting on progress is also required.

Enforcement proposals have relied mainly on national good faith stimulated by periodic reporting. International action has centered around commissions with fact-finding, conciliatory, and reporting powers. The use of international courts available on the initiative of injured individuals, though much discussed, has not been realized, either generally or regionally, though progress in that direction has been made in Western Europe. The use of the International Court of Justice for disputes between states concerning the application of human rights treaties is available for states which are parties to the optional clause. Apart from the European convention, procedures are limited to those initiated by states.

Special international remedies have been proposed for particular human rights, such as an international writ of habeas corpus, to give relief in cases of detention.[44] Individual petition is utilized in the Trusteeship system and is made available by the European human rights convention for nationals of states which have accepted the optional clause. It has been discussed in connection with the draft Covenant on civil and political rights but not accepted. The right of asylum has been urged as a final remedy if violations of civil liberties make life unbearable in a country. Under customary international law states are free, except as bound by extradition treaties, to grant asylum, but individuals have not had a right to demand it.[45] The right of emigration is asserted in the Universal Declaration (Art. 13) and the draft Covenant (Art. 12), but no right of immigration, nor is a right of asylum provided. Article 14 of the Universal Declaration asserts that "everyone has a right to seek and to enjoy in other countries asylum from persecution." It was originally proposed that the term "to be granted" asylum be included, but this was rejected and the phrase "to enjoy" inserted, thus continuing the freedom of states to permit or to refuse asylum. Furthermore, even this limited right "may not be invoked in the case of prosecutions genuinely arising from non-political crimes or from acts contrary to the purposes and

[44] Luis Kutner, "A Proposal for a United Nations Writ of Habeas Corpus," *Tulane Law Review*, 28 (1954), 417 ff.

[45] Manuel R. Garcia-Mora, *International Law and Asylum as a Human Right* (Washington, D.C.: Public Affairs Press, 1956), reviewed by Q. Wright, *University of Chicago Law Review*, 24 (1956), 202.

principles of the United Nations." The subject is not included in the draft Covenants.

This discussion indicates that the problem of implementing human rights is still in early stages of realization. In the meantime educational and political action has proceeded.

EDUCATIONAL ACTION

It is clear that the availability of information and the state of opinion in the world, after the enthusiasm of World War II had subsided, have not been sufficient to realize the principles of the Charter in the field of human rights. The United States, after rejecting the methods of human rights covenants, proposed a three-point program. It suggested that the United Nations appoint *rapporteurs* to study selected aspects of human rights, that each government make annual reports on development in the field for submission to the Commission, and that the United Nations establish advisory services on specific aspects of human rights, such as giving of technical assistance, providing scholarships, and arranging seminars.[46] The last of these proposals was approved by the General Assembly in 1955, and the Secretary-General was authorized to arrange for technical assistance on request of states. The Economic and Social Council approved the other suggestions in 1956. Members were requested to submit reports every three years, and a special study was authorized, "The Right of Everyone to Be Free from Arbitrary Arrest, Detention, and Exile."

It is feared that technical assistance will not be requested by countries which do not respect human rights, that national reports may be more self-congratulatory than informative, and that detailed studies may become a substitute for effective action. No great enthusiasm has, therefore, developed for the American program. Nevertheless, it may prove to have some value in developing information and preparing for action on specific human rights. In the meantime educational activity centering around the Universal Declaration and emphasizing the importance of respect for human rights has been carried on, particularly by UNESCO. The United Nations publishes a Human Rights Year Book providing information about national and international action in the field. Undoubtedly, in the long run, advance of

[46] Above note 39.

the United Nations program depends on the effectiveness of education and information, particularly in countries where human rights are likely to be neglected.

POLITICAL ACTION

The United Nations General Assembly has considered a number of situations where human rights were thought to be violated. The imprisonment of Cardinal Mindszenty and other religious leaders in Bulgaria, Hungary, and Roumania was considered by the Assembly on the basis of the peace treaties which these countries had ratified. The three countries refused to co-operate in setting up the tribunals to consider complaints on the observance of human rights as required by the treaties, and an advisory opinion was requested by the Assembly. The International Court of Justice advised that the matter was not within the domestic jurisdiction of these states, as they had claimed, but that the tribunals could not be set up wihout their co-operation.[47]

The General Assembly passed a resolution supporting the right of Russian wives of foreign nationals to leave the Soviet Union, especially if the husband was a diplomat (thus overruling the Soviet contention that the matter was domestic), on the ground that international obligations arising both from the diplomatic immunities of international law and from human rights were involved. Some results were achieved.[48] Less was achieved from the General Assembly's resolution concerning the kidnaping of Greek children during the invasion of Greece by Soviet satellites,[49] and practically nothing from its resolutions urging return of World War II prisoners of war and condemning forced labor, both directed in fact, though not in form, against Communist countries.[50]

The numerous resolutions criticizing discrimination in South African legislation and practice against Indians and natives have brought no tangible results. The South African government has claimed that the matter is within its domestic jurisdiction and beyond the As-

[47] Int. Court of Justice, *Reports*, 1950, p. 65; *Am. Jour. Int. Law*, 44 (1950), 745.
[48] Sohn, *United Nations Law*, pp. 670 ff.
[49] *International Organization*, 6 (1952), 239; 7 (1953), 71.
[50] *Ibid.*, 8 (1954), 94; 9 (1955), 122; 10 (1956), 623.

sembly's competence and has refused to consider the resolutions which have been passed. In the Indian case, agreements between India and South Africa appeared to make the matter one of international law.[51] In respect to the apartheid laws concerning natives, the only international obligation claimed was that which flowed from the Charter's human rights provisions. Because of doubt whether these established a positive legal obligation, the Assembly phrased its resolution in general terms on the theory that a general recommendation addressed to all members would not constitute "intervention," whereas a recommendation directed to South Africa alone might. The extensive debates on this question and the exhaustive reports of two special commissions, with abundant citation of international law authorities, have clarified the relationship between Assembly resolutions and the Charter prohibition against intervention in domestic affairs of members. The General Assembly has concluded that a matter is not "domestic" if it concerns an international obligation and that it is not "intervention" if the recommendation is in general terms. South Africa, however, has resisted these conclusions and has asked that an advisory opinion from the International Court of Justice be obtained, but the General Assembly has refused to make such a request.[52]

[51] The Assembly rejected by a vote of 24 to 19 with 6 abstentions a South African request, supported by the United States and the United Kingdom, for an advisory opinion on the Assembly's competence to deal with an Indian resolution calling upon South Africa to reverse its "general policy and legislative and administrative measures affecting Asiatics in South Africa so as to bring them into conformity with the principles and purposes of the Charter." It then adopted (32-15-7) a modified form of the Indian proposal referring to the danger that friendly relations between India and South Africa might be impaired and to the nonconformity of South African action with "international obligations of that country under agreements with India" but not to human rights provisions of the Charter (Joint Committee, November 21–30, and Plenary Meeting, December 7–8, 1946; Sohn, *United Nations Law*, pp. 592 ff.).

[52] The apartheid question was placed in the Assembly's Agenda in 1952, and the Assembly rejected South Africa's request for an advisory opinion by a vote of 45 to 6 with 8 abstentions. It established a Commission to study the problem, declared that racial discriminations are inconsistent with the pledge of members under Article 56 of the Charter, and called upon "all members to bring their policies into conformity with their obligations under the Charter to promote the observance of human rights and fundamental freedoms" (G.A.O.R. VII, Res. 616). South Africa regarded this resolution as *ultra vires* and refused further co-operation with the Commission or consideration of subsequent resolutions on the subject (Sohn, *United Nations Law*, pp. 627–628).

In the trusteeship areas, special United Nations procedures are provided for maintaining human rights, including the right of individual petition, and some results have been obtained. The extensive programs of the United Nations in resettling refugees and providing relief in Korea, Palestine, and elsewhere are related to human rights and have had a measure of success, but only through voluntary co-operation and contribution. States have usually been more mindful of national interest than of humanity in receiving refugees.

It would appear that political action cannot be effective in promoting respect for human rights unless there is a strong world public opinion behind that action and unless the state complained against is under clear international obligations. It would probably be desirable for the Assembly to obtain an advisory opinion of the Court when the issue of domestic jurisdiction is raised, as it usually is in these cases. In any case the total political situation should be considered and the probable consequences of a resolution carefully canvassed. The cause of human rights is not advanced by creating such resentments in accused governments that they refuse co-operation and perhaps withdraw from discussion.

CONCLUSION

It appears that, while the principle of respect for human rights is given some support in customary international law and is proclaimed in the Charter and these rights are to a considerable extent defined in the Universal Declaration, effective realization throughout the world is not likely until the moral ideas behind the conception of human rights are more generally accepted. Progress in this direction requires a reduction in international tensions and an approach to a more common understanding among the Western, Communist, and Bandung countries on the subject. The development of communications and cultural contacts and programs of information and education may, with more assured peace and reduction of tensions, contribute to this end.

In the meantime, progress is likely to be served by concentration on particular rights which are generally accepted in principle and upon which general treaties may be negotiated providing appropriate methods of implementation. Regional organizations may also make progress within the region, suggesting possible methods of advance of more general applicability. Finally, a major contribution would be the re-establishment of the leadership of the United States, which initiated the movement through President Roosevelt's Declaration of the Four Freedoms and which has achieved, through its constitutional experience, knowledge of the problems that may be useful in the international field.

[HERBERT W. BRIGGS]

CORNELL UNIVERSITY

The "Rights of Aliens"

and International Protection

of Human Rights

TO the student of international law, a striking feature of United Nations proposals for the international protection of human rights lies in the almost inarticulate major premise that international law should be extended to regulate certain legal relations between a State and its own nationals. Traditionally, international law has regulated certain relations between States and, more recently, between States and international organizations of States. There is even a substantial body of international law designed to control the behavior of a State in relation to some of its inhabitants, namely, resident aliens. The behavior of a State toward its own citizens has, however, been jealously reserved as a matter of domestic jurisdiction, largely escaping international legal concern or control. Proposals for the international protection of human rights thus encounter deeply entrenched legal concepts of the nature, scope, and function of international law as well as the traditional practice and behavior of States with reference to most of their inhabitants, their own citizens.

The radical nature of the changes proposed in legal concept and State practice is often discounted in the missionary urge to do something to improve the lot of the individual everywhere. If States whose constitutional and legal systems proclaim respect for basic human rights fail to guarantee them to their citizens, should not some form of international machinery be established to guarantee these rights within such countries? If it be true that the current trend in international law is against intervention in the internal affairs of States, should not legal theories of sovereignty and nonintervention nevertheless be modified to permit more frequent intervention to protect human rights?

A proposal that the United Nations should "assure" or "protect" human rights, instead of only "promoting and encouraging respect" for them (as provided in Art. 1, par. 3, of the Charter), was rejected at the San Francisco Conference, principally because "assuring or protecting such fundamental rights is primarily the concern of each State." In drafting the proposed Covenants on Human Rights, however, United Nations organs have assumed that the protection of human rights could be translated into terms of international law.

It seems appropriate, therefore, to examine the methods by which international law has established a regime for the protection of the rights of aliens in order to see what lessons have relevance to proposals to universalize these rights.

THE "RIGHTS OF ALIENS"

In few fields of international law has so great an opportunity been afforded for the development by judicial means of the rights and obligations of States as in the field of the international responsibility of States for injury to the lives and properties of resident aliens. Thousands of decisions by international tribunals have molded a jurisprudence whose object is the protection of the alien from arbitrary action by the State of residence. In general terms, the international responsibility of a State with reference to resident aliens may be summarized along the following lines.[1]

[1] See, generally, Research in International Law, Harvard Law School, *The Law of Responsibility of States for Damage Done in Their Territory to the Person or Property of Foreigners* (Edwin M. Borchard, reporter), *American Journal of International Law*, 23 (Special Number, April 1929), 131–239; Edwin M. Borchard, *The Diplomatic Protection of Citizens Abroad* (New York, 1915); Herbert W. Briggs, *The Law of Nations—Cases, Documents, and Notes* (2d ed.; New York, 1952), pp. 601–747.

The "Rights of Aliens"

A State is responsible under international law when it has a duty to make reparation for an injury to an alien as a consequence of an act or omission which is incompatible with its obligations under international law and which is attributable to that State.

The international responsibility of a State is determined by international law, specifically by international conventions, whether general or particular, establishing rules expressly recognized by the States concerned, by international custom, and by the general principles of law recognized by civilized States. A State cannot avoid international responsibility by invoking its constitution or municipal law.

International responsibility is incurred by a State if an injury to an alien results from an act or omission, incompatible with international law, of its executive or administrative authorities (organs, officials, or employees) within the scope of their authority or under cover of their official character. Responsibility for *ultra vires* acts of State authorities is recognized in the rule that a State is not relieved of international responsibility for the acts of its authorities by reason of the fact that they exceeded their competence under municipal law, provided that such behavior was under cover of their official character.

With reference to legislative acts, international responsibility is incurred by a State if an injury to an alien results from the enactment of legislation incompatible with international law or from the failure to enact legislation necessary for carrying out the State's obligations under international law.

International responsibility is incurred by a State if an injury to an alien results from an act or omission, incompatible with international law, of its judicial or administrative courts or of those of its authorities which are concerned with the administration of justice or the repression of crime. In particular, international responsibility can be incurred for acts of such organs where there has been denial, unwarranted delay, or gross deficiency in the administration of the judicial or remedial process; failure to provide those guaranties which are generally considered indispensable to the proper administration of justice; a manifestly unjust judgment; or failure to apprehend, prosecute, or punish persons charged with the commission of crimes against aliens.

International responsibility can also be incurred by a State if an injury to an alien is caused by an individual who is not a State official or by mob violence, where, in violation of its obligations under international law, the State has failed to exercise due diligence to prevent the injury.

The characterization of the international responsibility of a State in this field as an obligation to make reparation for its acts or omissions incompatible with international law assumes some practicable means for determining in a given case whether the acts or omissions charged are in violation of international law. That this function can best be performed in judicial proceedings is one of the reasons for the development of the rule of international law that an alien must ordinarily exhaust his local remedies before his State can present an international claim on his behalf. Other reasons for the rule are that when the alien enters a country he is required to abide by the local law and is expected to avail himself of the means provided by local law for redress of injuries and that the alien's State should avoid intervening until it is clear that justice has been denied the alien and that the State of residence is unwilling to right the wrong.

The rule of local remedies may be expressed in terms of its functions as follows: [2] The international responsibility of a State for an injury to an alien may not be invoked in the form of an international claim so long as local remedies, available to the injured alien under the law of that State and providing an effective, sufficient, and timely means of redress, have not been exhausted. Such resort to local remedies is required prior to the presentation of an international claim in order to determine whether or not an injury to an alien has in fact occurred; whether or not an act or omission is, in the circumstances, attributable to the State; whether or not such an act or omission is incompatible with international law; and, in the event of an affirmative finding on these points, whether that State is prepared to discharge its international responsibility by appropriate means. The exhaustion of local remedies as a condition of the receivability of an international claim may be waived where their availability, effectiveness, sufficiency, or timeliness is in dispute.

Both the findings of fact and law and the purported discharge of international responsibility are open to challenge by the alien's State; if they are deemed insufficient, an international claim may then be presented. The operation of the rule of local remedies has, however,

---

[2] See Herbert W. Briggs, "The Local Remedies Rule: A Drafting Suggestion," *American Journal of International Law*, 50 (1956), 921–927.

been beneficial in reducing the number of international claims while securing justice for the alien locally.

Although the object of the rules of international law setting forth the international responsibility of a State in this field may be regarded as the protection of the alien from arbitrary action by the State of residence, the rules are phrased in terms of the rights and duties of States. This approach is in conformity with the traditional practice of States of regarding the "rights of aliens" as the rights of the alien's State, since, under the orthodox view of the nature of international law, the alien himself has no standing in international law.

This orthodox view has been subjected to increasing challenge in recent years precisely because it is the alien and not his State that is the real object of protection and the real beneficiary of the rules.[3] Criticisms most often made of the regime established by international law for the protection of the alien and his property are that if the alien is unable to secure redress of injury through resort to local remedies he has no right to present an international claim in his own behalf but is dependent upon the State of his nationality to do so; that the State of his nationality can present a claim on his behalf only if the beneficial interest in the claim has remained continuously national from the time of injury to the time of the award (this deprives a State of the right to present claims on behalf of persons or their legal beneficiaries who were not its nationals at all relevant times and deprives stateless persons of an international remedy); that the State of his nationality is under no legal obligation to present his claim and may refuse to do so for extraneous political reasons or may delay, compromise, or abandon it, without accountability to him; and that if a State wins an award on his behalf it is under no legal obligation to remit it to him despite the uniform practice of doing so.[4]

It is, therefore, argued that the "rights of aliens" should be recog-

[3] See, for example, Philip C. Jessup, *A Modern Law of Nations* (New York, 1948); H. Lauterpacht, *International Law and Human Rights* (London, 1950); Marek S. Korowicz, "The Problem of the International Personality of Individuals," *American Journal of International Law*, 50 (1956), 533–562; P. E. Corbett, *The Individual and World Society* (Princeton, N.J.: Center for Research on World Political Institutions, Publication No. 2, 1953); Maurice Bourquin, "L'humanisation du droit des gens," in *La Technique et les Principes du Droit Public—Etudes en l'Honneur de Georges Scelle* (Paris, 1950), I, 21–54.

[4] See Manley O. Hudson, *International Tribunals—Past and Future* (Washington, D.C., 1944), p. 198.

nized as his rights and not those of his State. In other words, the State of residence should be regarded as owing obligations under international law directly to the alien and not merely to his State.

If attention is concentrated on the substantive content of the rules of international law stipulating rights and obligations with reference to aliens, a somewhat plausible case can be made for the suggestion. Unless, however, in addition to substantive rights the alien is granted procedural capacity under international law to secure those rights, the proposal may leave the alien in a weaker position than he is today.

If the alien has no enforceable legal rights under international law today, he is nevertheless the beneficiary of a corpus of rules of international law which obligate the State of residence to provide for him by municipal law a minimum standard of treatment—both substantive and procedural. Conversely, the State of residence has the right under international law to require the alien to comply with the local law. It is thus to the local law that the alien first looks for protection and for redress. In this respect he is on a par with nationals of the State of residence: they also must look to their municipal law for protection and redress. If, however, the State of residence fails to provide such protection or redress, the alien is the beneficiary of rules of international law which permit certain action by his State on his behalf. At this point, the alien is theoretically, and most often actually, in a better position than a national. Although, like the national, he may have no actionable right against the State of residence, his State has such a right and may take action leading to the redress of his injuries.

Whether or not the alien's State takes action on his behalf, it should be repeated, is beyond the control of the alien. Therefore, it is to prevent the sacrifice of the alien's interests to some extrinsic policy consideration of his State and to forestall the embroilment of States in relatively minor controversies that the alien should acquire in his own right the procedural capacity to pursue his claim.

Such a right must be derived from some system of law. Obviously, it cannot be the law of his nationality, since the municipal law of his State cannot operate to confer on him procedural capacity under the municipal law of the State of residence. The right to sue the State of residence can be—and has been in some circumstances—conferred on the alien by the municipal law of the State of residence. The local remedies to which the alien is required to resort under the rule of local remedies are of this kind, namely, remedies made available to him by the local municipal law. Such procedural capacity as the alien may in fact possess under the local law may include the right to sue citizens and other aliens; the right to sue government officials, employees, or agencies; possibly the right to sue the State itself. The right to sue the State or its higher organs or officials may not, however, be available to either aliens or citizens or may be available to citizens but not to aliens. Moreover, the law to be applied where an alien is party to litigation in a foreign court is most likely to be the municipal law of the State of residence, and the court will usually be unable to pass upon the conformity of that law with the requirements of international law. It is true that the courts of many countries will apply the substantive rules of treaties or of customary international law which have been received into the local law; but where this is done, that is, where a State complies with its international obligations, no basis for an international claim is likely to exist. It is situations where a State is charged with acts or omissions that are incompatible with its obligations under international law in which the alien needs procedural capacity against that State; and to be effectual it would seem that such capacity must be conferred by international law.

Many international claims tribunals have been set up to apply the rules and principles of international law as the test of the legality of the behavior of a State toward resident aliens. With a few exceptions, however—such as the Mixed Arbitral Tribunals and the Upper Silesian Arbitral Tribunal after World War I—procedural capacity to bring a suit was conferred on the alien's State and not on the alien himself.

It is this situation which the proposals are designed to modify, so that the alien can bring his own claim against a foreign State. There is a necessary twofold assumption underlying such proposals: not only must international law confer this procedural capacity upon the individual alien but also international law must be modified to set forth substantive rules of the international responsibility of States directly to aliens rather than to the alien's State.

With reference to the first assumption—the conferring of international procedural capacity on the alien—certain observations are in order.

First, the alien himself cannot establish this procedural capacity under international law. There is not in existence today any international court in which an individual alien can bring an action against a government. Not even the Court of Justice of the European Coal and Steel Community or the European Court of Human Rights permits such actions by individual aliens.

Second, a unilateral policy by a particular State of opening itself to suit by aliens in its own courts would be legally insufficient to confer capacity on the alien under international law.

Third, a unilateral declaration by a State accepting the jurisdiction of the International Court of Justice in cases brought against it by aliens would be legally insufficient unless the Statute of the Court were amended to confer jurisdiction *ratione personae* on that Court in such actions. By Article 34 of the Statute of that Court, "Only States may be parties in cases before the Court." Well over one hundred cases brought by individuals against States before that Court and its predecessor, the Permanent Court of International Justice, have been rejected without a hearing for lack of jurisdiction.

The minimum steps required are the conclusion of a treaty or treaties by which States agree to confer on a court the requisite jurisdiction and on aliens the necessary legal capacity. Two States could accomplish this as regards their citizens by a bilateral treaty. Instead of commencing with sets of bilateral treaties, it is conceivable that a number of States might agree in a multilateral treaty:

(1) to establish an appropriate International Claims Tribunal;

(2) to confer jurisdiction on it to hear claims brought by nationals of the participating States against any other State party to the treaty;

(3) to confer capacity under international law on nationals of the participating States (and perhaps on stateless persons) to bring actions *as aliens* against other participating States before the Tribunal;

(4) to stipulate the applicable law to be applied by the Tribunal

(a) by definition; or

(b) by reference and analogy to the existing rules of international law dealing with State responsibility.

Determination of the law to be applied by such an International Claims Tribunal is not the least of the difficulties. The international law establishing the responsibility of States has been developed for some centuries as inter-State law, and rewriting it by analogy in terms of direct State responsibility to individuals would be no easy undertaking. Moreover, this rewriting of international law by analogy would be unlikely to accomplish a complete change in the status of the alien. As Judge Manley O. Hudson has observed:

> The subjection of aliens to the law of the State within whose territory they may sojourn or act is a principle of almost universal acceptance. The direct relations between a State and an alien will usually be governed by that State's municipal law, the administration of which States generally are not disposed to entrust to any but their national courts. . . . Even if States were willing to provide that the inter-State law should be applied by analogy, they would probably be unwilling to relax the condition that local remedies be exhausted. . . .[5]

Although proposals for the establishment of a permanent International Claims Tribunal to which individuals should have direct access have been made over a period of years, the political obstacle of obtaining the consent of States has never been surmounted, and the rare instances in which *ad hoc* bilateral tribunals with such jurisdiction were created occurred a generation ago.

Indeed, interest has shifted from "the rights of aliens" to the more inclusive category of "human rights." If it becomes politically feasible to modify traditional international law to provide substantive and procedural rights under that law for the alien, why should concepts not be modified to confer comparable rights and capacity upon the citizen against his own State? The question poses problems less of logic than of policy and legal concept. Is it possible that States might be willing to translate the "rights of aliens"—a well-established category with which they are familiar—into individual rights with the necessary legal consequences and yet hesitate to follow this logic sufficiently to include all individuals, in particular their own nationals?

For the international responsibility of a State for denial of justice and official malfeasance or nonfeasance with regard to aliens there is no comparable body of international law stipulating the "rights of nationals" against their own State. It is true that there are in most States comparable concepts to protect nationals against arbitrary or illegal treatment; but these are matters of municipal law and policy, the administration of which is carefully reserved for national courts. The claim of a national against his own State seldom interests other States; and, in exceptional situations where the mistreatment of its nationals by a State is notoriously oppressive, the legal concern of

[5] *Ibid.,* p. 202.

other States, expressed in terms of humanitarian intervention, has always been challenged on grounds of domestic jurisdiction.

Customary international law does not tell a State what responsibility or what rights and duties it owes to its nationals. There have been exceptional situations, mostly based on treaty, in which international law does appear to provide standards for the treatment by a State of its own nationals. Thus the League of Nations system for the protection of minorities, imposed by the Great Powers upon about a dozen States after 1919, provided both the standards and an international guarantee for some citizens against the State. The legal and political implications, however, of employing international law as a shield against their State for "citizens with potentially centrifugal tendencies," led, as Erich Hula has observed, to the elimination of any provisions for the international protection of minorities as such from the proposed Covenants on Human Rights: "What has been accepted under duress as a special regime is not voluntarily acceptable even as a general scheme. The universality of the covenant has to be bought at the price of omitting from it any provisions specifically aiming at the protection of minorities of any kind." [6]

Conventions adopted under the auspices of the International Labor Organization provide another example of the way in which States have undertaken obligations to treat their nationals according to certain standards formulated in terms of international law; but the obligations are to other States, and by ratifying a convention the State acquires thereby no legal obligation under international law toward its own nationals. For purposes of illustration, suppose the United States becomes a party to an ILO convention stipulating that the maximum work week in factories shall be forty hours. This obligation is owed by the United States to other parties to the treaty. It does not confer legal rights to a forty-hour week on American workers unless the treaty is made United States law. This is clear if the treaty is not self-executing, and even if self-executing it is to American courts and United States law that the workers must look to obtain the benefits of the treaty. In this respect they are like the resident alien who must look to the local law for the rights stipulated in his behalf by inter-

[6] Erich Hula, "International Law and the Protection of Human Rights," in George A. Lipsky, *Law and Politics in the World Community*, Hans Kelsen *Festschrift* (Berkeley and Los Angeles, 1953), pp. 162, 171.

national law. Although other parties to an ILO convention may file complaints with the International Labor Office if they believe a party is not observing the treaty, labor conventions, as Hula observes,[7] fail to provide that mutuality of interests contained in the reciprocal rights and obligations of most treaties. States, therefore, lack a strong incentive to institute enforcement proceedings in the relations of another State with its own nationals.

In sum, the "rights of nationals" against their State are almost exclusively rights under municipal law. There is little customary international law on the subject, and there are only scattered and limited treaty provisions. Although hundreds of millions of people find aspects of their legal behavior indirectly regulated by the treaties to which their States are parties, the rights and obligations which directly govern their conduct and their procedural rights are those provided by their national law. The German-Polish Upper Silesian Convention of 1922, writes Professor Marek Korowicz, "was the sole instance in which for fifteen years individuals were authorized to sue not only a foreign State, but also their own States before an international body." [8]

The conclusion might, therefore, be reached that there is more basis in international law and practice for establishing the procedural capacity of the alien under international law, giving him both substantive and procedural rights against foreign States in his own right, than there is for endowing citizens with substantive and procedural rights under international law against their own States. It may be, however, that the time has passed for so limited an approach. The "human rights" approach is today dominating the field of such proposals and capturing popular imagination to such an extent that the granting of international legal personality to men only as "aliens" might not even be regarded as a politically sound first step.

THE INTERNATIONAL PROTECTION OF HUMAN RIGHTS

Stemming from provisions of the United Nations Charter which impose no stronger obligations upon Members of the United Nations than co-operation in the promotion and encouragement of respect for human rights and fundamental freedoms for all, United Nations

---

[7] *Ibid.*, pp. 167–169.
[8] Korowicz, *loc. cit.*, p. 561.

organs have devoted twelve years of study and conference to further-ing this aim. The General Assembly in 1948 placed its approval upon a Universal Declaration of Human Rights which has no legally bind-ing force but which expressed the consensus of United Nations Mem-bers (other than the Soviet bloc, Saudi Arabia, and the Union of South Africa) of the rights which should be granted to all persons, whether nationals or aliens. The Commission on Human Rights has prepared two draft Covenants—one on Civil and Political Rights and the other, promoted principally by the Soviet bloc, on Economic, Social, and Cultural Rights—for submission to the General Assembly and, even-tually, to States for acceptance as binding legal obligations under international law.

The reason for embodying fundamental rights in two treaties in-stead of one was closely related to the question of implementation. It was argued that civil and political rights were often immediately applicable "legal" rights of an "absolute" character, enforceable against unlawful action of the State, whereas economic, social, and cultural rights were "programme" rights which States would have to take positive action to create and promote.[9] On the basis of this distinction, the obligations of States and international measures of enforcement will be varied as between the two proposed Covenants.

No comprehensive examination will here be made of the substantive contents of the two draft Covenants. The civil and political rights include rights to life, liberty, travel, fair trial, privacy, opinion and information, peaceful assembly, association, marriage, nondiscrimina-tion and equality before the law. Economic, social, and cultural rights include the right to work, favorable conditions of work, trade union rights, social security, and rights relating to motherhood, childhood, marriage, family, adequate food, clothing, housing, health, education, culture, science, and a right to an adequate standard of living.

It is these rights, traditionally falling within the sacred domain of matters of domestic jurisdiction, which it is proposed to convert into obligations of international law regulating relations between a State and its citizens. Further analysis of the legal concepts implicit in this

---

[9] See United Nations Document A/2929, July 1, 1955, *Draft International Cove-nants on Human Rights, Annotation Prepared by the Secretary-General* (389 pp., mimeographed), pp. 23–24. Cited hereafter as UN Doc. A/2929.

program and the measures of enforcement which are envisaged may be useful.

The rules and principles of international law providing for the rights of aliens have developed through the centuries primarily as customary international law reflecting the practice of States and the decisions of international tribunals and have only occasionally been supplemented by treaties. As custom, the law had its roots in behavior patterns. Quite different is the current human rights approach which is intended to create by treaty—almost at one fell swoop—a whole new body of international law which, far from being rooted in custom, is in flat contradiction with the customary behavior pattern of States over the past centuries.

If the alien, as stated above, owes so much of his legal status to local law despite an eventual appeal by his State to standards of international law for his protection, the citizen is completely within the jurisdiction of his State. From the viewpoint of inter-State relations, the concept of the international responsibility of States is explicitly based upon the fact that a State acquires responsibility under international law for its conduct with respect to nationals of other States but never with regard to its own nationals. It is all very well to assume that every State is—or should be—interested in protecting the basic human rights of its nationals; but it is that State's interest and, under international law, it has the right to challenge the legal interest and concern of other States or even of international organizations in such matters. Perhaps international law should be modified in this respect, but it is well to bear in mind that since proposals for the international protection of human rights challenge traditional international law, practice, and behavior the measures designed for their implementation assume crucial importance.

By Article 2 of the draft Covenant on Civil and Political Rights, each contracting party "undertakes to respect and to ensure to all individuals within its territory and subject to its jurisdiction the rights recognized in this Covenant" without discrimination; to adopt the necessary legislative and other measures, not already in force, to give effect to the rights recognized in the Covenant; to ensure that any person whose human rights are violated shall have an effective remedy, preferably a judicial remedy, even against persons acting in an official capacity; and to ensure the enforcement of such remedies.[10] As an expression of desirable goals there is much to be said for these provisions. As obligations of international law their utility will depend upon the precision with which the rights recognized in the Covenant are drafted and upon the willingness of States to observe and enforce them, as well as upon international measures of enforcement.

Drafting the substantive articles of the Covenants raised an important problem: should each article be a brief general formulation of a right or should each right be set forth in detail as to scope, substance, exceptions, and the specific obligations of States in relation thereto? For example, during the discussion of the provision found in the first paragraph of Article 9 of the draft Covenant on Civil and Political Rights that "no one shall be subjected to arbitrary arrest or detention," no less than thirty limitations on the right were suggested.[11] On the whole, a general limitations clause seemed preferable to an inventory of exceptions. By Article 4 of the draft Covenant on Civil and Political Rights, States may derogate from some of their legal obligations under the Covenant in time of proclaimed public emergency, provided they do not otherwise violate international law or discriminate solely on grounds of race, color, sex, language, religion, or social origin. By Article 18 freedom of worship is subject to limitations of "public order," *inter alia,* and by Article 19 freedom of information may be abridged on grounds of "national security" or "public order." If these freedoms can "be abridged on the basis of such vague expressions as 'public order' and 'national security,'" it was argued in the United Nations, "such freedoms were in great jeopardy, indeed. In the name of 'public order' many a saintly character had been crucified, in the name of 'national security' many a patriot guillotined." [12] Despite this warning, the drafting of the articles varies considerably: some proclaim a right in the language of a manifesto, qualified by a general formula of exception, while others are set forth almost in terms of statute law.

The willingness of States to respect and ensure the human rights stipulated in the Covenant is a basic assumption arising from the fact that a State voluntarily becomes a party to the treaty. No one, however, questioned the necessity for enforcement measures. There was

[10] *Ibid.,* p. 47.   [11] *Ibid.,* p. 25; UN Doc. E/CN.4/95, Annex B, Part II.
[12] UN Doc. A/2929, p. 27.

agreement by the draftsmen that the Covenant would require implementation by national law and regulations and enforcement by local authorities. There was even provision (Art. 41) that available local remedies must normally be exhausted prior to any action by an international organ. The real debate turned upon whether there should be any international implementation, and, if so, what form it should take.[13]

It was argued that States, once having accepted the Covenant, would observe and enforce it locally. Mr. Koretsky (U.S.S.R.) observed that "he himself did not belong to a people who did not have confidence in their government."[14] It was further argued that all international measures of enforcement would be a violation of the sovereignty of States, of the domestic jurisdiction reserved to States by Article 2, paragraph 7, of the United Nations Charter, and of the system of international law regulating relations between States. Moreover, transforming a dispute between an individual and his own government into an international dispute would only increase possibilities of friction by encouraging intervention in the internal affairs of States.

These arguments did not find favor with the drafters of the Covenant. In 1950 the General Assembly rejected a proposal that it should recognize "that implementation of the Covenant fell entirely within the domestic jurisdiction of States."[15] Whether or not a matter was, by international law, one of domestic jurisdiction was relative; "by accepting the covenants, States parties would have entered into obligations of an international character and could hardly then claim that the provisions of the covenants were matters of exclusively domestic jurisdiction."[16]

The draft Covenant on Civil and Political Rights therefore provides[17] for the creation of a Human Rights Committee of nine members elected in their individual capacity and not as representatives of States. Complaints that a State is not observing its obligations under the Covenant can be brought before the Committee only by another State and after first complaining to the State charged with the infraction. The Committee will normally lack jurisdiction until avail-

---

[13] *Ibid.*, p. 28–31.
[14] UN Doc. E/CN.4/AC.4/SR.7.
[15] UN Doc. A/2929, p. 31n.
[16] *Ibid.*, p. 31.
[17] *Ibid.*, pp. 195–298, Arts. 27–50, with commentary.

able local remedies have been exhausted. The Committee may call upon the States concerned to supply relevant information, shall ascertain the facts, and make available its good offices to the States concerned with a view to effecting a friendly solution. In every case, the Committee shall, within eighteen months of its obtaining jurisdiction, draw up a report to be published by the United Nations, indicating the solution or, if none, whether the facts found indicate a breach of the Covenant. If the Committee has been unable to get the parties to agree to a solution, either the complaining State or the State complained of may seize the International Court of Justice of the dispute, the compulsory jurisdiction of the Court being established for this purpose by acceptance of the Covenant.[18] The parties to the Covenant are also under an obligation to submit to the United Nations reports on "the legislative or other measures, including judicial remedies, which they have adopted and which give effect to the rights recognized" in the Covenant.[19]

It will be noted that the enforcement procedures stipulated in the draft Covenant on Civil and Political Rights fail to give the individual any procedural capacity to pursue his own remedies before any international organ. Proposals for the creation of an International Court of Human Rights with jurisdiction to adjudicate claims brought by individuals or by States were rejected.[20] Also rejected were proposals to allow individuals the right of initiating proceedings before the Human Rights Committee by petition.[21] Arguments against the right of petition by individuals were closely patterned on the arguments employed against any international implementation of the Covenant: it would be contrary to traditional international law, and it might infringe the sovereignty of States and lead to intervention in their domestic affairs. There was also the argument that under current conditions reliance upon an individual right of petition promised less in the effective protection of human rights than enforcement proceedings initiated by States.

In favor of the right of petition it was argued that the Covenant "was unique in that States parties were to undertake specific obligations towards their own nationals." This involved "a voluntary relinquishment of some national sovereignty and not an invasion of

---

[18] *Ibid.*, pp. 268–270, Art. 46.   [19] *Ibid.*, pp. 289–294, Art. 49.
[20] *Ibid.*, p. 28.   [21] *Ibid.*, pp. 233–242.

it." Unlike most treaties, which set up mutual rights and obligations, a violation of the Covenant by which a State injured its own nationals was unlikely to cause another State to invoke enforcement measures: "past experience, especially of the minorities system of the League of Nations and the complaints procedure under the ILO Constitution, demonstrated that intervention of States to redress violations of human rights, even under treaty obligations, had been negligible and rarely fruitful." [22]

Since individuals were denied any procedural capacity to secure their rights under the draft Covenant on Civil and Political Rights, it was a foregone conclusion that they would be granted no such capacity under the draft Covenant on Economic, Social, and Cultural Rights. Although by Article 2 of the draft Covenant on Economic, Social, and Cultural Rights "each State Party hereto undertakes to take steps, individually and through international cooperation, to the maximum of its available resources, with a view to achieving progressively the full realization of the rights recognized in this Covenant by legislative as well as by other means" and without discrimination,[23] the so-called "measure of implementation" contained in Articles 17–25 of the treaty are scarcely enforcement measures. They provide only that States parties to the Covenant are obligated to make periodic reports which can be the basis "for study and *general* recommendation" by United Nations organs. The insertion of the word "general" in the phrase was defended as preventing the making of "particular recommendations to individual States." [24]

It is thus seen that the international protection of human rights envisaged in the draft Covenants does not go so far as do some current proposals for granting procedural capacity to aliens under international law. The decision to deny the individual any international procedural capacity under the draft Covenants means that the Covenants stop where proposals regarding aliens begin. It may be argued that, when the Covenants enter into force, the rights of nationals against their own State will be just as much rights under international law as are the rights of aliens—and this means rights without an international remedy within the control of the individual. Because the individual, whether as a national or as an alien lacks procedural capacity under

---

[22] *Ibid.*, p. 237.   [23] *Ibid.*, p. 56.   [24] *Ibid.*, pp. 345–346.

international law, some will be inclined to question whether the individual really possesses rights under international law.

As was noted above, the rights of aliens are traditionally expressed in terms of the rights of the alien's State, and the corresponding obligations of the State of residence under international law are obligations owed not directly to the alien but to his State. Under the draft Covenants on Human Rights, the language of obligation is insistent, but to whom are the obligations owed? Who is legally "injured" by a violation? States becoming parties to the Covenants undertake to "recognize," "respect," "grant," "ensure," or "guarantee" certain specified rights and liberties. Other articles are drafted in the language of rights, for example, "Everyone shall have the right to hold opinions without interference." However expressed, the obligations clearly rest upon the State party to the treaty. It is equally clear that the beneficiaries of these obligations are "all individuals within its territory and subject to its jurisdiction" (Art. 2).

What is not clear is whether the States which become parties to the Covenants intend thereby to confer upon their inhabitants substantive legal rights under international law or merely under their municipal law. The draft Covenants infringe in depth a field of traditionally domestic jurisdiction. In this sense they appear to be stipulating that henceforth international law shall regulate the relations of a State with its inhabitants, including its nationals. By a parity of reasoning, the language of the Covenants appears to clothe the individual with international legal personality to the extent of having substantive rights, and not merely benefits, conferred on him by the Covenants. And yet to secure these rights the nationals of a particular State are completely dependent upon the good faith of that State or upon the benevolent interest of another State willing to incur the odium of "intervention" on their behalf against their own government.

Whether the individual has substantive legal rights under the Covenants or merely receives benefits stipulated on his behalf can be regarded as a sterile legal question only where he obtains his rights. Where he is denied his rights or benefits, it becomes a crucial practical question whether the method of conferring upon him rights without remedies under international law is the most efficacious method by which the United Nations can fulfill its obligation of promoting and encouraging respect for human rights and fundamental freedoms.

The "Rights of Aliens"

It remains to be seen how many States will become parties to the draft Covenants on Human Rights and with what good faith they will accept in this field the conquest of their domestic jurisdiction by international law. To the writer, there is little evidence in the behavior of States with regard to their nationals or in the inter-State practice upon which international law is grounded to suggest that respect for human rights will be appreciably furthered by the methods envisaged in the draft Covenants. Putting words into a treaty and getting States to sign the pledge for a revolutionary reversal of current concepts and behavior promises as little in terms of effectiveness as a Kellogg Pact.

Most of the States of the world have long had constitutional provisions or basic laws guaranteeing civil liberties, and the newer States have facilely copied them.[25] It is not the absence of legal enactment but the mores of a community which permit neglect of civil liberties. The political and social environments which condition respect for human rights are local and infinitely varied. Uniform international "solutions" of such problems are suspect prima facie, the more so when couched in resounding legal abstractions. Changing the label of constitutionally formulated civil liberties into the international rights of man, aside from being historically retrograde, has little relevance to the conditioning environments. The differing environmental situations in more than one hundred political units will yield less to a uniform international legal code, with or without teeth, than to the patient promotion and encouragement of respect for human rights through political enlightenment and economic development.

[25] See Amos J. Peaslee, *Constitutions of Nations* (2d ed., 3 vols.; The Hague, 1956), *passim.*

V

COMPARATIVE ASPECTS

[ROBERT K. CARR]

DARTMOUTH COLLEGE

Observations by an American
on English Civil Liberties

AMERICANS have traditionally envied England's famed devotion to the cause of individual freedom. We have thought of England as a country in which respect for the law, a spirit of fair play, a concern for justice, and other similar national traits have combined to produce a social system in which civil liberties are secure. The American who has the good fortune to visit England finds little cause to revise this judgment—at least so far as outward appearances go. There is an air of calmness and a spirit of assuredness in England that seem to reflect faith in established institutions, trust in the common sense and loyalty of the people, and confidence in the integrity and fairness of public officials.

Communists spout their radical doctrines in Hyde Park without hindrance from the police or without stirring the wrath of super-patriots; Negroes, Hindus, and members of other minority groups go their way about London often garbed in strange raiment and appear to attract no special attention and not to encounter discrimination; criminal trials run their course at the Old Bailey, and everyone seems confident that justice has been done; Parliament transacts its business without benefit of noisy, controversial investigating committees; and everywhere are the friendly, weaponless policemen, who seem to symbolize a system of authority the aim of which is to help the individual find his way and solve his problems rather than to discipline him for transgressions against the law.

The American moves easily from these observations to the plaintive query: Why can't we be like the English? And he reminds himself that our political and legal institutions have much in common with those of England and that our social origins are more English than they are anything else. How valid is this comparison that we try so eagerly to make? Is the English civil liberty record as good as outward appearances suggest it is? And if the substance is as good as the shadow, what lessons does the English record hold for us? Careful attempts to answer questions such as these quickly lead to the not-surprising realization that things are not so simple as they seem.

One does not dig very far beneath the surface before he discovers that the Englishman's approach to the problems of civil liberty is in many ways indigenous to his country. England is a tiny land populated by a relatively homogeneous people.[1] It is thereby freed from many civil liberty problems which in the United States are substantially affected by the factors of geography and population. It is one thing to make individual freedom secure in a land the size of the State of New York in which sectional conflict is never more serious than, say, the ancient antagonism between Welshman and Englishman. It is something else altogether to achieve respect for the rights of each individual in a land that occupies a vast continental expanse and whose citizenry is derived from every race and nationality of the earth.

English society has also taken shape through long centuries of gradual development. Tradition is a powerful force making for a peaceful, stable social system and, in turn, for the security of individual rights. Contrast this slow evolution of English society with the development of our own fantastic melting-pot society into which were poured in less than a century some 40,000,000 immigrants, and it is easy to understand why the English are a more relaxed people than we are. This difference has profoundly affected the two nations' civil liberty records. For example, the relative absence of racial minorities has made it easy for the English to avoid the corrosive damage that racial

---

[1] Scotland and Northern Ireland are excluded from this analysis, for their civil liberty problems and practices are in many ways quite different from those of England.

antagonisms have done to American court procedures and to our sense of criminal justice.[2]

Homogeneity also helps explain the English sense of fair play, which often operates as a powerful force in preventing encroachments on the individual's rights. In recent decades the English public has become particularly insistent upon fair dealing for the individual who is caught up in the toils of bureaucratic red tape. A leading English editor told this writer that no press story commands a wider or more outraged audience in England than an episode in which "bloody mindedness" on the part of a person in a position of authority results in unfair action against a helpless individual. He added, "Such a story easily beats sex and murder for the headlines." Indeed, the postwar civil liberty case *par excellence* in England, the Crichel Down affair, was just such a story. Reaction was immediate and violent in England when, through seeming highhandedness by officials in the civil service, an Englishman failed to recover a piece of land, originally belonging to his wife's family, that had been taken through the power of eminent domain by the government for use as a bombing practice area but was no longer needed for this purpose. To be sure, the aggrieved man was no poor, friendless cockney, but a wealthy, intelligent country squire perfectly capable of pressing for a satisfactory recognition of his rights. This hurt the story not at all, however, and an aroused public opinion undoubtedly helped force the remedial steps that were ultimately taken to correct the injustices that this case brought to light.[3]

English "fair play," like all such so-called national characteristics, has its limitations and blind spots. The writer's two teen-age sons, who spent six months in London in 1955, were outraged when in the football "Cup Finals" at Wembley Stadium that year, following an injury to one of the leading players on the opening play of the game, his team had to play out the game one man short because "no substitutions are allowed." Fair play was seemingly forgotten when, at the annual meeting of a civil liberty organization in London in 1955, a labor union delegate took the floor and denounced the Negro im-

---

[2] Many of the famous cases of the last three decades, in which the United States Supreme Court has ordered new trials in state criminal cases because of serious deficiencies in the proceedings, have concerned Negro defendants.

[3] See R. Douglas Brown, *The Battle of Crichel Down* (London: The Bodley Head, 1955), for a somewhat partisan account of this complicated case.

migrants from Jamaica who were competing with him and his fellow members for jobs and housing.

It is also important to recognize that the homogeneity of the English people as a quality conducive to civil liberty is in some ways a vice masquerading as a virtue. Thus, the English are essentially a conservative people. For all their Tory-Labour political quarrels, they are not excitable, and they have a strong distaste for conflict and dissension. A former Director-General of the B.B.C. told the writer that if two participants in a radio discussion program cannot "find a good deal of common ground after twenty minutes of talking, the average listener begins to lose interest in them." And he added, "Finding common ground is an English tradition." Again, the abiding sense of tradition that influences strongly the English people goes far toward explaining the individual Englishman's acceptance of "his place in life"—a characteristic that may be a virtue when it comes to avoiding the bitter social conflicts out of which come civil liberty violations, but a vice in the way it leads to a denial of social opportunity. Admittedly the English class system is today in a state of flux. It is still a highly stratified one, however, and it has a long way to go before it achieves the fluidity of the American social system, particularly the latter's broad educational and economic opportunities for the young. Much emphasis has recently been placed upon the democratic inroads that have been made in the century-old aristocratic traditions of education in England. But the all-important examination that must be taken by the youngster at the age of "eleven-plus" still stands as a powerful barrier to the giving of a liberal arts education at the secondary school and university levels to any large number of English youngsters. Scholarships to the famed "public schools" and universities may now be available to bright students regardless of their social class or economic status, but the fact remains that the total number of students that these institutions can accept is, by American standards, extremely small. Thus, access to those walks of life that only this kind of education makes possible, namely, the professions and the higher levels of the civil service, is still extremely restricted. In a conversation with two members of the editorial staff of *The Economist* this writer mentioned the attractive personalities and high intelligence of English policemen, always so impressive to American visitors. He was told, by way of an explanation, that in the United States many of these men would undoubtedly have continued their education to a point where entry into business and the professions would have been their natural and inevitable goals.[4] Another journalist, an American expatriate, called England "liberal," but not "democratic." He insisted that control of English life is in the hands of a narrow social group numbering no more than 8,000 individuals.[5]

The virtues and faults in the English sense of calmness and conservatism that leads on the one hand to confidence in established ways of life and on the other to tolerance of those who harbor radical sentiments have been well illustrated in the postwar English attitude toward Communist activity on the domestic scene. The attitude has

[4] In its recent pamphlet, *Personal Freedom: Labour's Policy for the Individual and Society,* the Labour Party view is set forth in these terms: "There is no more important extension of personal freedom than a publicly provided system of education that ensures that the capabilities of each individual are developed to the full. Although we now have greater mobility between classes, ours is still a class-conscious society in which class distinction is based largely on educational privilege. Far from wanting to destroy the best kinds of education, however, we want to make them available to all" (p. 7). Christopher Hollis has written in a recent issue of *The Observer* (July 7, 1957): "It is clearly absurd to deny that the public school system as it at present exists is an affront to the principle of equality of opportunity. That is indeed its purpose."

[5] This same journalist doubted that English civil liberty cases are ever settled because the public becomes aroused and demands relief or justice in individual cases. Instead, members of the governing class pride themselves in doing what they think is proper, regardless of public clamor. Honor, duty, and reason are their guiding forces, not public opinion, said he. This position was somewhat borne out by a remarkable editorial that appeared in *The Times* on St. George's Day (April 23) in 1954. In part it ran: "The unforced cohesion of the English, it is commonly said, enables them to be tolerant of minorities. They, in fact, commonly say it themselves. But all that means is that, for the past 250 years, no minority in England itself has been strong enough to challenge the establishment—political and religious. When minorities outside England, but inside the United Kingdom, have threatened it the English have proved as capable of intolerance—and blundering intolerance at that—as anyone. . . . Because the establishment is so secure and so beneficial, there has grown up an attitude that it is neither wise nor expedient to question the foundations on which it rests. Both political and religious thinking in England suffer from this reluctance to ask the genuinely fundamental questions. Words—'class,' 'democracy,' 'rights,'—are given acceptable and meaningless definitions and are then used, not to aid thinking but as a substitute for it. . . . English society and English institutions live by preserving the forms but changing the reality. This is admirable and mature behavior. But it can only work in the long run if thinkers continue to look at the reality closely, and question what is happening beneath the forms (old and new). They are not doing it today. They have become much too English."

been decidedly *laissez faire.* There is no lack of laws in England defining crimes in the area of subversive activity, including even the vague
offense of sedition. But prosecutions of Communists under these laws
have been few in number. In particular, there has been no equivalent
of our Smith Act prosecutions in an effort to send the leaders of the
Communist Party in England to jail for advocating, or conspiring to
advocate, the overthrow of government by force or violence.[6] There
have been no sensational legislative investigations into the threat of
internal Communist subversion, no general loyalty tests for government
workers (there has been a "security check" in sensitive areas of public
employment that has been made progressively more rigorous) or for
teachers or lawyers or journalists, and no "Attorney General's list"
of proscribed organizations, membership in which renders the individual suspect as a subversive.

Some Americans have feared that the English view of their domestic
Communists as harmless cranks who can safely be given full freedom
to advertise their foolish notions has been a dangerous delusion. As a
matter of fact, successive revelations concerning Communist infiltration of certain English labor unions and provocation of strikes, as well
as the sensational developments in the Burgess-Maclean case, have
slowly led many Englishmen to wonder whether they have not been
underestimating the threat to their national security posed by the
native Communist movement. But this growing understanding of the
Communist threat has not stampeded the English into adopting any
of the more extreme methods of combating communism that have been
so popular in the United States.

The American observer who tries to be dispassionate in his evaluation of this phase of contemporary English life can perhaps draw
three conclusions: One, England has achieved at least as much security
against the internal Communist threat as has the United States,
through the use of far less "vigorous" methods than those we have
employed. Two, England's efforts to safeguard its national security

---

[6] In an unpublished manuscript, two English scholars, Professor W. J. M. Mackenzie of the University of Manchester and Professor Harry Street of the University
of Nottingham, write, "The best safeguard against extreme enforcement of [laws
defining the offense of sedition] has been the reluctance of juries to convict where
no manifest incitement to violence is proved." Contrast this attitude with the extreme proneness of American juries to convict in Smith Act cases.

have offered a minimal threat to civil liberties. Three, the basic problem with which England has been dealing here has almost certainly been a far easier one than we have faced, for the very reason that, as "a tight little isle," its basic way of life has deeper roots, its people are more instinctively loyal, and its public officers are more firmly committed to traditional ways of doing things and more strongly imbued with a sense of honor.

There is another and perhaps even more basic way in which the English and American civil liberty systems differ. Every American is aware that England has no written constitution and no formal bill of rights, which operate in the United States as such powerful safeguards of civil liberty. But it comes to him as a surprise to discover that England also makes much more sparing use than we do of statutes and court decisions as devices for protecting civil liberties.[7] He is particularly startled to discover that there is almost no direct counterpart in England of the United States Supreme Court decision setting forth a striking ruling on behalf of civil liberty for an entire nation to ponder and observe. Court decisions, of course, play their part in protecting an Englishman's civil liberties, but as often as not an English civil liberty "case" concerns only the administrative and parliamentary processes of government, and public opinion is the persistent and decisive force making for a sensible and "just" solution. It is here, as already suggested, that the English press plays such an important part. It is here also that such unique English institutions as the Royal Commission and Question Time in the House of Commons are powerful weapons for use when Englishmen undertake to do battle on behalf of civil liberty. More than one social problem in recent English history, in which a civil liberty issue was at stake, has been carried forward toward an acceptable solution through the re-

[7] Professors Mackenzie and Street write: "The law of civil liberties is derived in part from the principles of the common law which are in their general form obsolete; it flows in part from principles which belong primarily to private law and not to public law. The law has therefore none of the elegance usual in countries where the legal doctrine of civil liberties is based on a philosophical doctrine of the rights of man; it is capable of much improvement, and it is certainly not a model for imitation." And again: "The English think about liberties in terms of history, and not of guarantees. . . . Each liberty has been a position won in a battle to gain power or to restrain power; the familiar list of civil liberties is a list of what have at various times been key positions in English politics."

port of a Royal Commission.[8] Question Time is repeatedly used by backbenchers on both sides of the party aisle in the House of Commons to focus national attention upon civil liberty violations and, in particular, to bring pressure upon administrative officers to take remedial steps with respect to these violations.[9]

Civil liberties in England are based upon tradition, trial-and-error experimentation, and compromise arrangements far more often than they are upon constitutional guarantees, legal rules, or even moral principles. Arthur Goodhart, one of the keenest observers of English civil liberty practices, has put it, "The Englishman prefers to decide each concrete problem by itself, without worrying too much about theoretical consistency." And he quotes with approval Lord Morley's observation that England has "profound distrust of all general principles." [10] Thus, in protecting their civil liberties Englishmen have been influenced by recognition of the fact that social problems are marked by competing social interests and a conflict of opposing forces. Unless the victory in such a struggle is to go inevitably to the strongest of these forces, each competing interest is entitled to consideration in arriving at a solution.

Among other things, this means that when he is coping with a civil liberty problem (which he seldom recognizes as such, and almost never so labels, although he sometimes uses his own traditional phrase, "liberties of the subject"), the Englishman does not share the American's fear of political authority as the implacable enemy of liberty. Instead, he thinks of liberty and authority as overlapping concepts,

[8] For example, charges in 1928 that a girl secretarial worker had been subjected to "third degree" methods by police officers while being held on a morals charge led not only to a notable Royal Commission report on the reform of police methods, but a famed use of another unique English device, a "Tribunal of Inquiry," under an act of Parliament passed in 1921. See Herman Finer, "The British System," *University of Chicago Law Review*, Spring 1951, pp. 521–570, an extraordinarily interesting and informed article providing not only an excellent analysis of Royal Commissions and Tribunals of Inquiry but a systematic examination of all English equivalents to our legislative investigating committees.

[9] It should be noted that some scholars and observers, English and American alike, are inclined to believe that the efficacy of these devices—press, Royal Commission, Tribunal of Inquiry, and Question-Time—as safeguards of civil liberty has been exaggerated. But so, too, has the role of the American Bill of Rights and of United States Supreme Court decisions.

[10] Arthur Goodhart, *The British Constitution* (New York: British Information Services, 1946), p. 54.

as two phases of the same process in the sense that in every sensible and workable social arrangement in a democratic society there is some measure of authority and some measure of liberty.

A good example of this pragmatic approach to the development of civil liberties in England is found in its system of "soapbox oratory" which finds its most famed home in Hyde Park, always a fascinating spot for American tourists. Examination of the system leads to the conclusion that here the English have been much more concerned about achieving a common-sense, compromise solution to a troublesome problem than they have been to exalt the principle of free speech. No English court has ever attempted to establish such an unrestricted and sweeping constitutional right of street oratory as did the United States Supreme Court in 1939 in its decision in *Hague v. C.I.O.*[11] The Court's finding that "wherever the title to streets and parks may rest, they have immemorially been held in trust for the use of the public and, time out of mind, have been used for purposes of assembly, communicating thoughts between citizens, and discussing public questions" would strike a responsive chord in the breast of an Englishman. But the Court's insistence in that and later cases that the Constitution establishes a basic right of orators to use streets and parks, subject only to minimal interference by public authority to protect such competing interests as the orderly flow of traffic or avoidance of public disorder, would startle an Englishman. The English soapbox orator may not speak wherever his fancy dictates, for English law does not recognize any general right to hold public meetings in streets and parks. Instead, he must go to one of those relatively few spots, such as Hyde Park, that have been set aside for this purpose. And even here, he must watch his tongue. He is told by well-advertised police regulations that he may not use obscene, insulting, or abusive language and that he must avoid words likely to cause disorder or a breach of the peace. Similarly, he is forbidden to give racing or betting tips, sell any articles, or take up a collection. Moreover, he is expected to control his own audience, and if disorder threatens (which it rarely does), he may be told by a police officer "to close down." And to speak at certain desirable locations such as Trafalgar Square, he must first obtain permission from the Ministry of Works. A civil servant at this Ministry, which has responsibility for super-

[11] 306 U.S. 624 (1939).

vising the soapbox oratory system, told the writer that the system has developed on a "purely empirical basis." And he added, "It is typically British. We tell the orator, 'You have free speech, but you must not do certain things.'"

A comparison of English and American ways of handling the problem of street oratory suggests that we have worked out a splendid legal framework for this medium of expression, but that our practice in handling street orators in many an American community is grievously bad, whereas the English have been much less concerned about evolving a dogmatic legal principle in support of this aspect of freedom of speech and have concentrated instead upon working out in practice a system that is the envy of all other democratic countries.

His pragmatic approach to civil liberty problems has also made it easier for the Englishman than for the American to see that in many situations it is not liberty and authority that are in conflict but two or more civil liberties. Seeing this, he instinctively realizes that it helps very little in trying to find a solution to such a problem for high-minded people to use the sloganeering approach, "civil liberty must be defended." He sees instead that what is often called for is an evaluation of the conflicting interests present in the situation and the working out of a compromise settlement or the making of a decision that one interest should definitely take precedence over another.

A good illustration of the way in which Englishmen have been willing to make this choice between conflicting interests is seen in the area of freedom of the press. Here, too, a dogmatic assertion in law or moral principle in support of an ideal has been avoided. The English are just as aware as are Americans of the essential role played by a free press in a democratic society, but they have not hesitated to impose legal restraints upon the press at points where they feel that this is necessary in order to protect a competing civil liberty which is deemed to be superior to freedom of the press. One such competing interest which is regarded as superior is a man's good name and his right to privacy. Accordingly, the English law of libel places a much more drastic restraint upon the press than does American law. As one editor put it to the writer, he and every other newspaper editor in England must constantly ask themselves whether any item in their columns will "tend to lower the individual to whom it refers in the estimation of right-thinking persons generally, or to bring him into hatred, ridicule, or contempt, or to exclude him from the society of his fellow men." [12]

This protection against libel by newspapers extends even to politicians. Following the 1951 election in Britain, Winston Churchill brought a libel action against England's largest newspaper, *The Daily Mirror*, on the ground that its "Whose Finger at the Trigger" editorial attacks upon him during the campaign had unfairly implied that he was a warmonger. *The Daily Mirror* was sufficiently alarmed by the suit to make a settlement with Churchill out of court.[13]

Another competing civil liberty held to be superior to freedom of the press in England is the right of an accused person in a criminal case to a fair trial. Thus English law severely limits the manner in which criminal cases can be reported by the press. The vulgar, highly prejudicial fashion in which much of the American press reports such sensational crimes as the Sheppard murder case in Cleveland or the Denver plane-explosion case is absolutely forbidden in England. In particular, after an arrest has been made, English newspapers must rigidly restrict their stories to the bare reporting of factual developments.[14] Any English editor who fails to follow such a course is likely to find himself thrown into jail for contempt of court. Again, *The Daily Mirror* provides an example. In 1949 it published the lurid details of a series of "vampire" murders in London and implied that an unnamed man the police had taken into custody might be the perpetrator of these crimes. A court presided over by the Lord Chief Justice decided that there had been a deliberate pandering to sensationalism and sent

[12] The editor was quoting closely the conclusion on this point reached by Oswald S. Hickson and P. F. Carter-Ruck, in *The Law of Libel and Slander* (London: Faber and Faber, Ltd., 1953), p. 23.

[13] Hugh Cudlipp, *Publish and Be Damned!* (London: Andrew Dakers, Ltd., 1953), pp. 260–264.

[14] The recent trial at the Old Bailey of Dr. Adams on a murder charge has, moreover, stirred a controversy in England as to whether these restrictions are sufficiently severe. It was argued that several newspapers published sensational stories of mass poisonings and exhumed bodies long before Dr. Adams was charged with any crime and that his right to a fair trial was thereby jeopardized. The preliminary proceedings before the magistrates (which have replaced the grand jury hearing in England) were in this case public, and again, it was argued that the sensational evidence which the prosecuting authorities laid before the magistrates in this case prejudiced Dr. Adams' right to a fair trial. See *The Observer*, April 14, 1957.

the editor to jail for three months and fined his paper £10,000 for contempt of court.[15]

Perhaps the most astounding aspect to an American of these two restraints on the press is the universal approval of them that prevails in England. Even the author of the official history of *The Daily Mirror* admits that the paper "perpetrated a blunder" in its "vampire" case story. He writes that the "law is a good law. The Editor took his punishment and did not complain." [16] It does not occur even to newspaper people to think that "freedom of the press" is endangered by this restraint. Instead, the arrangement is evaluated in practical terms. The competing interests have been weighed, and the conclusion is drawn that the resulting adjustment of these interests is sensible.[17]

The contemporary English civil liberty record is not without its soft spots. The recent substantial immigration of Negroes into England from Jamaica and other islands of the British West Indies has produced "an emerging race problem" and has forced public officials and thoughtful citizens alike to recognize that racial prejudice and discrimination are not an American monopoly. On the surface, colored people may seem to be fully accepted in England. In the past this has been particularly true of colored students and government officials from the colonies. But in the last few years, as the number of Negroes entering England has risen to more than 25,000 a year, there has been a good deal of racial conflict in such centers as Birmingham, Liverpool, Leeds, and the Brixton and Paddington areas of London, particularly over jobs and housing and, to a certain extent, over Negro-white sexual relations. Fortunately, intelligent steps are being taken to cope with this problem before it gets out of hand, and it is unlikely that the English social scene will be marred by serious racial conflict.[18] But that any conflict at all should have appeared in such a tolerant, conservative society as that of England in the face of a Negro minority

[15] Hugh Cudlipp, *op. cit.*, p. 253.   [16] *Ibid.*, p. 254.

[17] Contrast this attitude with the quite different point of view that is set forth in James R. Wiggins, *Freedom or Secrecy?* (New York: Oxford University Press, 1956).

[18] On England's "emerging race problem" see Anthony H. Richmond, *The Colour Problem* (London: Penguin Books, 1955); M. P. Banton, *The Coloured Quarter* (London: Jonathan Cape, 1955); *Colonial Students in Britain,* a Report by PEP (Political and Economic Planning), 1955.

numbering about .25 per cent of the population throws a new light on the handling of the race problem in the United States where the Negro minority numbers 10 per cent of the population.

There is also growing concern among informed lawyers and students over the quality of English justice. The magistry of English criminal justice at the Old Bailey may be impressive. But some 95 per cent of all criminal cases in England are tried by local magistrates, most of whom, apart from those in London and a few other large cities, are not even trained in the law. According to Professor W. J. M. Mackenzie of the University of Manchester and Professor Harry Street of the University of Nottingham, most of these magistrates are appointed on a political basis, frequently from an elderly and conservative segment of the population. They write that these judges "often exhibit naked prejudice" and that "they believe police evidence on principle, and allow the police to exercise an illegal disciplinary control over the accused." [19] Another authority, Professor Glanville Williams of the University of London, states that the use of illegally procured police evidence in criminal cases has become a serious problem.[20] There has been a recent controversy over the use of wire tapping by the police, with bitter criticism of the Home Office for authorizing the police to obtain evidence by this method.[21] When, in 1954, a series of eminent publishers were prosecuted on the charge of having published obscene books, it was a shock to the English to discover how lacking in uniformity was the quality of justice meted out by their courts. In five cases that differed little on their facts, the results were two convictions, two acquittals, and, in the fifth case, two hung juries. Moreover, it was not so much the unpredictability of English juries that produced these erratic verdicts as it was the shockingly different charges to the jury made by the judges sitting in the cases.[22]

Perhaps the most disturbing aspect of the contemporary English

[19] Mackenzie and Street, *op. cit.*

[20] "Evidence Obtained by Illegal Means," *Criminal Law Review*, June 1955, pp. 339–349.

[21] *The Observer*, June 9, 1957.

[22] See the article by Roy Jenkins, MP, "Reforming the Censorship," *The Spectator*, March 22, 1957. A full account of these cases is found in Norman St. John-Stevas, *Obscenity and the Law* (London: Secker & Warburg, 1956). One of the publishers, Frederic John Warburg, supplies a fascinating account of his trial in "A Slight Case of Obscenity," *New Yorker*, April 20, 1957, p. 33.

civil liberty scene to an American is the measure of censorship that restrains such mass media of expression as the radio, the theater, and the cinema. During World War II the B.B.C. was forced to enter into a "gentlemen's agreement" with the Government that no legislative issue would be discussed over the air within fourteen days of the time that it was to come up for consideration in the House of Commons. The agreement lasted until 1955, when B.B.C. officials at long last threatened to repudiate this odious "14-day rule." Faced with such a threat, the Postmaster General reaffirmed the rule through an administrative order. In February 1956, however, the House of Commons established a Select Committee

> to consider whether any changes are desirable in the present methods of giving effect to the principle that there should be some limitation to the anticipation of parliamentary debates by broadcasting.

Following the report of this Committee the Government suspended the "14-day rule" for an experimental period of six months. The Prime Minister announced that the Government had

> received assurance from the B.B.C., the Independent Television Authority and the Independent Television Authority's Companies that, if the existing rule is suspended, they will continue to act in a way which does not derogate from the primacy of Parliament as the forum for debating the affairs of the nation.

In July 1957 the Government announced that the rule was "to remain suspended for an indefinite period." [23]

The most startling censorship in England is found in the legitimate theater. No play written within the last century can be performed anywhere in the United Kingdom unless it has been licensed for exhibition by the Lord Chamberlain, which means that the script of a play must be submitted in advance, revised if required, and approved for performance. The Lord Chamberlain's power is arbitrary and absolute. No playwright or producer has any right to a hearing when a play is being examined or to an appeal to any higher administrative agency or to the courts against an adverse ruling.[24] From the time of

---

[23] Information concerning these developments since 1955 has come to me from Sir William Haley, editor of *The Times*.

[24] Professors Mackenzie and Street write, "One can concede some merits in theatre censorship, without approving of censorship by an irresponsible official

the plays of Henrik Ibsen and George Bernard Shaw to those of Lillian Hellman, André Gide, Tennessee Williams, Arthur Miller, and Robert Anderson, many works of acknowledged dramatic merit have been denied licenses.[25] Informal inquiry at the Lord Chamberlain's office produced the statement that "it is pretty well understood that plays in the following categories will not be licensed: (1) those dealing with homosexuality; (2) those dealing with the royal family in critical terms; (3) those that are rude or unkind to living persons or persons recently dead; (4) those dealing with brutality for brutality's sake." But this writer was shown the script of Giraudoux's *Tiger at the Gates,* which was under consideration for a license, and it was clear that the blue pencil was also being used to delete lines suggestive of normal heterosexual behavior.

As is usual with censorship systems, the licensing of plays is marked by a number of inconsistencies. Music-hall programs and musical revues are largely immune from the Lord Chamberlain's control and are, accordingly, frequently marked by much vulgarity. In particular, crude jokes about homosexuality, discussion of which subject is barred from the "serious" theater, are a staple of music-hall comedians. As one informed observer put it to the writer, "There is more censorship in England of ideas than of vulgarity." Again, plays denied licenses can be performed by "art theatres" or "club theatres" to which the public has just about as ready access as it does to the commercial theater. A play performed under these circumstances, however, rarely reaches a wide audience.[26]

Theatrical producers and even some playwrights and critics strongly approve this system of stage censorship on the ground that once a play has been licensed by the Lord Chamberlain it is immune from attack by local police authorities or the Mrs. Grundys of the community. The editor of *The Times* told the writer that "the British like

working by undisclosed rules with an unqualified discretion free from judicial review, empowered to withdraw without reason a play whose performance has been previously approved."

[25] Among the plays which have been banned, at least for a time, in modern England have been *Ghosts, Mrs. Warren's Profession, Victoria Regina, The Green Pastures, Young Woodley, Parnell, The Children's Hour, The Immoralist, Cat on a Hot Tin Roof, The View from the Bridge,* and *Tea and Sympathy.*

[26] There are several moderately successful theaters of this type in London, but the recent spectacular development of the "off-Broadway" theater in New York has not been duplicated in London.

to get censorship out in the open where they can see it and where they know it functions relatively free from lobbies and pressures. The British won't stand for the D.A.R. and American Legion type of censorship of plays and movies that exists in America."

Many of England's intellectuals are disturbed by this power of the Lord Chamberlain, and about once every generation an abortive attempt is made to persuade Parliament to enact remedial legislation. Early in this century such a movement, in which Shaw and many of the other great figures of the theater of that time participated, resulted in a monumental report by a Joint Select Committee of the House of Lords and the House of Commons, but no legislation. Again, in 1949 a Private Member's Bill to end the censorship of plays passed the second reading in the House of Commons, after a brief, though notable debate.[27] But the shortage of parliamentary time, a factor that is responsible for the death of many worthy bills in Britain, prevented further action at that session.

A similar system of censorship lays a heavy hand on the English cinema. The system is sometimes defended as an entirely voluntary one on the ground that the British Board of Film Censors is a private rather than a governmental agency. But the censorship power wielded by this agency is made effective through the requirement imposed by local government authorities, who possess the power to license the operation of cinema theaters, that only films approved by BBFC may be shown. A BBFC license involves not only approval of the final film but scrutiny and approval of the script from which the film is made. Unlike the American film industry's voluntary censorship system or the play-licensing system in England, the BBFC has no "Code" which arbitrarily rules out certain themes or subjects from all films. Nevertheless the examination of films is rigorous, and most of the subjects automatically banned in the United States are excluded in England as individual films are examined.

Like the system of stage censorship, the English cinema censorship is often much admired.[28] In particular there is much praise for the

[27] The debate on the second reading is found in *Hansard* (March 25, 1949), vol. 463, cols. 715–798.

[28] See, for example, the laudatory article by Stephen Watts in *The New York Times,* February 7, 1954.

system of separating films into three categories in the licensing process. Those with a U (Universal) license can be seen by anyone; those with an A (Adult) license can be seen by a person under sixteen only if accompanied by a parent or guardian; those with an X license can be seen only by persons sixteen and over. It is argued that this plan allows for the licensing (with an X) of sophisticated films of a type that would be banned altogether in the United States either by the film industry's own censorship system or under state laws. But "going to the films" is very much a family affair in England, and thus a film with an X license is highly unlikely to be booked by the major chains that operate virtually all of the neighborhood and small city theaters in England, although it may be shown by a small theater in London and advertised as "the X-iest film in town!" [29]

There is a growing tendency among thoughtful people in England to wonder whether stage and film censorship is not partly responsible for the light and frivolous character of most contemporary English plays and films. In the main they avoid serious subjects—in particular, morbid themes or sociological problems.[30] Instead, playwrights and film scriptwriters depict the "joys and humors of the native scene" in scintillating drawing-room comedies and amusing "genre" pieces. For their serious West End theater fare, Londoners in recent years have been largely dependent upon Shakespeare [31] and contemporary plays imported from the Continent and the United States. John Osborne, whose *Look Back in Anger* and *The Entertainer* have recently burst upon the London theatrical scene like bombshells, may be the forerunner in a revival of serious playwrighting by Englishmen, but a startling aspect of the contemporary English theater remains the absence of a group of native playwrights of the caliber of Tennessee

[29] Some films are denied even X licenses. This was the fate of the American film, *The Wild One*, with Marlon Brando, a serious effort to deal with the social problem posed by "motorcycle bums." Apparently an X license was denied this film because of the fear that it might have a corrupting effect on English motorcycle operators, most of whom were presumably sixteen or over!

[30] Kenneth Tynan, drama critic of *The Observer*, has in the last few years repeatedly deplored the absence of serious English playwrighting.

[31] One of the most successful Shakespeare revivals of recent years in England has been the Stratford Memorial Theatre's performance of *Titus Andronicus* with Laurence Olivier and Vivien Leigh. Critics have taken delight in pointing to the play's resemblance to a modern "horror comic."

Williams, Arthur Miller, Lillian Hellman, William Inge, Robert Anderson, and Arthur Laurents.[32]

In 1954 even the English book business momentarily felt the heavy restraining hand of government. There is no censorship (in the sense of prior restraint) of books in England, although, as in the United States, the law carries heavy penalties for the actual publication of obscene books. Two approaches are open to the Government in prosecuting such cases. The first of these is prosecution for the common-law offense of obscene libel. The test of obscenity in these cases is still the nineteenth-century standard laid down in *Hicklin's* case, namely, "whether the tendency of the matter charged as obscenity is to deprave and corrupt those whose minds are open to such immoral influences and into whose hands a publication of this sort may fall." [33] " 'Tendency' is thus the essence of the common law offense, and it follows that if the necessary effect of a publication is to corrupt, then the motive of the defendant in publishing the obscene matter is not material." [34] The second approach is through a statutory offense defined by the Obscene Publications Act of 1857. Under this act any person can charge before local magistrates that a bookseller has obscene books in his possession and that an actual sale of such a book has occurred. The magistrates can order the police to enter the premises and seize the allegedly obscene books. The books are brought before the magistrates, and the bookseller is ordered to appear within seven days to show cause why the books should not be destroyed. Neither the publisher nor the author of the books in question has any right to be heard before an order to destroy is carried out. In the hands of conservative magistrates this law provides for bookburning with a vengeance!

The 1954 series of prosecutions under both these laws was apparently the end result of an increasingly reactionary point of view that had come to prevail in the Home Office. Seemingly, Labour and Conservative Home Secretaries alike did their part after the war to pave the way for the 1954 spectacle. Fortunately, there was a sharp adverse public reaction to the 1954 prosecutions. In the five common-law prosecutions of reputable publishers, the books in question were all

---

[32] The thesis that the censor may be partly responsible for this situation is strengthened by the fact that there is no dearth of serious writing among contemporary English novelists, poets, and essayists.

[33] L.R. 3 Q.B. 360 (1868). [34] St. John-Stevas, *op. cit.*, p. 126.

contemporary novels with considerable claim to literary merit. The admirable summing up for the jury by Mr. Justice Staple in one of these cases produced an acquittal and made a deep impression upon the English reading public.[35] Similarly, when the magistrates in Swindon ordered the destruction of a number of copies of *The Decameron,* a wave of revulsion against such stupidity swept through England, and the order was quashed on appeal.

The reaction to these prosecutions included the drafting by the English Society of Authors of an enlightened Obscene Publications Bill. Efforts to secure the enactment of this bill by Parliament have thus far failed, but the bill has provoked a very healthy debate on the subject of book suppression in England.

In spite of these soft spots, the American observer cannot fail to retain his respect for the strong spirit of individualism and the deep regard for basic civil liberties that are undeniably a part of the dominant mood in contemporary England. In his search for an exportable wisdom in these matters he is also bound to be impressed by the extent to which English civil liberties depend upon common-sense arrangements in which pragmatism and compromise play roles at least as important as those played by legal rules and moral principles. At the same time he cannot help wondering whether a somewhat stronger concern for the latter might not have enabled the English to avoid some part of the censorship that continues to limit freedom of expression in unfortunate ways. As it is, the English find it perhaps just a bit too easy to rationalize their censorship programs as serving common-sense needs.

The American also turns away from his observation of the English civil liberty scene with renewed appreciation of the very great progress we have made in this country in winning our own civil liberty battles—an appreciation that reflects the enormously greater problem we face here in safeguarding the liberties of a polyglot population occupying a vast continental expanse and an appreciation also of the high goal we have set for ourselves in trying to solve civil liberty problems in terms of constitutional principles, statutory standards, and judicial rulings, as well as by means of pragmatic arrangements and compromise agreements.

[35] See the *New Yorker* article referred to in note 22.

[MARIO EINAUDI]

CORNELL UNIVERSITY

Problems of Freedom

in Postwar Europe, 1945-1957

IT was in 1945, at the end of World War II, that the last of the totalitarian parties of Western Europe was destroyed. Beginning with fascism in 1922, totalitarianism had exercised for many years an unprecedented and monopolistic measure of power over a large part of Europe. This rule included total guidance and indoctrination of the people, extension of party and state power to all aspects of human life, and the use of terror as an instrument of policy. The crisis caused by totalitarianism was the greatest in Europe since the French Revolution. The denial of freedom was direct and brutal and reached deeply into the social fiber of the nations affected.

After the war, the determination on the part of the three countries most directly concerned to re-establish the essentials of a free society, though urgent and well-nigh universal, was not and could not be expressed in simple terms. What was the content of the freedom so anxiously sought? Were the free societies of tomorrow to find themselves helpless, as in the past, against the attacks of those who did not believe in freedom? Was the chief emphasis to be placed on individual or on social freedoms? How could these freedoms be defined constitutionally and what were to be their guarantees? How much could be learned from the painful experience of the European past and from the sturdy flowering of freedom in the Anglo-Saxon world? What was, finally, the relevance of the great expansion both of the power of Communist states and of the influence of Communist doctrine?

This essay will discuss some of the more significant problems of freedom in France, Germany, and Italy, from the time the new constitutions were framed to the present.

THE BILLS OF RIGHTS

The most urgent initial issue—from the end of 1945 when the first French Constituent Assembly met to the spring of 1949 when the Basic Law of the Federal Republic of Germany was approved—was that of writing into the new constitutions preliminary, yet basic, answers to the problem of freedom. Rights would certainly need for their implementation a legal framework against which they could be defined and defended. Constitutionalism and the successful defense of individual freedom had been, after all, parallel developments in the modern world. Rights had suffered under totalitarianism, for will had replaced law in the life of the community, and the community itself had ceased to exist as terror had tended to destroy all social ties. And even those who were dissatisfied with the eighteenth-century tradition of rights felt that the Constitution was an appropriate shelter under which to place their new economic and social freedoms.

Hence, recourse to the Constitution as an indispensable instrument in creating the conditions of freedom was to be expected. In each of the three countries the Constitution deals with some care with the problem of rights. But there are striking differences in the ways in which they do so.

The Bonn Bill of Rights shows clear evidence both of the authentic "federal" character of the new Germany and of the weight attached to the 1919–1945 experience. With the exception of a generic statement on public ownership in Article 15, the vast reach of economic rights is left to the states. Thirty years after the enactment of the Weimar Constitution, hailed then as the most modern constitution in the world for the extension of its jurisdiction to new fields of social rights, the Bonn Constitution gives us a Bill of Rights which on balance does not reach beyond the classical boundaries of the Western tradition of human freedom.

Nothing is said about the right to work, but Article 12 carefully guarantees to all Germans "the right freely to choose their occupation." More important than the definition of the contents of the welfare state is the definition of the rights which Nazism flouted. The right to the free development of human personality, the right to life, the inviolability of the freedom of the individual, the dignity of man, the right to teach, to move freely about, to establish private schools, the rights of conscientious objectors—these are the rights that above all matter.

The Constitution seeks to avoid the shortcomings of the Weimar Constitution and to eliminate the weaknesses of Article 48 which, through emergency action and constitutional dictatorship, had facilitated the destruction of republican institutions. Hence Article 18 specifies that, even though freedom of the press, of teaching, of assembly, and of association, among others, may be forfeited by anyone who uses them in order to attack the free democratic basic order, the forfeiture and its extent shall be pronounced only by the Federal Constitutional Court. Hence the provision of Section 2 of Article 19 stating that, even though a basic right may be restricted or defined by legislation, "in no case may a basic right be affected in its basic content." Hence the further provision under Section 4 of the same article giving the right of appeal to the courts to any person whose rights are deemed by him to be infringed by public authority. In this way a direct channel is opened between the citizens and the judicial system, which is raised to the position of protector of the Constitution and of the rights established under it. Finally, we should note Section 3 of Article 1 which, by making the basic rights "binding as directly valid law on legislation administrative and judiciary," seeks to avoid the danger of having the Bill of Rights construed later as a mere declaratory statement of policy of no juridical validity.

All evidence shows that it was not difficult for Germany to reach agreement on these constitutional provisions. The lesson had been learned, and there were not too many alternate roads to be followed.[1]

---

[1] Theodor Eschenburg provides a general discussion of the problem in his *Staat und Gesellschaft in Deutschland* (Stuttgart, 1956), especially ch. x, pp. 390–494. See also *Die Grundrechte: Handbuch der Theorie und Praxis der Grundrechte,* Franz Neumann, Hans C. Nipperdey, and Ulrich Scheuner, eds., especially vol. 2, *Die Freiheitsrechte in Deutschland* (Berlin, 1954). For a summary of the role of the judicial system, see C. R. Foster and G. Stambuk, "Judicial Protection of Civil Liberties in Germany," *Political Studies,* 1956, pp. 190–194.

On the other hand, France, the land of the Declaration of the Rights of Man, faced serious difficulties in trying to arrive at a fresh version of the principles embodied in the historical document of 1789. Both in 1945 and in 1946, a majority or near majority of the two Constituent Assemblies was controlled by Marxist parties looking with ill-concealed hostility or suspicion to the liberal and individualistic traditions of the revolution. Roger Garaudy could write lyrically on the eighteenth-century roots of French communism,[2] but a detailed restatement of the principles of the Declaration of Rights of Man meant support for doctrines of individual freedom which Marxism had always seen as an instrument for the domination of the capitalistic classes.

Communists and Socialists, as well as other parties of non-Marxian origin such as the Mouvement Républicain Populaire (MRP), could not, therefore, bring themselves to say simply, "The press is free and no laws shall be made abridging that freedom." They saw the "real" issues as those of the purpose for which the press exists (the press must be free to defend "democracy"), of the ways in which the press is financed (the press must be free from "special" interests), of the balance of power among parties (the press must represent organized political opinion), of the guarantors of press freedom (the state must see to it that the press is free).

In the end, the only practical solution proved to be that of proclaiming, in the Preamble of the Constitution, "that every human being, without distinction as to race, religion or creed, possesses inalienable and sacred rights" and of reaffirming "the rights and freedom of man and of the citizen ordained by the Declaration of Rights of 1789." Thus, with a summary appeal to a historical document, did the Constitution framers of the Fourth Republic dispose of the matter of personal and civil rights. Certainly this was not a very satisfactory way of dealing with the issue of human freedom which had been at stake in the struggle against totalitarianism.

As was to be expected, fewer difficulties were met in outlining certain new economic and social principles in the subsequent paragraphs of the Preamble. Often they turned out to be either a re-statement of what should have been obvious and noncontroversial ("Everyone may defend his rights and interests by trade union action and may join

[2] *Les Sources Françaises du Socialisme Scientifique* (Paris, 1948).

the trade union of his choice"; "The right to strike may be exercised within the framework of the laws that govern it") or a mere expression of hope concerning the future. This is, of course, a mood frequently found in economic bills of rights. For they have traditionally become documents in which politicians, at no cost to themselves, offer happiness, wealth, and security to all. The language is at times meaningless (what are the conditions necessary to the development of the individual and of the family?): at best it reflects a generic attempt to anticipate for a future state of affairs happier than the one prevailing at present.

The different way in which political and economic rights were approached reveals one of the problems in the reconstruction of European constitutionalism. There is reluctance to impose the austere and harsh conditions of authentic constitutionalism: the rule of law, respect for due process, the stringent application of procedural norms in all activities of the police and of judicial authorities. The cleansing of custom and the lifting of the moral habits of the community do require a sustained, deliberate, and immediate effort on the part of those charged with the responsibility of government.

But to promise full employment, rest and leisure, universal education, and modern housing does not engage heavily the responsibility of anyone. Everybody concerned realizes that these are long-range policies or even utopian statements. It will even be wholly legitimate to pursue policies which will lead to directly opposite goals. No one can challenge as unconstitutional a budget that will surely lead to unemployment or that will use most of the public revenues for purposes of destruction and not of welfare. But a government action encroaching upon press freedom could at least be challenged if the Constitution did effectively guarantee press freedom. Therefore, it is much better to have the Constitution wax eloquent about the right to obtain employment, but remain silent about press freedom.

The Italian constitution makers went about their job diligently. The result was the longest and most elaborate Bill of Rights of postwar Europe, made up of a statement of fundamental principles in 11 articles, followed by four chapters of particulars with 43 more articles.

Some of the traditional freedoms are defined in simple and clear terms, such as personal freedom, inviolability of the home, freedom of movement within the country, freedom of assembly and of associa-tion,[3] freedom of expression. In other instances the language is less satisfactory, as in the case of press freedom. Article 21 authorizes the seizure of periodicals by the police without judicial sanction (such sanction must be sought within 48 hours; but this is a meaningless guarantee for the daily press). Article 19 guaranteeing religious free-dom may be difficult to reconcile at all points with Articles 7 and 8 dealing with the special position of the Catholic Church.

The Italian Bill of Rights is quite generous in its social and eco-nomic promises. All have a right to work. Families are to be protected, health is a fundamental right, schools are open to all, and thrift is to be encouraged. Sometimes it appears that the purpose of the Bill of Rights is to salvage something from the relics of the corporate states, as when Article 39 recognizes the possibility of trade unions signing collective labor contracts with binding effects on all persons belong-ing to the categories covered by the contract in question. At other times, the economic thought behind a particular clause is platitudinous. (Article 42: "Property is public or private. Economic goods belong to the state, to associations or to private individuals.") Clearly all groups, all schools of thought are to find something in the Bill of Rights to satisfy their interests or to confirm their prejudices. But the same is true of this as of all other economic bills of rights: it will receive its meaning only from the sum total of legislation and of concrete achieve-ments over the next fifty years.

JUDICIAL REVIEW AS AN INSTRUMENT OF FREEDOM

In both Germany and Italy judicial power has been given important roles in the defense of freedom and of the general principles of the Constitution. As we have seen, Articles 18 and 19 of the Bonn Con-stitution bring the voice of the courts, and in particular of the Fed-eral Constitutional Court,[4] to bear in the definition, the defense, and

[3] Clause 12 of the so-called "Transitional and final provisions" states, however, that "the re-organization in any form whatsoever of the dissolved Fascist Party is prohibited."

[4] The Court is established under Arts. 92 and 94 of the Constitution. The law of March 12, 1951, fixed the details of its organization. The members are elected by the Bundestag and by the Bundesrat (secs. 5–7). So far, there have been no de-cisions under Arts. 1, 18, and 19. The 1951 organization law allowed an almost

the limitation of basic rights. We shall see below the decisive role of the Constitutional Court under Article 21.

But it is Article 93 that establishes judicial review, by giving jurisdiction to the Federal Constitutional Court, on the application of the Federal Government, of a land government, or of one-third of the members of the Bundestag, to settle "cases of differences of opinion or doubts on the formal and material compatibility of federal law or land law with this Basic Law." Within the limits it imposes, Article 93 may give substantial scope to the defense by the Court of the essential principles of the Constitution.[5] It represents the victory of a doctrine that had been defeated at the Weimar Convention in 1919.[6]

Italy has made a more sweeping grant of power to its Constitutional Court. Organized under Title Six of the Constitution, the Court is given in Article 134 jurisdiction over "controversies relating to the constitutional legitimacy of laws." According to Article 136 any law declared unconstitutional by the Court loses all validity on the day after

---

unlimited right of appeal to the Court for individuals claiming violations of constitutional rights (sec. 90). From 1951 to 1956 the Court was swamped by approximately 3,000 such complaints, of which only 6 or 7 were decided in the appellant's favor. But a revision in 1956 of the 1951 law gave the Court the right to decide which of these appeals it would hear (sec. 91a). I owe this information to the courtesy of Dr. Gerhard Loewenberg, of Mt. Holyoke College.

[5] The Court may also intervene under Art. 100, which requires any lower court to obtain the decision of the Federal Constitutional Court whenever a law the validity of which is pertinent to its decision is considered unconstitutional.

[6] The prevailing mood at Weimar was well represented by Hugo Preuss who strongly supported judicial review of legislation and who thought that even in the silence of the Constitution the judicial system would exercise this power (see his *Staat, Recht und Freiheit* [Tübingen, 1926]). To prevent this from happening, the minority sought to write into the Constitution a positive prohibition of judicial review of legislation, admitting it, however, whenever 100 members of the Reichstag requested it. This proposal (which, in reverse, is close to the present language of Art. 93) failed of adoption, and the Constitution was silent on the matter (cf. Theisen, "Verfassung und Richter," *Archiv des Oeffentlichen Rechts*, 1925, pp. 260 ff.). Between 1924 and 1927 a number of higher tribunals, according to the expectations of Preuss, moved toward judicial review and proclaimed themselves the "protectors of the Constitution," even though in the meantime attempts to set up judicial review through legislation had come to nothing. But the growing German crisis could not permit judicial review to establish itself. The forerunner of the new times was Carl Schmitt who, in protest against the *Politisierung der Justiz,* saw in the President the true protector of the Constitution (see his *Hüter der Verfassung* [Tübingen, 1931]). On current developments, cf. H. Nagel, "Judicial Review in Germany," *American Journal of Comparative Law*, 1954, pp 233–241.

the publication of the sentence of the Court. A constitutional law dated February 9, 1948, clarifies further the jurisdiction of the Court and makes it possible for private citizens to bring suit to test the constitutionality of laws.

But the Constitutional Court was inaugurated only on April 23, 1956, that is, with a delay of more than eight years. The main roadblock had been the application of Article 135 concerning the equal sharing of the power to appoint the fifteen judges of the Court by Parliament, the President, and the Judiciary.[7] Parliament failed until 1956 to elect its quota of judges, while the Cabinet tried until 1953 to claim for itself the appointment of the five presidential judges. Of the two deadlocks, the second was the most dangerous. Had the Cabinet point of view prevailed, one of the important presidential constitutional prerogatives would have been abrogated. The Constitution, by distributing the appointment of the members of the Court in equal parts between the President, the Parliament, and the Judiciary, wanted to prevent any of them from dominating the majority of the Court. Had the Cabinet, depending upon the support of a parliamentary majority, been able to select five judges, the parliamentary majority would in the end have controlled ten out of the fifteen members of the Court. It was odd to find the dominant Christian Democratic Party, which in the Constituent Assembly had been the most vocal proponent of judicial review, support in the five years from 1948 to 1953 legislation which would have deprived the President of his constitutional power of appointment. The conclusion is inescapable that while from a rhetorical point of view Christian Democracy favored the Constitutional Court, from a practical political point of view it was doing its best to make of it a mere party appendix.

Only after it became obvious that the efforts to nullify the spirit and the letter of the Constitution would lead to a most severe crisis did the required law on the functioning of the Constitutional Court get through Parliament.[8] When finally the Constitutional Court got under way, it surprised public and political opinion by moving with the ut-

[7] Art. 135 of the Constitution fixed the membership of the Court at fifteen judges appointed for twelve years, five by the President of the Republic, five by a joint session of the houses of Parliament and a three-fifths majority, and five by the highest courts of the land.

[8] Law of March 11, 1953. Art. 4 stipulates that "the Constitutional Court judges, whose appointment belongs to the President, are appointed by his decree."

most speed in eliminating some of the more obvious anomalies in the field of civil and political rights.

After the enactment of the Constitution in 1948, the police laws of 1931, which, needless to say, had been written in order to strengthen the hand of the Fascist dictatorship, had remained in full force and had continued to be applied by police authorities in important areas affecting freedom of religion, of association, of speech, of the press, and of the person. They made it possible for police authorities to prevent political or religious meetings, to use repressive measures such as forced domicile, to harass people who were guilty only of trying to move from one city to another in order to find a better job. While examples of police misbehavior were not sufficiently numerous or important to alter the general atmosphere of freedom that prevailed in the country, they were sufficiently significant and persistent to warrant the resentment and the anxiety which they caused.[9]

Beginning with its first decision of June 5, 1956, and continuing through the summer and fall of that year, the Constitutional Court declared unconstitutional the most obnoxious provisions of the police laws of 1931. The Court did this in spite of the efforts of the government to deny the jurisdiction of the Court over laws preceding the enactment of the Constitution of 1948. The decision of June 5, 1956, strengthens press and thought freedoms guaranteed by Article 21 of the Constitution, by voiding those provisions of the police laws which required advance police authorization for the distribution of printed materials. The decision of June 14, 1956, supports Articles 13 and 16 which guarantee personal freedom and the freedom to travel and sojourn freely in any part of the national territory, by voiding the law authorizing police authorities to force the return of citizens to their home towns. The decision of June 19, 1956, again supports Article 13 by voiding a long series of police "admonitions." The "admonition" of persons whose activities are viewed with suspicion by the police seriously curtails the freedom of movement of the individuals affected. The Court finds it to be a "juridical degradation" and to provide a measure of police surveillance which is the result not of a judicial decision but of uncontrolled administrative authority.

These and many other decisions, some of them concerning religious

---

[9] See a detailed analysis of the problem by Achille Battaglia, "Giustizia e politica nella giurisprudenza," in *Dieci Anni Dopo, 1945–1955* (Bari, 1955), pp. 317–408.

freedom, show that the Constitutional Court considers its function in the defense of the Bill of Rights as a central one and that it is not afraid to reach decisions which the government has found uncomfortable. For the wholesale voiding of police laws is forcing the legislative and executive branches to reconsider in the light of the requirements of a democratic society the problem of the relationship between public authority and the citizen. The Court has dashed the complacency of politicians and of administrators who, under the shelter of generic constitutionalism, felt that daily life could proceed much as it had in the past, even when it was the Fascist past. And it has introduced into constitutional life a concept of judicial review which is a radical departure from Italian legal traditions.[10]

POLITICAL PARTIES AND THE "FREE AND DEMOCRATIC BASIC ORDER"

The rule of totalitarian parties was bound to influence public discussion of the place of parties in a democratic state and in particular to raise the issue of their regulation by either constitutional or statutory law.

Speaking in the Constitutional Committee of the first French Constituent Assembly, the Socialist leader and president of the Committee, André Philip, favored regulation: "Political parties cannot any longer be considered as mere associations. . . . As an intermediary between the people and the legislator, the party must be protected, but its democratic organization must also be assured. It will have, therefore, to accept certain rules. Its financial resources must be known." [11] But even though a majority of the Constitutional Committee approved the outlines of the Philip proposal,[12] nothing further was heard about it, and both Constitution and legislation have been silent about parties on all questions of substance, excluding of course electoral matters.

---

[10] The decisions of the Court are published in *Raccolta Ufficiale delle Sentenze e Ordinanze della Corte Costituzionale* (Rome). The decisions referred to in the text are in vol. I (1956), at pp. 25, 41, 117.

[11] Assemblée Nationale Constituante, *Séances de la Commission de la Constitution*, December 7, 1945, p. 63.

[12] The vote was 22 to 18, with Socialist and MRP members in the majority, Communist and Conservative members in the minority, *ibid.*, p. 64. See also Pascal Arrighi, *Le Statut des Partis Politiques* (Paris, 1948).

It was left to Germany to start on the road of party regulation and to link it to the fundamental question of a "free and democratic basic order." The Bill of Rights, as we have seen, refers in Article 18 to the "free democratic basic order" as the order embodied in the Constitution. But this is not the only reference to it in the German Constitution. A second is found in Article 21 dealing with political parties.

Section 1 of Article 21 recognizes the existence of parties as participants "in forming the political will of the people." They can be freely formed. But they are bound to certain standards, one being the conformity of their internal organization to democratic principles, the other the public accounting of the sources of their funds. Pending the enactment of the needed federal legislation, the two requirements will remain for the most part generic declarations of principles.[13]

Quite different is the legal significance of Section 2 of Article 21: "Parties which, according to their aims and the behavior of their members, seek to impair or abolish the free and democratic basic order or to jeopardize the existence of the Federal Republic of Germany, shall be unconstitutional. The Federal Constitutional Court shall decide on the question of unconstitutionality." For here the Constitution provides the specific instrument through which parties seeking to impair the "free and democratic basic order" are to be destroyed.

Twice the Federal Constitution Court has accepted jurisdiction under Section 2 of Article 21. On October 3, 1952, the Court declared the unconstitutionality of the neo-Nazi Socialist Reich Party (SRP), and on August 17, 1956, that of the German Communist Party (KPD).[14]

---

[13] The 1956 election law does make things difficult for parties which cannot prove they are governed by an executive committee elected according to democratic principles. See Carl J. Schneider, "Political Parties and the German Basic Law of 1949," *Western Political Quarterly*, September 1957, pp. 534 ff. The most recent document on party legislation is *Rechtliche Ordnung des Parteiwesens* (Frankfurt, 1957), xvi, 246 pp., a report drawn up by a distinguished committee of academicians and published in August 1957 under the auspices of the Minister of the Interior, who introduces the report with cautious words on the difficulty and the unprecedented nature of the problem. The committee itself is equally cautious. In general, opinion is unfavorable to regulation. See F. A. von der Heydte, "Freiheit der Parteien," in *Die Grundrechte,* pp. 457 ff.

[14] The SRP decision occupies the first 79 pages of the first volume of the decisions of the Federal Constitutional Court: the KPD decision, 308 pages long, fills most of the fifth volume. The full documentation of the KPD trial, including government and party documents, proceedings before the first Senate of the Federal Constitutional Court, and the Court's decision, has been brought together in *KPD-Prozess: Dokumentarwerk*, Gerd Pfeiffer and Hans-Georg Strickert, eds. (3 vols. of 975, 946, 780 pages; Karlsruhe, 1955–1956).

With these decisions of unconstitutionality, the parties were dissolved.[15]

What is important about the decisions is that the Court not only had to prove that the two parties were systematically seeking to impair the "free and democratic basic order" with their programs and activities, but also had to describe the nature of the "free and democratic basic order" itself, an order not to be identified with the specific Bonn constitutional system. In so doing, the Court has provided the scholar with a definition of liberal democracy and of the values which give substance to the Bill of Rights which is of considerable interest in the history of constitutionalism in postwar Europe.

Certain key principles are to be borne in mind, the Court maintains in its opinion of October 23, 1952, when a decision has to be reached on the elimination of a party from the political life of a country. The importance of parties in a democratic state is so exceptional that such a step can be justified not because they may oppose this or the other institution, but only when

they want to subvert the highest values of the free and democratic constitutional state. These values shape the free and democratic basic order which the constitution considers fundamental in the general organization of the state. . . . Ultimately the basic order is founded on the idea that in the order of creation man is endowed with unique worth and that freedom and equality are lasting foundations of state unity. Because of this the basic order is one based on values. It is the very opposite of the totalitarian state which, as monopolistic master, rejects the rights of man, freedom and equality.[16]

Coming to grips with the task of giving a more specific content to this idealized basic order, the Court calls it "a government of laws which, having rejected violence and despotic rule, is based on the self-determination of the people according to the will of the majority, on liberty and on equality." The fundamental principles of such an order must include as a minimum:

respect for the human rights contained in the Basic Law and above all for the right of the person to life and free development, sovereignty of the people, separation of powers, responsibility of the government, legality of the

[15] See secs. 43–47 of the Law of March 12, 1951, on procedure and consequences. The Court can transfer party assets to the federal or state governments.

[16] Urteil vom 23 October 1952, Festellung der Verfassungswidrigkeit der Sozialistischen Reichspartei, *Entscheidungen der Bundesverfassungsgerichts,* II, 12.

administration, independence of the judiciary, the multi-party system with equal chance open to all parties, including the right of the formation and exercise of a constitutional opposition.[17]

In the KPD decision of August 17, 1956, the Court stresses the care with which it will proceed. Both the wholesale rejection of values and the concerted attack on the system must be shown. But the Constitution reflects the belief that certain basic principles, once approved in a democratic manner, become absolute values and, as such, must be defended resolutely against any attack.[18] This is why the limitations imposed by Article 21 on the freedom of political organization must be accepted.

In a liberal democracy, the Court holds,

the dignity of the individual is the highest value. It is unassailable. It must be respected and protected by the state. Man is a "personality" capable of shaping his life in a responsible manner. Therefore neither his behavior nor his thinking can clearly be determined by his class position. Rather he is considered capable, and expected to balance his own interests and ideas with those of others. For the sake of his dignity the largest possible scope of his development must be ensured. In the political and social field this means that it is not enough if some authority endeavors, no matter how well, to look after the welfare of its "subjects." Rather the individual is expected to participate as much as possible in community decisions. It is the duty of the state to open the way for him to do this. . . . Freedom of thinking is of paramount importance in the liberal democracy. It really is the premise for the successful functioning of the system; it saves it from paralysis and reveals the many possibilities for the solution of specific problems.[19]

This is uncompromisingly strong and classical language that must be taken as a welcome sign of the new strength of freedom in Germany today. Even the possibility that "class" may influence the conduct of man is frowned upon by the Court. It comes, therefore, as a surprise to see the Court develop the view that, by virtue of Section 1 of Article 21 ("Parties shall participate in forming the political will of the people"),

---

[17] *Ibid.*, pp. 12–13.

[18] Urteil vom 17 August 1956, Verfahren über den Antrag der Bundesregierung auf Feststellung der Verfassungswidrigkeit der Kommunistische Partei Deutschlands, *Entscheidungen*, V, 133–140.

[19] *Ibid.*, pp. 204–205.

the Constitution has deliberately taken the step of constitutionalizing political parties. Since they have been lifted to the rank of institutions of constitutional law, parties have at the same time made their entry among the
"integrating factors" of state life. . . . Certainly, one must not exaggerate
the duties that will result for the parties from the integration task. Opposition parties must retain freedom of movement. A party bent upon seeking
fundamental reforms must be permitted to criticize the existing order and
must be allowed to carry out propaganda capable of reaching the masses of
the people. This always means a certain cheapening of political ideas, their
"adaptation" in other words to the emotional needs of the masses. . . . All
this is harmless and not objectionable from a constitutional point of view, so
long as the party in its conduct shows it is always aware of acting as a
political party within the framework of a liberal democracy.[20]

These are curious words, which betray a certain impatience with
party life and an anxiety to endow parties with manners so proper
that the trivialities and vulgarities of democratic life shall be effectively
repressed. The Court seems to be reading too much into a generic
constitutional recognition of the importance of parties. There is a
wide gap of principle between it and the doctrine that makes of parties
agencies of public law, regulated by the state and in effect part of its
structure.

It is true that the Constitution does impose certain standards of behavior on the parties (internal democracy and financial publicity)
and threatens them with dissolution if they undermine the free and
democratic basic order. But while the Constitutional Court has been
able to satisfy itself twice as to the existence of conditions warranting
dissolution, the legislative branch has been unable as yet to give substance to the standards of behavior and to what the Court calls the
"constitutionalization" of political parties. The truth is that this is a
risky path and one that in a constitutional democracy had better be
left untrodden.

ADMINISTRATIVE PROTECTION OF FREEDOM

If the French constitutional foundations of rights appear to some
critics to lack the desirable degree of specificity, their statutory foundations are strong and detailed and have for long provided an adequate

[20] *Ibid.*, pp. 388–389.

basis for the defense of freedom. For example, the laws of 1833, 1850, and 1875, by allowing the reopening of private schools, have restored to the educational system some of the flexibility which had disappeared during the revolutionary period. Religious freedom relies on the law of December 9, 1905, on the separation of Church and state. Freedom of the press rests to a large extent on the law of July 29, 1881. Freedom of assembly is based on the law of June 30, 1881, as well as on the law of March 28, 1907, which removed the last restriction of prior notice to police authorities. Paradoxically enough, the law of July 1, 1901, aiming in the first place at the regulation or dissolution of religious congregations, has become the foundation stone of freedom of association.[21]

These are only some of the more important examples of statutory protection of freedoms. Taken together with a quite resolute reliance on the Declaration of 1789, they have furnished an impressive arsenal of weapons to the agency that has become a chief protector of freedom in France, the Council of State. It is to this administrative tribunal that one has to look for the best guarantee of individual rights against executive interference, even though its jurisdiction is limited to the control of administrative acts and does not extend to that of the behavior of judicial authorities or of the police placed under their control or to the question of the constitutionality of laws.

The Courts have tended to spend their best efforts in the protection of property rights which are for the most part well defined and such as to lend themselves to clear pronouncements of right and wrong. The Courts can, in settling private disputes, contribute to the protection of the citizen's freedom. But the Courts have shown far greater reluctance to interfere when the state is involved. Government violations of the rights of privacy, of the home, of individual safety, of association have shown up the uncertainties and the hesitancies of the Courts. As a distinguished French jurist has stated:

The over-all impression derived from an analysis of judicial jurisprudence is not altogether satisfactory. A two-fold effort should be required of the judge in the future. He must carry his inquiries deeper when the conflict is one between public power and private persons. . . . Secondly, we think it unjust to establish a hierarchy of freedoms exclusively favoring property rights.

[21] Georges Burdeau, *Manuel de Droit Public: Les Libertés Publiques, Les Droits Sociaux* (Paris, 1948).

Personal freedoms must get at least equal protection. We need here a revision of the values accepted by the Courts.[22]

This is a statement that will call to mind similar issues, long and hotly debated in the United States, concerning the "preferred position" to be given by the Courts, and especially the Supreme Court, to personal freedoms over economic rights. As the debate has been proceeding over the last thirty years, many advances and retreats of the "preferred position" defenders have been witnessed.[23] It is not too much to say, perhaps, that in recent years the Supreme Court has once more moved strongly forward and that there is much that could be taken from its doctrines by European judges to increase their daring and their freedom of movement when dealing with government abuses of power.

Indeed, much could be learned by them from the jurisprudence of the Council of State, the strongest of the French administrative courts, which has been playing an increasingly significant role in the field of civil rights. The Council of State, because of its split personality, has often presented foreign scholars with baffling problems of interpretation. The Council is, first of all, an essential element in the operation of the executive branch of the government. It is the adviser of cabinets and of public administrators. It co-operates in the formulation of legislative proposals. It is made up of the more trusted and the more able civil servants. And it is because of this strong position in the inner councils of state that the Council of State has been able to perform so effectively its second task, that of the supporter of the individual against the usurpations and illegalities of public agencies.[24]

[22] Roger Pinto, "La protection des droits de l'homme par les tribunaux judiciaires en France," in Conseil d'Etat, *Etudes et Documents* (Paris, 1949), III, 28.

[23] A valuable and up-to-date discussion is found in Bernard Schwartz, *The Supreme Court* (New York, 1957).

[24] "Some Englishmen envy the Frenchman who can apply to the *Conseil d'Etat* to have an administrative decision quashed or to be given compensation on the ground that he has been unjustly treated; for the *Conseil d'Etat* is in the peculiarly favorable position of being staffed by officials who are perfectly familiar with administrative problems but are at the same time completely independent of the government. In Britain, the administrator who is called upon to give a decision is part of the government, whereas the judges, even when they have power to examine administrative acts, may lack the administrator's special knowledge and so fail to exercise it wisely" (Lawson, in *Law and Government*, Brierly, ed. [London, 1948], pp. 119–120; quoted by Jacques Donnedieu de Vabres, "La protection des droits de l'homme par les juridictions administratives en France," in Conseil d'Etat, *Etudes et Documents*, III, 47–48).

Freedom in Postwar Europe

In France, as in other countries, the influence of legislative power and of legislation has been declining. Perhaps one of the beneficial by-products of legislative impotence has been that fewer laws, bad or good, have emerged from the legislative machine. But, of necessity, the influence of executive and administrative action has increased. One has therefore to look at least as much to executive and administrative malpractices as to legislative violations of fundamental freedoms, in trying to measure the dangers facing the citizen.

Because of this the expanded role of the Council of State and its readiness to take on the burdens of protector of the broad principles upon which republican institutions are founded are viewed with much interest and satisfaction. As a member *extra ordinem* of the executive family whose standing and power are unchallenged, since they rest on the strongest of foundations, the Council of State is in an enviable position to interpret properly the meaning and consequences of executive action. It can bridge the gap between judicial and executive branches which has rendered the Courts so reluctant to verify government activities. The Council of State operating from within the executive with unlimited jurisdiction can act as a check on it.

The Council of State will, therefore, protect individual freedom. It will grant indemnities in case of arbitrary arrest. The Council said in 1947:

Perhaps we belong to an old generation and perhaps we remain attached to obsolete conceptions, but we persist in believing that the principle of *habeas corpus* remains the foundation of republican freedoms and that our public law continues to be controlled by Article 7 of the Declaration of the Rights of Man. No one can be accused, arrested, or detained except in cases determined by the law and according to the forms prescribed by the law.[25]

The Council will protect collective freedoms such as freedom of assembly and freedom of association. It will defend the principle of the equality of all citizens in their treatment by public agencies. It will maintain the principle of the nonretroactivity of laws. As the Council said in 1948, in a decision involving a retroactive increase of power rates affecting a newspaper:

One of the essential characteristics of modern law in a civilized country is that it rests on a small number of fundamental principles which, being the

[25] Case of Alexis and Wolff, *Recueil Sirey,* 1948, III, p. 103.

fruit of a long evolutionary process, aim to maintain the dignity of the human person, the freedom and the equality of citizens. France can undoubtedly take pride in the fact that she has been one of the first countries to state, with the Declaration of Rights of 1789, the existence and the supremacy of such principles. Administrative Courts can be proud of the jealous care and the inflexible intransigence with which they have guaranteed their maintenance and growth, and have avoided all action opposed to them. Among these essential principles we must include those of the non-retroactivity of administrative decisions and of the equal application of public charges to all.[26]

The rights of the defense are protected by the Council of State, including the right of a civil servant to have access to the dossier affecting him. Protected also are local autonomies and the participation of private citizens and bodies in the management of public corporations, when that participation is guaranteed by law.

Not the least interesting aspect of this massive intervention is, as we have seen, the readiness to call into play the highest and more philosophical document upon which modern French civilization rests, the Declaration of the Rights of Man. There does not seem to be much doubt in the view of the Council of State concerning the binding validity of the principles of 1789. The conclusions of Donnedieu de Vabres appear fully justified:

Administrative justice has acquired a great role in the formation and application of the law of freedom. This law has multiple sources. It proceeds first of all from a few great proclamations which have awakened and impressed public opinion. It flows next from a few basic laws which organize public freedoms and determine their guarantees. But it would remain a dead letter . . . if it didn't have the support of an independent jurisdiction permeated by a liberal spirit. The political controls of public opinion and of parliament are not adequate for the defense of the rights of man: that defense requires an unceasing and daily vigilance; it needs the sanction of judicial and of administrative tribunals.[27]

No recent intervention of the Council of State has seemed more decisive and more significant than that of May 28, 1954, in the so-called National School of Administration case.[28] The facts, in brief, were

[26] Case of Journal L'Aurore, *Recueil Sirey*, 1948, III, p. 69.

[27] Donnedieu de Vabres, *op. cit.*, p. 49.

[28] Case of Barel *et al.*, *Recueil Sirey*, 1954, III, pp. 97 ff.

these. In establishing the list of candidates admitted to the 1953 competitive examination for admission to the National School of Administration, the Secretary of State for civil service affairs, attached to the office of the Prime Minister, ruled against the admission of seven candidates out of a total of 1,350. The notification of the exclusion gave no reason for it, and the five candidates who appealed to the Council of State did so on grounds of excess of power.

When the press started to give publicity to the case, it began to be generally assumed that the five candidates had been excluded because they were Communists. In the absence of any clear statement on the part of the Laniel government, which had retreated behind a veil of silence, public anxiety increased. On October 15, 1953, the association of teachers on the faculties of laws approved a motion stating that the power to draw up a list of candidates admitted to participate in competitive examinations must be exercised in conformity with Article 6 of the Declaration of the Rights of Man. ("All men being equal, they are equally to be admitted to all public offices and employment according to their capacity and without any distinction other than those due to their virtues and skills.") On November 13, 1953, a debate took place in the National Assembly in the course of which the government defended its discretionary powers and refused to offer any explanation. By a vote of 355 to 214 the Assembly took notice of the fact that the Council of State had full jurisdiction in the matter and that indeed it had already accepted it.[29]

The Council, aware of the great importance of the issue, had also decided to move ahead with the utmost speed. The appellants' contention was that the exclusion from the examination was due solely to political reasons. In reply, the government limited itself to say that the exclusion was based on its discretionary power and that political considerations had played no role. Invited, on March 19, 1954, to produce within eight days all files concerning the five candidates, the government failed to reply for two of them and failed to give any satisfaction for the other three, leaving without reply a final request from the Council dated May 19.

The Council of State ruled that it had the right to require the production of all relevant documents so that the allegations of the plaintiffs could be verified. The Council ruled that if the government has the

[29] *Journal Officiel: Débats,* November 14, 1953, p. 5077.

right to establish the qualifications to be found in candidates aspiring to civil service positions it cannot, without violating the principle of equality of access on the part of all Frenchmen to public employment, eliminate from the list any candidate solely on the basis of his political opinions.

In the face of official silence, the Council found that the allegations of the plaintiffs that they were eliminated from the list only because of their political views were proved. Therefore the request of the plaintiffs to have the government decision voided because of excess of power was to be granted. The Council based its decision on all relevant ordinances and decrees and on "the Constitution of the French Republic of October 27, 1946."

It should be noted, first of all, that the Council of State obviously attached particular importance to the case since the National School of Administration was involved. There was no thought of curtailing the right that any government possesses in the assignment of its civil servants among the various careers and positions open to them. In the selections of the occupants of sensitive or policy-making posts, the government has a freedom of choice which is not subject to serious challenge. But one of the basic ideas which presided over the foundation of the National School of Administration after the war was that it would serve as a clearing house where the best of the young people of the country were to be brought together and carefully trained to provide the future administrative elite of France. It was a democratic experiment because it set out to break down the restrictive policies of some of the great administrative bodies of the state in the selection of their members. If the precedent to permit the government to proceed without explanation to a political screening of the candidates to the school was allowed to go by unchallenged, then the purpose of the school would be destroyed. The issue was not that of the right of Communists to occupy high administrative positions. The question was that of the right of all qualified French citizens to have access to the most important school of public administration.

In the second place, the speech of the Socialist leader Jules Moch in the National Assembly of November 8, 1953, shows that there was widespread uneasiness at the thought that the McCarthy techniques would begin to make their appearance in France. It is perhaps because of this concern that the Council of State insisted so strongly on the duty of the government to produce the evidence upon which its decision was based, as well as on the need of reaching a decision in time to permit the five appellants to have their names included in the 1954 list of candidates.

Finally, it should be noted that to establish its case the Council of State used the Constitution. We know that the appeal to the Constitution or to a constitutional law can no longer be considered a novelty in Council proceedings. But since the Council was concerned with Article 6 of the Declaration of the Rights of Man with its guarantee of equality of access to public employment, the reference to the Constitution may properly be construed as extending to the Preamble, the only part of the Constitution which refers to the Declaration of the Rights of Man of 1789. Once again, the Council, by implication at least, has recognized the binding validity of the Preamble and of the documents and principles which it supports.[30] This is a welcome position. Given the uncertainties that the elusive language of the Preamble has created, it is only through the steady accumulation of a body of jurisprudential doctrine that its values can acquire substance and precision.

In conclusion, as Mathiat writes:

The Barel decision must be registered as a great decision in the book of liberalism, a book in which the Council of State has already written so many admirable pages. Who can say that in countries without administrative jurisdiction, even in Great Britain, a judicial body could have reached a better judgment, with greater independence, on such a burning issue.[31]

FREEDOM OF THE PRESS

The task of the restoration of a free press met with the greatest complexities in the country that had suffered the briefest eclipse of demo-

---

[30] This is a conclusion which André Mathiat, the able commentator of the Barel decision (*Recueil Sirey,* 1954, III, pp. 97–103, at 100), is not quite ready to reach. See his entire note for a discussion of some of the points raised in the text.

[31] Mathiat, *ibid.,* p. 103. Cf. also C. J. Hamson, *Executive Discretion and Judicial Control* (London, 1954), especially the first chapter, for a most illuminating discussion of the Barel proceedings. Both the decision of the Council and the "conclusions" of the "government commissary," Letourneur, together with a note by Professor Waline, have been published in *Revue du Droit Public et de la Science Politique,* April–June 1954, pp. 509–538.

cratic institutions. France was torn among conflicting viewpoints concerning the nature and purpose of press freedom and felt deeply the need to redeem some of the aspirations of the Resistance.

The initial engagement in the "ideological" battle was fought early in 1946, when the first Constituent Assembly made its attempt to write a Constitution.[32] As it emerged from the debates, under the sponsorship of the Socialist-Communist majority, Article 14 read: "Every man is free to speak, write, print and publish; he can by means of the press or any other means, express, diffuse and defend any opinion in such measure as does not abuse this right, notably as it does not violate freedoms guaranteed by the present declarations." This meant, if it meant anything, that the complex of political and economic rights and freedoms to be guaranteed by the Constitution was placed above debate and that any discussion by the press tending to cast doubts on the validity or the admissibility of any of them was ruled out.

The debates in the Constituent Assembly showed that those who feared a restrictive application of Article 14 were not obsessed by shadows. The non-Marxist minority was defeated when it proposed to add to Article 14 the words "Freedom of the press is guaranteed." It was equally voted down when it pressed for the abolition of prior government approval for the publication of newspapers. The majority was clearly out of sympathy with the appeal of Edouard Herriot whose thesis was that the personal right of individual expression through the press was just as strong in 1946 as it was in 1789 and had not been weakened by the acceptance of desirable changes in the economic system.

The majority was siding with the Communist deputy, Madeleine Braun, when she called freedom of the press a slogan, to be classified together with that of economic freedom—as if the restrictions which may have to be applied to the production and trade of economic goods, could equally well be applied to the production and trade of ideas. The French people, however, having elected in the fall of 1945 a Constituent Assembly responsible for a document which could have given legal sanction to the suppression of freedom of the press, repudiated that document in the spring of 1946 by a wide margin.

---

[32] The attentive reader does not have to be reminded that what is under discussion here is the proposed Constitution drafted by the first Constitutional Assembly and rejected in the referendum of May 5, 1946.

But the Assembly had been busy not only at the ideological level. An even more dramatic struggle had been going on at the same time concerning the physical plant, the walls within which newspaper offices were sheltered and the presses upon which the papers were printed.

Few have realized the unprecedented nature of the revolutionary measures undertaken in France during the summer of 1944. At one stroke, without exception, all the daily newspapers of France which had not promptly stopped publication following the Nazi occupation were suspended, the use of their titles made forever impossible and their eventual reappearance made exceedingly difficult.

No other country made a more determined attempt to sweep away the past in order to build a better future. The guilt of the French press was deemed to have been so great that apparently no half measure was thought adequate. Only by doing away altogether with the press which had continued to appear, no matter what the individual extenuating circumstances might have been, under the Nazi or Vichy regimes could the honor of France be redeemed and a truly free and responsible press be built. Thus courageously did the new France face the task of the country's moral reconstruction.

The beginnings of the new era are found in a circular issued early in 1944 by the French Committee of National Liberation, which provided: one, for the suspension of the publication of all newspapers having continued to appear for more than fifteen days after the Armistice of June 25, 1940, in the zone under German occupation or for more than fifteen days after November 11, 1942, when the whole country passed under German control; two, for the permanent banning of the names of those newspapers; three, for the creation of a new press to take the place of the old. This program was to be fulfilled as soon as the liberation of France occurred, as indeed it was.

It soon became apparent that even with the later ordinance of May 5, 1945, the reappearance of some of the old newspapers could not be prevented, for in case of acquittal from all charges of collaboration with the enemy, the courts might revoke the suspension, and the paper thus acquitted could bring action to recover the use of its plant in order to reappear, with a new name. Two new decrees were issued on November 2, 1945, in order to safeguard to a greater extent the position of the new press. But these were temporary measures. Final action was required. On April 16, 1946, with practically only Communist and Socialist votes (the MRP abstaining), the Assembly approved the bill which from 1946 to 1954 was the most important law affecting the French press.[33]

The law provided in Article 1 for the temporary transfer to the state of all assets of the newspaper enterprises falling within the chronological limits established at the beginning of 1944. This meant the transfer to the government of 286 printing plants and of the assets of 482 dailies. While information and publicity agencies were included in the scope of the law, scientific and technical periodicals were exempted if, within one month of the publication of the law, they could be placed on a list of permitted periodical publications prepared under conditions to be fixed at the discretion of the Minister of Information after consultation with the appropriate syndicalist organizations.

The intention of the Assembly was to make it as difficult as possible for the old press to reappear. But the government, in introducing the bill, felt that exceptions should be made for those newspapers whose owners or editors had been jailed or sent to concentration camps by the Nazis and had been therefore physically unable to control the activities of their papers during the occupation.

To Fernand Grénier, spokesman for the Communist Party, this appeared as an intolerable concession. He summoned up visions of newspaper owners and editors who, with diabolical cunning and foresight, had gotten themselves sent to concentration camps at the last hour ("deportés de la dernière heure," he called them). He therefore offered an amendment which reversed the original intent of the bill by making the transfer mandatory even in the case of political victims who were left with the probably meager and certainly meaningless consolation of trying to sue for damages those responsible for their plight.[34]

[33] Law No. 46-994, May 11, 1946, *Journal Officiel: Lois et Décrets,* May 12, 1946.

[34] The text deserves quotation in full: "The owners and principal shareholders of the enterprises thus transferred to government ownership, who can prove that, at the date referred to in the law, they had been placed in the impossibility of maintaining the effective direction of their enterprise, as a consequence of the application of exceptional laws, or because they were prisoners of war, or political prisoners, or deported, will be able to start action for damages against those who in their absence abusively placed their enterprise in the conditions which render necessary the present transfer of ownership."

To avoid embarrassment, the amendment was approved without a roll call. It became Article 2 of the law.

Article 9 provided for the setting up of a government corporation, the Société Nationale des Entreprises de Presse, to manage the newspaper properties thus transferred to the state. Pending the passage of permanent press legislation, no indemnities were to be paid to the former owners, no sale was to be permitted, nor any lease made for more than six months.

The net effect of the Law of 1946 was to make the position of the government overwhelmingly powerful, as long as permanent legislation was not enacted. Many newspapers never paid in full the rent or the other charges to which the SNEP was entitled. Some have therefore survived as partly subsidized government newspapers. This was a state of affairs not entirely new, especially for part of the Paris press. But what was a restricted private vice in the past almost became a universal public virtue after 1946.[35]

These uncertainties finally came to an end in 1954 with a law which, silently recognizing the political impossibility of any general press legislation, set for itself the limited but praiseworthy objective of putting an end to SNEP control of press facilities.[36] In effect, current users of those facilities will be able to buy them, at prices reflecting present values. Former owners will then be reimbursed. No attempt will be made to distinguish, among the buyers, between Resistance and non-Resistance groups. The 1954 law defeats, it is true, the high hopes of the more idealistic leaders of the Resistance.[37] But the with-

[35] On the French press in this period, see Jean Mottin, *Histoire Politique de la Presse, 1944–49* (Paris, 1949); Francisque Gay, "La structure des entreprises de presse," *Cahiers Politiques,* May 1945, pp. 23–43; "La presse, IVème pouvoir, 1944–1950," a special issue of *La Nef,* August–September 1950; and the useful journal of the Institut Français de Presse, *Etudes de Presse,* published irregularly since 1946. Cf. also the informed and critical comments on the persistent deficit operations of SNEP contained in the five reports issued between 1949 and 1956 by the Commission de Vérification des Comptes des Entreprises Publiques.

[36] Law 54-782, August 2, 1954, *Journal Officiel,* August 5, 1954. For the report of the press committee, see *Journal Officiel: Documents,* Annexe 7919, February 26, 1954, pp. 262 ff. For the debates in the National Assembly, see *Journal Officiel: Débats,* May 7, 11, and 20, 1954, pp. 2192 ff., 2298 ff., and 2537 ff. The final debate took place on July 20, 1954, *ibid.,* pp. 3349 ff. The vote was 449 to 101, the opposition being represented by the Communists.

[37] On the hopes of the Resistance, see Francisque Gay, "En face de la presse nouvelle," *L'Aube,* Paris, January 6, 7, and 10, 1948. On the 1954 law, see the

drawal of the state from a critical area of economic control is a great gain for the press. At the very least it will fortify the existing press, which is by all odds a better press than France has had in a long time.

ALGERIA AND FREEDOM

The evidence that has so far been gathered in these pages might support the preliminary conclusion that European freedom, public and private, has come back from the depths of totalitarianism in a way that many pessimistic observers of the postwar scene had not thought possible. Old and new institutions, from the Council of State in France to the new Constitutional Courts in Germany and Italy, have often taken firm stands in defense of freedom. Debate has flourished in the midst of a cultural climate more exciting than at any time in the interwar years. Aware of the proximity of the Soviet Union, Western Europe has been true to her tradition.

But it is clear that this texture of freedom is a delicate one, likely to be torn by unusual pressures of events or by fears of impending calamities. The reflective and calm strength of peoples conscious of the power and depth of their constitutional system has not always been present on a continent still too insecure and caught in midpassage by the rush of events.

France, as Charles Morazé has written, is a mirror of all the hopes and difficulties of Europe and of mankind.[38] In it we can see reflected the strengths and weaknesses of European states and societies, for historical circumstances have placed on France more burdens than on any other continental country. They are burdens for which all of Europe must share responsibility.

The Algerian war has provided a key test of freedom in Europe since 1954. Its repercussions have been varied and intimately linked with all aspects of individual rights and of constitutionalism. The issues have been sufficiently clear to permit a precise measure of the course and meaning of events.

The war that France has been waging in Algeria has been a danger-

anonymous article "1944–1954: De la rinovation de la presse à la loi de Moustier, *Le Monde,* August 6, 1954.

[38] *Les Français et la République* (Paris, 1956).

ous one for freedom and democracy everywhere. Military necessity has been invoked to justify methods of repression which no free community can sustain without destroying itself.[39] Exceptional laws, meant originally for Algeria, have been extended in their application to the territory of metropolitan France.[40] The Army itself—and all its members are, in principle, the proud wearers of the shield of freedom of the Armies of NATO—has become at times an agency of terror, from which Moslem and French alike have suffered.[41] Important dailies and weeklies have been subjected to legal suits [42] and to numerous

[39] The use of terroristic methods by French authorities in Algeria has been discussed in a large body of increasingly critical literature. See the striking reportage of the editor of *L'Express,* Jean-Jacques Servan-Schreiber, in his *Lieutenant en Algérie* (Paris, 1957), together with the weekly "Bloc-Notes" of Mauriac in the same journal. See also Pierre-Henri Simon, *Contre la Torture* (Paris, 1957), Georges Arnaud and Jacques Vergès, *Pour Djamila Bouhired* (Paris, 1957), and the account of one of the survivors, Henri Alleg, *La Question* (Paris, 1958). On Alleg's book and on the role of torture in the modern world, see Jean-Paul Sartre, "Une victoire," *L'Express,* March 6, 1958. For a perceptive sociological appraisal of the Algerian problem, see Germaine Tillion, *L'Algérie en 1957* (Paris, 1957). Of particular interest, because of the eminence of the author, Raymond Aron, is *La Tragedie Algérienne* (Paris, 1957). To his proposal for the recognition of an Algerian state, Jacques Soustelle, former de Gaullist leader and governor of Algeria, gave an uncompromising reply in *Le Drame Algérien et la Décadence Française* (Paris, 1957). For the Communist point of view, see Marcel Egretaud, *Réalité de la Nation Algérienne* (Paris, 1957).

[40] The Law of March 16, 1956, granting to the government special powers to fight the rebellion in Algeria, was extended to France by the Law of July 26, 1957, which permits the assignment to "forced residence" up to 21 days of persons who otherwise would under ordinary law escape punishment. Maurice Duverger has seen in this law the danger of concentration camps ("Les camps," *Le Monde,* July 20, 1957).

[41] While in military custody, the distinguished Algerian lawyer Ali Boumendjel committed "suicide" and the young mathematician Maurice Audin "disappeared." René Capitant, a well-known de Gaullist Resistance leader and member of the Paris Law Faculty, stopped teaching as a result of the death of Boumendjel, a former student: "As long as such practices . . . shall be tolerated by the government of my country, I shall not be able to teach in a French law faculty" (*Le Monde,* March 26, 1957). On December 2, 1957, in a solemn session of the Sorbonne, the Faculty of Sciences granted the doctorate in mathematics to Audin, following a "defense" of the dissertation by the professor under whose direction Audin had just completed his work at the University of Algiers.

[42] One example is the suit by military authorities against the editor of *L'Express,* Jean-Jacques Servan-Schreiber, for the publication of the articles later collected in *Lieutenant en Algérie* (now published in English translation by Knopf [New York, 1957]). Another example is the joint suit brought by the National Federation of French Paratroopers and the French government against *Le Monde* (*Le Monde,*

seizures [43] by the government whenever they ventured to publish too candid recitals of events.

But the press, the universities, important sectors of public and political opinion, and, lately, the Church have reacted with intensity and vigor. On April 5, 1957, the government announced the appointment of a Commission to Safeguard Individual Rights and Freedoms. After extensive inquiries, a general report was turned over to the Prime Minister on September 14, 1957. When, three months later, the government had failed to publish the report, *Le Monde* proceeded to do so in full.[44] The government also permitted a committee of the International Commission against Concentration Camps to visit Algeria during the summer of 1957. Its report has been published by the press [45] and has been followed by supplementary evidence prepared by a distinguished academician for the most influential conservative daily of France.[46]

As in the similar instance of a 1953 report on Tunisian affairs, the 1957 documents on Algeria could well bring about the strengthening of the forces of freedom. More important, in the long run, than the painful reluctance of recent French governments to face up to the truth, is the hope that these sober investigations and accounts of African excesses may ultimately lead to basic changes in mood and policy.

Today many are prepared to see these issues of freedom—a generation ago still considered a remote matter—as affecting the vital core

---

July 20, 1957), for publication on March 22, 1957, of an article by Maurice Duverger pointing to the danger to democracy caused by the existence in Algeria of a quasi-political military power, that of the paratroopers commanded by General Massu. The paratroopers' association has now withdrawn its suit. It is probable that the French government will not press it either, for the minister responsible for the original suit, André Morice, is no longer in office.

[43] Among the weeklies, *L'Express, Demain,* and *France-Observateur* have repeatedly been seized, either in France or in Algeria. The latest sufferer is Sartre. The January 1958 issue of his literary journal, *Les Temps Modernes,* was seized. The seizures are based either on the decree of March 20, 1939, on military security or, more frequently, on what is an illegitimate interpretation of Art. 10 of the Code of Criminal Procedure which authorizes prefects to seize copies of a publication in order "to establish" proof of an alleged crime against the internal or external security of the state. The point is that the seizure of the entire issue of a publication, which is what police authorities do, is not needed "to establish" proof.

[44] December 14, 1957.   [45] *Le Monde,* July 27, 1957.

[46] See the article by Louis Martin-Chauffier, in *Le Figaro,* August 13, 1957.

of civilization which must above all be "a moral rule." [47] The fervor and sense of urgency that pervaded the Dijon gathering of October 1957 [48] for the defense of individual rights are proof of the fact that Western Europe is alive to the nature of the dangers that threaten it and to the significance of the values of the way of life that it has once more tentatively regained since 1945. But it must be realized that the interests, passions, and tendencies set in motion by the African crisis are of such intensity that they are not going to be easily countered.

[47] *Ibid.*

[48] The meetings were held at the University of Dijon and were sponsored by notable names among the leaders of French political life, such as former President Auriol, Pierre Mendès-France, and André Philip; by deputies and senators belonging to many different parties, such as Daniel Mayer, Pierre Cot, Léo Hamon, Michel Debré; by journalists, such as H. Beuve-Méry and Pierre Lazareff; by lawyers, public servants, and scholars, such as the vice-president of the Council of State, René Cassin, Letourneur (of the Barel case), Gilbert Grandval, J. J. Chevallier, Roger Pinto, Alfred Grosser, and René-William Thorp. Some of the reports presented at the meetings are printed in *Les Cahiers de la République,* November–December 1957 and January–February 1958.

VI

JURISDICTIONAL, INSTITUTIONAL, AND PROCEDURAL ASPECTS

[WILLIAM ANDERSON]

UNIVERSITY OF MINNESOTA

The Bill of Rights,

the Fourteenth Amendment,

and the Federal System

TO deal with the questions posed by this topic is by no means to cover the entire field of civil liberties and civil rights under the United States Constitution. The topic itself is rather awkward to handle. I will consider primarily how and to what extent the Bill of Rights has been "nationalized," that is to say, made applicable to the states through the Fourteenth Amendment, and with what consequences to the division of powers and the relations between the national and state governments. This may seem like too narrow a topic, and it will be hard to stay strictly within these bounds; but toward the end of the article I will touch upon the broader question of state versus national protection of civil rights under federal-type constitutions.

Several questions need to be considered. To what extent and in what sense have any provisions of the United States Bill of Rights been held by the Supreme Court to operate as restrictions upon state as well as federal action? To the extent that they have been so construed, has it been possible to make the decisions effective against the states? Have the decisions brought about an actual transfer of legislative power in the matters concerned from the state legislatures to Congress? If not, what are the causes? If grave discrepancies are found between what the Supreme Court says the states should do and what the United States Congress and executive department are willing and able to do to induce reluctant states to comply with Supreme Court rulings, what are the consequences of such Supreme Court decisions for national-state relations under the federal system? We have here a number of questions not simply about what the Supreme Court has said in declaring the law, but on what are the practical consequences of its decisions for the operation of the federal system. Not all these questions will be answered in this article.

"The Bill of Rights" is the designation usually given to the first ten or, more technically, to the first eight amendments to the United States Constitution. It is with the meaning of the first eight amendments that I use the term "The Bill of Rights" in the title to this article, although in fact, if all the provisions of the Constitution that declare and presumably guarantee rights to individuals against government or, alternatively, put limits on the powers of national and state governments in the interests of individual rights were brought together in one separate document, the list would include much more than the first eight or ten amendments.

Upon even cursory examination, the Bill of Rights is found to consist of several different types of provisions covering a number of subjects. The First Amendment obviously states several distinct substantive rights of individuals, the freedoms of speech, press, religion, peaceful assembly, and petition, but these are couched in the form of prohibitions against legislation by Congress. The rest of these amendments assert rights in general language without specific reference to Congress, but certainly with no mention of the states either. Other substantive rights stated in the Bill of Rights are those to bear arms, to be free in one's house against the quartering of troops, and to have just compensation for property taken for public use. At the other end of the scale are rights that are primarily procedural and related to the judicial process, indictment by grand jury, jury trial, confrontation of witnesses, right of counsel, no compulsory self-incrimination, and so on. Still others are to some extent both substantive and procedural rights, such as the right against unreasonable searches and seizures and against excessive bail and cruel and unusual punishments. Then there is the Due Process Clause in the Fifth Amendment, asserting the general right not to be deprived of the substantive rights of life, liberty, or property without due process of law, which was later repeated in the Fourteenth Amendment and which has also been found to have both substantive and procedural aspects.

All things considered, therefore, the Bill of Rights provisions cover large parts of the fields of property and civil rights that are so important among the powers of the states and provinces as distinguished from the central government in present-day federal systems, but covers them negatively, as denials or limitations of powers.

When the Supreme Court in 1925 decided the famous *Gitlow* case,[1] many persons seemed to think that it was as important for the Holmes-Brandeis dissent reaffirming the "clear and present danger" doctrine of the *Schenck* case [2] as for what it actually decided. The decision was in effect to incorporate the First Amendment guarantees of freedom of speech and press into the concept of "liberty" in the Fourteenth Amendment Due Process Clause and thus to make those two constitutional liberties effective against the states as well as against the national government. There followed a good deal of public discussion of "nationalizing the Bill of Rights," which meant in effect the making of the entire Bill of Rights fully operative against the states and thus to have a single standard of individual rights for both the national and state governments to observe and protect. In fact, there has been some expansion of the concept of the *Gitlow* decision so that, for example, the entire First Amendment is now generally conceded to be applicable against the states [3]—but what about Amendments 2 to 8, inclusive?

As is well known, the Constitution submitted to the people as they assembled in the state ratifying conventions in 1787 and 1788 contained no bill of rights. Certain members of a number of state conventions when ratifying "this constitution for the United States of America" (Preamble), as well as considerable bodies of citizens throughout the states, were disappointed at this lack of a bill of rights. In compliance with a tacit but general understanding on the subject, leaders in both houses of the first Congress proceeded with plans to

[1] 268 U.S. 652 (1925).   [2] Schenck v. United States, 249 U.S. 47 (1919).
[3] On this broadening of the scope of the Gitlow doctrine, see *The Constitution of the United States of America: Analysis and Interpretation*, Edward S. Corwin, ed., Senate Document No. 170, 82d Congress, 2d Session (1953), pp. 757 ff., and cases there cited.

draft appropriate constitutional amendments to submit to the states, which, when adopted, would constitute a bill of rights in the Constitution.[4] James Madison in the House was one of the principal draftsmen.

Alexander Hamilton had already argued in *The Federalist*, Number 84, against the addition of a bill of rights to the Constitution on the grounds (a) that it was unnecessary, since the powers conferred on the national government by the Constitution were not such as would give rise to legislation by Congress that would infringe on personal rights, and (b) that it was dangerous, because to prohibit the central government from doing things like restraining the liberty of the press, "when no power is given by which restrictions may be imposed, . . . would afford a colorable pretext" to the national authorities "to claim more [powers] than were granted."

This line of argument by Hamilton was not sufficiently persuasive to stem the tide, but it showed that Hamilton held the general view that the bill of rights proposed for the national Constitution was intended by its proponents to establish limits on the new national government only and not on the states. That this view was not held by all persons is shown by what happened in the committee in the first House of Representatives to which the drafting of constitutional amendments for a bill of rights was referred. James Madison, chairman of this House committee, a former member of the Federal Convention and himself an author of many of *The Federalist* papers, was so impressed with the importance of the freedoms of conscience and utterance against invasions by any and all public authorities that he included in the draft he laid before his committee the following: "No State shall violate the equal rights of conscience, or the freedom of the press, or the trial by jury in criminal cases."[5] This was in addition to a parallel prohibition against Congress. He argued, among other things, and had his experience in Virginia to support him, "that the State Governments are as liable to attack these invaluable privileges as the General Government is." In a revised form, which included also a protection for the freedom of speech, this prohibition against

[4] For a recent short history of the movement, see Robert A. Rutland, *The Birth of the Bill of Rights, 1776–1791* (1955).

[5] See Charles Warren, "The New 'Liberty' under the Fourteenth Amendment," 39 *Harvard Law Rev.* 431 (1926), reprinted in *Selected Essays on Constitutional Law* (Chicago, 1938), Book 2, pp. 237–266. This reprint will be cited hereinafter.

state action was approved by both the committee and the whole House, but the Senate struck out the proposal from the seventeen sent over to it by the House.

The congressional draftsmen who drew up the Bill of Rights amendments directed only the first one specifically against Congress. The seven following amendments, from 2 through 8, were either purposely or (is it possible?) inadvertently written in such general language as to be potentially applicable against both the national and state governments. "No person shall be held to answer for a capital, or otherwise infamous crime. . . . In all criminal prosecutions, the accused shall enjoy the right to a speedy and public trial. . . . Excessive bail shall not be required" are typical provisions.

Against what governments were these supposed to apply? Lawyers evidently began very early to try, for one reason or another, to persuade the courts that these amendments to the federal Constitution were applicable also against the states. This question finally reached the United States Supreme Court from the State of Maryland in the eminent domain case of *Barron v. Baltimore,* decided in 1833.[6] Chief Justice Marshall wrote the decision for a unanimous Court.

The specific question was whether the just compensation provision of the Eminent Domain Clause of the Fifth Amendment did or did not apply against the City of Baltimore, a public corporation of the State of Maryland. If it did not, there would be no federal question, and the Supreme Court could not take jurisdiction of the case. Since the Amendment did not in its own words specify to which governments it applied, the Chief Justice had to seek extrinsic evidence on the point, and particularly such evidence as would indicate the intentions of Congress in proposing the Bill of Rights. This he did with great acuteness and cogency, using other parts of the text of the Constitution itself, the history of its approval in the state conventions, and the demands for a bill of rights to protect citizens against the new national government as evidences that the Bill of Rights was not intended to apply against the states; and so it was ruled by a unanimous Court that the Bill of Rights as a whole was directed against "the general government, not against those of the local governments."

This decision set the course for judicial construction of the Bill of Rights from that day on, but did not quiet all dissent. Other cases

[6] 7 Pet. 243.

arose in which lawyers argued for the application of the principles of the Bill of Rights against state action, but in vain.[7] Their reasoning seems to have been, as in *Barron's* case, that since the provisions of the Bill of Rights are "in favor of the liberty of the citizen" they "ought to be so construed as to restrain the legislative power of a state, as well as that of the United States." They were in effect asking the courts to make the law as they wished it to be. This was especially true of their efforts, when defending persons accused of crime, to get the courts to apply the federal Bill of Rights standards of procedure to the conduct of state trials.

The adoption of the Fourteenth Amendment in 1868 introduced new elements into the constitutional situation. Adopted as it was after the end of the Civil War to seal the victory of the Union over the forces of secession and to assure the Negroes of their newly won freedom, it was nevertheless couched in general language that seemed to foreshadow sweeping changes in the federal system of government. It overrode the *Dred Scott* decision with all its confusion on the subject of citizenship and established national citizenship for all persons born or naturalized in the United States and subject to the jurisdiction thereof, and made state citizenship subordinate thereto. It also provided that "no State shall make or enforce any law which shall abridge the privileges or immunities of citizens of the United States; nor shall any state deprive any person of life, liberty, or property, without due process of law; nor deny to any person within its jurisdiction the equal protection of the laws."

These clauses held forth a new promise to litigants who decided to attack state legislation injuriously affecting their property and civil rights. To some extent the Thirteenth and Fifteenth Amendments gave new hope also, but the Fourteenth was most frequently invoked. It was much broader than the others in what it covered and also in the three lines of attack that it seemed to offer—that is, by way of charging violations of privileges or immunities, or due process, or equal protection, or a combination of any two thereof, or all three at once. Was it the purpose of the framers of the Fourteenth Amendment to make the whole federal Bill of Rights effective against the states? The Amendment does not specifically say so, but it did put upon the federal courts a new responsibility, namely, to decide in proper cases brought

[7] See Warren, *op. cit.*, pp. 241–242.

before them whether state laws to which litigants objected actually violated any part of the Fourteenth Amendment. Any piece of state legislation affecting human life, liberty, or property, or the privileges or immunities of United States citizens, became a potential subject of federal court jurisdiction.

This portended not only a great increase in the jurisdiction and work of the federal courts, but an almost wholly new federal activity in supervising the work of the states. The federal courts were clearly not to be left to perform this supervisory function alone. The Fourteenth, like the Thirteenth and the later Fifteenth Amendment, specifically authorized Congress to enact appropriate laws to enforce the Amendment. And where enforcement is called for, the executive branch is obviously going to have to do the work. Thus the Civil War Amendments made a substantial change in the old federal system. Potentially, at least, they imposed upon the entire apparatus of the national government, legislative, executive, and judicial, the task of seeing to it that no state deprived any person of life, liberty, or property without due process of law, or denied to any person within its jurisdiction the equal protection of the laws, or abridged the privileges or immunities of citizens of the United States. Here was indeed a Pandora's box, but whether it contained ills or blessings remained to be seen.

It was clearly up to Congress to say how much and what manner of enforcement there should be. It was for the Supreme Court, however, to determine and to say what the new amendments meant in law. Is it surprising that the first reaction of the Court was to recoil in dismay and to try to minimize the importance and the scope of the amendments?

Turning to the clauses of the Fourteenth Amendment for their legal support, several groups of litigants in early cases of major importance were doomed to serious disappointment in the Supreme Court. Five years after the Amendment had gone into effect, a group of butchers in Louisiana who had been forced out of work by a state law giving a monopoly in the butchering business to one company found every one of their three pleas under the Fourteenth Amendment and their one under the Thirteenth Amendment (involuntary servitude) rejected by the Supreme Court.[8] The majority of the Justices (the vote was 5 to

[8] Slaughter-House Cases, 16 Wall. 36 (1873).

4) held that the right to engage in the butchering trade was not a "privilege or immunity" of "citizens of the United States" as such, that it was not a property right protected by the Fourteenth Amendment Due Process Clause, and that the litigants were not denied equal protection by the state law. Indeed the Privileges or Immunities Clause of the Amendment was dealt a blow from which it has never recovered. The majority asserted that, with a few exceptions only, "the entire domain of the privileges and immunities of the citizens of the states . . . lay within the constitutional and legislative power of the states, and without that of the federal government." Also, they said, it was not the purpose of the Fourteenth Amendment "to transfer the security and protection of all the civil rights . . . from the states to the federal government." The Court's emphasis was clearly upon the preservation of the existing division of powers between the nation and the states, not upon the personal rights claimed by the butchers.

All three of the Civil War Amendments ended with clauses that empowered Congress to enforce their provisions by appropriate legislation. In 1875, Congress enacted the Civil Rights Act to ensure to all persons in the United States, without regard to race or color, the full and equal enjoyment of the accommodations of inns, public conveyances, theaters, and so on and to punish those who violated this act. Eight years later, in 1883, the Supreme Court declared the act unconstitutional insofar as it provided for the direct federal punishment of individuals violating the act instead of merely negativing or "correcting" improper legislation by the states.[9] Again the theme of the Court was that the protection of civil rights is a power vested in the states and not in the national government and that the Fourteenth Amendment made no change in this division of powers. The Negroes who were the plaintiffs in the *Civil Rights* cases thus suffered a defeat in their cases comparable to that of the unemployed butchers in the *Slaughter-House* cases. From their viewpoint the Fourteenth Amendment was proving to be a weak support on which to rely. Even with Congress and the Executive on their side, they lost in the Supreme Court.

The reluctance of the Supreme Court majority to find in the Civil War Amendments, and especially in the Due Process Clause of the

[9] Civil Rights Cases, 109 U.S. 3 (1883).

Fourteenth, an adequate basis for declaring in favor of substantive restrictions upon state legislation cannot be understood without considering the circumstances and the issues of the times. In the late sixties and early seventies the Radical Republicans in control of Congress were pushing through legislation to supplant state legislation on civil and political rights and to provide for direct federal enforcement thereof. So important a departure from the once prevailing concepts of the nature of the federal system was being opposed by conservative people both in the South and in the North. In the years that it took to enact such legislation, to put it into effect, and to bring litigation under it through the lower courts and up to the Supreme Court, there was considerable time for thought and for consideration of the probable consequences of the reconstruction program to the federal system. Furthermore, by the time some of the major cases reached the Supreme Court, the radical reconstruction plans had been dropped, the issues of the Civil War were slowly being put into the background, and the new economic and industrial developments in the nation were capturing public attention.

The first reaction of the Supreme Court Justices to the Fourteenth Amendment Due Process Clause seems to have been that it provided procedural protections only and not substantive prohibitions against state legislation. Before any important connections between the new Due Process Clause and the federal Bill of Rights could be established, it was necessary for the Court to see in the clause potentialities, at least, for both procedural and substantive restrictions on state action. These insights came, in the course of time, in response to the demands of businessmen, corporations, and property owners generally for the protection of property rights. But the Court refused to lay down in advance any general principles for construing the Due Process Clause. The Fourteenth Amendment itself provided no such general explanation of its meaning, and the Court preferred, in the language of Justice Miller in 1878, to proceed to the task of defining due process "by the gradual process of judicial inclusion and exclusion, as the cases presented for decision shall require." [10] For the protection of property rights against state action the Supreme Court presently found, however, not only the Due Process Clause of the Fourteenth Amendment, but also the doctrines of natural law and "natural equity" to be use-

[10] Davidson v. New Orleans, 96 U.S. 97 (1878).

ful. As early as 1875 the Court invalidated a local property tax, which was to be spent to move a private industry into the city, as not being for a public purpose and supported its conclusion by references to "the social compact" and "the essential nature of all free governments" as putting certain things "beyond the control of the State." [11] Twenty-two years later it applied the Fourteenth Amendment Due Process Clause in an eminent domain case in such a way as to hold that the taking of private property for public use without compensation to the owner is unconstitutional, re-enforcing its views with references to "natural equity" and a "deep and universal sense of justice." [12] Thus, the rights of property began to be protected against state action by the Fourteenth Amendment. It did not escape notice that the decision last cited was quite different in its outcome from the one in *Barron v. Baltimore* and that the Court had in effect written into the Fourteenth Amendment Due Process Clause the provision "nor shall private property be taken for public use, without just compensation," which appears as a distinct element in the Fifth Amendment but not at all in the Fourteenth. Thus in a sense the Court had used a principle or provision of the federal Bill of Rights to interpret "due process" in the Fourteenth Amendment and had made one substantive "due process" restriction on the state governments identical with a specific provision in the federal Bill of Rights.

The connection thus made between restrictions on the states in the Fourteenth Amendment and the federal Bill of Rights was useful to attorneys in later constitutional cases. If one specific provision of the original Bill of Rights could be written into or used in interpreting the Fourteenth Amendment, and thus be made to apply against the states, why could not others? And if to protect property rights, why not to protect life and liberty, too, which precede property in the Due Process Clause of the Fourteenth Amendment?

When it came up against this argument in cases where attorneys argued that the procedural safeguards in the Bill of Rights affecting federal criminal and civil cases should apply equally against the states, the Court proved reluctant to yield. It was still following the process of case-by-case inclusion and exclusion. In 1884 in the case of *Hurtado*

[11] Savings and Loan Association v. Topeka, 20 Wall. 655 (1875).
[12] Chicago, B. & Q. R. Co. v. Chicago, 166 U.S. 226 (1897).

v. California,[13] attorneys for a man convicted of murder in a state court upon "information" and without indictment by a grand jury argued that the Fourteenth Amendment due process requirement in this case should be construed to include the Fifth Amendment grand jury requirement as employed in federal criminal cases. This the Court refused to do. It held that due process in criminal cases is not always and everywhere the same and that the Fourteenth Amendment was not intended to require every state to follow the same procedures, but rather to forbid arbitrary methods and such as do not give a fair hearing to the accused.

The general principle of the *Hurtado* decision, that the various specific procedural safeguards in the Bill of Rights are not necessarily essential to criminal due process in the states under the Fourteenth Amendment, has been followed in subsequent cases, despite strong dissents by a number of Justices in many cases. In 1908 the Court rejected the plea that the Fifth Amendment right against self-incrimination is one of the privileges and immunities of citizens of the United States that the states are forbidden by the Fourteenth Amendment to abridge and that they are required to recognize in their own criminal proceedings.[14] The almost unanimous decision written in this case by Justice Moody, with only Justice Harlan dissenting, was well reasoned and has so far withstood all attacks.

The high-water mark of these attacks up to date was reached in the *Adamson* case in 1947.[15] A majority of five specifically reaffirmed the *Twining* decision, but four Justices dissented vigorously and at considerable length. The minority Justices took the position that "the specific guarantees of the Bill of Rights should be carried over intact into the first section of the Fourteenth Amendment." These dissenters based their conclusion largely upon a new reading of the evidence concerning the intentions of the framers of the Fourteenth Amendment, but also on the proposition that the majority view left the Supreme Court untrammeled in its development of the rules of due process under the Fourteenth, whereas the Bill of Rights provided

---

[13] 110 U.S. 516 (1884).

[14] Twining v. New Jersey, 211 U.S. 78 (1908). This decision includes an excellent summary of the cases up to that date.

[15] Adamson v. California, 332 U.S. 46 (1947).

definite and specific standards for state as well as federal due process. Justice Frankfurter of the majority wrote an able concurring opinion in reply to the dissenters, and scholars outside the Court have added notable contributions to the discussion.[16]

While the Supreme Court has thus continued to reject the idea of the complete incorporation of the specific procedural safeguards of the Bill of Rights into the Fourteenth Amendment Due Process Clause,[17] it has on a case-by-case basis developed a general concept or theory of the procedural due process that the Fourteenth Amendment requires of the states and has even given it a certain amount of specific content drawn in part from the Bill of Rights. Reviewing a number of cases in point when writing the majority decision in the *Palko* case, Justice Cardozo said:

In these and other situations immunities that are valid as against the federal government by force of the specific pledges of particular amendments [referring to the First and Sixth] have been found to be implicit in the concept of ordered liberty, and thus, through the Fourteenth Amendment, become valid as against the states. . . .

The line of division may seem to be wavering and broken if there is a hasty catalogue of the cases on the one side and the other. Reflection and analysis will induce a different view. There emerges the perception of a rationalizing principle which gives to discrete instances a proper order and coherence. The right to trial by jury and the immunity from prosecution except as the result of an indictment may have value and importance. Even so, they are not of the very essence of a scheme of ordered liberty. To abolish them is not to violate a "principle of justice so rooted in the traditions and conscience of our people as to be ranked as fundamental."

Various Justices have tried to rephrase this "principle of ordered liberty" or due process that should apply to state procedures depriving persons of life, liberty, or property, but, except where they purposely quoted each other, no two have come up with the same words. One example is: "that fundamental fairness essential to the very concept of justice." In deciding one case after another they have agreed

[16] See, for example, John Raeburn Green, "The Bill of Rights, the Fourteenth Amendment, and the Supreme Court," 46 *Michigan Law Rev.* 869 (1948), and Charles Fairman, "Does the Fourteenth Amendment Incorporate the Bill of Rights? The Original Understanding," 2 *Stanford Law Rev.* 5-139 (1949).

[17] The decision in Palko v. State of Connecticut, 302 U.S. 319 (1937) on the issue of "twice in jeopardy," is one of the important utterances on this subject.

upon some fairly definite propositions: "Liberty is something more than exemption from physical restraint . . . condemnation shall be rendered only after trial. . . . The hearing, moreover, must be a real one, not a sham or a pretense." Other propositions are: that forced confessions may not be used as evidence, that in the more serious criminal cases the accused has a right of counsel, that convictions based on official misrepresentations to the accused are barred—and a number of others.[18] On the other hand, the Court does not hold the states to the Bill of Rights rules on self-incrimination, grand jury indictment, twelve-member unanimous jury, the use of improperly obtained evidence, and certain other points.

In short, Amendments 2 to 8, inclusive, in the Bill of Rights have not been made fully applicable to the states; that is, they have not been "nationalized." Something approaching that result may be achieved in time, but this would require many more decisions by the Court and the reversal of a number of its past decisions. As the judicial process operates only on the cases that happen to be brought into Court, any real "nationalizing" of the Bill of Rights by this method is most unlikely. On the other hand, if the minority view in the *Adamson* case were to become the majority view, so that all eight amendments in the Bill of Rights were suddenly to become applicable to the states through the Fourteenth Amendment, there would be tremendous confusion in the field of state civil and criminal procedure.

Let us now return for a moment to the *Gitlow* decision, in which the Supreme Court in effect wrote the First Amendment freedoms of speech and press into the Fourteenth Amendment as a partial definition of "liberty" in the Due Process Clause. As already mentioned, subsequent decisions have completed the work of the *Gitlow* decision, so that today all the substantive guarantees of the First Amendment are applicable against the states.

Thus, by a curious paradox, the one amendment in the Bill of Rights that is directed specifically and solely against Congress has come to be applied by the Supreme Court, and in full, against the states, as a result of the Court's interpretation of "liberty" in the Four-

---

[18] For a more complete listing and discussion of the points the Court has decided concerning due process requirements under the Fourteenth Amendment in criminal cases see Corwin, ed., *op. cit.*, note 3 above, pp. 1096–1139.

teenth Amendment Due Process Clause; whereas Amendments 2 to 8, inclusive, which are general in their wording, are not so applied. Furthermore, although the Court once said that the Due Process Clause was intended to have a procedural effect, the procedural clauses of the Bill of Rights do not, as such, impress the Court as applicable to the states, whereas the substantive restrictions of the First Amendment are so applied by it.

Clearly, in the *Gitlow* decision the Supreme Court made an important adjustment in its scale of values. Whereas in the *Civil Rights* cases, and even to some extent in *Twining* and similar decisions, the Court gave priority to the importance of preserving the old federal system and guaranteeing the reserved powers of the states in matters of property and civil rights, the *Gitlow* decision shows a shift to the idea that the First Amendment liberties of individuals have priority in importance over the federal division of powers between the nation and the states. This shift was easy to make in the *Gitlow* case because the Court was planning to and did uphold the constitutionality of New York's anti-criminal-anarchy law. But surely some of the Justices foresaw that they were opening the door to a new field of activity for themselves in reviewing state legislative acts and state court decisions on freedom of speech and press; that logically the other First Amendment liberties would have to be included in their new definition of liberty; and that in time Congress and the executive branch of the national government would have to be drawn in to help enforce the Court's decisions. This is not to imply that their decision was wrong, but merely to say that they knew what they were doing in finally giving some content and meaning to the word "liberty" in the Fourteenth Amendment Due Process Clause. How much new litigation has come to the Supreme Court under the *Gitlow* ruling I have not endeavored to determine, but it has been a great deal. Inevitably the national government as a whole has become more or less involved in the protection of civil rights against the states. This has been no small change in the federal system.

Justice Sanford's decision in the *Gitlow* case gave no reasons for the holding that the First Amendment freedoms of speech and press are a part of Fourteenth Amendment "liberty," but subsequent opinions have added something. For example, in the *Palko* decision (1937) Justice Cardozo distinguished between the less fundamental procedural rights in the Bill of Rights and the more basic, even indispensable, First Amendment rights, as follows:

We reach a different plane of social and moral values when we pass to the privileges and immunities that have been taken over from the earlier articles [*sic*] of the Federal Bill of Rights and brought within the Fourteenth Amendment by a process of absorption. These in their origin were effective against the federal government alone. If the Fourteenth Amendment has absorbed them, the process of absorption has had its source in the belief that neither liberty nor justice would exist if they were sacrificed. . . . This is true, for illustration, of freedom of thought and speech. Of that freedom one may say that it is the matrix, the indispensable condition, of nearly every other form of freedom.

Thus the Supreme Court subsequently explained its choice between competing values.

It is not my intention to enter into the controversy between the main schools of thought on the problem of "nationalizing" the Bill of Rights. In general both sides leave me unconvinced. Here are two "due process" clauses in the Constitution that are practically identical in wording. Of them the Supreme Court once said that the Fourteenth Amendment clause "operates to extend . . . the same protection against arbitrary State legislation, affecting life, liberty, and property, as is offered by the Fifth Amendment" against congressional legislation.[19] It happens that neither side of the current controversy is arguing for this position; certainly those who wish to nationalize the whole Bill of Rights are demanding a great deal more; and if the decisions on the two due process clauses were lined up side by side it would quickly appear how wide of the mark this early statement is.

The identity of the words prove practically nothing as to the meanings of the two clauses in operation—and how could they be expected to? The clauses were adopted at different times, seventy-seven years apart, and were drawn up by different persons with undoubtedly a variety of different intentions or purposes, none of them very clear and none of them defined in the text; and they were put into different contexts in the Constitution. One was to limit a single national government which exercises a number of granted powers of nation-wide scope; the other was to limit a large and increasing number of states that exercise an extensive range of undefined "reserved" powers of

[19] Hibben v. Smith, 191 U.S. 310 (1903).

limited territorial scope. They were interpreted by different bodies of Supreme Court Justices at different times in different kinds of cases and under different social, economic, and political circumstances. Each clause has been and is being developed by actions of the courts, the Congress, the Executive, and by the states, in such a way as to reveal the blemishes and weaknesses as well as the beauties and strengths that result from the work of many hands, not always skilled, and from an ever-changing stream of fortuitous circumstances. In a judicial sense the Supreme Court has the last say (for the time being) on what each clause means, but it has clearly not been the purpose of the Justices merely to bring about an identical interpretation of the two due process clauses, although on a few points a close approximation to identity may be found. The Fourteenth Amendment clause has been subjected to a great deal of interpretation and has developed a surprising amplitude of meaning, while the Fifth Amendment clause has been the subject of far fewer decisions, although it is nearly twice as old.

The proponents of the policy of nationalizing the federal Bill of Rights, that is, of making all the first eight amendments applicable to the states just as fully as to the national government, have clearly not succeeded in convincing a majority of the Supreme Court. Neither have they been able to make their proposal an issue of national party politics. The discussion is confined very largely to legal circles, including law reviews. Deeply concerned with the proposal are many persons who would like to see the civil rights of the people expanded and better protected by means of having the presumably higher standards of the federal Bill of Rights become the controlling criteria in all courts and the binding rules for all legislative action as well.

The arguments of the proponents have been addressed largely to the Supreme Court, in the hope of getting the Justices to reverse themselves. Should they ever be turned in other directions, new issues would arise. One obvious and direct method to achieve their purposes would be to try to get Congress to propose a new constitutional amendment, or perhaps a redraft of the Fourteenth, that would make it clear that due process in all the state courts would have to comply with the Bill of Rights requirements. If the framers of the Fourteenth Amendment did intend this, they quite obviously did not make their intention clear. To write into their proposed amendment, as they did, just one clause out of one of the eight Bill of Rights amendments, and expect this to be interpreted as writing in all portions of the entire eight, was not good draftsmanship. A new amendment might clear up at least part of the uncertainties.

This method of proceeding by means of a new amendment would have the advantage of permitting the various issues to be distinguished and to be discussed separately. Should a grand jury indictment be required in all state criminal cases? What standards should apply to state trial juries as to numbers, unanimity, and so on? What should be the rules on double jeopardy, on self-incrimination, on search and seizure? Has the Bill of Rights proved so satisfactory on all these and other points that every state should be required to conform? Is it not more likely that if such questions were opened up there would be reasonable proposals to modify some sections of the Bill of Rights even as they apply to the national government? The possibilities are rather intriguing.

An important question to consider in drafting a new amendment would be the effect it would have on the basic structure of the federal system. The division of powers between the national and state governments is inevitably involved. Under the original Constitution the protection of life, liberty, and property was left largely within the jurisdiction of the states. The Civil War Amendments made important changes in this arrangement by imposing new and potentially very sweeping restrictions on state powers. The freedom of the states to be different, one from another, in their public policies was thereby reduced considerably, but the Supreme Court in applying the new limitations has clearly softened their effects. As a result the states still have extensive freedom of action, in some respects perhaps more than they had fifty years ago. Any changes that result from "nationalizing" any part or all parts of the Bill of Rights, and requiring every state to conform thereto, will to that extent limit the powers of the states. The gains to be made in the better protection of civil rights by any such change need to be weighed against any undesirable effects that may come from further restricting the powers of the states to develop their own policies and institutions. I confess to a strong predisposition in favor of greater protection of civil rights, whether by state or national action, and I am on record as being an unperturbed upholder of national action where it seems to me to be desirable.[20] But I also want to see substantial supporting evidence, to hear cogent arguments, and to have a fairly clear picture of the consequences, before giving approval to any basic change in the federal system.

Before a change is made, whether by a Supreme Court reversal of past decisions, or by a new constitutional amendment, to apply the entire federal Bill of Rights, or most of it, against the states, some attention should be given also to the constitutional provisions and experiences of other comparable federal systems. Of these there are two, Canada and Australia. Both have faced the same broad question as the United States faces—shall property and civil rights be protected primarily by state action (which involves permitting diversity) or by national action (which almost necessarily requires uniformity of action)?

Offhand I cannot point to anything in their experience to help the United States, and especially not to strengthen the case for nationalizing the Bill of Rights. Neither one has a bill of rights in its federal constitution. Neither has two complete systems of courts, federal and state, like the United States, and on the other hand their respective supreme courts (called the High Court in Australia) have a fairly general appellate jurisdiction and power of review over state and provincial courts, and not just in federal cases.

Canada has by specific constitutional provisions (B.N.A. Act) assigned education and "property and civil rights" exclusively to the provinces, but on the other hand the whole field of criminal law and marriage and divorce (except for the solemnization of marriage) is vested entirely in the Dominion.[21]

Australia, through its Commonwealth Constitution, reserves to the states the powers they had previously exercised that were not granted to the Commonwealth government, but the powers granted to the Commonwealth include those over marriage, divorce, and matrimonial causes, including related issues of parental rights and guardianship; naturalization and aliens; immigration and emigration; invalid and old-age pensions; regulations concerning the people of any race other

---

[20] See my work, *The Nation and the States: Rivals or Partners?* (Minneapolis, 1955).

[21] British North America Act, 1867, as amended to date, secs. 91, 92, 93.

than the aborigines; and a few others that may have civil rights implications.[22] Thus the Australian Constitution is also not on all fours with that of the United States in its division of powers. For example, an exceptional provision forbids the Commonwealth to "make any law for establishing any religion," [23] but there is no comparable provision against a state making any such law. In both Canada and Australia the provinces and states exercise a great deal of control over civil liberties; while the central governments are excluded therefrom in large part. As the United States faces special problems of civil rights in the Southern states, so Canada has a special situation in Quebec.

Perhaps even more important than a survey of the civil liberties experiences of other federal systems would be a study of the feasibility of enforcing uniformity of civil rights through federal action in the United States. The recent desegregation decisions affecting public schools, parks, and swimming pools illustrate some of the difficulties. Although those desegregation cases that involved states were decided on the basis of the Equal Protection Clause,[24] the decision that concerned the District of Columbia schools was put squarely on the basis of deprivation of liberty without due process.[25] Said the Court:

Liberty under law extends to the full range of conduct which the individual is free to pursue, and it cannot be restricted except for a governmental objective. Segregation in public education is not reasonably related to any proper governmental objective, and thus it imposes on Negro children of the District of Columbia a burden that constitutes an arbitrary deprivation of their liberty in violation of the Due Process Clause.

With "neither purse nor sword" in hand, the federal courts stand on the battle front facing the resistance of determined local communities backed by their state and local governments. A federal marshal is but one against many. Congress seems to be unable or unwilling to give the courts strong support through new legislation. The demands of individual Senators for a right of unlimited obstruction, combined with the exigencies of party politics, have resulted in

[22] The Commonwealth of Australia Constitution Act, especially secs. 51, 107.
[23] *Ibid.*, sec. 116.
[24] Brown v. Board of Education of Topeka; Briggs v. Elliott; Davis v. County School Board; Gebhart v. Belton: 347 U.S. 483 (1954).
[25] Bolling v. Sharpe, 347 U.S. 497 (1954).

the adoption of Senate rules of debate and closure of debate that give a minority of Senators representing a single section of the country a veto power over the majority. There is good reason to believe that the most important of these rules are unconstitutional, but only the Senate can change them, and it is not so inclined.[26] As a result, civil rights legislation is very difficult, if not practically impossible, to enact. The 1957 Civil Rights Act is the first important civil rights act to be put on the books since the end of Reconstruction. Through this failure to enact enforcing legislation, effective weapons are withheld from the President; and the executive department is thus unable to back up the courts effectively.

The problem of the constitutional power of Congress to enact legislation to protect civil rights and civil liberties against state action presents some interesting complications. There is no specific grant of power to Congress to legislate thereon, and there is the First Amendment itself to contend with. On the positive side stand the Necessary and Proper Clause and the enforcing clauses in all three of the Civil War Amendments. These should be sufficient to sustain the power despite the decision in the *Civil Rights* cases.[27] The latter decision has already lost some part of its old authority, and sufficient congressional ingenuity to meet the objections therein raised to the act of 1875 can hardly be doubted.

Furthermore, how is such legislation to be enforced? Does anyone seriously believe that sending federal troops or even a large number of federal enforcement officers into a recalcitrant community is the way to bring about the enforcement of civil rights?

I do not have the answers; I merely raise some questions that I consider pertinent and important. The enforcement of civil rights is an exceedingly difficult thing when community sentiment and local authorities unite in opposition. The central government is clearly not adequately equipped at present to cope with the problem. It is true that federal court decisions overruling state court decisions have

[26] See William Anderson, *1949 Supplement to American Government* (1946) and *The National Government of the United States (1946)* (New York, 1949), pp. 9–14; reprinted in the *Congressional Record*, February 18, 1957, Appendix, A 1132–1133. See also William Anderson and Edward W. Weidner, *American Government* (4th ed.; New York, 1953), pp. 557–559.

[27] Civil Rights Cases, 109 U.S. 3 (1883).

a considerable effect and that court injunctions and contempt proceedings also achieve something, but, without more effective means
of enforcement, there are many things that court action alone cannot
accomplish. The effects on the federal system of constant friction
between national and state authorities over issues of civil rights cannot be lightly brushed aside.

[ROBERT FAIRCHILD CUSHMAN]

NEW YORK UNIVERSITY

Procedural Due Process

in the Fifth Amendment

BEYOND a doubt the most colorful clause in the Constitution is the provision in the Fourteenth Amendment stating that no person shall be deprived of life, liberty, or property without due process of law. No other clause has so powerful an appeal to the scholar, for in its history one can trace the role of judicial power, the growing pains of the labor movement, and the struggle for the freedoms of speech, press, and religion. With a wealth of material it illustrates the growth of the United States and its struggle toward democratic government. In defense of the Due Process Clause in its "substantive" aspect, the Supreme Court exercises the power to review the wisdom and reasonableness of state policies, and it is upon this aspect, therefore, that generally the scholar's attention is focused.

As a result of this focus of attention, two things tend generally to be overlooked. First, due process has a "procedural" side, which deals not with the wisdom of policies but with the mundane machinery of the state. Second, the Fifth Amendment also contains a Due Process Clause, which limits the national government just as the Fourteenth Amendment limits the states. This paper is an inquiry into the way in which the Due Process Clause of the Fifth Amendment has served its purpose as a *procedural* check upon the national government.

The words "substantive" and "procedural" have long been used to distinguish between two fairly well defined aspects of due process of law. Procedural due process deals with the way in which a policy is carried out and protects the interest of the public in having it carried out in accordance with certain forms and procedures. Substantive due process, on the other hand, deals with the merits of the policy itself and protects the interest in having the government pursue only fair and reasonable policies. A few examples well illustrate the distinction involved here.

In 1838 Samuel Swartwout, who for eight years had been collector of customs for the port of New York, fled the country leaving a shortage of nearly one and a half million dollars, which he had failed to turn over to the government. Federal law provided that in cases of this kind the United States marshal could seize the property of the defaulting tax collector and sell it for what it would bring. This particular seizure was accomplished by the administrative branch of the government entirely without resort to a court of law. The Solicitor of the Treasury simply issued what was called a "distress warrant" authorizing the seizure, and the marshal seized the property. The Supreme Court passed upon the validity of this procedure in *Murray's Lessee v. Hoboken Land and Improvement Co.*[1]

That the warrant now in question is legal process, is not denied. It was issued in conformity with an Act of Congress. "But is it due process of law?" The Constitution contains no description of those processes which it was intended to allow or forbid. It does not even declare what principles are to be applied to ascertain whether it be due process. It is manifest that it was not left to the legislative power to enact any process which might be devised. The article is a restraint on the legislative as well as on the executive and judicial powers of the government, and cannot be so construed as to leave Congress free to make any process "due process of law," by its mere will.[2]

Upon examination the Court found that this sort of administrative process was long known to the English common law and hence was all that was "due" under the Fifth Amendment. There is little question that *procedural* due process was involved here, despite the fact that an act of Congress was involved. What the Court was interested in was the process used, and had the Court found this process invalid, Congress could obviously have continued its policy of collecting money from defaulting tax collectors by substituting judicial process for

[1] 18 How. 272 (1856).　　　　[2] *Ibid.* at 276.

the invalid administrative one. Its ultimate policy was not in jeopardy, only the procedure by which it was to be executed.

In the three other cases in which the Due Process Clause of the Fifth Amendment appeared prior to 1873, the Court was apparently dealing with substantive due process. Here involved was not the mere method of enforcement, but the legislative policy itself. In *Bloomer v. McQuewan,*[3] a man named Woodward had patented a planing machine and sold to McQuewan the right to build and use such machines during the life of the patent. When the patent expired, Congress renewed it by a special act, whereupon Woodward assigned to Bloomer the exclusive right to build and use the machine. McQuewan claimed that Congress could not thus take away his right to use the machines he had built. With this the Court agreed.

If such could be the interpretation of this law, the power of Congress to pass it would be open to serious objections. . . . The right to construct and use these planing machines, had been purchased and paid for. . . . And a special Act of Congress, passed afterwards, depriving the appellees of the right to use them, certainly could not be regarded as due process of law.[4]

The serious objections were unnecessary, however, since Congress had not (according to the Court) intended to interfere with McQuewan's use of his machines.

Far better known are the phrases connoting substantive due process in Chief Justice Taney's opinion in the famous *Dred Scott* case [5] holding invalid the Missouri Compromise Act. "An Act of Congress which deprives a citizen of the United States of his liberty or property, merely because he came himself or brought his property into a particular Territory of the United States, and who had committed no offense against the laws, could hardly be dignified with the name of due process of law." [6]

Substantive due process was again involved when, during the Civil War, Congress passed an act which made United States Treasury notes legal tender for the payment of debts. In *Hepburn v. Griswold* [7] the Supreme Court, three Justices dissenting, held the act void. Not only was Congress delegated no explicit power to declare such notes

---

[3] 14 How. 539 (1852). [4] *Ibid.* at 553.
[5] Dred Scott v. Sanford, 19 How. 393 (1856). [6] *Ibid.* at 450.
[7] 8 Wall. 603 (1870).

legal tender, but no such power could be implied because such action was forbidden by the Fifth Amendment. The Court explained:

> The only question is whether an Act which compels all those who hold contracts for the payment of gold and silver money to accept in payment a currency of inferior value deprives such persons of property without due process of law. . . . It is difficult to conceive what Act would take private property without due process of law if such an Act would not.[8]

While the distinction between *procedural* and *substantive* is fairly clear in these early discussions of due process, problems do arise in a number of cases in which the job of deciding which kind of due process is involved becomes difficult and delicate. Such a case is raised by a statute that creates a presumption of guilt from otherwise innocent circumstances. The Federal Firearms Act of 1938 made it a crime for anyone who had been convicted of a crime or was a fugitive from justice to receive any gun or ammunition which had moved in interstate commerce. To facilitate the operation of the federal act, the law provided that "the possession of a firearm or ammunition by any such person shall be presumptive evidence that such firearm or ammunition was shipped. . . . [in interstate commerce] by such person in violation of this Act."

In holding the statute void in *Tot v. United States*,[9] was the Court applying procedural or substantive due process? If it was procedural, then it should be possible to substitute another procedure for the invalid one that would still permit the execution of the policy of Congress. But what was the policy of Congress in this case? If it was to punish persons who have not, in fact, carried guns in interstate commerce, then obviously no substitute procedure would do the trick, since Congress has no authority to punish the carrying of firearms generally and must achieve such a policy by indirection or subterfuge. On the theory, therefore, that the only purpose of the presumption was to achieve ends beyond the power of Congress, this was substantive due process. The substantive right of the defendant was the right not to be punished for an act which Congress had no delegated authority to make a crime. This, however, would seem to be a right protected by the delegation of powers concept and the Tenth Amendment, rather than by a guarantee of due process of law. On the other

[8] *Ibid.* at 624. [9] 319 U.S. 463 (1943).

hand, if one assumes that Congress was merely trying to make easier the punishment of persons who have carried guns in interstate commerce, this was procedural due process. It is the right of the defendant to have a fair process for the proof of his guilt, and he could, of course, have been proven guilty by an alternative process—the usual one of introducing evidence of guilt to refute a presumption of innocence.

Even more difficult is the job of deciding what kind of due process is involved in holding statutes "void for vagueness." In an effort to prevent profiteering during World War I, Congress made it a crime to "make any unjust or unreasonable rate or charge in handling or dealing in or with any necessities." This, the Court held, denied due process because it was so vague as not to provide an ascertainable standard of guilt.[10] A man has a right to know what conduct is forbidden so that he can conduct his affairs legally. Is this a procedural right or a substantive right? What is the policy of Congress involved, and could another procedure be substituted without abandoning that policy? It seems apparent that it would not be possible to substitute a valid process. The vice is vagueness, and it can be cured only by a statute which defines a crime more explicitly. In failing to define a crime clearly, Congress has adopted a policy of punishing those things a jury thinks the law forbids, while by defining it explicitly Congress is punishing those things Congress wishes to forbid. Each is a policy of Congress, and not a policy that can be achieved by an alternative process. It is thus a substantive right, and its protection involves substantive due process.

Although the distinction between procedural and substantive due process is today largely of academic interest, at one time in history it was of crucial concern. Not only was procedural due process the first kind to emerge, but until nearly the close of the nineteenth century it was strongly contended that the procedural application was the only legitimate one, that the review of policy under due process was a usurpation of political power by the courts. The Due Process Clause traces its ancestry back to the thirty-ninth chapter of Magna Carta, in which the King promised that "no freeman shall be taken and imprisoned or disseized or exiled or in any way destroyed, nor will we go upon him or send against him, except by a legal judgment of his peers or by the law of the land." By the time Magna Carta was

[10] United States v. Cohen Grocery Co., 255 U.S. 81 (1921).

reaffirmed in the Statute of Westminster in 1354, the phrase "law of the land" had given way to "due process of law," although in state constitutions drafted before the passage of the Fifth Amendment the term "law of the land" was usually the one employed. Whichever the term used, however, the meaning was the same. The great jurist Lord Coke held that due process was intended to guarantee the process required by the common law, especially trial by jury. And while scholars tend to agree that Coke was mistaken in this, the important fact remains that the framers of the Constitution and its amendments placed reliance upon Coke. What the framers meant by the clause, therefore, is probably the meaning given the phrase by Coke.

Whatever may have been the intent of the framers of the Fifth Amendment concerning the propriety of substantive due process, it is not easy to prove anything regarding the attitude of the Supreme Court. It was sixty years before the Court began to interpret the clause, and once it did begin, three of the first four cases spoke in terms of substantive due process.[11] But when, in the *Slaughterhouse* cases in 1873,[12] the Court began interpreting the same clause in the Fourteenth Amendment, it made clear that the substantive application of the clause involved "no construction of that provision that we have ever seen, or any that we deem admissible." [13]

CRIMINAL PROCEDURE

Regardless of the conclusion one reaches as to the propriety of substantive due process, one would be justified in expecting the clause to have its principal importance as a procedural check, especially as a check upon criminal procedure.[14] It is not surprising, therefore, to find the Court in the years after the *Slaughterhouse* cases invoking the Fifth Amendment's Due Process Clause to protect a defendant's right to criminal procedure. In three such cases the Court relied on the clause to sustain a defendant's case against the government. *Hopt v. Utah* [15] held that it was a denial of due process to conduct part of a trial in the absence of the accused; and *Crain v. United States* [16]

---

[11] See notes 1–7 above.   [12] 16 Wall. 36 (1873).   [13] *Ibid.* at 81.
[14] In no case involving civil procedure in the federal courts has the due process clause been successfully invoked.
[15] 110 U.S. 574 (1884).   [16] 162 U.S. 625 (1896).

held that a criminal must be required to plead to indictment before
he could be tried. In *Hovey v. Elliott* [17] the Court held that a lawyer
had a right to be heard in his own defense before being punished for
contempt of court.

The amazing thing is that in only two cases since the turn of the
century has the Court applied the due process clause as a check upon
criminal procedure. One of these was a case [18] similar to *Hovey v.
Elliott;* the other was the *Tot* case discussed above. For all intents
and purposes, the Court has written off the Due Process Clause of the
Fifth Amendment as a check upon criminal procedure. In 1943, however, the date of the last criminal due process cases under the Fifth
Amendment, a new doctrine emerged that may make further reliance
on the Due Process Clause in this area unnecessary.

Three members of the McNabb family, a clan of Tennessee moun-
taineers, were arrested on suspicion of selling illegal whiskey and for
killing one of the revenue agents who had come to arrest them. They
were taken to the federal building in Chattanooga where they were
held in detention for several days, instead of being arraigned immediately before a judge or United States commissioner, as the law
required. Confessions obtained during this illegal detention were admitted at their trial, and they were convicted. In *McNabb v. United
States* [19] the Court refused to consider whether the confessions were
inadmissible because they were obtained under such circumstances
as to deny due process of law—a determination they would have made
had the case come to them from a state court under the Fourteenth
Amendment. The Court explained:

In the view we take of the case . . . it becomes unnecessary to reach the
Constitutional issue pressed upon us. For, while the power of this Court to
undo convictions in state courts is limited to the enforcement of those
"fundamental principles of liberty and justice" . . . which are secured by
the Fourteenth Amendment, the scope of our reviewing power over convictions brought here from the Federal courts is not confined to ascertain-
ment of Constitutional validity. Judicial supervision of the administration
of criminal justice in the Federal courts implies the duty of establishing
and maintaining civilized standards of procedure and evidence. Such standards are not satisfied merely by observance of those minimal historic safe-

[17] 167 U.S. 409 (1897).   [18] Cooke v. United States, 267 U.S. 517 (1925).
[19] 318 U.S. 332 (1943).

guards for securing trial by reason which are summarized as "due process of law" and below which we reach what is really trial by force.[20]

The Court's approach to the problem of fair criminal procedure is clearly revealed in this statement. Far from being a guarantee of common-law procedure, due process is not even a guarantee of a procedure sufficiently fair to meet "civilized standards." It protects a person against a trial by force, and that is all. Small wonder, in view of the elaborate procedural guarantees contained in the rest of the Bill of Rights, that due process is not a useful check upon court procedure.

In seven cases since the *McNabb* case the Court has applied the *McNabb* rule to require civilized standards in the administration of criminal justice in the United States courts. Moreover, the *McNabb* rule has become in these few years a far more versatile instrument of procedural control than the Due Process Clause of the Fifth Amendment. Two of these cases [21] involved the same application of the rule as that involved in the *McNabb* case itself; confessions were excluded as evidence on the ground that they were obtained while the accused was being illegally detained in violation of the rule requiring his immediate arraignment. In two other cases [22] the Court relied on the ruling in the *McNabb* case to order a new trial where the rules regarding the proper selection of federal juries had been ignored, although the Court has made clear that these departures from fair procedure would not necessarily have violated the Due Process Clause of the Fourteenth Amendment had they occurred in a state court.[23]

In *Rea v. United States* [24] a federal agent obtained evidence against

[20] *Ibid.* at 340.

[21] Upshaw v. United States, 335 U.S. 410 (1948); Mallory v. United States, 354 U.S. 449 (1957).

[22] Thiel v. Southern P. Co., 328 U.S. 217 (1946); Ballard v. United States, 329 U.S. 187 (1946).

[23] In Fay v. New York, 332 U.S. 261 (1947), the Court pointed out that the Ballard and Thiel decisions "were not constrained by any duty of deference to the authority of the State over local administration of justice. They dealt only with juries in federal courts. Over federal proceedings we may exert a supervisory power with greater freedom to reflect our notions of good policy than we may constitutionally exert over proceedings in state courts, and these expressions of policy are not necessarily embodied in the concept of due process."

[24] 350 U.S. 214 U.S. (1956).

a possessor of narcotics by stealing it in violation of the Fourth Amendment guarantee against unreasonable searches and seizures. Since such evidence is inadmissible in a federal court, the federal case against Rea was dismissed. Evidence of this kind is not, however, inadmissible in a state court under the Due Process Clause of the Fourteenth Amendment, and the agent filed a complaint in the state court and volunteered to turn the stolen narcotics over to that court as evidence. The Supreme Court, considering it unfair for the federal agent to benefit by his wrongdoing, applied the *McNabb* rule and enjoined his turning it over to the state court.

Mesarosh v. United States [25] involved a quite different use of the *McNabb* doctrine. Mesarosh (Steve Nelson) had been convicted under the Smith Act for conspiring to advocate the overthrow of the government by force and violence. One of the seven witnesses against Mesarosh had perjured himself in similar cases before other tribunals. The Supreme Court ordered that he be given a new trial on the grounds of the *McNabb* decision. "This is a federal criminal case, and this Court has supervisory jurisdiction over the proceedings of the federal courts. If it has any duty to perform in this regard, it is to see that the waters of justice are not polluted." [26]

One of the most spectacular cases of the 1956 term of the Court also appeared to involve the *McNabb* rule, although the Court left this in doubt by not referring to the *McNabb* case explicitly. Jencks, an officer of a labor union, was convicted of swearing falsely that he was not a member of the Communist Party. Testimony against him was given by two undercover agents for the F.B.I., Harvey Matusow and J. W. Ford. These agents had made written reports to the F.B.I. covering the periods and episodes concerning which they testified, and it was Jencks's contention that these reports, could he but get access to them, would refute the oral testimony given at the trial. The Supreme Court ruled that Jencks must be allowed to examine the F.B.I. reports involved, and it was not necessary that he show in advance what conflict of testimony the production of the reports would show. "A requirement of a showing of conflict would be clearly incompatible with our standards for the administration of criminal justice in the federal courts and must therefore be rejected. . . . We hold further,

[25] 352 U.S. 1 (1956).   [26] *Ibid.*

that the petitioner is entitled to inspect the reports to decide whether to use them in his defense. . . . Justice requires no less." [27] Doubts have been raised whether this last statement is not, in fact, a reference to due process rather than the *McNabb* rule. But considering the much closer relationship between justice and the *McNabb* rule than exists between due process and justice, such doubts seem unwarranted. Congress has since passed a statute authorizing the federal judge to determine which F.B.I. files are relevant to the defendant's case.

ADMINISTRATIVE PROCEDURE

Although almost no use has been made of the Due Process Clause as a check upon federal criminal procedure, in over a dozen cases it has been invoked as a check upon the procedures employed by the administrative agencies of the Federal Government. Even here the clause has been limited to two or three types of cases. The first type includes problems arising out of the treatment of aliens and immigrants, largely because Congress has provided that the rights of this group (which has no power of political retaliation) should be handled by administrative agencies. As early as *Fong Yue Ting v. United States* [28] in 1893, the Court made it clear that the deportation of an alien was not a criminal punishment and could properly be done by administrative action without denying due process of law. Such action must, however, extend a hearing to the alien,[29] and the fact that an alien may have entered illegally does not mean that he can be confined at hard labor without a jury trial.[30] In addition, a person who is outside the country and claims to be a citizen, while not entitled to a jury trial on the question of his citizenship,[31] is entitled to a fair hearing.[32] On the other hand, a resident who claims to be a citizen is entitled to prove the fact in a jury trial.[33] By 1922 the alien problem appeared settled, and although other alien rights have been before the court in litigation, in no case has the Court held the Due Process Clause to have been violated.

[27] Jencks v. United States, 353 U.S. 657 (1957).   [28] 149 U.S. 698 (1893).
[29] Chin Yow v. United States, 208 U.S. 8 (1908).
[30] Wong Wing v. United States, 163 U.S. 228 (1896).
[31] United States v. Ju Toy, 198 U.S. 253 (1905).
[32] Kwock Jan Fat v. White, 253 U.S. 454 (1920).
[33] Ng Fung Ho v. White, 259 U.S. 276 (1922).

Procedural Due Process

With the solution of the alien problem, the Court turned the quenching stream of due process on the blaze of administrative regulations designed for the control of the economic system. Starting in the 1920's, the Court's activity in this area reached its height during the 1930's when it struck down as a denial of due process a total of six administrative practices, two [34] on the ground that they should have been judicial procedures and four [35] on the ground that the administrative procedure which was employed did not meet the test of due process.

But the fate of administrative due process appears to have been the same as that which befell criminal due process, for not since 1938 has the Court held an administrative procedure void under the Due Process Clause of the Fifth Amendment. As in the case of criminal procedure, the Court has found ways of enforcing its concept of fairness without resorting to the Constitution. For the most part, these involve accepted judicial techniques, such as statutory interpretation and construing the intent of Congress.

In *Estep v. United States* [36] the Court relied upon this method to achieve what it believed was fair administrative action. Estep was a Jehovah's Witness who had refused to submit to induction into the armed forces on the ground that he was a minister of the Gospel and that the draft board should have exempted him under the provisions of the Selective Service Act. He was convicted in federal district court of having refused to submit to induction, and since the act specifically provided that the "decisions of . . . [local draft boards] shall be final" on matters of classification, the district court refused to listen to his plea that he had been improperly classified. The Supreme Court, noting that "we are dealing here with a question of personal liberty," was unwilling to

infer that Congress departed so far from the traditional concepts of a fair trial when it made the actions of the local boards "final" as to provide that a citizen of this country should go to jail for not obeying an unlawful order of an administrative agency. . . . The provision making the decisions

[34] Crowell v. Benson, 285 U.S. 22 (1932); St. Joseph Stock Yards Co. v. United States, 298 U.S. 38 (1936).

[35] Heiner v. Donnan, 285 U.S. 312 (1932); Atchison, T. & S.F.R. Co. v. United States, 284 U.S. 248 (1932); Morgan v. United States, 304 U.S. 1 (1938); Consolidated Edison Co. v. National Labor Relations Board, 305 U.S. 197 (1938).

[36] 327 U.S. 114 (1946).

of the local boards "final" means to us that Congress chose not to give administrative action under this Act the customary scope of judicial review which obtains under other statutes.[37]

An even more striking application of the method of statutory interpretation was relied upon by the Court in the leading case of *Wong Yang Sung v. McGrath*.[38] In passing the Administrative Procedure Act (APA), Congress had spelled out in considerable detail what ingredients it considered essential to a "fair" administrative hearing—ingredients which raised hearings given under the statute far above the minimum level required by due process of law. The APA, however, required this kind of hearing only "in every case of adjudication required by statute," and the statutes did not require a hearing in the procedure for deporting an alien. The Court held, however, that Wong Yang Sung (a Chinese illegally in the United States) could not be deported without giving him the kind of hearing required by the APA. The Constitution, after all, required that he be given a hearing, and "we would hardly attribute to Congress a purpose to be less scrupulous about the fairness of a hearing necessitated by the Constitution than one granted by it as a matter of expediency." [39] The importance of the *Wong Yang Sung* case itself has been partially reduced by the passage of the Immigration and Nationality Act of 1952, which exempts immigration procedures from the APA and sets up special and somewhat less scrupulously fair procedures regarding the admission and deportation of aliens. But the doctrine of *Wong Yang Sung* has been extended to hearings involving interstate commerce [40] and the post office [41] in which a hearing is required by the Constitution. A long step has thus been taken toward providing fairer hearings in these areas than either due process or the specific action of Congress has seen fit to provide.

Although the Court has been successful in obtaining fair administrative procedure through the use of statutory interpretation, an even greater advance appears in store as a result of the application of the *McNabb* rule to administrative procedure. In 1957 the Supreme Court reversed the findings of the Subversive Activities Control Board that the Communist Party was a "Communist action" organization within

[37] *Ibid.* at 122.   [38] 339 U.S. 33 (1950).   [39] *Ibid.* at 50.
[40] Riss & Co., Inc. v. United States, 341 U.S. 907 (1951).
[41] Cates v. Haderlein, 342 U.S. 804 (1951).

the meaning of the Communist Control Act. Some of the testimony before the board had admittedly been perjured, but the board had concluded that there remained enough reliable evidence to justify its decision. Citing the *McNabb* case, the Court held that "fastidious regard for the honor of the administration of justice requires the Court to make certain that the doing of justice be made so manifest that only irrational or perverse claims of its disregard can be asserted." [42] The importance of this attitude toward administrative procedure can hardly be overestimated.

ANALYSIS

Why is it that "due process of law," a guarantee designed to ensure the individual certain fair procedures in the dispensation of justice, especially criminal justice, should have proved so dim a light in the constitutional sky and finally flickered out entirely? One answer, of course, lies in the nature of the Bill of Rights itself. Most of the provisions of that important document constitute an explicit guarantee of certain procedural safeguards. There is little call to rely on due process when the Constitution expressly forbids such things as trial in the absence of a jury, grand jury indictment, legal counsel, and the right to know charges and confront witnesses. These provisions leave little scope for the operation of due process of law in the field of criminal procedure, and the fact that they do not apply in the field of administrative procedure undoubtedly accounts for the greater use of due process in this area. But why not rely on due process rather than on some form of quasi-due process such as the *McNabb* rule? Certainly the versatility of the Due Process Clause of the Fourteenth Amendment justifies the feeling that it could be made to serve any end the Court wished to make it serve. But this reckons without the attitude of the Court toward any constitutional check, and especially one so vague and malleable as due process. The revolution of the late 1930's in which the Court renounced its role as political censor of the fairness and wisdom of Congress has left an indelible mark on the judicial process. The Court, no less than the public, likes to think of the Constitution as the fundamental law. And it knows, too, that this fundamental law must do two things if it is to achieve the respect

[42] Communist Party v. Subversive Activities Control Board, 351 U.S. 115 (1956).

of the people: it must serve the needs of the people without standing in the way of popular rule, and at the same time it must remain fairly stable for long periods of time. If these two ends are to be achieved, the Constitution must not protect rights that the people do not wish protected and must not protect different rights today from those it protected yesterday. It must, therefore, guarantee only those minimums upon which there is virtually unanimous agreement.

The Court has, moreover, shown remarkable reluctance to interfere with the criminal process of the states. It prefers to let the states, with their own constitutions and political processes, work out procedures that meet their particular needs. If it were to insist upon certain procedures in federal courts as essential to due process under the Fifth Amendment, it would be forced into the delicate problem of explaining why the Due Process Clause of the Fourteenth Amendment did not make the same procedures applicable to the states.

In this view the rise of the broad concept of "civilized standards" enforced by a "supervisory power," which we have called quasi-due process, is easy to explain. The Court, aware of the political realities, knows how difficult it is to get anything concrete enacted into law. All statutes are the result of compromise, and a law enacting vague promises is much more easily passed than one containing specific guarantees. A determined minority can block almost anything it dislikes thoroughly enough. But the Court knows, too, that this works both ways. If a statute, however vague, can be found to contain a requirement of a high order of procedural fairness, there is little likelihood that minority opposition in Congress will be able to enact a statute providing a lower order of fairness. And it makes little difference to a defendant whether his rights are protected by statute or by the Constitution. If, on the other hand, the Court misjudges the temper of Congress, as it did to some extent in *Jencks v. United States* and *Wong Yang Sung v. McGrath,* it can assume that the protection it has extended is not something desired by the people of the country. It can thus acquiesce in the statutory change, the will of the people is allowed to prevail, and that august document the Constitution will stand in dignity unruffled by the whole affair.

[R. G. WHITESEL]

UNIVERSITY OF IOWA

Congress: Old Powers, New Techniques

THE congressional tides of dissatisfaction have been running high. Most of all, Congress has been dissatisfied with Congress; but the President, the administration, the political party system, the Supreme Court, and even the Constitution have felt the pressure.[1] The main causes of this dissatisfaction, however, have been bureaucracy and communism, and it is in reaction to these two problems that Congress has been the most active in developing, from its own powers, new methods and techniques. In so doing it has pushed against both the separation of powers doctrine and the Bill of Rights of the Constitution. Furthermore, although the new congressional techniques seem to be essentially different in the two areas, there are certain underlying similarities.

SEPARATION AND DELEGATION OF POWERS

Under our constitutional system of separated powers each branch of the Federal Government is possessed of a formidable assortment of powers, sufficient to ensure its own equality and to ensure that the irresponsible exercise of powers by any other branch will not long go unchecked. This equilibrium has sometimes appeared to be en-

[1] The number of constitutional amendments introduced in Congress increased from 71 in the Seventy-ninth Congress to a record high in the Eighty-third of 156.

dangered, but no branch has ever been able to secure any great advantage over the others for more than a relatively short period. Partial explanation of this is to be found in the willingness of each branch to observe and maintain the constitutional equilibrium, and only occasionally does a clear-cut test of the separation of powers doctrine develop, as it did in the *Steel Seizure* case.[2] The ruling in that case is extremely valuable in relation to the long-brewing issue of executive prerogative, but the real division of the Court seemed to be bottomed on the existence or nonexistence of a national emergency, and the reasoning of the Court is of doubtful value in clarifying the actual operation of the separation of powers doctrine. Certainly the Court's statement that "the Constitution limits his [the President's] functions in the lawmaking process to the recommending of laws he thinks wise and the vetoing of laws he thinks bad"[3] is to attribute to the Constitution an ignorance of functions it probably should resent. Justice Jackson's explanatory formula in his concurring opinion comes closer to recognizing what is happening to executive-legislative relations within the constitutional framework of separated powers.[4] His formula, however, can be read to say simply that the Court cannot be expected to police executive-legislative relations unless it is assured of the support, or at least the neutrality, of either the President or Congress. Such a reading may be too big a truth.

Despite our endeavors to keep the powers, functions, and activities of the branches semantically packaged together, the separation of powers doctrine has become less and less descriptive of how government actually operates. There are four major reasons for this: First, though the separation of powers has provided each branch with a

---

[2] 343 U.S. 579 (1952).   [3] 343 U.S. 587.

[4] "1. When the President acts pursuant to an express or implied authorization of Congress, his authority is at its maximum, for it includes all that he possesses in his own right plus all that Congress can delegate. . . .

"2. When the President acts in absence of either a congressional grant or denial of authority, he can rely upon his own independent powers, but there is a zone of twilight in which he and Congress may have concurrent authority. . . . In this area, any actual test of power is likely to depend on the imperatives of events and contemporary imponderables rather than on abstract theories of law. . . .

"3. When the President takes measures incompatible with the expressed or implied will of Congress, his power is at its lowest ebb, for then he can rely only upon his own constitutional powers minus any constitutional powers of Congress over the matter . . ." 343 U.S. 635–637.

defense against what it conceives to be the improper advances of the other branches, the modifying system of checks has always been available to justify seduction if not rape. The second reason is that no branch of government, being possessed of a complex of constitutional powers, hesitates overlong to employ any of its powers simply because its use would be out of context in the strict separation of powers sense. The President uses his purely executive powers in the legislative process; Congress uses its legislative power in the executive process. The third reason is that the very nature of the legal process makes conformation to a tripartite explanation very difficult. The legal process consists of but two stages, lawmaking and law executing, and it is almost impossible in practice to determine exactly where one stage ends and the other begins. Seldom can Congress spell out the first element of a law, the condition, so complete, so direct, and so precise in its command to those liable to its second element, the sanction, that all that remains is the execution of the law by reference to the sanction. Ordinarily any law will involve the other two branches to some degree in the condition-determining, lawmaking stage of the legal process. However, as long as the involvement of the other branches can be categorized as an adjunct of executive or judicial power, the separation of powers doctrine will give the appearance of having determined the location of the function. The fourth reason is the emergence of the modern pattern of legislation, marked by redelegation of constitutionally delegated power, whereby Congress so involves the other branches in the legal process that their activities cannot be easily categorized under their own constitutional powers but must be attributed to the delegated power.

The proposition that Congress cannot delegate powers without violating the separation of powers doctrine has been resolved by interpreting the doctrine as prohibiting only the delegation of whole, or final, power. Thus the Constitution is not violated if Congress delegates what amounts to legislative power provided it is something less than its own original power to enact a law. Moreover, what amounts to judicial power may also be delegated, even though Congress itself does not possess any general judicial power, provided such delegation does not possess the attributes of finality. Indeed, Congress by delegation may even blend what amounts to legislative, executive, and judicial powers, provided none of the ingredients is exercised completely independently. As Professor Nutting said in reviewing the earlier Supreme Court decisions which supported the nondelegation doctrine:

If these conclusions are correct they raise the question as to whether the doctrine that delegated powers may not be redelegated has any significance in modern constitutional law. Never literally true, it appears that the maxim is no longer even substantially accurate. Practical necessity seems the only limitation left as far as delegability is concerned. It is not true, as long as the Schechter and Panama cases are not overruled, that there are no limitations whatever, but such limitations as remain are determined by the rule of reason rather than the doctrine of non-delegability. Thus the power of the legislature is limited here, as in other respects, by the vague boundaries of due process. *Delegata potestas non potest delegare* has been swallowed by the fifth and fourteenth amendments. The question is not, "May powers be delegated?" but "Is it reasonable to make this particular delegation in this specific case?" In determining the questions the character of the field, the type of administrative agency and the need for regulation are all relevant. If Congress has basic power in the field and if it has been as specific in delegating that power as circumstances permit, then the delegation seemingly will be sustained.[5]

These conclusions have been reinforced by later Supreme Court decisions, especially those sustaining the exceptionally broad delegations of power to the Office of Price Administrator during World War II.[6]

The process of delegation has affected all branches. The dividing line between acceptance or rejection by the judiciary of any delegation of power to it by Congress has been simply whether the delegation reinforced or restricted the judicial power. The principal beneficiary of congressional delegation, however, has been the executive branch. The tremendous growth of that branch is often cited as direct evidence of the increase of governmental activities and functions generally, but only the process of delegation will explain how that increase has been reflected almost exclusively in the growth of administrative machinery. If the same increase in governmental functions is assumed, Congress presumably could have distributed the load by proportionate

[5] Charles B. Nutting, "Congressional Delegations since the Schechter Case," 14 *Mississippi Law Jour.* 367 (1942). Robert E. Cushman came to the same conclusion in *The Independent Regulatory Commissions* (New York, 1941), pp. 433–434: "In fact the doctrine of non-delegability could safely be scrapped as long as due process of law remains the effective safeguard it is now."

[6] Yakus v. United States, 321 U.S. 414 (1944); Bowles v. Willingham, 321 U.S. 503 (1944).

increases in congressional and judicial machinery directly under Congress and the judiciary. That the disproportionate increase has resulted from delegations of legislative and judicial power is also evidenced in the development of what we know as administrative law. Administrative law, if the title was employed at all prior to 1900, meant the law that controlled administrators and ordinarily covered the judicial remedies available to challenge administrative action. With greater and greater resort to delegation of both legislative and judicial authority, administrative law came to mean, and now means, not only the law that controls administrators but also the law that administrators make and adjudicate. Today's treatise on administrative law generally begins and ends with a constitutional question, but the intervening material must be statute-oriented.

Before any delegation can occur, of course, Congress must determine what job it wants done, spell out whatever limits, standards, and procedures the delegatee is to follow, provide a suitable organization and location in the government hierarchy, and provide the financial and other means to perform the task. These are difficult determinations to make. Indeed, most of them now require the participation of existing executive agencies, with the result that executive and legislative functions become all the more intermingled, informally and formally, as Congress delegates power in order to do a better job of delegating power. Coupled with the other factors that tend to make the President the Chief Legislator of the nation, the commingling of legislative and executive activities has reached the stage where it is now possible to defend quite adequately the proposition that in the determination of public policy it is the executive branch which proposes and the legislative branch which accepts or rejects. Most legislative proposals originate in the executive branch, and ordinarily any bill which does not is "cleared" with the appropriate administrative agency and the Bureau of the Budget. It is the President's legislative program which has become the standard for evaluating the legislative record of Congress, complete with box scores. On the whole, it would seem that no branch of government could "yield" as much of its basic role as Congress has to the executive branch without upsetting the constitutional tripartite equilibrium.

What is not so well understood, however, is the degree to which Congress has compensated for this sharing of its legislative role by increasing its share in executive and administrative activities. It has had no other choice. To "recapture" its legislative power would have required abandonment of the pattern of modern legislation—a pattern developed not so much by choice as by necessity. The problem was not the elimination but the control of delegated authority exercised by the administrative bureaucracy. To this problem of control, by compensation and adjustment, Congress is directing its complex of powers, and consequently we do not yet have a functional term that satisfies both separation of powers terminology and descriptive needs. "Oversight" comes closest.[7]

CONGRESSIONAL OVERSIGHT OF ADMINISTRATION

As the oversight function develops, Congress is deciding by trial and error the answers to three basic questions: What powers are available and effective? Who shall exercise the powers? What are the effective and proper limits of penetration into the administrative process? Congress has no lack of powers available. The dimensions of its own executive powers—senatorial approval of treaties and appointments—are well established. The judicial power of impeachment is available but unsuitable. Inevitably, however, the oversight powers must flow largely from the reservoir of legislative powers.

The close relationship between legislating and overseeing can be seen in the problem of imposing better statutory "prenatal" and "postnatal" controls on the exercise of delegated powers. Congress has been paying increased attention to the problem, not only on an agency by agency basis, but on an over-all or horizontal basis, as in the Government Corporation Control Act and the Administrative Procedures Act. The latter has drawn especially heavy praise from many quarters.[8] Similarly worthy of praise are the unglamourous jobs performed by Congress in "codifying" statutes on a subject or agency basis. All of

[7] There is an interesting account in Bertram M. Gross, *The Legislative Struggle* (New York, 1953), pp. 136–138, of the inability of Congress to find the right word to describe this function for purposes of the Legislative Reorganization Act. "Supervision," "scrutiny," "watchfulness," "surveillance"—all seemed too weak or too strong.

[8] "The Act marks the beginning of a new era in American administrative law in that Congress has at last recognized the importance, even though inadequately, of administrative procedures" (Arthur T. Vanderbilt, *The Doctrine of the Separation of Powers and Its Present Day Significance* [Lincoln, Neb., 1953], p. 88).

these statutory enactments produce better, more responsible administration, and all of them reduce the need for, and facilitate, congressional oversight.

Indispensable to any form of oversight is the right to know what the administrative agencies are doing. There are no hard and fast rules governing the myriad communication practices used between Congress, or Congressmen, and the President, or administrators. If the other avenues of communication prove unsatisfactory, Congress can resort to the ultimate in informational demands: the conduct of a full-scale investigation using compulsory process. Here the President as Chief Executive has some degree of immunity and can extend this immunity in some disputed degree to subordinate officials, but without such immunity an administrator is likely to be a reluctant witness. His vulnerability is too great. The challenges to the investigative power that have revealed its constitutional limits have seldom arisen in oversight investigations, where the process is not likely to run afoul of individual immunities or encounter the difficulty that the scope of the inquiry does not square with the scope of the power. Moreover, it is not the "last resort" aspect of the investigative power that has accounted for its increased use by Congress. What Congress has discovered is its potentialities for securing publicity and for influencing and even controlling action. It serves the purpose of the British Question Hour; it even serves as a congressional equivalent of the President's taking his criticisms of Congress "to the people." Indeed, it has proved so sharp a tool that Congress has used it for purposes far beyond that of securing information or exercising administrative oversight. It has been used, on occasion, as a substitute for legislation, administration, and even adjudication.

Congress could choose to disregard all its other powers, but as long as it controlled the lifeblood of administration—appropriations—it would be able to exercise almost comprehensive oversight of the administration. It is normal for members of Congress who are not members of appropriations committees to resent the legislative power that the separation of legislative and appropriation functions in Congress allows the appropriations committees to wield. But they are strong defenders of the system to the extent that it allows Congress to exert a second-stage, second-look control over administrative programs. It is almost axiomatic in Washington today that the more general the authorization, the greater the degree of postauthorization control will be, until in many instances policy decisions are made in dollar terms. The leading examples of this are found in those programs where policy is the most difficult to nail down in statutory form—as in the fields of defense and foreign aid. While the efforts of Congress to reassert some of the control over the nation's purse strings that it lost to the administration during the wars tend to take the form of economy and efficiency campaigns, the Battle of the Budget would be little more than a skirmish if policy were not at stake.

Who exercises the powers that are appropriate to the oversight function? The foregoing incomplete summary of the powers Congress uses in administrative oversight speaks of Congress in the singular even though power may be exercised by congressional agencies or even individuals. Congress may delegate oversight powers inside and outside of Congress. While the General Accounting Office is the best example of a congressional "arm," independent commissions such as the Civil Service Commission should also be considered agencies of Congress in some degree. For some administrators, some members of Congress may well *be* Congress. Normally, however, the agencies of administrative oversight will be the congressional standing committees, which, since the passage of the Legislative Reorganization Act of 1946, have been charged specifically with the responsibility of watching over the administrative agencies in their legislative jurisdiction. The oversight record of the committees has not been uniformly good, but any serious shortcomings in the system seem to be the result of defects in the committee system itself, for if committees are essential to the legislative process, they would seem to be equally essential to the oversight process. It is possible that administrative oversight might be sharpened if the organization of the committee systems more closely paralleled the organization of the executive branch, but the benefits derived from the present arrangement, where some committees are based on other congressional functions, would then be lost. It is also possible that the gravitation of members to committees having jurisdiction over some activity close to their own or their constituents' interests, and the resultant bias in favor of that activity, may have different implications for oversight responsibility than for legislative responsibility. Perhaps committees, like independent regulatory commissions, are susceptible to the degenerative disease "administrativitis." [9] All that is certain is that, barring a complete reorganization of Congress, the primary agency of congressional oversight of administration will be the committee.

By far the most important and most difficult problem for Congress to determine in connection with its oversight function is not what powers to use, or whom to charge with the responsibility, but how deep into the administrative process itself to penetrate. Should it so use its awesome powers, formally and directly, to take part in the actual conduct of administrative affairs? The question must be stated as one of wisdom rather than legality, for Congress can do so if it chooses. Removal is considered to be an executive function, and the only power Congress can employ directly to remove a federal officer is that of impeachment. It can, however, achieve the same result indirectly by resort to its legislative powers and remove the job from the man. Motive in such an instance is seldom justiciable—unless the case be so flagrant that it could be held a bill of attainder. Appointment similarly is an executive function, extremely modified in practice by the power of senatorial confirmation, but Congress can itemize qualifications for appointment in such a way as to name the candidate.

The newer and more direct techniques have developed as variations on the practice of attaching activating or terminating conditions to delegated powers. Congress by repeal can terminate any statute at will. It also can include in a statute a specific expiration date, or an automatic termination date, as many of the President's war-emergency powers terminated with the war. Congress also can delegate a power and attach conditions to its activation, providing that the power shall not be exercised until or unless a certain specified state of events exists, as it has done in tariff laws and "stand-by authority" laws. The variations we are concerned with here, as methods of oversight, are those whereby Congress makes the activation or termination conditional upon some future nonstatutory action by Congress or some part of Congress. The terminal condition of the Lend-Lease and Emergency Price Control Acts was a concurrent resolution of Congress. The condition antecedent to the execution of an administrative order or rule may be a delay period during which time the legislature may take affirmative or contrary action. The Attorney General, for example, is required to report to Congress the names of certain aliens liable to

[9] Paul H. Douglas, *Ethics in Government* (Cambridge, Mass., 1952), p. 30.

331

deportation; then Congress by concurrent resolution can order the deportation; or, if Congress takes no action within a specified time, the deportation proceeding is canceled.[10] The Apportionment Act of 1941 makes the procedure for apportioning Representatives automatic unless Congress chooses to take contrary action.

Congress also has used a similar device enough times to have made the expression "legislative veto" a part of our governmental vocabulary. There have been several versions, but the basic pattern of the legislative veto is to delegate initiating authority, require the delegatee to lay his implementing order or rule before Congress, and allow the order to go into effect unless Congress takes some sort of negative action within a specified time. The various Reorganization Acts, delegating authority to the President to propose changes in administrative organization, have differed as to how much of Congress should be involved in this legislative veto—both houses by concurrent resolution or only one by simple resolution.[11] Whether by one or by two, the idea is spreading. The legislation under which the government disposed of its synthetic rubber facilities required that the administration negotiate the sales and then report the prospective sales to Congress, any or all of which could be disapproved by majority vote in either house within a period of sixty days.[12]

OVERSIGHT BY COMMITTEE VETO

If Congress can exercise this kind of veto power by concurrent or simple resolution, can it delegate such power to its committees? Can it delegate authority to an administrative agency and require as a prerequisite condition to the specific exercise of that authority that the administrator secure approval of one or more congressional committees? The question has not reached the courts—nor is it likely to—but Presidents have undertaken, with varying degrees of consistency and intensity, to convince Congress that it possesses no such power. In 1933 the President vetoed a bill authorizing a joint committee to make the final decision as to whether any refund of taxes over $20,000 should be made and to fix the amount. The Attorney General had advised

[10] U.S. Code, title 8, sec. 155.

[11] In this reversal of legislative initiative and executive veto it must be remembered that the one-house veto is a heavier hand to lay on presidential action than the two-house veto.

[12] Public Law 205, 1953; 67 Stat. 408.

the President that previous Presidents had vetoed bills, as obnoxious to the Constitution, because they attempted to entrust members of the legislative branch, acting ex officio, with executive functions in the execution of the law.[13] Following the veto, Congress substituted a provision requiring that no such refund be paid until the joint committee had thirty days to study the proposed action.

In 1954 Congress utilized a "veto" device involving "committee justification." Congress and the administration were not in agreement as to just what government operations in competition with private enterprise ought to be abandoned, so the House Appropriations Committee recommended that the Department of Defense Appropriations Act include a proviso: "No part of the funds appropriated in this act may be used for the disposal or transfer by contract or otherwise of work traditionally performed by civilian personnel unless it has been justified before the appropriate committees of Congress . . ."[14] The proviso was amended during the course of its legislative history, but the final act included a "committee veto" provision: "Provided that no such disposal or transfer shall be made if disapproved by either committee within the ninety-day period by written notice to the Secretary of Defense."[15] Although the President signed the bill, he sent a special message to Congress protesting the proviso as an unconstitutional invasion of executive power. Since "Congress has no right to confer upon its committees the power to veto executive action or to prevent executive action from becoming effective," the President stated that he would regard the provision as invalid unless otherwise determined by a court of competent jurisdiction.[16] The problem did not reach the court; the Secretary of Defense did not take action to dispose of any of the facilities he knew Congress was attempting to protect by the proviso—a naval ropewalk at Boston figured most prominently in the congressional debates—and the committees concerned had no occasion to test their power of disapproval.

A similar situation developed when Congress included two pro-

---

[13] *Opinions of the Attorney General of the United States,* 37 (1932–1934), 56. The opinion contains a good summary of the earlier vetoes.

[14] *Congressional Record,* May 12, 1954, p. 5305. The same bill also contained a proviso: "No part of any funds appropriated in this act shall be available for the moving of any major permanent facility until the use of such funds has been specifically justified before the appropriate committees of Congress." This second proviso was defeated on the floor of the House.

[15] Public Law 157, 1955; 69 Stat. 321.   [16] House Document 218, 1955.

visions in the Military Construction Act of 1956 that would have prevented the Department of Defense from taking action in connection with construction of certain guided missile site facilities and military housing projects "until the Secretary of Defense shall have come into agreement with the Armed Services Committees." The provisions so violated the President's understanding of "the fundamental constitutional principle of separation of powers" that he vetoed the measure.[17] Congress promptly deleted the entire missile site authorization to which one proviso had been attached and changed the other proviso to a requirement that the military housing programs be sent to the Armed Services Committees and wait 180 days before taking effect unless earlier approved by the committees, thereby solving one of the problems by refusing to delegate power and the other by varying the oversight technique.

Immediately after the adjournment of the Second Session of the Eighty-fourth Congress, the President again was faced with legislation including the "committee veto" device of legislative oversight. The Small Reclamation Projects Act of 1956, which authorized federal contract assistance to state and local public agencies in the financing of certain reclamation projects, stipulated:

No such contract shall be executed by the Secretary prior to sixty calendar days . . . from the date on which the project proposal has been submitted to both branches of the Congress for consideration by the appropriate committees thereof, and then only if neither such committee, by committee resolution and notification in writing to the Secretary, disapproves the project proposal within such period: *Provided,* that if both such committees, in the same manner and prior to the expiration of such period, approved the project proposal, then the Secretary may proceed to execute the contract: *Provided further,* that in the event either committee disapproves the project proposal, the Secretary shall not proceed further unless the Congress has approved the same.[18]

The President approved the bill only because Congress was not in session to receive a veto message and because he was assured that the general merit of the act could be saved by appropriate amendment of the objectionable provision at an early date in the next session of Congress. Until that time, he advised Congress, the only action he would approve under the Act would be preliminary planning.[19]

[17] House Document 450, 1956.   [18] Public Law 984, 1956; 70 Stat. 1044.
[19] House Report No. 25, 85th Congress, 1st Session, pp. 3–4.

Congress: New Techniques

The next Congress, anxious to get the program under way, did not choose to pursue the President's challenge that the provision violated the constitutional separation of powers. Instead, it sought oversight alternatives between the extremes of requiring each small project to be individually authorized by legislation and of requiring no more than appropriate reports from the Secretary of the Interior. One alternative considered was the requirement of a 60-day waiting period. Another alternative considered was to set a dollar figure for such projects, above which figure specific congressional authorization would be required and below which administrative discretion would be checked, after the fact, by review of reports. The alternative chosen, however, was to retain the committee veto, but shift its impact to the appropriations process. The act, as amended, provides a 60-day waiting period for review of the Secretary's findings and approval of small projects. This period gives the Senate and House Interior and Insular Affairs Committees an opportunity to review and act upon the project proposals by committee resolution of disapproval directed to the Senate and House Appropriations Committees. If either legislative committee so disapproves a project within the 60-day period, appropriation of funds may be made only if the project is specifically authorized by legislation.[20] Under this arrangement the action directly inhibited is not that of the administrator but of the appropriators. Nevertheless, the end result is substantially the same. Although the legislative committees cannot veto the projects directly, they retain the power to block appropriations for projects they disapprove.[21]

[20] The text of the provision is as follows: "No appropriation shall be made for financial participation in any such project prior to sixty calendar days (which sixty days, however, shall not include days on which either the House of Representatives or the Senate is not in session because of an adjournment of more than three calendar days to a day certain) from the date on which the Secretary's findings and approval are submitted to the Congress and then only if, within said sixty days neither the House nor the Senate Interior and Insular Affairs Committee disapproves the project proposal by committee resolution." Public Law 47, 1957; 71 Stat. 49.

[21] The Public Building Act of 1949, as amended, includes a similar restriction on the federal lease-purchase program: "No appropriation shall be made for purchase contract projects which have not been approved by resolutions adopted by the Committees on Public Works of the Senate and the House of Representatives." Public Law 519, 1954; 68 Stat. 519. See also the Watershed Protection and Flood Prevention Act: "No appropriation shall be made for any plan involving an estimated Federal contribution to construction costs in excess of $250,000, or which includes any structure which provides more than twenty-five hundred acre-

No President has protested against any oversight technique on the grounds that Congress did not possess ultimate power to make the decision involved in the oversight. If Congress wants the government to operate a ropewalk, it has ample power to bring that about; if it does not want a ropewalk, it has ample power for that purpose, too. The protests have stressed, instead, interposition and interference with the general constitutional power of the President to see the laws faithfully executed. But what Congress sees, initially at least, in initiating any oversight action is not the executive power of the President, but the delegated authority of some administrative agency. The executive branch is too big and subject to too many centrifugal forces for Congress to identify all administrative activities with the President, and the fact that Congress has contributed more than a little to this atomization of authority makes the identification more difficult. The many well-established reciprocal lines of power running horizontally between Congress and administrative agencies nominally under presidential control sometimes obscure the vertical lines of responsibility on either side. The committee veto device certainly obscures the vertical lines of responsibility in Congress as much as it does in the executive branch. It is an attempt on the part of Congress to delegate power to an administrative agency and at the same time delegate independent concurrent administrative power to a congressional committee. All the other oversight techniques by which committees have been included formally in the process have required some congressional action to affirm or reject the committee action. Requiring that a proposed order lie before a committee for even 180 days before taking effect still leaves with the committee the eventual burden of securing full legislative action if it wishes to intercede. Even the one-house legislative veto conforms to the legislative process because in our bicameral system one house can exercise an absolute veto on positive legislative action. Furthermore, as far as I know, Congress has never formally delegated to its committees any final legislative authority, either positive or negative. Even the "life and death" power of committees over bills is exercised in a framework of recommendations and potential appeals within the parent organization. This is not true of

---

feet of total capacity unless such plan has been approved by resolutions adopted by the appropriate committees of the Senate and the House of Representatives." Public Law 1018, 1956; 70 Stat. 1088.

the committee veto device which, in effect, foreshortens and fore-stalls both the legislative and administrative process.

Are there any practical considerations justifying the use of the committee veto technique in preference to some other method of oversight? Apart from any consideration of timesaving, which seems almost irrelevant in view of the total time-distribution problem in Congress, the underlying, though not sharply voiced, theme in the floor discussions in Congress has been that the committees, being specialized and expert in the particular area, can be trusted to make at least as good a decision as the House or Senate would make.

The business of trusting experts, in and out of Congress, is not a new one in the national legislature. In earlier days the interests for which legislative recognition was sought were few and relatively simple. Congress seemed to contain, within itself, all the factors of representation, information, advocacy, deliberation, and judgment necessary to adjust the conflicting interests. "The average member knew, or thought he knew the answers." [22] As public issues became slightly more complex and became political party issues, the answers could be sought in terms of party principles. As the industrial age and its tremendous increase in demands for statutory remedies presented more and more complicated questions to Congress, additional reliance was placed upon the concept of a representative assembly being a "court." Competing interests were expected, in adversary proceedings before committees or through advocates on the floor, to present the facts requisite to congressional judgment, preferably on a "yes or no" basis. But since advocates operate under no affirmative obligation to develop any more of the facts than are necessary to support the desired decision, the soundness of judgment depended on all the interests being in court, including public interests which the court itself represents. Congress, faced with expert knowledge employed for a purpose, had to seek expert knowledge divorced from the special interests and did so by expanding and intensifying fact-finding and research activities of existing administrative agencies. However, as the power to decide naturally gravitates to the fact finders, so it did from Congress to the executive branch, hastened by the process of delegation. The executive branch developed its own interests, and even early congressional resort to independent regulatory

[22] Ernest Griffith, *Congress: Its Contemporary Role* (New York, 1951), p. 55.

commissions was as much a defense against the particularistic interests of administrative agencies as it was an expression of its own.

In the meantime, distrustful of private experts and executive experts alike, Congress sought to develop its own sources. Not only were staff agencies, such as the legislative Reference Services, created but the standing committees, which by virtue of their subject jurisdiction and seniority had become repositories of legislative experience, were encouraged to develop expert specialization. The Legislative Reorganization Act of 1946 confirmed the trend toward legislative specialization and consolidated in the standing committees much of the oversight function which had been performed by select or special investigating committees.[23] The development of permanent, professional committee staffs made it possible at least to approach administrative oversight as a process of expert and continuous intervention. It was also hoped that the committee specialization would eventually solve the problem of liaison between Congressmen, as well as Congress, and the administration. If all had gone according to plan, the committees might well have been considered so expert in their respective areas that Congress could formalize further its already great reliance on committee judgment. This has not been the case. The record of the committees in their exercise of the oversight function has not been such as to justify claims of final authority.[24] Moreover, the more expert they become, the more imperative it will be for Congress to oversee its own overseers. The watchdog problem is without end.

[23] The act also confirmed a second level of oversight: the well-established power of the Appropriations Committees to oversee administrative activities in connection with budget scrutinization.

[24] The *Congressional Record* contains many such confessions: "We in Congress are helpless. There are 50 members of the House Committee on appropriations, and 23 members of the Senate Committee on appropriations. The time of these members is fully occupied. All we can do is to hear the representatives of the executive branch of the government who came before us to support the President's budget. They may be correct; they may not be correct. But we have no sure way to uphold or repute their testimony. Sometimes a member of the House or a Senator may detect something and may raise a question about it. The committee may eliminate a particular item or reduce it. But of the thousands of items which are contained in the budget, very few of them receive the scrutiny which they should receive before Congress votes to pay the expenses which such items represent" (April 4, 1957, p. 4564).

338

THE FUTURE OF CONGRESSIONAL OVERSIGHT

Apart from the constitutional and practical deficiencies of the committee veto technique, the wisdom and efficiency of the entire process of congressional oversight has been sharply questioned.

The methods and instrumentalities used by Congress may at times be extremely useful, but on the whole and in the long run, they are unsatisfactory because neither house of Congress, as now established, is qualified for efficient, unified, and continuous administrative supervision. Plural bodies, much smaller and better selected, are universally considered unfit for administrative control. Even if the administrative agencies were solely responsible to Congress, control would still be inefficient, probably more so.[25]

The indictment against the existing system of congressional control is impressive. It is basically control over details, not over essentials. It is negative and repressive rather than positive and constructive. It reflects fear rather than confidence. It is sometimes irresponsible. It is based on no rational plan but is an accumulation of particulars whose consequences are seldom seen in perspective. Congress has done both too much and too little in trying to discharge this phase of its responsibilities.[26]

The indictments continue to be sound. There are, however, certain assumptions which would seem to govern any discussion of what can and should be done about congressional oversight as an instrument of government. First, there is little likelihood that the fundamental structure of our constitutional system, which makes the task of oversight difficult at least and impossible at most, will be radically altered in the foreseeable future.

Second, within the present constitutional system, Congress will continue to exercise its powers of administrative supervision. The process of delegation is too essential to modern government. The possibility of clearly distinguishing the making of policy from the execution of policy is less real than ever before, if such a possibility ever did exist. The wisdom of the precept that Congress should tend to policy and not to actual administration does not fit even the harsh

---

[25] Arthur C. Millspaugh, *Toward Efficient Democracy* (Washington, D.C., 1949), p. 240.

[26] Leonard D. White, "Congressional Control of the Public Service," 34 *Am. Pol. Sci. Rev.* 1 (February 1945).

facts of American political life in that the hard core of the popular requests for "errand-boy" services of Congressmen consists not of favors but of demands for intervention in the administrative process. Congress has encouraged and could better institutionalize this aspect of the "errand-boy" function, but it cannot be ignored or abandoned. Not only will Congress continue its oversight activities—it will increase and intensify them. That has been the trend ever since the close of World War II, and the most serious problems in the nation today—national security, economic welfare, and technological change —are conducive to increased presidential legislative leadership, administrative discretion, and congressional frustration. In the history of American law, the Age of Legislation, in which legislators and judges tend to predominate, is being displaced by the Age of Administrative Law, in which administrators and experts tend to predominate.

Third, it seems almost certain that little will be done to establish any type of higher, over-all agency in Congress or any high-level joint machinery between Congress and the executive branch that might help integrate the legislative and oversight functions. The power position of the standing committees militates against the former, and the difficulties of increasing party responsibility work against both. Indeed, if the voters are pursuing consciously a doctrine of separation of political power and intentionally electing Congressmen and the President from opposing parties, it will be difficult enough to maintain informal harmonious co-operation between White House and Capitol, let alone establish formal co-ordinating machinery between the two branches.

If these assumptions are correct, the setting in which legislative oversight of administration is conducted is going to remain fundamentally unchanged. Nevertheless, even though Congress cannot really reform itself,[27] there are a great many things that might be done to reduce the severity of the indictment against congressional oversight.

It seems all too obvious that better legislation might be expected. More careful delegation, within more precise limits, under clearer standards, with more direct responsibilities, would not eliminate the need for oversight, but it would certainly simplify the task and reduce the possibility of abuse. So also would additional "horizontal" administrative control legislation, like the Administrative Procedures

[27] James M. Burns, *Congress on Trial* (New York, 1949), ch. viii.

Act. Oversight functions of the "congressional arms," particularly the General Accounting Office, might be expanded. Supplementary legislation and clarifying resolutions might more effectively provide administrative directions in some instances rather than informal "understandings" among administrators and legislators.[28] Certainly one of the prime, and presently most neglected, considerations in the enactment of any bill vesting considerable discretion in an administrative agency should be the desirability or necessity of including special oversight devices. The experience gained from the use of the various terminating and activating techniques has been valuable and should be put to more systematic use. Committees could so organize their activities that a more systematic, continuous review of administration would result. Galloway has reported on scattered committee activities that show promise not only for improving committee oversight but also for helping Congress as a whole to supervise or assist the committees—intercommittee activities, joint watchdog committees, committee reports evaluating agency operation, conferences at the committee or staff level with agency officials.[29] It may be expecting too much, but the elimination of some of the friction between legislative and appropriations committees would be helpful. The budget process is so complicated that simple solutions are out of the question; Congress has tried the idea of a legislative budget, as a standard against which to check the executive budget, without much success, but it has resisted many proposed reforms in the budget process that it suspected might diminish its control.[30]

It is much easier to summarize what Congress must do under any circumstances if oversight is to be effective, wise, and responsible. In short, it must avoid detail, and it must not allow oversight to become actual administration. The objections to Congress's doing anything in detail are not based on theories of power but on considerations of utility. If Congress has the power to legislate on a subject, it has the power to legislate in as much detail as it desires; if it has the power to oversee the administration of a law, it has the power to check into

[28] Cushman, *The Independent Regulatory Commissions*, p. 449.

[29] George B. Galloway, *The Legislative Process in Congress* (New York, 1953), pp. 612–616.

[30] Thirty-eight members of the House Committee on Appropriations on July 30, 1957, addressed a joint letter to the House membership objecting to an accrued expenditures budget bill as an "installment-buying-dollar-down-contract-authority-hodgepodge."

the smallest details of that administration. Detail is not necessarily inconsequential; there are many seemingly insignificant details in the process of administration no less fateful than the famous horseshoe nail for want of which the battle was lost. But concern for detail is a quicksand. It is the silent, passive, unperceived consumer of time and effort. "The hazard is that a body like Congress, when it gets to detail, ceases to be itself; it acts through a fraction which may be a fraction." [31] In addition, it tends to deal with a fraction of the problem as if it were the whole. Congress eventually discovered not only that excessive concern for detail in legislation led to neglect of other duties for want of time but also that excessive detail in a statute can defeat the purpose of the statute. It now is learning the same lesson in regard to the discharge of its oversight responsibilities. It cannot hope to review administration in all detail. It cannot check on every dollar spent, or decision made, or even policy followed, by administrators. It must make selective choices, in a continuous process, of what to review and in what detail. The "provisional order" device would be self-defeating, for example, if it were applied universally to all rules and orders issued under legislative authority. There is also the great danger that concern for details in the oversight process will lead Congress, or its committees or members, into the greater error of actually administering rather than supervising. Congress has neither the design for, nor the capacity to be, an administrative agency. To the extent that it attempts to be, it destroys the justification and meaning of its oversight function.

Although misuse or abuse of power is never a matter of small concern in our governmental system, it should be remembered that the whole issue of congressional oversight of administration falls within the greater issue of legislative-executive relations. Congress cannot battle bureaucracy, either wisely or foolishly, without encountering active presidential power. Thus, the committee veto technique was an attempt on the part of Congress to begin and end a governmental process of lawmaking and law executing in the same branch, but the intermediate process of delegation and oversight brought the executive power almost automatically into play. A more difficult situation would be presented if one branch of the government possessed powers flexible

---

[31] A. W. Macmahon, "Congressional Oversight of Administration: The Power of the Purse II," 58 *Pol. Sci. Quart.* 414 (1943).

enough to encompass a complete process of lawmaking and law executing without coming into direct conflict with either of the other two branches, even though the attempt ultimately might carry to the constitutional boundaries defended by the judiciary generally. Although the circumstances were unusual, the provocations great, and the degree of popular support high, just such a situation developed when Congress began to adapt its investigative power to new uses in the battle against subversion and disloyalty.

GOVERNMENT BY INVESTIGATION

From past experiences in time of war it could have been expected that, in estimating the subversive threats of fascism and communism, Congress would err on the side of national security interests in the enactment of legislation, delegation of authority, and the exercise of oversight. What could not have been completely anticipated was that circumstances would prompt Congress to attempt to develop, entirely within its own resources, a self-contained system for identifying and eliminating one of the threats. The first, and crucial, part of a three-part process was committee investigation, conducted with full authority to compel, by subpoena, the appearance of witnesses, place them under oath, and initiate contempt proceedings against those who were recalcitrant. The customary functions of congressional investigations in the past had been: first, to develop the information and facts essential to the exercise of the legislative and other express constitutional powers of Congress; second, to oversee the activities of the administrative agencies engaged in the execution and enforcement of law; and third, to inform the public of the facts pertinent to some matter of public concern. As Carr points out [32] the propriety of the informing function of Congress, though not grounded in the specifics of the Constitution, has always been accepted and defended, but the committees investigating subversion and disloyalty tended to invert these functions and emphasize the third almost to the exclusion of the other two. The second part of the process was to attempt to do by investigation and publicity what apparently was too difficult a job to do by legislation. The committees defined, but only by inference,

---

[32] Robert K. Carr, *The House Committee on Un-American Activities* (Ithaca, N.Y., 1952), pp. 6–7.

such terms as "un-American," "disloyal," and "subversive," as a basis for approving or disapproving conduct of individuals and groups. The final part of the process was to complete what amounted to the full cycle of governmental activity, embodying some combination of executive and even judicial activity in the process of investigation and disclosure.

In 1943 Congress attempted to condense the legislative-executive-judicial process by prohibiting the payment of the salaries of three federal employees whose activities they judged subversive as a result of committee disclosure. The reaction of Congress to the Supreme Court's denunciation of this procedure as a bill of attainder [33] was an almost successful attempt in the House of Representatives to undo the Court's decision by refusal to appropriate to the Court of Claims the necessary funds to pay the judgments confirmed by the Supreme Court. The decision was flatly denounced by some members of Congress as a crippling of Congress in its efforts to purge the government of persons proved to be disloyal and subversive. But if what Congress wanted was to purify the federal service on its own terms, it had ample powers to accomplish that purpose by statute, setting loyalty and security standards as high as it desired, or, if incapable of such precision, by the process of statutory delegation and oversight. Such an approach would not guarantee constitutionality, since due process of law requires a basic degree of precision and certainty, but it would have dealt with the problem and not just the evidence of the existence of a problem.

The same considerations came into play in congressional attempts to condense the legal process of identifying and coping with the problem of disloyalty of private individuals. The legislative-executive-judicial process was sometimes so compressed that committees gave at once the appearance of being legislatures, prosecutors, grand juries, and even judges instructing a jury of public opinion.

The extent to which this process unnecessarily and unconstitutionally deviates from the American tradition is still being spelled out. There have been Supreme Court rulings restricting powers of congressional investigating committees and their imitating state counterparts. Indeed, if the progress of law is due to the lawbreakers, the Bill of Rights is considerably indebted to congressional investigations.

[33] United States v. Lovett, 328 U.S. 303 (1946).

Congress: New Techniques

Unfortunately, the total price of unconstitutionality is always too high. Part of the cost that Congress must pay for neglecting proven techniques while engaged in the search for quick solutions is to be seen in the chaotic, contradictory condition of our national security laws and programs. No one at the present time seems quite sure that the enforcement of the Communist Control Act of 1954 would not stultify enforcement of other security legislation. Yet Congressmen are demanding that Congress shore up the damage they think the "Civil Liberties Court" has done to the structure of national security. It would appear that the greater need for congressional activity is to remedy the weaknesses of a structure not entirely squared with either the Bill of Rights or effective use of constitutional power. One of the most difficult tasks within the framework of a constitutional democracy is the balancing of national security interests and interests of individual freedom. So delicate is this adjustment that it requires the best efforts of the entire society, and the attempt of any part of that society—even a majority—to monopolize the responsibility is both dangerous and unwise. The partial, not total, responsibility of Congress for achieving the best possible system of national security consistent with civil liberty, by deliberate resort to methods which are both constitutional and wise, still remains.

The current history of congressional attempts to meet the problems of bureaucracy and national security does not as yet reveal any real lack of congressional power. The difficulty, instead, has been the marshalling and employment of existing powers.

In the trial-and-error search for effective techniques of legislative oversight of administration, Congress has tried many promising procedures, but in placing more and more reliance on its committees, it has tended to delegate more and more final authority to them. The most extreme form of this has been to authorize committees to veto proposed exercises of administrative authority. Whether the committee veto is considered to be in the nature of an executive or a legislative act, it is subject to constitutional challenge either as an unlawful delegation of final legislative power or as an unlawful infringement of the separation of executive and legislative powers. Furthermore, apart from the legal issues, the technique does not seem to have any inherent advantages over other more legitimate methods.

345

Aspects of Liberty

In the trial-and-error search for effective methods to employ against subversion, Congress has tended to place more and more reliance on its committees and has allowed them to exercise more and more authority by way of investigative power. Although the constitutional challenges here have not stemmed from the separation of powers doctrine, the abuse of that doctrine has been the more obvious simply because legislative oversight of delegated administrative power has not been involved. That there are no easy solutions to the problem of legislative oversight does not justify congressional uses of power which overreach the necessity and the desirability of both the process of delegation and the constitutional division of government authority.

BIBLIOGRAPHY

Robert Eugene Cushman: A Bibliography

Compiled by Harold Frank Way, Jr.

BOOKS

1917

Excess Condemnation. Doctoral dissertation, Columbia University. New York: D. Appleton and Company. 323 pp.

1925

Leading Constitutional Decisions. New York: F. S. Crofts and Company. Editions also published in 1929, 1932, 1935, 1936, 1937, 1940, 1946, and 1950; 11th ed., Appleton-Century-Crofts, Inc., 1958. 483 pp.

1931

American National Government. Coauthor, Samuel P. Orth. New York: F. S. Crofts and Company. 717 pp.

1941

Independent Regulatory Commissions. New York: Oxford University Press. 780 pp.

1956

Civil Liberties in the United States: A Guide to Current Problems and Experience. Ithaca, N.Y.: Cornell University Press, 248 pp.

1958

Cases on Constitutional Law. Coauthor Robert Fairchild Cushman. Appleton-Century-Crofts. 1,100 pp. (approx.)

MONOGRAPHS

1937

"The Problem of Independent Regulatory Commissions." President's Committee on Administrative Management, The Brownlow Committee. Washington, D.C.: Government Printing Office. 37 pp.

ESSAYS AND ARTICLES

1913

"Voting Organic Laws." *Political Science Quarterly,* vol. 38, pp. 207–209.

1915

"Analysis of the Popular Vote on Constitutional and Legislative Proposals in the General Election of 1914." *New Republic,* vol. 2, no. 18, supplement, March 6, 1915. 24 pp.

"City Planning and the Courts." Illinois Municipal League, *Proceedings,* Second Annual Convention, University of Illinois, November 2 and 3, 1915. 18 pp.

"Voters' Leagues and Their Work." *National Municipal Review,* vol. 4, pp. 286–290.

1916

"Recent Experience with the Initiative and Referendum." *American-Political Science Review,* vol. 10, pp. 532–539.

1917

"American Municipalities in War Time." Illinois Municipal League, *Proceedings,* Fourth Annual Convention, University of Illinois, December 7, 1917, 5 pp.

"Woman Suffrage on the Instalment Plan." *Nation,* vol. 105, pp. 633–634.

1918

"Municipal War Works." *University of Illinois Bulletin,* vol. 15, no. 23, February 4, 1918. 16 pp.

"What Every One Should Know about War Legislation." *University of Illinois Bulletin,* vol. 15, no. 32, April 8, 1918; reprinted in *American Review of Reviews,* vol. 58, pp. 82–84.

1919

"National Police Power under the Commerce Clause of the Constitution." *Minnesota Law Review,* vol. 3, three separate issues, pp. 289–301, 381–389, 452–463.

1920

"Marshall and the Constitution." *Minnesota Law Review,* vol. 5, pp. 1–31.
"National Police Power under the Postal Clause of the Constitution." *Minnesota Law Review,* vol. 4, pp. 402–440.
"National Police Power under the Taxing Clause of the Constitution." *Minnesota Law Review,* vol. 4, pp. 247–281.

1921

"Constitutional Decisions by a Bare Majority of the Court." *Michigan Law Review,* vol. 19, pp. 771–803.

1922

"The Social and Economic Interpretation of the Fourteenth Amendment." *Michigan Law Review,* vol. 20, pp. 737–764.

1923

"The History of the Supreme Court in Résumé." *Minnesota Law Review,* vol. 7, pp. 275–305.
"Non-Partisan Nominations and Elections." *Annals of the American Academy,* vol. 106, pp. 83–96.

1934

"Offenses against the State Government and Its Administration." Reports of the Commission on Administration of Justice in New York, *Legislative Document,* no. 50, S, pp. 1–27.
"Social and Economic Control Through Federal Taxation." *Minnesota Law Review,* vol. 18, pp. 759–783.

1935

"Our Antiquated Judicial System." *Annals of the American Academy,* vol. 182, pp. 90–96.

1937

"Memorandum of the Special Committee on the Constitution." National Policy Committee. Washington, D.C. 16 pp.

"Must the Constitution Be Amended?" Address before the National Consumers' League, New York City, December 15, 1936; printed under the extension of remarks of Senator Robert F. Wagner, in *Congressional Record*, vol. 81, pp. 117–118, 75th Congress, 1st Session; reprinted in *Reference Shelf*, vol. 11, no. 4, pp. 147–152.

"State Governments Today." *Political Quarterly*, vol. 8, pp. 530–541.

1938

"The Role of the Supreme Court in a Democratic Nation." In *The Edmund L. James Lectures on Government*, vol. 1, pp. 47–62. Urbana, Ill.: University of Illinois.

"The Supreme Court and the Constitution." *Public Affairs Committee Pamphlet*, no. 7. 48 pp.

"The Supreme Court Legislates." *Areopagus*, vol. 6, pp. 1–2.

1939

"Constitutional Status of Independent Regulatory Commissions." *Cornell Law Quarterly*, vol. 24, two issues, pp. 13–53, 163–189.

"In Memoriam: Max Shepard." *Areopagus*, vol. 8, no. 1, pp. 4–5.

1940

"Memorandum of the Special Committee on the Function of Administrative Agencies." National Policy Committee. Washington, D.C. 29 pp.

"Safeguarding Our Civil Liberties." *Public Affairs Committee Pamphlets*, no. 43. 31 pp.

1941

"Civil Liberties in Time of National Defense." *Vital Speeches*, vol. 8, pp. 142–143.

"National Defense and the Restriction of Civil Liberties." *University of Kansas City Law Review*, vol. 9, pp. 63–76.

"Supreme Court and Constitutional Law." In *The American Year Book*. New York: Appleton & Company. Pp. 42–59.

1942

"The Case of the Nazi Saboteurs." *American Political Science Review*, vol. 36, pp. 1082–1091.

"Impact of the War on the Constitution." In *Impact of the War on America.* Ithaca, N.Y.: Cornell University Press. Pp. 1–25.

"What's Happening to Our Constitution?" *Public Affairs Pamphlet,* no. 70. 34 pp.

1943

"American Government in War-Time: Civil Liberties." *American Political Science Review,* vol. 37, pp. 49–56.

"Purge of Federal Employees Accused of Disloyalty." *Public Administration Review,* vol. 3, pp. 297–316.

"Some Constitutional Problems of Civil Liberties: Freedom of Speech and Press under the Constitution, The Negro and the Constitution, Our Interned Citizens—the Problem of Japanese Evacuation." *Gaspar Bacon Lectures.* Boston: Boston University. Pp. 335–378.

1944

"The Basic Concepts of Our Federal Constitution." *We, the People* (Indianapolis, Ind.), vol. 2, no. 1, September 17, 1944.

"Civil Liberties after the War." Presidential Address of Robert Eugene Cushman, Delivered at the 39th Annual Meeting of the American Political Science Association, January 22, 1944, Washington, D.C. *American Political Science Review,* vol. 38, pp. 1–20.

"Our Constitutional Freedoms: Civil Liberties, An American Heritage." National Foundation for Education and American Citizenship and the Public Affairs Pamphlet Committee. New York: Public Affairs Committee. 32 pp.

"The Texas 'White Primary' Case—Smith v. Allwright." *Cornell Law Quarterly,* vol. 30, pp. 66–76.

1945

"Safeguarding Our Civil Liberties." *Public Affairs Pamphlets,* no. 43, revised. 31 pp.

1946

"Keep Our Press Free." *Public Affairs Pamphlets,* no. 123. 32 pp.

"Human Rights under the United States Constitution." *Yearbook on Human Rights,* vol. 1, pp. 323–326.

1947

"Civil Liberties in the Atomic Age." *Annals of the American Academy,* vol. 249, pp. 54–65.

"Laws of the Land." *Survey Graphic,* vol. 36, pp. 14–18.

"President's Loyalty Purge." *Survey Graphic,* vol. 36, pp. 283–287.

1948

" 'Clear and Present Danger' in Free Speech Cases: A Study in Judicial Semantics." In *Essays in Political Theory Presented to George H. Sabine.* Milton R. Konvitz and Arthur E. Murphy, eds. Ithaca, N.Y.: Cornell University Press. Pp. 311–324.

"In the Matter of Editorializing by Broadcast Licensees." Statement before the Federal Communications Commission, March 1, 1948, Representing Cornell University. F.C.C. Docket no. 8516.

"New Threats to American Freedom." *Public Affairs Pamphlets,* no. 143. 32 pp.

"Our Civil Rights Become a World Issue." *New York Times Magazine,* January 11, 1948, p. 12.

"Repercussions of Foreign Affairs on American Tradition of Civil Liberties." *Proceedings of the American Philosophical Society,* vol. 92, pp. 257–263.

"Ten Years of the Supreme Court: 1937–1947, Civil Liberties." *American Political Science Review,* vol. 42, pp. 42–52.

1949

"Freedom v. Security in the Modern World." *Physics Today,* vol. 2, pp. 14–19; reprinted in *Bulletin of Atomic Scientists,* vol. 5, pp. 69–72.

1951

"American Civil Liberties in Mid-Twentieth Century." *Annals of the American Academy,* vol. 275, pp. 1–8.

1953

"Academic Freedom and Responsibility." Reprinted from the *Cornell Daily Sun.*

"Tolerance in Contemporary America." *Listener,* vol. 50, August 20, 1953, pp. 291–292.

LEGAL SERIES

"Constitutional Decisions of the Supreme Court in the October Term." *American Political Science Review,* vol. 20 (1926) through vol. 42 (1948).

"Public Law in the State Courts: Judicial Decisions on Public Law." *American Political Science Review,* nineteen separate articles, vol. 11 (1917) through vol. 22 (1928).

Cushman Bibliography

ENCYCLOPEDIC WRITINGS

Dictionary of American Biography
David Josiah Brewer, vol. 2, pp. 22–23
James Brooks Dill, vol. 5, pp. 309–310
John Forest Dillon, vol. 5, p. 311
Samuel Calvin Tate Dodd, vol. 5, p. 311
John Marshall Harlan, vol. 7, pp. 269–270
Ward Hunt, vol. 9, pp. 394–395
John Lansing, vol. 10, pp. 608–609
Richard Vliet Lindabury, vol. 11, pp. 269–270
Henry Brockholst Livingston, vol. 11, pp. 312–313
Samuel Nelson, vol. 13, pp. 422–423
Charles Cooper Nott, vol. 13, pp. 579–580
Walter Chadwick Noyes, vol. 13, p. 591
Cuthbert Winfred Pound, vol. 21, supplement, pp. 606–607
Smith Thompson, vol. 18, pp. 471–472
Montgomery Hunt Throop, vol. 18, pp. 511–512

Encyclopedia of the Social Sciences
John Adams, vol. 1, p. 434
The Alien and Sedition Acts, vol. 1, pp. 635–636
Civil Liberties, vol. 3, pp. 509–513
Constitutional Amendments, vol. 2, pp. 21–23
Contract Clause, vol. 4, pp. 339–341
Due Process of Law, vol. 5, pp. 264–268
Equal Protection of the Laws, vol. 5, pp. 572–574

Encyclopedia Americana
Direct Legislation, edition of 1955
Federal Judiciary, edition of 1922
Franchise Tax, edition of 1955
Law Merchant, edition of 1955
Legislative Reform, edition of 1955
Municipal Debts, edition of 1922
Municipal Home Rule, edition of 1922
Municipal Ownership, edition of 1922
Municipalities, edition of 1955
Proportional Representation, edition of 1955
Public Utilities, edition of 1955